The re-emergence of small enterprises:
Industrial restructuring
in industrialised countries

The re-emergence of small enterprises: Industrial restructuring in industrialised countries

Edited by W. Sengenberger, G. Loveman and M. J. Piore

International Institute for Labour Studies   Geneva

Copyright © International Labour Organisation (International Institute for Labour Studies) 1990

Short excerpts from this publication may be reproduced without authorisation, on condition that the source is indicated. For rights of reproduction or translation, application should be made to the Editor, International Institute for Labour Studies, P.O. Box 6, CH-1211 Geneva 22 (Switzerland).

ISBN 92-9014-465-3

First published 1990

Second impression 1991

The responsibility for opinions expressed in signed articles, studies and other contributions rests solely with their authors, and publication does not constitute an endorsement by the International Institute for Labour Studies of the opinions expressed in them.

Copies can be ordered from: ILO Publications, International Labour Office, CH-1211 Geneva 22.

Preface

This reader presents case studies and a synthesising introductory chapter, on developments in the structure and organisation of small and medium-sized enterprises (SMEs) from the world's six largest industrialised market economy countries (France, Federal Republic of Germany, Italy, Japan, the United Kingdom and the United States of America). These studies were part of a project launched in 1986 by the International Institute for Labour Studies (IILS) within its 'New Industrial Organisation' Programme. In addition to the above-mentioned countries, the project covered three smaller countries, namely Switzerland, Norway and Hungary. For reasons of limited space, the reports from these latter countries are not included in the present volume. Instead, they are published in the IILS's Discussion Paper Series. Relevant statistical findings from these countries, especially those that concern the quantitative aspects of small firm development, are, however, reported in the introductory chapter of this reader.

At the core of the studies is the proposition that during the 1970s the trend towards larger scale in business organisation was stopped and even reversed in most industrialised nations. In fact, today a larger proportion of workers is employed by SMEs compared to ten years ago. The studies document this important reversal in the size structure, they present the prevailing explanations and viewpoints available in the national context to account for the change, and they discuss a number of implications, especially those which are relevant for labour and labour institutions. Beyond this central focus the studies collate and synthesise what is known in each of the nine countries on the nature and composition of the SME sector, and its status and role within the economy as a whole.

In this regard the project differs markedly from the host of recent SME research which focuses primarily on the individual small firm. Yet, to understand the peculiar world of small business, to explain its performance, and to draw adequate policy conclusions in this area, a more macroscopic approach emphasising the role of SMEs within the larger framework of industrial organisation and industrial restructuring would be absolutely essential.

Developments in the SME sector allow us to capture a major dimension of the present period of transformation in industrial organisation, and even in industrial society at large. There are mounting signs that this transformation is not limited to the market economy countries, but is gradually pervading the countries of Central and Eastern Europe as well. For this reason Hungary was included in the project, as we knew that significant restructuring had occurred there and had been the subject of research.

The ongoing changes in the size structure of production and employment have potentially vast implications for labour standards and terms of employment, and it is thus of great significance to the International Labour Organisation. Practically all aspects of labour with which the ILO is concerned are in some way affected by the size of the business organisation: wages and other forms of compensation, working hours, employment security, occupational health and safety, the collective organisation of workers and employers, industrial relations, etc. *De jure* and *de facto* standards, terms and practices vary a great deal according to the size of organisational units, implying that any shift in the size structure will affect the nature and quality of employment and work.

What, however, the expansion of employment in smaller firms eventually means for labour is to be seen as an open question, the answer to which will depend greatly on the type and direction of policies pursued in the years to come.

This project may be seen as a venture in international comparative research which offers an enormous potential for insight, comprehension, and learning, not only for the community of researchers and scholars, but for practitioners as well. Forming networks of researchers and research groups, and thus expanding the scope of theorising and policy formulation beyond national boundaries, appears nothing but natural in a world that is increasingly characterised by the internationalisation of capital, commodity, and labour markets. It is certainly true that the comparative analysis of business and labour organisation is beset with formidable problems of language barriers, information gathering, comparability of data, and national idiosyncracies in approach and methodology. The proper response to these hurdles is not, however, to retreat, but rather to engage in increased efforts at cross-national exchange and co-operation.

We are especially appreciative of the support given to this study by the late Elimane Kane during his years as Director of the IILS. In addition, we wish to thank all the members of the working group formed to advise the Institute on this project. We also wish to thank Hazel Cecconi, Hilary Mueller and Jacqueline Premat for their valuable contributions to the editing, typing and formatting of this book. The cover was designed by Ximena Subercaseaux.

The Editors

Contributors

Jean-François Amadieu: Research Associate, Ministère de l'Education nationale, Conservatoire national des Arts et Métiers, Laboratoire de Sociologie du Travail et des Relations professionnelles, Paris.

Giacomo Becattini: Professor of Economics, University of Florence, Italy.

Kazutoshi Koshiro: Professor of Economics, Yokohama National University, Yokohama, Japan.

Gary W. Loveman: Assistant Professor, Graduate School of Business Administration, Harvard University, Boston, USA.

David Marsden: Senior Lecturer in Industrial Relations, The London School of Economics and Political Science, London, UK.

Michael J. Piore: Professor of Economics, Massachussetts Institute of Technology, Cambridge, Massachussetts, USA.

Werner Sengenberger: Head, New Industrial Organisation Programme, International Institute for Labour Studies, Geneva.

Stephanie Weimer, Research Associate, Institut für Sozialwissenschaftliche Forschung, e.V., Munich, Federal Republic of Germany.

Table of contents

	Preface. *Werner Sengenberger, Gary Loveman, Michael J. Piore*	v
	Contributors	viii
1	Introduction - Economic and social reorganisation in the small and medium-sized enterprise sector. *Gary Loveman and Werner Sengenberger*	1
2	France. *Jean-François Amadieu*	62
3	Federal Republic of Germany. *Stephanie Weimer*	98
4	Italy. *Giacomo Becattini*	144
5	Japan. *Kazutoshi Koshiro*	173
6	United Kingdom. *David Marsden*	223
7	United States of America. *Michael J. Piore*	261

1 Introduction: Economic and social reorganisation in the small and medium-sized enterprise sector

Gary Loveman and Werner Sengenberger

I. The wider socio-economic context of SME studies

Just a decade ago the idea that small enterprises might be seen as the key to economic regeneration, and a road to renewed growth of employment and the fight against mass unemployment, may have seemed eccentric or even absurd. Today, this view seems much less far-fetched. On the contrary, many observers from different traditions and political orientations embrace the idea, though they may disagree on why and how small firm expansion and dynamism have arisen.

SMEs used to be a largely mute, or marginal, subject in economics and the social sciences. There used to be a widely shared understanding on how industrial society evolves, according to which small business was considered largely as a vestige of an earlier period of economic development. In their seminal book on *Industrialism and industrial man*, Kerr, Dunlop, Harbison and Myers viewed it as imperative to industrialisation that "the technology and specialisation of the industrial society are necessarily and distinctively associated with large-scale organisations" and "economic activity is carried on by large-scale enterprises which require extensive co-ordination of managers and the managed..." [Kerr et al., 1960, p. 39].

Large-scale units[1] of production and employment, organised by the dynamic centre of the economy, the giant, vertically integrated corporation, were themselves part of a more encompassing, coherent *model of economic and social development*, whose essential ingredients were:

- *mass production* of standardised products, built on specific capital equipment and technology;
- *market expansion* to minimise cost and to assure the absorption of the output of mass produced commodities;

---

1. Throughout this volume the term "enterprise" relates to a separate legal entity, while "establishment" means a single place of work which may be part of a larger multi-establishment enterprise. The term "firm" is used synonymously with enterprise. "Unit" is used to refer to either enterprises or establishments.

- Keynesian-type *demand management policies* and *income stabilisation schemes* to assure stable and continuous mass purchasing power;
- a Taylorist-type *work organisation*, built on an extensive division of labour, narrowly defined jobs with a low work content, correspondingly little training and skill formation, the separation of the planning and execution of work, a related gulf between blue-collar and white-collar work, an extensive managerial apparatus organised along hierarchical control, bureaucratic administration, and close supervision.

This coherent model of production, consumption, and work organisation has been termed "Fordism" (for an elaborated discussion, see Piore and Sabel [1984]). Yet, the model had even wider ramifications. It put its stamp not only on the way people work, produce and consume, but also on how people live. Standardised leisure activities, urbanisation and suburbanisation, and finally the devolution of regionalism and localism - not just in economic activities, but in cultural life - can be seen as collaterals to that paradigm.

The model of industrialisation pervaded not only the Western market economy countries. Significant elements, notably mass production and the centralisation and integration of productive organisations, could be found in the Central and Eastern European planned economy countries, as well as in parts of the developing world. Certainly, not all structures and institutions conformed to this concept. But the exceptions and deviations were generally seen to play a residual role or were a left-over, bound to disappear as economic development proceeded.

The facts seemed to be in accord with this model, at least until the early 1970s. Most studies revealed that capital ownership was continuously concentrating, and enterprises and establishments were growing in size. Small firms were expected to gradually wither away, due to inferior organisation, poor management, and backward technologies.

The mainstream theoretical notions offered plausible explanations for why this should happen. Industrial economics emphasised the principle of positive economies of scale and predicted a tendency towards larger units of production, or sought to find optimal plant size. Practically every textbook offered Adam Smith's famous example of the pin factory to illustrate the theory of the degressive cost of increased production scale attributable to the specialisation of labour, machines and equipment, as well as the more profitable use of technology at higher capacity levels. The physical "law" of scale efficiencies appeared to be especially relevant in the domain of mass and process production industries.

A dynamic force in the direction of "bigness" was also assumed in the Marxian tradition of social science, though here it was not as much attributed to technical efficiencies as it was to the process of growing capital concentration and centralisation that is considered inherent in the capital accumulation process under the capitalist mode of production. Small enterprises would remain only in areas of production "which modern industry has only sporadically or incompletely got hold of" [Marx, 1934, pp. 5, 7, 8].

Introduction 3

Against this background of widely shared beliefs, it is astonishing to see, within less than a decade, a profound change in view. What happened to refocus attention on smaller firms, which had previously been considered anachronistic? First, spectacular cases of large enterprises running into economic difficulties and shedding employment arose in nearly all countries; on the other hand, the small firm sector or parts of it seemed to travel relatively well through the period of economic turbulence that started in the early 1970s; and in the late 1970s the David Birch story, claiming that small firms created the majority of new jobs in the United States, spread quickly around the world [Birch, 1979].

A revival of smaller units of employment occurred not only in the United States, but also elsewhere in the industrialised world. In terms of employment growth small firms looked better than large ones or showed - as in some European countries with aggregate employment losses - a smaller rate of decline. The OECD concluded in 1985 that in several of its member states a tendency towards the concentration of workers in small firms could be found, even after accounting for shifts in industrial structure or sectoral composition. Furthermore, they found that "small firms have been particularly important in net job growth over the past 10 or 15 years. The same holds, perhaps with a little bit more certainty, for establishments" [OECD, 1985, p. 80].

From these observations a growing number of politicians and organisations concluded that a new dynamic of small firm growth might lead the way out of the unemployment problem, and recommended the active encouragement and financial support of the small firm sector. Orthodox economists enthusiastically embraced the idea of the "new entrepreneurship", as it seemed to speak in favour of competitive markets and finally disprove the efficacy of market intervention and regulation. Small firms were seen now as carrying innate qualities, such as competitiveness and innovativeness, that were superior to large firms. They were also viewed as showing more drive and better providing a needed element of flexibility. While this view can be found in an OECD document of 1982, the OECD employment report of 1985 stated more soberly that more detailed knowledge is required as to why small firms have on average been associated with a greater capacity for job growth, and what the externalities of jobs created by the small firm sector are [OECD, 1985, p. 10].

Indeed, there has been as yet little discussion about the nature of the shift of employment towards smaller units. Those who assume innate small firm characteristics of greater efficiency and flexibility were led to believe that this could expand economic activity without losses elsewhere in the economic system. There has been little concern for the question of whether the growth of employment in small firms is indeed independent from what is going on in the large firm sector; whether, for instance, the small firms absorb the labour resources that are shed by the large firms so that the structural shift merely amounts to a displacement effect.

The trade unions have perhaps been the most worried about the apparent shifts in the size structure of employment. Many unions have their organisational strongholds in the large firm sector, and it has normally been the big firm where the pattern and pace for gains in wages and other terms of employment have been set. Collective worker influences, at least *de jure*, have generally been better established in large than in small companies. Thus, *ceteris paribus*, the shift toward smaller establishments inevitably confronts workers' organisations with the threat of shrinking membership, loss of organisational strength and loss of influence and participation. Hence, on top of the negative impact for unions stemming from the sustained slack in the labour market, there seemed to be a structural factor at work that could weaken the unions, lead to a severe loss of their influence, and consequently have a negative impact on the functioning of industrial relations.

Yet it is important to guard against rushing into premature and overly general conclusions as to both the origins and the economic and social implications of the shift toward smaller units. Both the social scientist and the policy maker have reason to look into the matter carefully.

Doubts may be raised as to whether it is the size dimension of business organisation *as such* that plays the crucial role in determining economic efficiency and vitality; and also, whether there is something inherent in large or small firms that could make one or the other particularly apt as job generators. If there were an intrinsic superiority in the economic performance of small enterprises, why should their relative share of employment first decline and then grow again? Similarly, large units are not inexorably stricken with rigidities and lack of responsiveness on their markets and in their production systems, nor are small firms necessarily more flexible or dynamic. Without denying that there are certain technical efficiencies associated with the scale of production, it need not follow that there is a natural law that inescapably puts dimension or size of business units at the root of superior economic performance.

Against the tenet of physical determinism of economic organisation is the claim that economic performance crucially depends on the *social organisation* of activities. While large firms may enjoy advantages through a more powerful market position, positive economies of scale or scope, and better utilisation of services like Research and Development (R & D), marketing, advertising, distribution etc. which require certain minimum investments, small firms can overcome their disadvantages and gain similar efficiency, or a different sort of efficiency, if they organise their production and ancillary services on a communal basis. Thus, for example, a number of small producers of the same product and in the same area, or industrial villages of firms producing different products, may organise their purchase of energy, raw materials and equipment jointly; and in grouping together and forming associations and consortiums, they can also overcome the lack of political influence which small firms typically face if they act on their own. The well-known "industrial districts" in what has become known as the "Third Italy" provides evidence of such communal organisation [Bagnasco, 1977; Brusco, 1982; Becattini, 1987; Pyke et al., 1990].

Yet, if the notion of an intrinsically inferior or superior performance of small business organisation is dismissed, and, furthermore, if it is assumed that this shift in the size distribution of business is more than a statistical

Introduction

artefact (as, for example, caused by the growth of the service sector with smaller average firm size), how then can the move to smaller units in most countries since the early 1970s, documented in the country studies in this book, be accounted for?

In essence, two kinds of interpretations are offered. Both direct attention to the larger socio-economic environment in which the reversal took place. The first maintains the logic of technical-organisational efficiency, but claims that as a result of largely exogenous developments some basic parameters in the efficiency equation were altered in favour of smaller units. For example, it is asserted that the much increased turbulence in the international markets, the instability of demand, and more differentiated consumer tastes, render the mass production of standardised goods in large production units unprofitable or obsolete. In addition, the advent and diffusion of new technologies, based on micro-electronics, is seen to lower capital costs and permit the efficiency gap between long and short runs of production to shrink, thereby enhancing the cost competitiveness of small-scale production.

A second line of reasoning steps out of the narrow efficiency logic. It attributes a much more critical role to social or political organisation. It asserts that there is - within limits - a strategic choice of how to organise production, employment, and work. Which option is chosen is ultimately decided by "politics", i.e. the dominant groups in society, the power relations among them, and the institutions they create. Sabel [1981] and Piore and Sabel [1984], for example, hold, contrary to the conventional view, that the victory of the mass production paradigm over the craft system earlier in this century was by no means inevitable. It was not based on an inherent technological superiority or greater dynamism. Rather, it was a product of politics: property rights, distribution of capital and wealth, Fordist-type regulation, etc. As a consequence, the course of industrial development can produce rather different results in different societies, and it can be redirected. The period starting in the 1970s could be seen as one of a "second industrial divide", in which reorientation and transformation of industrial organisation took place.

II. Substantial international size differences in employment units

"Small enterprise" or "small- and medium-sized enterprises" are elusive concepts. They do in fact hide a large heterogeneity in the types of firms. The country studies testify that the definitions, conceptions, and available typologies vary from one country to another. Depending on the institutional or historical context, major criteria for structuring the SME sector are the legal status (as in France), the ownership status (as in Hungary), the distinction between "craft" and "industrial" firms (as in the Federal Republic of Germany), independent and subordinate firms (as in Japan), or small firms in small-firm industries versus small firms in industries where large enterprises dominate or where there is a mixed size composition. Such structural variety, within and across national boundaries, will have to be taken into account when analysing the SME sector.

Another frequently raised question concerns the statistical definition of "small", "medium" and "large" with regard to firm size. Usually, underlying this question is the expectation that somebody comes up with a precise answer to what a small firm is. If the respondent does not live up to this expectation, or if the answer is "it depends" (on the country, the industry, the time period, etc.), the conclusion drawn is often that it would be futile or meaningless to conduct a comparative statistical analysis on the size structure of enterprises.

We believe that underlying this sort of reasoning is a misconception of what the analysis of the size composition of a production system is intended to do. There is no value as such in studying size dimensions and, consequently, there is no need to provide uniform definitions. The concern with the scale of enterprises or establishments is meaningful only in a relative or comparative context. That is, if significant differences in the size structure of regional or national economies can be identified, or if this structure changes over time, this may say something about the scope and latitude for industrial organisation in relation to regional, national or historical institutions. It is, then, sufficient to set ad hoc or convenient statistical conventions aimed at revealing as much as possible of the variation in the size composition. After all, despite the formidable problems with measurement and comparability of the data, size is still one of the most accessible indicators of productive organisation across countries. Instead of worrying about what a "small firm" is, the energy of the researcher is better spent studying why there are such remarkable differences in the size distribution of enterprises, not only in the economy as a whole, but in various sub-sections.

Table 1 provides evidence that among the countries included in this study the scale of organisational units varies a great deal. For example, if one follows the OECD definition of a small enterprise as one with fewer than 100 employees, then the share of small enterprises in total employment ranges from roughly 43 per cent in the Federal Republic of Germany to nearly 70 per cent in Italy. The employment share of medium-sized enterprises, with 100 to 499 employees ranges from 12 per cent in Italy to 18 per cent in France, while the shares of large firms with more than 500 employees varies widely from 18.5 per cent in Italy to 41 per cent in the United States.

To some extent the differences in the size structure reflect varying sectoral and industrial compositions. Since employment in SMEs is in all countries more important in the service sector than in manufacturing, it can be expected that countries with a larger service sector have smaller average scale of organisational units. But taking, for example, the manufacturing sector (Table 3) separately, major international differentials remain. This suggests that size differences are not purely compositional.

Even more pronounced dispersions in the size composition are revealed at the *establishment* level. Table 7 presents the figures at the total

Introduction

economy level while Table 10 gives data for the manufacturing sector. The latter, for example, shows that manufacturing establishments with fewer than 20 employees account for 3.4 per cent of all workers in Hungary, 7.4 per cent in the United States, but roughly 35 per cent in Italy and Japan. Taking the available information for the category of "small" establishments with up to 100 employees, the extreme cases are Hungary (17 per cent), and the United Kingdom (26 per cent) on the low end, and Japan (56 per cent) and Italy (59 per cent) on the high end. Employment shares of large manufacturing establishments range from slightly less than 20 per cent in Italy to almost 47 per cent in the United Kingdom.

Again, it could be argued that these sectoral differences reflect the fact that manufacturing contains a different industry composition with different size in different countries. Yet, the substantial international variance in the size structure remains at a more disaggregated level. Although there has been no systematic collection of official information in this study, casual knowledge does exist of large differences in the size of production units in particular industries. To take a few illustrations, Norway and Sweden organise most of their bread production on a mass scale in a few larger firms, while the Federal Republic of Germany still has more than 30,000 firms in bread baking, most of which are small craft bakers that produce and sell for local markets of just a few housing blocks. In beer brewing, there are more than 1,000 enterprises of various size categories in the Federal Republic of Germany, but only four large firms in Japan. In British beer brewing, after a massive concentration process, a number of small breweries offering real ale and other specialities have reappeared. Similarly, small artisan bakeries have come back on the scene after a long phase of decline in Britain, whereas in the Netherlands there has been a continuous strong shrinkage of their number.

One has to dig deeply into history to understand why and how the structures have developed in this way. One would have to draw upon national systems of regulation such as a law dating from World War I that prohibits bread baking during the night hours in Germany and that clearly puts the artisan baker at an advantage over the larger industrial producer. In some cases, one might even have to go further back in history and look into the evolution of guilds and crafts and inquire why they have survived in some countries and eroded in others. To understand the peculiar Japanese industrial structure of today it helps to study inherited historical organisational patterns, such as the ancient agricultural village, the traditional hierarchical social order, and the *Zaibatsu*, which played a key role in industrial modernisation following the *Meiji* period. The *Zaibatsu* were big compounds of numerous directly and collaterally affiliated subsidiary companies closely knit together. They were completely disbanded by the occupying forces after World War II, but reappeared in the form of industrial groups following the peace treaty.

III. Recent shift to smaller units

In addition to the wide international variance in the size distribution of production, the most important empirical result to emerge from the country reports is that there has been a recent increase in the share of total employment in small enterprises and establishments which are defined as those with fewer than 100 employees.[2] In general, the increase has been at the expense of large enterprises and establishments. While the magnitude of the increase varies considerably from country to country and across sectors, its significance rests primarily on the fact that it signifies the reversal of a substantial downward trend in the employment shares of small units that had prevailed for many decades. Indeed, Tables 2, 4, 8 and 11 show that the time series behaviour of small unit employment shares has followed a "V" pattern in which declines through the late 1960s-early 1970s are reversed and small unit employment shares increase into the 1980s. The "V" pattern is evident both for enterprises and establishments, and for the total economy and manufacturing. What is remarkable about this finding is not that the recent growth in small unit employment shares has been enormous in all countries, but rather that the pattern of decline and then growth is so robust over such a wide sample of countries, sectors, size distributions, and institutions.

The remainder of this section is divided into three parts. The first section discusses the size distribution data in more detail. The next section addresses a series of important issues that arise in the interpretation of these data. The third section summarises and evaluates relevant evidence from the job generation literature.

1. A more detailed review

Data on the size distribution of employment vary enormously in coverage and frequency across the six countries included in this volume. The data are better for establishments than enterprises, and for manufacturing than other sectors. What emerges from these data, however, is a clear picture of a recent general trend toward smaller units of production.

Tables 1 and 2 show enterprise size data at the total economy level of aggregation. Despite significant cross-national differences in the size distribution, the employment share of small enterprises has reversed a downward trend and risen significantly in all nine countries[3] which were part of this study. In addition, the same result has been reported for other countries, such as Canada [see Laroche, 1989]. Even in countries exhibiting

---

2. The OECD size definitions are the standard used throughout this volume. However, there are many deviations on a country-by-country basis, so the reader is advised to consult the many notes to the tables.

3. The information from the three other countries forming part of this project (Hungary, Norway, Switzerland) will be published separately at a later date (see Foreword).

Introduction

very different size distributions, such as Italy and the United States, the time series behaviour of the small enterprise employment shares have been very similar. Furthermore, in all cases except Switzerland, small enterprise gains have coincided with large enterprise losses, as the employment shares of medium-sized enterprises have remained fairly stable.

Changes in the total economy size distribution may be influenced significantly by a sectoral recomposition of employment from goods to services production, because average enterprise and establishment size is smaller in the latter. The best way to examine this issue is to decompose the aggregate change into three parts: across sectors (compositional), within sectors, and an inter-action component.[4] These calculations have been performed for three of the nine countries in our sample. In Japan (1973-83) and France (1975-81), 75 and 45 per cent, respectively, of the increase in *very* small (fewer than 29 employees in Japan; fewer than 20 employees

Table 1: Employment shares by enterprise size, total economy

Country	Year	< 20	21-99	100-499	500+
United States	1982	45.7		13.0	41.3
Japan	1985	37.8(1)	17.9(2)	17.3	27.0
France	1985	25.8	20.4	18.3	35.5
Germany, Fed.Rep.	1970	17.2(3)	24.3(4)	18.3	40.3
Norway	1985	47.2(5)	10.2(6)	10.0(7)	32.6(8)
Switzerland	1985	46.3(9)		27.1(10)	26.5
Italy	1981	53.2	16.1	12.2	18.5

Notes:
(1) 1-29 employees.
(2) 30-99 employees.
(3) 1-10 employees.
(4) 10-100 employees.
(5) 0-49 employees.
(6) 50-99 employees.
(7) 100-199 employees.
(8) 200+ employees.
(9) 1-49 employees.
(10) 50-499 employees.

Note: Most of the tables in this chapter were compiled from information contained in the various country reports contained in this volume, or in those published separately in the IILS Research Report series.

---

4. This is commonly termed "shift-share" analysis.

Table 2: Employment shares by enterprise size, time series for the total economy

	1959	1962	1965	1968	1971	1974	1977	1979	1982	1985
Japan										
Small(1)	46.7	43.8	43.8	45.0	45.5	46.5	48.3	49.3	48.8	
Small(2)					53.3	54.4	56.9	57.3	56.6	55.7
Small and medium(1)(5)	54.6	53.3	53.7	55.0	55.9	57.0	58.9	60.2	60.0	
Small and medium(2)					70.0	70.4	72.7	73.6	73.1	73.0

	1958	1963	1967	1972	1977	1982
United States						
Small	41.3	39.9	39.9	41.3	40.1	45.7
Small and medium	55.1	52.9	53.2	53.5	52.5	58.7

	1971	1979	1985
France			
Small	39.0	43.4	46.2
Small and medium	57.4	60.7	64.5

	1907	1925	1961	1970
Germany, Fed.Rep.				
Small(3)	57.8	47.6	40.4	37.9
Small(4)	72.9	61.5	54.9	52.3
Small and medium(4)	72.9	61.5	54.9	52.3
Small and medium(6)	86.2	76.0	70.4	68.8

	1951	1961	1971	1981
Italy				
Small	60.2	63.5	61.6	69.3
Small and medium	73.0	77.1	74.4	81.5

	1929	1939	1955	1965	1975	1985
Switzerland						
Small(7)	54.2	60.2	52.5	45.4	46.1	46.3
Small and medium	81.2	83.4	82.0	78.9	77.4	73.4

Notes: Small: fewer than 100 employees.
Small and medium: fewer than 500 employees.
(1) *Basic Survey of Employment Structure*
(2) *Annual Report of the Labour Force Survey.*
(3) 1-49 employees.
(4) 1-199 employees.
(5) 0-299 employees.
(6) 1-999 employees.
(7) 1-50 employees, 1929-1939; 1-49 employees 1955-1985.

Introduction

in France) enterprise employment shares was due to compositional shifts [OECD, 1985, p.7]. The United States study in this volume reports that just under 50 per cent of the shift to small enterprises from 1973 to 1984 was due to changes in the sectoral composition of employment. Therefore, while compositional effects are clearly important, there remains a significant within-sector shift to smaller units.

Another way to see the within-sector changes in the size distribution is to examine the more comprehensive manufacturing enterprise data given in Tables 3 and 4, which also indicate that the shift to smaller enterprises is not a purely compositional effect. Table 3 shows that, again, there is enormous international variance in the size structure of manufacturing, while Table 4 shows that, with the exception of Switzerland, the small enterprise employment share has been rising at the expense of large enterprises. Hungary and the United Kingdom are the most striking examples of increased relative employment in small manufacturing enterprises. Finally, the most recent Japanese data reveal a modest decline in the employment share of small manufacturing enterprises during the latest recession. More recent data is necessary to determine whether the downturn continued into the subsequent business cycle recovery.

Table 3: Employment shares by enterprise size, manufacturing

Country	Year	< 20	21-99	100-499	500+
United States	1982	17.6		12.7	69.7
France	1979	10.7	17.9	22.0	49.4
Germany, Fed.Rep. (1)	1983		16.0	24.8	59.2
United Kingdom	1981	27.1(2)		36.9(3)	29.2(4)
Japan	1983	27.8(5)	19.3(6)	19.6	33.3
Norway (7)	1985	14.0(8)		36.3	49.6
Hungary (9)	1985	0.6(10)	2.0(11)	18.9	78.5
Switzerland	1985	17.7	23.5	28.2	30.6
Italy	1981	33.7	21.8	18.5	26.0

Notes:
(1) No data for enterprises with fewer than 20 employees. Shares thus apply only to population of enterprises with more than 20 employees.
(2) <100 employees.
(3) 10-199 employees.
(4) 1,000 + employees.
(5) 1-29 employees.
(6) 30-99 employees.
(7) No data for enterprises with fewer than 50 employees. Shares thus apply only to population of enterprises with more than 50 employees.
(8) 50-99 employees.
(9) State and co-operative sectors.
(10) <50 employees.
(11) 51-100 employees.

Table 4: Employment shares by enterprise size: Time series for manufacturing

Japan	1919	1935	1949	1955	1972(3)	1975(3)	1979(3)	1980(3)	1982(3)	1983(3)		
Small	45.0(1)	48.0(1)	51.0(1)	57.0(1)	43.0	45.0	49.0	49.0	47.0	47.0		
Small and medium	78.0(2)	83.0(2)	77.0(2)	85.0(2)	63.0	65.0	68.0	68.0	67.0	67.0		
United States	1958	1963	1967	1972	1977	1982						
Small	20.6	19.1	16.3	16.2	16.2	17.6						
Small and medium	37.1	34.5	30.4	28.9	29.0	30.3						
France	1971	1979										
Small	26.4	28.6										
Small and medium	49.5	50.6										
Germany, Fed.Rep.(4)	1963	1970	1976	1977	1980	1983	1984					
Small	14.0	12.5	13.1	15.9	15.4	16.0	16.2					
Small and medium	39.6	37.3	38.0	40.4	39.9	40.8	41.1					
United Kingdom (5)	1971	1972	1973	1974	1975	1976	1977	1978	1979	1980	1981	1982	1983
Small	15.5	16.0	15.3	16.0	16.6	17.0	17.1	17.3	17.5	18.8	20.3	21.1	22.0
Switzerland	1965	1985										
Small (6)	34.8	29.7										
Small and medium	71.0	69.4										
Italy (7)	1951	1961	1971	1981								
Small	50.5	53.2	50.5	55.3								
Small and medium	67.4	72.0	69.2	73.9								

Introduction

	1938	1949	1951	1954	1959	1964	1969	1974	1979	1982	1983	1984	1985
Hungary													
a) State (8)													
Small	87.1	62.9	50.1	33.4	2.1	0.7	0.4	0.3	0.2	0.2	0.2	0.2	2.2
Small and medium	97.2	89.4	91.7(9)	91.6(9)	22.0	10.0	7.5	7.4	5.4	5.5	5.7	5.8	16.9
b) Small firms(10)										23.0	20.4	28.5	
c) Industrial co-operatives(11)													
Average size(12)		30.2	29.9	88.3	114.5	198.5							
Small							19.0	13.8	3.1	2.9	2.8	3.0	3.0
Small and medium							86.4	83.5	63.7	68.3	69.5	68.0	68.0
d) Small co-operatives(13)										14.5	25.5	36.8	
e) Private small-scale industry(14)		269.4(15)	92.6	67.6	100.5	59.2	101.9	48.8	43.9(16)	121.4	131.5	139.0	143.5

Notes:
(1) 5-99 employees.
(2) 5-999 employees.
(3) From OECD [1985], Chart 13.
(4) 63-76 data are not comparable with 77-83 data due to inclusion of the *handwerk* sector only in the latter period. Also data covers only enterprises with 20 + employees.
(5) Data from Storey and Johnson [1987], Table 4.
(6) 1-49 employees.
(7) Excludes NACE divisions 21 and 23.
(8) Data through 1954 refer to the share of total enterprises by size. 1959 and subsequent data refer to employment shares.
(9) 101-1000 employees.
(10) Number of "new small organisations" a new statistical category introduced to account for new independent forms resulting from break-ups of larger firms. Includes subsidiary companies. Subsequent data are employment shares.
(11) Data through 1964 are average employment per co-operative.
(12) Average number of employees per co-operative.
(13) Same as (8), except for co-operatives.
(14) Total employment, in thousands.
(15) 1948 data.
(16) 1978 data.

The services data, shown in Tables 5 and 6, are much more anecdotal and fragmentary. The services sector is defined in so many different ways that international comparisons of the size structure are not very meaningful. The time series evidence is even thinner, and does not suggest any clear trend. What is perhaps most notable in the services data is the existence of sectors, such as banking and insurance, where the typical enterprise is quite large, and eating and drinking establishments and personal and commercial services, where most enterprises are quite small.

Establishments are production units, and shifts in their size structure are obviously conceptually distinct from that of *enterprises*, which are ownership units. Which entity is most appropriate depends on precisely what issues are being addressed; more specifically, whether the emphasis is on production or control. The data in the nine country studies indicate, however, that the movement in both cases is toward higher employment shares in small units: enterprises are getting smaller, at least in part, because establishments are getting smaller.

Table 5: Employment shares by enterprise size, service sector

Country	Year	< 20	21-99	100-499	500+
United States (1)	1982	60.1		17.1	22.8
Germany, Fed.Rep. (2)	1970	39.0(3)	23.4(4)	11.8	25.7
United Kingdom					
Banking	1983			1.5(5)	95.5(6)
Insurance	1983			4.8(5)	80.0(6)
Japan	1983	40.4(7)	16.6(8)	16.7	26.2
Italy (2)	1981	71.1	9.2	6.1	13.6
Switzerland	1985				
Retailing, hotels, repair			64.0(9)	19.6 (10)	16.4
Banks, insurance, real estate, rental services			15.1(9)	24.4(10)	60.5
Consulting, planning, commercial services			80.2(9)	14.8(10)	6.6
Traffic, transport, communication			20.4(9)	14.8(10)	64.8

Notes: (1) "Selected service" industries.
(2) Includes wholesale and retail trade, which are not included for other countries in this table.
(3) 1-9 employees.
(4) 10-99 employees.
(5) Share of enterprises with 10-199 employees.
(6) Share of enterprises with 1,000 + employees.
(7) 1-29 employees.
(8) 30-99 employees.
(9) 1-49 employees.
(10) 50-499 employees.

Introduction

Table 6: Employment shares by enterprise size, time series for services

	1958	1963	1967	1972	1977	1982
United States (1)						
Small	69.5	67.3	65.4	63.5	59.0	60.1
Small and medium	84.0	81.7	81.0	79.3	75.7	77.2

	1961	1970
Germany, Fed.Rep. (2)		
Small	66.0	62.4
Small and medium	75.8	74.2

	1965	1985
Switzerland		
Retailing, hotels, repair		
Small (3)	63.4	64.0
Small and medium	85.1	83.6
Banks, insurance, real estate, rental services		
Small (3)	29.1	15.1
Small and medium	58.3	39.5

Notes:
(1) "Selected services".
(2) Includes wholesale and retail trade, which are not included in United States data.
(3) 1-49 employees.

Table 7: Employment shares by establishment size, total economy

Country	Year	< 20	20-99	100-499	500+
Japan	1981	49.4	27.6	11.2	11.7
United States	1985	26.9	29.0	23.9	20.2
Germany, Fed.Rep.	1983(3)	27.3	22.4	22.6	27.7
Switzerland	1985	42.6	26.7	19.6	11.1
Italy	1981	50.7	21.7	14.9	12.7

Notes:
(1) 100-299 employees.
(2) 300 + employees.
(3) Data from Employment Statistics; excludes self-employed.

Table 8: Employment shares by establishment size, time series for total economy, recent data

Japan	1969	1972	1975	1978	1981								
Small	70.1	71.5	73.8	76.1	77.1								
Small and medium (1)	83.1	84.2	85.6	87.5	88.3								
United States	1962	1965	1970	1975	1978	1979	1980	1981	1982	1983	1984	1985	
Small	51.3	51.5	49.5	54.0	54.4	54.1	54.3	54.5	55.1	56.1	55.9	55.9	
Small and medium				76.9	77.7	77.6	78.1	78.5	78.6	79.2	79.4	79.8	
Germany, Fed. Rep. (2)	1977	1978	1979	1980	1981	1982	1983	1984	1985				
Small	47.0	47.4	47.9	47.7	48.3	49.0	49.7	50.2	49.6				
Small and medium	70.4	70.7	71.1	70.9	71.4	71.9	72.3	73.0	72.3				
Italy	1951	1961	1971	1981									
Small	67.2	61.6	69.3	72.4									
Small and medium	82.6	82.2	85.0	87.3									
Switzerland	1975	1985											
Small	66.2	69.3											
Small and medium	88.2	89.0											

Notes: (1) 1-300 employees.
(2) Data from Employment Statistic; see: Cramer [1987].

Introduction

The pattern of international variation in the size structure identified for enterprises also holds for establishments: Japan, Italy and Switzerland have relatively large shares of employment in small establishments, while the United States and the Federal Republic of Germany have larger shares in medium and large establishments (Table 7). The time series data (Table 8) again display a noticeable "V" pattern for small establishments, as well as a decline in large establishment employment shares. Early time series data (Table 9) for the Federal Republic of Germany, the United States and Switzerland show a long and steady decline in small establishment employment shares into the late 1960s-early 1970s, with a significant blip during the Great Depression (more on this latter point below).

Table 9: Employment shares by establishment size, time series, historical data

	1882(6)	1895(6)	1907	1925	1933	1950	1970	
Germany, Fed.Rep. (1)								
Small (2),(4)	78.0	70.4	62.9	53.3	62.0	56.8	43.6	
Small and medium (2),(5)	88.1	84.4	79.7	69.9	76.4	73.0	63.2	
Small (3),(4)	-	-	57.6	49.3	56.6	53.9	42.1	
Small and medium (3),(5)	-	-	76.8	67.4	73.0	71.2	62.2	
	1909	1919	1929	1933	1939	1947	1967	1977
United States (7)								
Very small (8)	14.4	10.3	9.8	10.0	9.5	7.2	5.6	6.5
Small (9)	37.8	29.2	29.1	30.8	30.0	25.0	23.2	25.3
	1905	1929	1939	1955	1975			
Switzerland								
Small	76.0	70.6	73.5	66.6	66.2			
Small and medium				87.0	88.2			

Notes: (1) For total economy, census data.
(2) Includes the self-employed in the small category.
(3) Excludes the self-employed altogether.
(4) Up to 50 employees.
(5) Up to 200 employees.
(6) No self-employed data for these years.
(7) Manufacturing sector; Census of Manufacturers data.
(8) Fewer than 20 employees.
(9) Fewer than 100 employees.

The manufacturing establishment size data is the most comprehensive in this study, as time series data are available for all nine countries (Tables 10 and 11). The evolution of the manufacturing establishment size distribution over time provides the clearest case in the sample for an international "V" pattern. In all the countries in Table 11 except Switzerland, the employment shares of small establishments rise in the late 1970s or early 1980s, reversing downward trends in previous periods. The increase is again particularly striking for Hungary and the United Kingdom. The Swiss data for the decade are difficult to interpret because the employment shares oscillate significantly from one observation to the next, but the sharp decline from 1975 to 1985 is clearly inconsistent with the trend in the other countries in the sample. Perhaps more importantly, in Japan and the United States, the trend toward larger shares of employment in small establishments was reversed in the early-mid 1980s, which is consistent with the Japanese enterprise level developments reported above. The data from the other countries, at least so far, do not suggest that the reversal is, like the "V" pattern, an international phenomenon in manufacturing.

Finally, the existence of comparable enterprise and establishment data is important for consideration of a closely related issue: namely, decentralisation of production within large enterprises. Declining large enterprise employment shares are not sufficient to address this issue, since they are consistent with a declining number of increasingly large establishments. However, if the dynamics of establishment and enterprise size distributions of employment in an industry both favour smaller units, then the hypothesis of decentralisation within large firms gains further credence. The data, in fact, support such a hypothesis for most cases where comparable data exist; e.g., Japan, Italy, the United States, France, the Federal Republic of Germany and the United Kingdom. Nonetheless, to make the case conclusively requires data on the average number of establishments per large enterprise, since otherwise the true results may be lost in aggregation. The British report provides such data for the 100 largest firms from 1970 to 1983. These data show an increase in the average number of establishments per large enterprise and a decline in average employment per establishment, thus demonstrating decentralisation of large enterprises in the United Kingdom.

Table 10: Employment shares by establishment size, manufacturing

Country	Year	< 20	20-99	100-499	500 +
Japan	1983	35.0(1)	21.0(2)	17.0(3)	27.0(4)
United States	1985	7.4	20.2	33.8	38.6
United Kingdom	1983		26.2	27.0	46.8
France	1981(5)	25.0	22.0	26.0	27.0
	1981(6)	21.8	23.0	27.1	28.1
Norway	1985	17.8	30.6	15.3(7)	36.4(8)
Germany, Fed.Rep.	1970		33.4	25.3	41.1
Switzerland	1985	19.6	26.9	30.6	23.0
Hungary (9)	1985	3.4	14.9	32.9	48.8
Italy	1981	35.5	23.8	21.1	19.6

Notes:
(1) 1-29 employees.
(2) 30-99 employees.
(3) 100-299 employees.
(4) 300+ employees.
(5) "Industry" including self-employed.
(6) "Industry" excluding self-employed.
(7) 100-199 workers.
(8) 200 + workers.
(9) State and co-operative sectors.

Introduction

Table 11: Employment shares by establishment size: Time series for manufacturing

	1957	1962	1967	1971	1977	1980	1982	1984	
Japan									
Small	59.0	52.0	53.0	51.0	56.0	58.0	56.0	55.0	
Small and medium (1)	73.0	68.0	69.0	67.0	71.0	74.0	72.0	72.0	
	1974	1976	1978	1980	1981	1982	1983	1984	1985
United States									
Small	24.4	25.4	25.3	25.2	25.6	26.9	28.0	27.4	27.6
Small and medium	57.2	58.3	58.3	58.2	58.8	59.9	61.7	61.3	61.4
	1906	1926	1931	1936	1954	1966	1974	1981	
France									
Small	75.0	63.0	59.0	61.0	52.0	48.0	45.0	47.0	
Small and medium	88.0	81.0	79.0	79.0	75.0	74.0	72.0	73.0	
	1930	1948	1954	1963	1970	1974-1975	1978		
United Kingdom									
Small	28.9	26.8	24.1	20.2	18.4	19.7	26.2		
Small and medium	61.6	59.0	56.5	50.9	45.4	45.0	53.2		
	1952	1963	1974	1984	1985				
Norway									
Small	58.4	50.6	45.1	48.3	48.4				
Small and medium (2)	70.7	64.3	60.0	64.4	63.7				
	1963	1970	1976	1977	1980	1984			
Germany, Fed. Rep. (3)									
Small	20.0	18.5	19.6	18.7	18.3	18.6			
Small and medium	48.2	46.6	48.3	48.0	47.6	48.5			

continued overleaf

Table 11: Employment shares by establishment size: Time series for manufacturing (continued)

Switzerland	1955	1965	1975	1985						
Small	43.6	37.8	38.4	33.3						
Small and medium	80.1	76.8	78.3	77.0						

Hungary (4)	1959	1964	1969	1974	1979	1980	1981	1982	1983	1984	1985
Small	10.6	5.2	8.3	8.6	8.4	8.5	8.6	8.7	8.4	8.5	14.2
Small and medium	33.1	21.1	31.4	24.6	35.6	37.8	37.7	38.0	38.1	38.2	45.6

Italy (5)	1951	1961	1971	1981
Small	54.2	56.9	54.6	59.1
Small and medium	74.6	78.5	76.9	80.3

Notes: (1) 100-299 employees.
(2) <199 employees.
(3) 1963-76 data are not comparable with 1977-84 data due to inclusion of the *handwerk* sector only in the latter period.
(4) State sector.
(5) Excludes NACE divisions 21 and 23.

2. Problems in interpretation of the employment share evidence

The employment share data provide fairly conclusive evidence of a relative shift in employment to smaller units in recent years, but this method of empirical inquiry has a number of shortcomings with respect to gaining a rich understanding of actual changes in industrial organisation. The fundamental problem arises in the inability of share data to inform explicitly on both changes of size taking place in existing firms over time, and changes introduced by the dynamics of firm births and deaths. These changes, which are identifiable using longitudinal data, are obscured almost entirely in share data. Examples are many, but consider the following problems. The same rise in the employment share of small enterprises may result from employment decline among large firms but constant employment in existing small firms, births of small firms and stable employment in large firms, employment growth among existing small firms at a rate exceeding that of large firms, and substantial employment loss among several large enterprises that over time move through the size distribution into the small firm sector, etc. Of course, a small firm employment share decline can result from dynamic growth of small firms through the size distribution. These examples illustrate the point that exactly the same employment share changes can be generated by vastly different phenomena having widely varying implications for new industrial organisation. The problems in this regard are very similar to those of job generation studies, but in the latter case the data permit the research methodology to control more carefully for these factors.

A closely related empirical problem, that has increased in importance significantly in recent years, is that large enterprises often have very many legally independent subsidiaries. While the subsidiaries are *de jure* independent, they are *de facto* part of the large enterprise and should be accounted for accordingly. The relationship between the ostensibly independent firms is virtually impossible to track in current large samples, but the failure to do so may seriously jeopardise inferences drawn from the unadjusted data. Bade [1983], for example, found that in 1983 the 32 largest German manufacturing enterprises had in excess of 1,000 legally independent subsidiaries, and the number grew by almost 50 per cent from 1971-1983. Developments of this sort have obvious implications for the sort of conclusions that might be drawn from a more superficial review of the data presented in this overview. If the phenomenon identified by Bade is international, the results discussed above must be seen as an *upper bound* on the true movement to smaller enterprises.

A further important consideration is that, after all, employment is only one of many potential dimensions by which to analyse changes in industrial organisation, and the dimensions which are most relevant for empirical work should be derived, or follow, from a well articulated theory of new industrial organisation. Of course, in the end, the empirical work is always constrained by data availability, but this fact should not impede the understanding that a theory may suggest that other indicators are better, or more appropriate, for testing hypotheses. In the United States, for example, the declining manufacturing employment share is considered by many to be evidence of deindustrialisation, while for others it is the logical, and desirable, result of a rate of productivity growth exceeding that of other sectors. It may be that changes in industrial organisation are best captured by changes in the size distribution of profitability, value-added, capital investment, unit labour costs, innovation (patents), in-process inventories, or a myriad of other non-employment variables. If, for example, a large enterprise reduces employment but increases its capital stock so as to keep output constant, this is obviously a different development in terms of industrial organisation than if large enterprise employment declines because *production* is actually shifting to smaller firms. The country reports contain a variety of important non-employment data that is very useful in understanding national developments in the size structure. Unfortunately, comparable data is not available in enough countries to permit international comparison.

What would constitute an ideal data set for research will be considered elsewhere, and ultimately you must "dance with girl you brought to the ball". For better or worse the employment share data are the most comprehensive available in this project for the purposes of international comparison, so it is important to now weigh critically what can be learned from them. Perhaps the most significant cause for concern that the increasing small unit employment shares does not reflect any fundamental changes in industrial organisation favouring smaller units is that there is compelling evidence in the data that the "V" pattern may be generated largely by the *counter-cyclicality* of small firm employment shares. If these shares rise in recessionary periods as large firms reduce employment, there is an employment decline in industries like durable or capital goods which are produced primarily by large units, and new and small firm employment rises (part-time work, subcontracting, etc.), this is a much different matter than if there is a *trend* increase in small firm employment.

The best way to investigate this issue, given the available data, would be to regress the employment shares on cyclical variables to determine if a trend exists and, if so, in what direction. The United States study in this volume includes such an analysis. The small manufacturing establishment employment share is regressed on cyclical variables and a time trend for the period 1969 to 1984. The results indicate an important, statistically significant counter-cyclical relationship *and* a postive trend. The similar regression for large establishments yields a statistically significant cyclical relationship and a negative trend. The shift to small establishments, therefore, remains after controlling for the effect of the business cycle.

In the absence of this type of analysis for the other countries, OLS (ocular least squares) must be employed: that is, the time series data must be examined to consider whether cyclical effects have played a large role. A first pass at this procedure suggests that there are at least three reasons for thinking that cyclical factors have been important. First, the "V" pattern crudely fits the prosperous 1960s/stagflation 1970s experience, and individual country data often fit rather closely with even the more detailed cycles in the 1970s/early 1980s. In other cases there is evidence of a cyclical effect around a positive trend similar to what was found in the regression analysis of the

Introduction

United States data. This can be seen by looking at first differences of the British manufacturing enterprise time series.

For most other countries the time series are inadequate to test for cyclical influences, but in the case of Japan the data are adequate yet give mixed results. On the one hand, the Japanese data up to 1980 do not seem to display much cyclical sensitivity. This may be due in part to the superior macroeconomic performance of Japan over the period but, in fact, this makes the Japanese small unit experience even more outstanding. Industrial employment growth from 1970 to 1983 was higher in Japan than in any of the other eight countries and GNP growth exceeded the OECD average throughout the period, yet the small unit share grew steadily and substantially. On the other hand, the most recent time series data for total economy enterprises and manufacturing enterprises and establishments reveal a reversal in the trend toward smaller enterprises since roughly 1980. Output and rate of return on capital data in the Japanese report also show a sharp deterioration in the relative profitability and output of small enterprises and establishments since 1980. While the overall Japanese experience cautions against extrapolating these recent results to other countries, the recent Japanese and United States data raise questions about the sustainability of the trend to small units during the recent recovery.

A third reason for concern about cyclical influences stems from data from the Great Depression. In French manufacturing establishment data, German economy establishment data, and Japanese total economy enterprise data, there are very large increases or blips, coincident with the Great Depression during what are otherwise significant negative trends in small unit employment shares. Thus, there is a historical precedent for the claim that increased small unit employment shares are a product of bad times.

One commonly cited cyclical explanation for small firm growth appears not to have played an important role: self-employment. Self-employment and new firms started by the self-employed are generally considered to be a significant counter-cyclical response to rising unemployment. However, a recent study by the OECD [1986] concludes that the level of self-employment is insensitive to the business cycle. It is not, therefore, likely to have affected the size distribution of employment.

In sum, this section has raised several issues that counsel caution in the interpretation of the employment share data. The data are, unfortunately, inadequate to permit a more rigorous empirical analysis that would control for the business cycle, sectoral recomposition, etc. and calculate what portion of the shift to smaller units was a "genuine" change in industrial organisation. These shortcomings do not, however, imply that nothing can be learned from the data, or that nothing substantive has happened. Indeed, the fact that a long-standing trend toward larger units has been reversed in all nine countries spanning such a wide range of size structures, institutions, levels of economic performance, etc. suggests that something quite important and fundamental has taken place. Furthermore, the fact that a shift to smaller units was coincident with bad economic times need not by any means imply that the shift was part of a stable relationship between the business cycle and the size structure, supported by an unchanged regime of industrial organisation. Quite the contrary, the bad times might have been symptomatic of institutional crisis and flux, of which change in the size structure of business organisations was an important part. Alternative explanations for the shift to smaller units of employment are considered in the following section.

3. Job generation

Much of the attention devoted to small firms in recent years resulted from research, beginning with Birch [1979] in the United States, claiming that small firms were responsible for creating a disproportionate share of new jobs. The process of job generation is indissolubly connected with the evolution of employment shares, but there is no unique mapping between the former and periodic observations of the latter. The job generation methodology is based on longitudinal data that tracks enterprises or establishments over time, whereas employment shares are simply cross-section snapshots of the size distribution at different points in time. The aim of job generation studies is to account for employment changes by size class, distinguish between employment changes from firm births and deaths and *in situ* expansion or contraction, and to control properly for movements of firms across size boundaries. Changes in employment shares over time can be the result of an infinite number of combinations of these factors. Thus, longitudinal job generation studies are necessary to attribute employment changes explicitly to firms of different sizes.

Unfortunately, job generation studies, such as those of Birch [1979] suffer from very severe methodological problems:

- failure to properly adjust for sample selection bias resulting from firm deaths;
- inadequate and biased sectoral representation in the sample over time;
- biased reporting of employment by firm.

A detailed critique of the job generation methodology is not pursued here, but may be found in the literature discussed below. In what follows, we present a brief review of the empirical findings from the job generation literature, with a general caveat that the results, particularly Birch's results, are highly controversial. For this reason, we base our analysis in this chapter on the more conservative employment share evidence.

Birch's [1979] pioneering study stimulated so much additional work, at least in part, because of its strong claims for the job generation performance of small firms. For the period 1969-76, Birch found that small enterprises contributed 82 per cent of net job growth in the United States private economy. Subsequent work by Armington and Odle [1982] using the same data base, first for Brookings and later for the United States Small Business Administration [1985], found small enterprises responsible for 39 per cent and 53 per cent of net job creation for the periods 1978-80 and

1976-82, respectively. Studies of the American case suggest that the superior job generation performance of small firms was due to both higher *in situ* growth and greater job creation by new firms. Small firms are reported to have been better job creators across a wide range of industries, but to have performed relatively best in terms of job growth in declining industries. Birch argues that the employment dynamic of individual firms is quite volatile with "winners" and "losers" often exchanging positions in consecutive years. Teitz et al. [1981] point out that, in California, small firm job generation was concentrated in only a few firms, while most experienced very modest employment changes.

Birch [1987] recently published updated and far more comprehensive United States job generation results. The data for 1981-85 confirm his earlier findings: 88 per cent of net job creation was in enterprises with 1-19 employees, and small enterprises with fewer than 100 employees accounted for essentially all net job creation. Small firms were again found to be superior both in terms of *in situ* expansion and job creation from start-ups and closures. In the latter case, very small firms created more than half the total, but very large firms (more than 500) were also important contributors. Large firms are less likely to die, but more likely to contract. Job creation by medium and large firms was particularly erratic, while it varied much less among small firms.

Finally, Birch [1987] stresses the tremendous turbulence experienced by firms of all sizes during this period. He finds that big losers in previous periods have the highest odds of being big winners in subsequent periods, and vice versa, while stable firms are the most likely to die. As in Teitz et al. [1981], it is the few big winners that create the lion's share of the jobs: from 1981-85, the 18 per cent of firms that grew fastest created 86 per cent of the net new jobs.

In addition to a variety of other detailed methodological criticisms, the job generation literature was recently called into question by Jonathan Leonard's [1986] work in the United States. Leonard argues that firms have long-run, or equilibrium configurations from which they are temporarily disturbed. Thus, they occasionally find themselves somewhat larger or smaller than their long-term mean employment. The process of transitory fluctuation around this mean has an inherent statistical bias with respect to job accounting of the Birch and Evans variety, as transitorily small firms will gain jobs during their path back to equilibrium, and vice versa for temporarily large firms. The argument is, therefore, that "regression to the mean" will generate high rates of job creation (loss) for small (large) firms, but the result is, in fact, a statistical artefact of the equilibration process. In a period of rapid structural change, when there is a significant shift from old to new industries, the small unit employment share will rise as old firms shrink below their optimum and young firms have not yet reached their optimum.

Leonard tests this stochastic model using United States longitudinal data on firms in existence from 1974-80 (i.e. excludes births and deaths). His results suggest that, if his model of optimum firm size is appropriate, the conventional finding of a negative relationship between employment growth and size is nothing more than regression to the mean. Brownyn Hall [1986], conversely, estimates a similar model and rejects "regression to the mean" for a different manufacturing sector sample. She argues instead that differences in investment and R & D outlays explain truly superior job creation performance by small firms. Thus, this new dimension of the debate is by no means resolved either.

Leonard makes a related point using his longitudinal data on employment shares. The employment share analysis presented earlier in this section compared cross sections wherein enterprise/establishment employment shares were defined in terms of the current year size class. An alternative method is to compare shares calculated using base or terminal period size classes; e.g. 1980 employment by 1980 size class versus 1974 employment by 1980 size class. Using this technique Leonard finds that establishments that are small tend to grow, thereby reversing earlier employment declines. This is another implication of regression to the mean.

The United States report in our project considers the problem of consistency between the job generation results and changes in the employment shares. This comparison suggests that the magnitude of reported small firm job generation is hard to justify given observed changes in employment shares unless very many firms classified as small at the beginning of the period grew into larger size classes by the end of the period. There is evidence that this occurred, at least for a few very successful small firms, but the question of consistency remains largely unresolved.

Recent work by Evans [1987] involving a much different methodology confirms the finding that employment growth is inversely related to size in the United States. Evans uses United States manufacturing data from 1976 to 1982 to estimate the relationship between employment growth, firm size and age. He finds that employment growth decreases with size *and* age, and these results are robust to alternative assumptions regarding sample censoring (exit firms) and functional forms of the growth relationship. Evans' finding that growth decreases with size given age, and vice versa, is consistent with Birch's [1979; 1987] similar results, despite very different methodologies. Thus, while young firm growth is abnormally high, small firms continue to grow faster than large firms even after many years. The life-cycle model of firm growth is therefore applicable, but does not tell the entire story in the United States.

Finally, the most comprehensive analysis of a United States manufacturing job growth by establishment size is conducted by Dunne, Roberts and Samuelson [1987] using the longitudinal data set of all manufacturing plants present in the 1967, 1972, 1977 and 1982 Census of Manufacturers. They find a tradeoff between growth rates and survival rates, and variance across ownership types:

> When compared with small plants, large plants have lower failure rates and lower growth rates if they survive. Large multi-unit plants have both lower failure rates and higher growth rates if successful than large single-unit plants. The latter plants have negative growth rates even when they survive [Dunne et al., 1987, p. 31].

However, the failure rate is substantially higher for smaller plants:

> The average failure rate for plants with 5-19 employees is 12.7, 34.4 and 104.7 per cent higher than for plants with 20-00, 100-249, and more than 250 employees, respectively. One way of illustrating the tradeoff is to note that, in order to keep the total number of employees in the 5-19 size class constant, the surviving plants would need average growth of 64.2 per cent between the two census years (10.4 per cent annually). The relevant question, then, is not whether successful small plants have faster rates of employment growth, but whether their growth rates are large enough to compensate for their attrition rates [ibid., pp. 32-29].

Following Birch's work, job generation studies have been undertaken in many OECD countries, and the results of many of these studies are summarised in the country reports, OECD [1985], and Storey and Johnson [1987]. Storey and Johnson summarise the SME employment creation literature for the United Kingdom, the Federal Republic of Germany, and France, and Table 12, taken from their paper, gives an overview of the more important empirical findings. Note that the figures are percentages of base year employment, so that a given growth rate translates into many fewer jobs for small firms than for large firms.

Hence, despite the relatively strong performance of SMEs, the job losses of large enterprises were sufficient to dominate aggregate employment performance. Thus, despite employment gains among SMEs, total employment fell in nearly all samples that include firm closures. While these figures are not comparable to those of Birch, it is now easy to see how SME job creation can be simultaneously modest in absolute numbers, and very large as a percentage of net job creation. Furthermore, while SMEs generated jobs in both phases of the business cycle, their rate of job generation appears to be counter-cyclical. SMEs would therefore be likely to have particularly strong relative rates of job creation during the poor macroeconomic growth period of the past 10-15 years.

Storey and Johnson cite two other important caveats to the results. First, the distribution of job gains and losses within size groups is far from uniform: a large proportion of new jobs (job losses) come from a small number of firms. Table 13, also taken from Storey and Johnson, shows that very few of the firms that started the period in the smallest size category grew past the very small size group by the end of the period. However, the vast majority of new jobs were created by the few firms that did expand substantially.

Second, Storey and Johnson point out that, given the minor (major) job losses from the contraction or closure of small (large) firms, it is relatively easy (hard) for a few "winners" to compensate for the losers. Thus, there is a natural bias favouring small firms in this sort of job growth accounting. In addition, many of the jobs ostensibly created by small enterprises may ultimately have their source in large enterprises via subsidiary or multi-establishment connections.

Table 12: Job generation studies in Europe

Country/Area	Time period	Coverage	20	20-49	50-99	100-499	500+	Total
United Kingdom								
East Midlands	1968-1975	Manufacturing	+0.4	+0.3	+0.2	-0.3	-0.9	-0.3
Northern England	1965-1976	Manufacturing	+0.2	+0.1	+0.0	-0.1	-1.0	-0.8
Northern England	1976-1981	Manufacturing	+0.2	-0.0	-0.2	-1.6	-3.8	-5.4
United Kingdom	1972-1975	Manufacturing	0.0	0.0	-0.0	-0.0	-0.1	-0.1
United Kingdom	1971-1981	All sectors	+0.8	-0.1	-0.0	-0.1	-1.4	-0.7
United Kingdom	1982-1984	All sectors	+2.0	+0.3	-0.0	-1.0	-2.2	-0.9
Northern Ireland	1971-1981	Manufacturing	+0.1	-0.0	-0.2	-1.2	-1.9	-3.2
Germany, Fed. Rep.								
FRG (sample) (1)	1974-1981	All sectors	+0.2	+0.2	+0.2	+0.2	-0.5	+0.3
FRG (4 regions)(1)	1974-1980	All sectors	+0.8	+0.7	-0.0	-0.2	-0.5	+0.8
North Rhine-Westfalia	1978-1984	Manufacturing	-0.2	-0.3	-0.3	-0.9	-1.3	-3.0
Ruhr and Frankfurt	1975-1980	All sectors	+1.1	-0.4	-0.4	-0.5	+0.5	+0.3
France								
Poitou-Charentes	1972-1984	All sectors	+1.0	+0.7	-0.1	-1.9	+0.5	+0.2
France	1981-1983	All sectors	+0.0	-0.1	-0.1	-0.4	-0.4	-1.0
Ireland								
Ireland	1973-1980	Manufacturing	[+0.7]		+0.3	-0.3	-0.2	+0.6

Note: (1) Survivor analysis only.

Introduction

Table 13: Jobs created in expansions of small firms (1)

	\multicolumn{6}{c}{Employment size group at end of year}	
	0	1-19	20-49	50-99	100-499	500+	Total (n)
United Kingdom, 1982-84							
% of firms	10.6	87.7	1.2	0.3	0.1	0.02	560 250
% of jobs in expansion	-	0.0	23.1	19.7	22.0	28.3	550 000
France, 1981-83							
% of firms	30.5	64.7	4.5	0.2	0.09	0.005	22 200
% of jobs in expansion	-	0.0	57.0	16.1	23.5	3.2	15 805
Poitou Charentes, 1972-84							
% of firms	61.9	33.3	4.2	0.5	0.06	0.06	1 682
% of jobs in expansion	-	0.0	47.8	14.5	6.6	31.1	2 483
Ireland, 1973-80							
% of firms	25.9	65.5	6.2	1.7	0.7	0.0	1 980
% of jobs in expansion	-	na	na	na	na	na	34 587

Note: (1) "Small firms" defined as fewer than 20 employees, apart from Ireland - fewer than 25 employees.

Hull's [1986] review of German job generation studies supports these points, but is more sceptical about the evidence for small firm dynamism. In his own research, Hull disagrees with Birch's finding that size, and not age, is the key factor in job growth. Regression analysis of a sample of 458 small independent manufacturers in Northern Germany suggests that "it is more the youth of small firms than their size which 'makes' them grow" [p.24].

Hull's most general criticism of the claims of job generation studies is to be found in a footnote which shifts the burden of proof back to the proponents by correctly pointing out the need for historical perspective:

> The results of the new micro-based job-generation studies do not necessarily indicate that a new age of the small firm has dawned, as sometimes appears to be inferred. That conclusion could only be justified on the basis of comparable micro-level evidence for earlier periods by showing that small firms have increased their employment contribution of late... But comparable evidence for earlier periods is generally lacking [Hull, 1986, p. 40].

For the Federal Republic of Germany, additional information on job creation is presented in Table 14 which was not available when the German report was written. It is based on data from a sample of 3,300 industrial establishments. It shows for the period from 1975 to 1986 that the percentage of net employment growth was the larger the smaller the size class of the establishment. By far the largest net increase was recorded in establishments with up to 20 employees [Fritsch, 1989, p. 22]. Since the data include only the survivor firms, and as the failure rate is larger for small firms than for larger ones, caution is required in inferring from the data that smaller firms are more successful in job creation. The Italian report reviews the recent important work of Contini and Revelli [1987], and the Norwegian report reviews job generation studies for Norway; the main conclusion to be drawn from these studies, which span a wide range of geographical regions, time periods, sectors, and methodologies, is that SMEs are creating jobs at a time when large enterprises have experienced declining employment. The Italian job generation story is very much like that of Birch in the United States, but the results are even more striking for very small Italian firms.

Table 14: **Employment changes between 1975 and 1986 by size of establishment, manufacturing industry, in the Federal Republic of Germany**

Establishment	Under 20	20-49	50-99	100-199	200-499	500-999	1 000 and +	Total
Gross increase	6 528	7 505	8 846	9 632	11 846	12 483	60 015	116 855
Gross losses	-898	-2 964	-3 957	-4 569	-8 118	-9 734	-46 063	-76 303
Net change (absolute)	5 630	4 541	4 889	5 063	3 728	2 749	13 952	40 552
Share of employment stock in 1975	1.7	4.6	5.6	7.8	13.1	12.0	55.4	100.0
Share of employment stock in 1986	2.6	5.1	6.0	8.1	12.8	11.6	53.9	100.0
Share of gross increase	5.6	6.4	7.6	8.2	10.1	10.7	51.4	100.0
Share of gross losses	1.2	3.9	5.2	6.0	10.6	12.8	60.4	100.0
Net change (in %)	65.3	19.2	17.1	12.7	5.5	4.5	4.9	7.9
Share of gross increase/ share of employment stock in 1975	3.4	1.4	1.4	1.1	0.8	0.9	0.9	-
Share of gross losses/ share of employment stock in 1975	0.7	0.8	0.9	0.8	0.8	1.1	1.1	-

Source: Fritsch [1989], p. 23.

A final note on employment creation research comes from the Japanese report, wherein a particular type of small enterprise, the venture business, is identified. Venture businesses are small enterprises distinguished by having "products or technology based on intensive R & D specialising in certain areas of new technology and maintaining high profitability". Koshiro tests for the "employment generating ability" of venture businesses vis-à-vis ordinary small firms by estimating the increase in employment from a unit increase in sales for the two groups. The results suggest that venture firms increase employment faster for a given increase in sales, and may thus be expected to have unusually high job creation potential. If, of course, the venture firms also have abnormally rapid sales growth, the employment results will be magnified.

In sum, a conservative review of the job generation literature suggests that small firms account for at least their share of employment creation, but the net new jobs result from a very dynamic process of expansion and contraction within the small firm sector. Large employment gains occur only in a few small firms, as most small firms start and remain small throughout their existence.

The job generation studies show that the employment dynamic accompanying new firm formation and business closures is very important to the net employment contribution of small units. Data in several country reports suggest that small firm employment share gains may have come, in part, from net additions to the stock of firms in recent years. Time series evidence for the Federal Republic of Germany, France, Japan, and Hungary shows that the population of enterprises has risen significantly in the first half of the 1980s. In general, the increase has resulted from a rise in new firms more than offsetting an increase in closures. Storey and Johnson [1987] draw the same conclusion from their sample of EC countries.

Hull, however, cites very interesting German data on new firm registrations which suggest that simple measures of firm births and deaths may not correspond to economically meaningful changes in the population of firms. A sample of new firms registered in 1981 or 1983 shows that roughly 25 per cent of "new firms" were in fact takeovers or other continuations of existing business, and another 25 per cent were not their founder's sole source of livelihood. Thus, only approximately 50 per cent of the registrations were for "genuine start-ups providing the founder's sole source of livelihood" [Hull, 1986, p. 18]. In the United States, new business data are further suspect because of the frequent and growing use of a variety of "paper corporations" for purposes of tax and litigation avoidance. Therefore, data suggesting recent increases in both the population of firms and their volatility must be interpreted rather cautiously.

The country reports also include a variety of measures of enterprise formation by sector. In all cases new firm formation is proportionately highest in the services and wholesale and retail trade sectors and in particular branches such as catering. Manufacturing and construction have below average rates of firm births.

The precarious prospects for the survival of new enterprises, the vast majority of which are small, are well known, and are reflected in the fact that the probability of survival rises significantly with size. The longer odds faced by small firms are evident in Birch's [1979] findings that the percentage of firms existing in 1969 that survived to 1976 in the United States was 40, 65, 70, and 80 for very small, small, medium, and large enterprises, respectively. Similarly, in the United Kingdom two-thirds of new businesses fail in their first two-and-a-half years, and in the Federal

Republic of Germany 37 per cent of 1985 insolvencies were in firms less than four years old. However, Birch [1987] reports that in the United States from 1981-85, the odds of an *establishment* closing were essentially constant across size classes. The same was true for the percentage of employees laid off by enterprise size.

Marsden's report in this volume shows that in the United Kingdom firms that do persevere in the early years often have very long lives: for example, firms active at least seven years in 1970 had median ages, "ranging from 19 years in retail and motor trades to 22 years in manufacturing and 69 years in construction". This apparently bi-modal life expectancy distribution resulted in a median age at death of nearly four years for all sectors of the British economy in 1981. In addition, Marsden notes the surprising uniformity of this statistic across individual sectors.

The young average age of most business failures explains part of the correlated rise of both births and deaths in recent years, since many of the latter follow with a short lag from the former. Furthermore, Hull argues that many recent births in the Federal Republic of Germany have been induced by poor economic conditions in general and high unemployment in particular, and those undertaken as "last-ditch" attempts to provide livelihood to the founder may rest on especially shaky ground. The failure rate among these firms might therefore be expected to be abnormally high as either good times draw the entrepreneur back into dependent employment or bad times topple the weak firm.

In reviewing the new firm formation data the implications for small unit employment creation bear repeating, ambiguous though they may be. First, it seems clear that internationally the vast majority of small new firms either remain small indefinitely or fail. Thus, their contribution to employment creation is modest. The few remarkably successful new small firms account for much of the total increase among small firms. Second, some studies [United States Small Business Administration, 1985; Gallagher and Stewart (United Kingdom), 1984] suggest that employment growth rates for new large firms are roughly equal to those of small firms, thus perhaps yielding a substantial number of jobs despite fewer new firms. Third, many of the thorny empirical problems discussed above also apply here.

Finally, the notion of *net* job creation is also very elusive in the case of new firms. If new firms reflect a redistribution of production from existing firms, as would be the case with subcontracting, entries not involving significant innovations or new products, or entry into industries with inelastic demand, the employment gains of new firms certainly have ambiguous welfare implications. Consequently, even settling the apparently unresolvable empirical debate may not provide a clear answer to the more substantive questions about the role of new and small firms in raising aggregate welfare.

IV. Labour compensation, working conditions and industrial relations

If there is indeed a shift to production by smaller enterprises or establishments, the relative compensation and working conditions offered by SMEs are critical, since a new industrial organisation entailing a deterioration in compensation, hours worked, etc. is not an attractive development. An appropriate way to compare two jobs is to ask whether workers with equal marginal products, or abilities, receive equal total utility from both jobs. However, it is extremely difficult to make such a comparison in practice, since many job and worker characteristics are not observable, workers have heterogeneous tastes over the range of job characteristics, and particular jobs may be part of a training or search process yielding important non-wage benefits. Keeping in mind, nonetheless, what would be an ideal comparison, there is a variety of crude indicators in the country reports which suggest that, on average, remuneration and working conditions are, and have historically been, inferior in small units.

Table 15 shows that *wages* are an increasing function of enterprise and establishment size. In some cases, such as small firms in the United States and very small firms in Japan, wages are just over half those of large firms. Wage differentials are much narrower in the Nordic countries, and in the Federal Republic of Germany where comprehensive industry-wide bargains are often applicable to all employers, including industries with many small firms. While Table 15 shows that small firms in the Federal Republic of Germany pay male workers in manufacturing approximately 90 per cent of what large firms pay, another study which examined monthly incomes for the years 1980-81 showed little difference between establishments with fewer and establishments with more than 50 employees. Female workers could gain more than male workers from employment in large plants. Controlling for gender, education, seniority, and working time, establishment size had a positive and significant effect on wages. Again, the size effect was larger for female than for male workers [Brüderl and Preisendörfer, 1986].

The figures in Table 15 differ substantially in definition and coverage, but two important international conclusions are nonetheless clear from the data. First, small firms pay lower average wages than large firms in all countries in the sample. Second, wage gaps between large, medium and small enterprises/establishments differ substantially across countries. The time series evidence is much more limited. The Japanese report presents three time series by firm size: average monthly regular pay; average monthly cash earnings (shown in Table 15); and average hourly earnings. It is interesting to look at these three series together, since they show how regular pay, bonuses, and hours worked interact to affect wage differentials by size of enterprise. The regular pay and cash earnings series display very similar fluctuations for each size group from 1965-84, but the differentials in the latter case are substantially larger because bonuses are primarily a large firm phenomenon. The differential for total hourly earnings is even larger for very small firms, owing to longer hours worked, but is roughly the same as monthly cash earnings for firms with 30-499 employees. The pattern over

Table 15: Average wages by enterprise size (1), percentage of wages in largest employment size group

Country	Year						
France (2)	1978	10-99 82.9	100-499 86.3	500+ 100.0			
Germany, Fed.Rep. (3)	1978	89.7	92.2	100.0			
Italy (3)	1978	85.4	92.7	100.0			
Japan (4)	1982	77.1	82.9(5)	100.0(6)			
United States (7)	1983	57.0(8)	73.8	100.0			
Norway (9)	1982	20 88.0	20-44 92.0	45-89 94.0	90-179 95.0	180 100.0	
Japan (10)	1984	5-29 59.3	30-99 70.0	100-499 83.4	500+ 100.0		
Germany, Fed.Rep. (11)	1978	10-49	50-99	100-199	200-499	500-999	1000+
Blue-collar		80.0	79.0	80.0	82.0	86.0	100.0
White-collar		64.0	74.0	79.0	80.0	85.0	100.0
United Kingdom (12)	1980	25-49	50-99	100-199	200-499	500-999	1000-1999	2000+
Semi-skilled		76.0	86.0	85.0	91.0	94.0	97.0	100.0
Skilled		82.0	88.0	86.0	94.0	95.0	97.0	100.0
Clerical		82.0	86.0	87.0	89.0	89.0	89.0	100.0
Middle management		82.0	85.0	85.0	87.0	92.0	94.0	100.0
Switzerland	1979	1-19(13)	20-49	50-99	100-199	200-499	500-999	1000+
Total economy		82.5	86.3	87.6	88.9	93.8	93.1	100.0
Industry and crafts		80.9	81.4	82.3	83.9	88.6	87.7	100.0

Introduction

Time series data

		5-29	30-99	100-499	500+	
Japan (10)	1965	65.9	78.3	86.7	100.0	
	1970	64.9	76.2	85.8	100.0	
	1975	64.9	75.6	86.2	100.0	
	1980	61.7	72.7	83.6	100.0	
	1984	59.3	70.0	83.4	100.0	

		25-90	500+			
United Kingdom (14)	1970	85.0(15)	100.0			
	1980	93.0(15)				

		20	20-99	100-249	250-499	500-999	1000+
United States (15)	1974	78.0	70.6	71.1	73.2	80.3	100.0
	1976	69.4	69.4	70.6	72.0	79.9	100.0
	1978	65.1	65.8	67.7	70.3	78.5	100.0
	1980	66.0	66.2	68.5	71.4	79.6	100.0
	1982	62.3	65.1	68.2	70.8	78.6	100.0
	1984	60.4	62.9	65.6	68.9	77.1	100.0

Notes: (1) Italy, Norway, first German series, and second United Kingdom and United States series are for establishments, all others are for enterprises.
(2) Hourly pay, manual manufacturing workers.
(3) Hourly pay, male manual manufacturing workers.
(4) Monthly scheduled earnings for regular employees in private non-agricultural sector.
(5) 100-999 employees. (6) 1000+ employees.
(7) Usual weekly earnings for wage and salary earners in private non-agricultural sector.
(8) 1-99 employees.
(9) Data on blue-collar workers from Norwegian Employers Federation, adjusted for worker and job characteristics.
(10) Average monthly cash earnings of regular employees in all industries except services.
(11) Total labour cost per hour in manufacturing, mining, and construction.
(12) Workplace industrial relations survey for whole economy, establishments.
(13) Unweighted average of earnings for the 1-3, 4-5, 6-9, and 10-19 employee size groups.
(14) Average weekly earnings for manual workers in small engineering firms.
(15) 25-99 employees. (16) Annual payroll per employee in manufacturing establishments.

time in all cases is a trend increase, with temporary declines in the oil-shock recessions of the 1970s. The differentials have risen substantially since the late 1970s and are at historically very high levels. The fluctuation and increase in differentials has been much more pronounced for small versus medium-size firms.

The United States manufacturing data also display a steady increase in wage differentials by establishment size. Differentials widened for all size groups below 1,000 workers from 1974 to 1984, but the increase was especially large for very small establishments.

The only other intertemporal evidence comes from a comparison of 1970 and 1980 average weekly earnings for manual workers in small engineering firms in the United Kingdom. These data show a very significant decline in the differentials, suggesting a relative shifting out (back) of labour demand curves for small (large) firms, since the small firm employment share rose coincidentally with small firm relative wages.

Supporting evidence for a decline in wage differentials comes from an attempt in the Japanese report to adjust differentials for differences in worker age, education, occupation, and experience. This method is in the spirit of the "ideal comparison" outlined above, and it shows a significant narrowing of differentials in monthly regular pay for male manufacturing workers from 1961 to 1972, and further from 1972 to 1984. It also shows that there are significant differences in the career profile of earnings by firm size, with the adjusted small firm differential being small if not negligible for workers under 40, but quite significant for workers over 50. Koshiro attributes this to the fact that many blue-collar workers in small firms achieve white-collar or ownership status around age 40. Indeed, the ability of some small firm employees to earn "entrepreneurial-like" incomes introduces considerable variance into the earnings distribution of small firm employees. The Japanese report shows that while the low tail of the small firm earnings distribution lies well below that for large firms, the high tail lies substantially above the highest earnings in large firms.

The adjusted differentials calculated by Koshiro, nonetheless, almost undoubtedly understate the true size of compensation differentials. By using regular monthly pay rather than total hourly earnings, the adjustment fails to capture the higher bonuses and shorter hours in large firms. United States studies using more sophisticated techniques have consistently found that observationally equivalent workers in similar jobs earn considerably less in small firms. In a systematic review of American data, Brown and Medoff [1989] show that differences in labour quality can explain no more than one-half of the total establishment size differential. This differential is estimated to be roughly 10 per cent across establishments one standard deviation below the average size to one standard deviation above. Furthermore, Brown and Medoff find independent positive effects of enterprise and establishment size. Alternative explanations for the differentials - differences in working conditions, product market power, and union avoidance - are found to contribute little empirically. Hence, much of the United States size differential remains unexplained. However, even this is an understatement of the pecuniary disadvantage of small firm employment, since it fails to

Introduction 37

account for non-wage compensation such as medical insurance, pension benefits, etc. There is little doubt that fringe benefits are much higher for large enterprise employees. While this may be due in large part to more extensive unionisation of large firms, the OECD [1985, p. 79] reports that in the United States the differential by size is even more pronounced for non-union firms. Comprehensive data on fringe benefits is notoriously hard to find. However, the Japanese and British reports document substantially lower non-wage compensation in small enterprises establishments, and Table 16 taken from OECD [1985] shows that in the United States and Japan compensation differentials are very large, and may perhaps be even wider than wage differentials in these countries. The table also suggests that the preponderance of part-time workers, who are typically exempt from fringe benefits, in small firms may explain part of the difference.

Skill composition data in a few of the country reports suggest that compensation differentials are not likely to follow from an *overall* lower skill level in small firms. The French report gives detailed occupational data by firm size for 1979 and 1983, which indicate that small firms employ roughly the same proportion of skilled production workers, but proportionately more white-collar workers and fewer unskilled workers than large firms. The difference narrowed somewhat from 1979 to 1983, as large firms reduced their share of unskilled workers quite significantly. The British report shows that small engineering firms (25-99) have a much higher share of skilled workers than large firms, and the difference increased from 1970-80. The small firms also have a slightly higher share of unskilled workers, but the large firms have a much greater share of semi-skilled workers. Similarly, Storey and Johnson [1987] cite evidence that the skill level of manufacturing employees is higher in small enterprises in the United Kingdom and Federal Republic of Germany. In the Federal Republic of Germany, 76 per cent of male manual small firm workers are rated as skilled, as opposed to 60 per cent in large firms. There is no difference in the share of workers rated as unskilled workers, but the proportion of those rated as semi-skilled is much higher in large firms. In a study based on social security data, it turned out that larger establishments employ greater shares of highly educated personnel, but also larger proportions of unskilled workers [Cramer, 1987]. Finally, Hotz-Hart reports that in Switzerland, small firms have a higher share of workers with no training, but, like the large firms, have a high share of craftsmen. The larger firms, of course, have much more of their employment devoted to non-production activities such as marketing and personnel.

Becattini argues in this volume that, at least so far as industrial districts in Italy are concerned, standard compensation and working conditions data do not adequately describe worker welfare. Living conditions and working conditions are tightly interconnected, and many benefits in the former (e.g. training and social relationships) may offset shortcomings in the latter.

Table 16: Non-wage compensation by firm size

				Enterprise size (Number of persons employed)			
United States	Year	1-24	25-99	100-199	500-999	1000+	
Health insurance coverage (%)	1983	35.4	64.9	75.1	79.1	86.3	
Pension or retirement plan coverage (%)	1983	17.3	40.7	63.9	74.3	87.9	
Average years of tenure with current employer (years)	1983	4.5	5.2	6.0	6.8	9.0	
Part-time employment (proportion of employment in each size group (%))	1983	31.8	16.6	15.8	14.1	12.2	
Japan	Year	1-29	30-99	100-299	300-999	1000-4999	5000+
Average cost per regular employee of obligatory welfare services(1)(%)	1982	-	70.5	71.8	81.2	92.6	100.0
Average cost per regular employee of non-obligatory welfare services(2)(%)	1982	-	28.7	30.4	41.6	60.5	100.0
Retirement allowance at mandatory retirement (%)	1982	-	22.1	46.7		100.0	
Average years of tenure with current employers (years)	1982		7.9(3)	9.1		12.2	
Part-time employment (proportion of employment in each size group (%))	1983	15.1	8.8	7.5(4)	7.4(5)	8.4	

Notes: (1) Employer payments for pension schemes, health insurance, etc.
(2) Company housing, canteens, recreational facilities, etc.
(3) 10-99.
(4) 100-499.
(5) 500-999.

Sources: United States, data supplied by BLS based on the May 1981 Special Pension Supplement to the Current Population Survey; Japan, Ministry of Labour, *Yearbook of labour statistics*, and Bureau of Statistics, *Labour force surveys*.

The dimension of working conditions for which the best, and perhaps only, international comparative data exist is *hours worked*. The Japanese, French and British country reports contain data suggesting that small firm employees work more hours than large firm employees, but the discrepancy has narrowed in recent years. Table 17 reproduces a portion of the data, and shows that while total hours worked have declined in the past 15 years for all workers, the decline has been significantly greater in small firms. There remains, however, a substantial small/large differential, but the differential is rather modest between medium and large firms. In Japan the longer hours for small firm employees result from more work days per week, more hours per day, and fewer holidays and vacation days.

Introduction

Table 17: Hours worked by enterprise size

Japan	Total monthly hours worked, all industries				
Size	1970	1973	1975	1980	1984
5-29	195.9	190.1	182.7	184.5	182.9
30-99	187.8	183.3	175.5	177.8	177.5
100-499	186.3	182.0	171.9	174.2	175.2
500+	185.4	179.8	166.6	174.4	176.1

United Kingdom	Weekly hours worked for all workers in small engineering firms	
	1970	1980
25-99	45.7	43.5
500+	42.0	41.3

France	Total annual hours worked, commerce and industry
	(see figure 4 in French report)

From the perspective of understanding the growth of small units, the compensation and working hours data are also interesting in so far as they shed light on the important issue of differences in *unit labour costs* by firm size. Unit labour costs are, of course, a function of compensation and productivity, and thus have sufficiently stiff data requirements. Little is known about how they vary by firm size. The British report gives labour productivity data showing significant advantages for large establishments, which appear to have increased in recent years. If so, compensation differentials may be insufficient to give smaller firms any significant current unit labour cost advantage. Table 18 from Sengenberger [1987] shows that labour productivity is an increasing function of establishment size in the United Kingdom, France, Italy, and the Federal Republic of Germany. In addition, Table 19 shows that unit labour costs were a monotonically decreasing function of establishment size in Japan in 1978. The inferior labour productivity of small establishments, due in large part to much lower capital-labour ratios, was sufficient to more than offset substantially lower wages.

The differences in compensation and working conditions are reflected in a very strong positive relationship between size and *unionisation rates*. The French, British, Norwegian and Japanese reports contain data on trade union coverage by enterprise/establishment size, all of which show that small unit employees are covered by collective bargaining agreements to a much lesser extent than are large unit employees. For example, in Japan in 1985 the unionisation rates in the private sector were 60, 24, 7 and 0.5 per cent for firms with 500+, 100-499, 30-99, and 1-29 workers, respectively; in Norway in 1980 the rate of union membership by establishment size ranged monotonically from 18 per cent for fewer than five workers to 67 per cent

Table 18: Indices of labour productivity by firm size: Germany (Fed.Rep.), France, Italy and United Kingdom

Establishment size	Germany (F.R.)	France	Italy	United Kingdom
1000+	100.0	100.0	100.0	100.0
500 - 999	86.2	87.3	96.0	100.0
100-499	85.5	85.7	87.0	91.3
20-99	84.7	116.1	75.0	83.8

Source: Eurostat, *Structure and activity in industry*, 1978, Vol. 15; Sengenberger [1987].

Table 19: Indices of wages, productivity, unit labour costs, and the capital-labour ratio by firm size in Japan

Establishment size	Wages	Value added per employee	Unit labour costs	Capital-labour ratio
1000+	100.0	100.0	100.0	100.09
500-999	85.5	89.3	98.7	83.3
300-499	81.9	81.3	100.7	77.6
200-299	74.7	72.6	102.9	57.8
100-199	67.6	64.2	105.3	46.3
50-99	60.3	53.0	113.8	36.4

Source: Nippon, *A chartered survey of Japan, 1981-82*, Tokyo, Kokuseisha, 1981, S.51.

for 200+ workers; only 25 per cent of British private sector establishments with 1-24 workers recognised trade unions in 1980, while the equivalent figure for establishments with 200+ workers was 91 per cent; and in France in 1985, 9.1 per cent of workers in establishments with 11-49 workers were not covered by an industry-wide, company or plant agreement, while all workers in establishments with 500+ workers were covered. In the Federal Republic of Germany, where union density declines with establishment size as well, the frequent extension of collective agreements to the entire industry means that small unit coverage is not so much below that of large units, but in the United States the difference is quite large.

One obvious reason for the less extensive unionisation of small firms is their concentration in industries which have historically been relatively less organised. The Japanese report shows that unionisation rates in wholesale and retail trade, services, and construction are well below those of industries for which the size structure favours large firms. French data for 1985 show that four times as many tertiary workers were "uncovered" than were industrial workers.

Time series data in the French and Japanese reports give conflicting results on changes in unionisation rates in recent years. In France there was a decline of well over half the percentage of "uncovered" workers in small units from 1981-85, as small units participated strongly in the general trend that resulted in the percentage of uncovered workers in all size units falling from 11 to 4.4 per cent. In Japan, on the other hand, private and public sector unionisation rates have fallen since at least 1970, and the decline has been at least as strong overall for SMEs as for large firms.

Finally, there is evidence that industrial disputes, as manifested by *strikes*, are less common in small firms. British data on work days lost, and number of stoppages, per employee, show both series rising significantly with manufacturing plant size for 1971-73. Prais et al. [1981] report a similar positive relationship for the United States and the Federal Republic of Germany for 1965-75, but with less significant size-related differences. Marsden points out that the differences in the level of industrial disputes may have important relative cost-of-production implications favouring small firms, observable in the form of larger buffer stocks and excess capital in large firms.

While these results can be summarised cautiously by saying that - on a statistical basis - workers are largely less well off in smaller enterprises and establishments, the question again is whether this is inevitably so. Is the quality of work and employment necessarily related to organisational size? And would a further expansion of small-unit employment inescapably entail a downward slide in the conditions of labour?

It can be plausibly argued that it is not the size dimension as such that matters. A union's capacity for mobilising workers and gaining organisational strength may not be crucially related to enterprise or establishment size. In fact some of the most effective union organisation in the United States can be found in small-scale industries such as printing, trucking, construction and ladies' garments [see Piore and Sabel, 1984]. In many countries the earlier strong base of trade unions was in the craft sector and it frequently was not at all easy for unionism to set foot in the large-scale mass production industries.

There are instances where unionism covers small business. In Sweden many small and even very small firms in metal-working and other manufacturing industries are highly union organised and wages are approximately on a par with those paid by large producers. This, of course, is mainly the outcome of very high union density, solidaristic wage policies and the related emphasis on egalitarian wage structures that have been followed in Sweden over the past 30 to 40 years. The highly uniform wage standards across economic sectors, regions and firm size groups has squeezed the inefficient small firms with a lower capacity to pay out of the market.

There is also a serious issue of how certain statistical indicators of job and employment quality are to be interpreted. For example does the lower job stability found in smaller firms and establishments, as measured by job tenure or accession and separation rates, necessarily mean more insecurity to the worker? It often does, but it also depends on whether or not institutions exist to take care of the social consequences of the instability problem; or even better, that make arrangements under which instability or discontinuity at the level of individual firms is not passed through into employment insecurity. If there is some central labour market agency, such as a hiring hall (as in United States construction) that redistributes the workers who lose their jobs as a result of a shrinking or disappearing business, the loss of a job in a particular firm may not be a disaster. Likewise, if there are well established occupational-type labour markets with standardised skills that act as channels of inter-firm mobility, then fairly high rates of job changes may be conducive to the functioning of the market. Inter-firm mobility may help the worker to accumulate skill and experience and at the same time help the firm to adjust its labour volume to changing market conditions, as well as enrich its human resources.

Nevertheless, it is probably safe to say that on average the effective employment security is weaker in smaller firms than in large firms. This may be seen, among other things, as the result of establishing or extending internal labour markets in large enterprises in the course of a sustained period of employment growth and stable demand in the post Second World War period. Employment protection legislation was built or extended on the basis of this development, at least in Europe, with the result that the effective protection of workers from the risk of dismissal was increasingly dependent on the workers' employment in a particular firm or plant. This again could be seen as a particular historical configuration rather than a sort of structural inevitability linked to particular types of firms.

To take a final example, several of the country studies report much lower strike activity (incidence of days lost through work stoppages) in small compared to large enterprises (establishments). Should this be interpreted as a sign of less "muscle" of the worker in the small firm, representing an inability of workers to voice problems and have their interests represented? Less open militance and conflict may not say very much about the true strength of worker representation, just as frequent strikes as such may indicate both strength and weakness of the worker organisation vis-à-vis the employer. It is also useful to look at the pattern of work stoppages more closely. In Italy, for instance, it has been found that workers in the small firm industrial districts go on strike more frequently than the average Italian worker, but the stoppages are typically of short duration.

It is likely that the variation in wage payments, fringe benefits and the physical working environment is larger in the small firm sector than it is among the big firms. It is also more likely to find the sweat-shop among small firms merely because of the lower visibility of small firms. But at the same time, some of best employment standards and working conditions are found in small firms. For Norway it is reported that the physical and social environment is the best in the small enterprises. Surveys about job satisfaction in various countries have repeatedly produced the result that satisfaction levels are inversely related to establishment size. Some of the country reports, such as those on the United Kingdom and the Federal Republic of Germany, also indicate that the average skill level of workers (at least for blue-collar workers) is higher than in the large firms. In several countries, small firms are engaged in apprenticeship training more than large firms. So the extensive heterogeneity of social standards and conditions in the small firm sector is in itself an argument that speaks against a "natural" law of inferiority of small firms.

V. Why the shift to smaller units?

Despite important methodological caveats, the nine country studies taken together present a convincing case for a shift in employment to smaller units of production. The fact that such a shift has occurred across a wide sample of industrialised countries is a new and surprising finding in most quarters, and accordingly little attention has been devoted to formulating explanations. A variety of hypotheses are discussed in the context of the individual national experiences, but these hypotheses have not been tested rigorously at the national level, nor have they been considered in terms of their explanatory power across countries. There is, however, considerable uniformity in the types of explanations put forth in the country studies, and they fall roughly into the following groups:

1. No real shift - statistical fallacy.
2. Transitory shift from business cycle, but no structural change.
3. Small firm cost advantages.
4. Government and managerial liberalisation.
5. Flexible specialisation.

1. Statistical fallacy

The most sceptical argument is that the observed shift to smaller units is merely a statistical illusion arising from one or more of the factors discussed above; in particular, sectoral recomposition and transitory deviations from optimum size (regression to the mean). Advocates of this position would argue furthermore that non-employment indicators are necessary to substantiate the case for a reorganisation of production favouring smaller units. Implicit in this position is the adherence to optimum efficient size, as determined strictly by the production technology and factor prices, as the sole determinant of an equilibrium size distribution of production. A case for a shift to smaller units would therefore have to be built on evidence of a change in technology favouring smaller units.

The country reports do not support this interpretation, for many reasons. First, what is perhaps the most striking empirical result from this study is the shift to smaller units of employment across such a wide range of institutions *and* existing size structures. The existence in the first place of a wide variance in the size structure which, we have argued, is often a function of factors other than optimum scale, is not supportive of the sceptical position. Indeed, the long-term existence of such a large share of small units alongside very large units in many industries is anomalous to this viewpoint. Furthermore, the persistence of differences in compensation, working conditions, etc., suggests a large role for factors other than unique optimum size. The country reports, moreover, often include a variety of non-employment data by size which suggest that employment share gains are not alone as measures of a shift in organisation. Finally, admittedly modest attempts to adjust for purely statistical effects such as changes in sectoral composition suggest that a substantial "pure" effect remains.

2. The business cycle

The business cycle has almost certainly affected the size distribution, but the evidence suggests that:

(i) the business cycle alone does not account for the shift to smaller units;

(ii) the recent business cycle downturn was coincident with an institutional crisis. Therefore, the coincidence of changes in the size structure with recession does not imply a stable historical response by the size structure to business cycle fluctuations. The recent experience is therefore not a repetition of the Great Depression, after which the employment shares of small units continued a long run decline;

(iii) the shift took place in countries with widely variant macroeconomic conditions, such as Japan, the United Kingdom, and Hungary;

(iv) higher employment shares have remained for small units well into the expansion in the 1980s.

The evidence produced in this study does not, therefore, favour an exclusive, or dominant, role for the business cycle.

3. Cost advantages

The country studies present considerable evidence that labour costs are lower in small units. The time series data, where they exist, suggest increased differentials in recent years. While most of the data fail to adjust for worker characteristics, it is almost certainly true that similar workers earn less in small units, particularly when non-wage compensation is accounted for (flexibility is discussed below). Furthermore, decentralisation and subcontracting from large to small units may be a means for evading labour standards, and many conglomerations of small firms have arisen in regions where such abuses have been widespread. Consequently, lower labour costs are an obvious candidate for explaining for the growth of small units. While this hypothesis, too, has not been tested rigorously, there are many reasons for doubting that it has been the central factor.

First, in most countries many years ago, wage differentials were wide, and in some cases increasing, while small unit employment shares fell. Second, there is no obvious relationship between the size of the differential

Introduction

and the growth of small unit employment shares. Italy, for example, has relatively small wage differentials and relatively large employment share gains by small units. Third, and perhaps most fundamentally, it is very hard to argue for a central role for wage differentials without first having a good understanding of why the differentials have existed historically. In the United States, at least, the persistence of large unit wage premiums - and even larger compensation premiums - for observationally equivalent workers, along with the persistence of inter-industry wage premiums, remain as unsolved mysteries.[5]

There is no doubt that lower labour costs favour the use of labour over capital in small units, and vice versa in large units, and this clearly works in the direction of the observed changes in employment shares. Unit labour costs, however, do not always favour small units because higher capital/labour ratios in large units increase large unit labour productivity. In fact, in many countries changes in unit labour costs favour large units (e.g. see the French and United Kingdom reports in this volume). In sum, the fact that smaller units face lower labour costs may have had something to do with their relative employment gains, but the evidence in the country reports suggests that the differentials were, at most, facilitators to other, more fundamental factors.

4. Liberalisation

During the period of increasing small unit employment shares, many countries, under conservative leadership, undertook a variety of tax reduction and deregulation initiatives. Many observers credit these policies with unleashing the entrepreneurial spirit of small firms, and thus enhancing their relative growth. The premise in this line of thought is that small firms are innately dynamic, or "beautiful", and that government intervention has historically impeded their performance, perhaps to a greater extent than large firms. Liberalisation, therefore, is seen as a boon to small firms.

A related argument, advanced most notably by Bluestone and Harrison [1982] in the United States, is that production by smaller units is part of a broad managerial initiative aimed at reducing worker power, lessening the influence of unions, etc., via decentralisation. Decentralisation may involve the shrinkage of establishments owned by large enterprises, or subcontracting to small firms work formerly done in-house. The data cited above from the United Kingdom, for example, support the notion of decentralisation within large firms, although the causes are not yet fully understood. A similar view, popular in business schools, is that breakthroughs in management science, which are best applied in small units, are making small units both more attractive and more prosperous. In Europe - and in the United Kingdom report specifically - it is often noted that the recession and labour market slack of recent years has facilitated a

---

5. See Gibbons and Katz [1989] for a very good empirical and theoretical discussion of inter-industry wage premia in the United States.

reassertion of managerial control which has resulted in a down-sizing of organisational units.

Again, research in this field has not progressed sufficiently to weigh carefully the merits of these positions. However, the weight of the international evidence does suggest that a fundamental force, cutting across widely varying legal, political and institutional structures, is at work in influencing the size distribution. These supply-side and managerial factors may be relevant in specific instances, but they do not have the uniformity and timing necessary to fully explain the data. (For example, the beginning of the shift to small units in countries such as the United States (mid 1970s) preceded most of action cited above.)

5. Flexible specialisation

The explanation for the shift to smaller units that is most pervasive and persuasive in the country reports involves the Piore and Sabel [1984] notion of a crisis in the institutional structure based on mass production and a movement toward an alternative based on flexible specialisation.[6] Flexible specialisation, it is argued, is being pursued both by independent small firms and by the decentralisation of large enterprises. Mass production depended on stable and growing markets to profit from reduced unit costs associated with production by highly specialised, dedicated labour and capital inputs. Large hierarchical firms emerged as organisations to co-ordinate the specialised vertical relations, while small, more flexible firms served a variety of less stable, more idiosyncratic markets.

Slowed growth, greater international competition and increased uncertainty in product and factor markets in the 1970s made specialised goods and more flexible techniques preferable to mass production. Final demand also changed, as consumer tastes increasingly favoured customised goods and services. Italian analysts argue that during this period large firm cost structures had become quite rigid, particularly with respect to labour costs and industrial relations.

Flexible specialisation was not new to small firms, but in large firms radical reorganisation was needed to create smaller, more horizontally co-ordinated organisational units in which the establishments owned by the corporation behaved more like associations of independent small firms. Small unit employment share gains therefore result both from the dynamism of small enterprises, and the down-sizing of establishments owned by large enterprises. (See Loveman [1989] for an empirical analysis of the shift from mass to flexible production in the United States, the United Kingdom and the Federal Republic of Germany.) It is important to note, however, that in this story decentralisation is not a "low road" premised on cost reduction and sweated labour - as described above - but rather is a "high road" effort

---

6. This argument is presented in much greater detail in Piore [1988] and is only summarised here.

to reinvigorate large enterprises by combining the dynamism of small entities with the labour standards, compensation, R & D, etc. of large enterprises.

On the supply side, the reports argue that technological change, particulary in micro-electronics, has reduced or eliminated small firm disadvantages in production costs by making competitive capital goods available at prices affordable to small firms. Indeed, the new breed of "flexible" capital equipment is considered to be especially well suited to a small firm strategy favouring small batches of customised products. Moreover, Becattini argues in this volume that the location of the most productive R & D activities has moved from large private corporations to universities and governments. R & D has thus increasingly become a public good - or has become less costly - and is available to small firms, which has enhanced their competitive position.

Flexible specialisation requires an institutional structure much different from that associated with mass production. The most salient characteristics of this structure are akin to those observed in industrial districts, and they may apply both to small firms and decentralised large enterprises. They are:

(i) technological dynamism;

(ii) the combination of extensive co-operation and vigorous competition;

(iii) location within a community or social structure, which may be based on the family, unions or political parties, or a corporation.

At least superficially, there seems to be no simple relationship between the degree of development of such institutions and changes in the size distribution of production. The United Kingdom, for example, would perhaps rank among the lowest in terms of the institutional structures outlined by Piore and Sabel, yet it has had one of the most significant shifts to smaller units. This is, of course, due in large part to the very serious problems experienced by large firms in the United Kingdom, but it nonetheless points out the difficulties in trying to develop some sort of mapping between institutions and small firm performance. Italy, conversely, is considered to have extensive inter-firm co-operation and organisation, and the shift in employment to smaller units has been quite significant. Becattini discusses the argument often made in Italy that the highly successful Italian industrial districts are largely the result of an unreplicable historical accident: the districts inherited peculiar circumstances from existing agricultural and industrial structures that are very conducive to the development of industrial districts.

Relations between large and small firms have also changed as a result of the new economic environment. There is evidence of increased use of subcontracting by large firms to small firms, and the Japanese report discusses at some length the pros and cons of such a development. If large firms simply use small firms as insulation from business cycles, exploit their cheaper labour to reduce costs, make them bear unwanted inventory costs, or otherwise keep them in a state of dependency, an increase in subcontracting is unlikely to be a desirable phenomenon for small firms. If, instead, large firms enter into long-term collaborative arrangements with subcontractors wherein the goal is to improve product design and quality via shared expertise and experience, the effect on small firms is much more favourable. At this point anecdotal evidence exists for both cases and it is not possible to discern a dominant international trend in either direction.

VI. The choice in SME development

The previous discussion of the issues leaves us with a double-faced argument. On the one hand there are numerous indications that:

(i) the economic performance of small enterprises is, on average, inferior to that of large enterprises; productivity levels as well as profit rates appear to be lower, the capacity for innovation and technological improvement smaller;

(ii) the average social standard of the quality of jobs and the conditions of work are inferior in the small firm.

On the other hand, we have argued that there is nothing inevitable or inescapable about this result; it is not the outcome of some natural law that links economic and social performance to the size dimension of business. Rather, to the extent that there is lower quality of employment found in small firms it is the effect of a particular historical and institutional configuration under which large firms have fared more favourably.

Actually, there is a very large variation and heterogeneity of competitiveness and economic vitality as well as social standards among small firms, both within and across national economies. Thus, there are sweat-shops as well as highly flexible, stable, innovative and independent categories of small firms, often with polyvalent workforces, good pay and extensive autonomy for the worker. The business strategy of these firms is often based on product quality or differentiated products, or on flexible specialisation. It normally requires a skilled workforce and well developed occupational labour markets. The small firms or communities of small firms with good economic and social performance suggest that there is, in terms of competitive strategy, a real alternative to the low cost/low productivity/poor social standard configuration in which many small firms find themselves.

A key to understanding the wide variance in small firm performance and development lies in their "competitive strategy", notably in their links to other firms or institutions. Due to their limited economic, financial, personnel and political resources, small firms, acting alone, are rarely in a position to gain the strategic behaviour generally enjoyed by large companies and therefore they require some sort of supportive structure that allows them to compensate for their lack of resources. Basically there are three ways of overcoming this shortcoming: (1) special protection, privileges or support transferred to them by the state or some other public authority; (2) a foster relationship with a large enterprise, or an intermediary organisation (such as a bank, university, etc.) which provide various types of resource transfers; (3) creating a community of small firms which, through collective self-organisation and co-operation, may compensate for the weakness endemic to individual small firms.

Each of these support systems creates a particular "social organisation" of the market. They tend to shape the ultimate social position of the small firm in the economy: its role in the division of labour, its degree of autonomy and dependence, and its hierarchical position in the industrial structure.

The country reports indicate that each of the types of support systems is relevant, but it also appears that particular support structures are more developed in some countries than in others. Moreover, each of them has historical predecessors so that it is possible to speak of a heritage of historical solutions to the resource and control problems. Consider these support systems in turn.

1. State intervention

The state may intervene in multiple ways to lend support to small business: attribute special rights or privileges, or supply resources or subsidies. One prominent type of state support is certification, i.e. a sort of exclusive right to particular firms, trades, or professions to perform particular tasks or services, or to produce particular goods, justified usually by reference to some public interest in exclusive treatment. Typical examples are doctors, lawyers, pharmacists, i.e. instances in which health and safety are at stake.

Historically, perhaps the most important small firm sector that benefited from public protection, was the crafts and guilds. State intervention has not been the only support structure for crafts. Often the craft system is based on collective self-organisation (see below) and there are numerous examples where the crafts came to depend on larger organisations or on some capitalist for their survival. This happened, for example, when the crafts, due to their limited financial capacity, could not afford to buy new expensive machinery and equipment or, as was the case with silk weavers, purchase expensive materials in advance. In these instances, which were especially frequent at the early stages of industrialisation, the crafts became subject to the putting-out system and lost part of their previous autonomy.

Throughout the middle ages, and even today, craft organisation has been built on a varying mix of public regulation and self-organisation, the latter often being dependent on the former. In medieval times, public authorities accorded the privilege of exclusive production and servicing in particular domains - food production, for example - to particular craft organisations. In return, the crafts were held accountable for ensuring the proper supply and care of the entire population at reasonable prices. The satisfactory organisation of these tasks was left to them. There existed a kind of social contract between the governments and the crafts, based on an exchange of rights of jurisdiction and "satisfactory" services.

As a result of this (external and internal) regulation there was a twofold restriction of entry into the market: one in the product market concerning the restriction of entry to licensed firms, and one in the labour market limiting access to employment to apprenticed workers. The latter was normally part of the rules set by the crafts in order to ensure a certain level of skill and craftsmanship deemed necessary for the quality of the product or service. According to a frequent rule, masters could have only one apprentice at a time to ensure proper training. Essentially, the blend of state regulation and self-organisation in the craft sector prevails to the present day, even though the exclusive rights given to the crafts were cut back as a result of nineteenth century business liberalisation laws.

In some areas there is an almost permanent struggle by crafts to regain some of the earlier exclusive rights. This can be observed in the Federal Republic of Germany where, among the countries in this project, the craft sector is still numerically most significant, employing more than four million workers (or one in six of the total labour force). In manufacturing the majority of firms are craft firms, and their share in the total shows remarkable stability through the business cycle.

There are no strict rules today according to which the crafts are forced to employ exclusively apprenticed workers. But, in fact, they generally do so anyway, knowing well that the quality of labour is essential for the quality of their product or service as well as their versatility; criteria on which their competitiveness vis-à-vis products of industrial producers are grounded. The state, however, assists the crafts (and also industry) in the generation and maintenance of occupational-type labour markets with a kind of enabling law, as well as public institutions, that design and readjust curricula for vocational training. Practical implementation is done under the influence of employers' associations and labour unions, both of which have formal rights of representation in the craft chambers (*Handwerkskammern*) set up under public law. There is no doubt that this regulation favouring standardised comprehensive vocational training and occupational labour markets throughout the country is one of the key reasons why the crafts have retained importance in the Federal Republic of Germany (as well as in the German Democratic Republic, Switzerland, Austria, Denmark and some other countries).

To safeguard or improve their position in the product market many crafts tend to continuously call upon the government to extend their rights of exclusivity. For example, in certain services, such as automobile maintenance and repair, the craft association argues that it would be in the public interest of road safety that this business be left exclusively to "qualified" firms and their fully trained, competent workers.

In fact, the crafts have succeeded here and there in gaining quasi-monopolies or exclusive rights and jurisdiction in some areas, but, by and large, they currently have to rely on effective self-organisation to maintain their competitive edge through supplying "trademark" commodities and services. The state accords the craft firm the title "Master Firm", but leaves it to the craft to generate and reproduce superior "products" through adequate organisation.

State intervention, of course, is by no means limited to the craft sector. The country reports document a new debate and a number of recent legislative and administrative activities intended to support the small firm in general. In terms of policy there appear to be various crucial issues in this regard. Should the public support consist of direct financial assistance or "real services" in the sense of creating or supporting institutions and organisations that potentially favour small business (such as consultation, technology transfer, etc.)? Furthermore, should small firms be exempted from obligations and duties in order to improve their competitive position? The latter issue is often debated against the background of almost continuous allegations by small entrepreneurs and small firms associations that at present the state, through regulation and subsidies, puts the small firm at a disadvantage (this charge is especially widespread in Switzerland).

While the question of public small business promotion is not a central issue for this project, it could, nevertheless, be hypothesised that "money" alone will not ultimately assure economically vital small firms. To the extent that the reports address this issue, the message is that effective "social organisation" - that is, rooting small business in a co-operative social network and tying to it social relations - appears to be more important for their competitiveness. Monetary assistance, such as tax exemptions (in general, or in the early years of new firms), may produce the undesirable effect of increased turnover of small firms, with resulting heightened employment instability. This might occur if the monetary assistance entices more people to establish firms which lack competence and the financial stamina to sustain themselves in the long run.

In recent years, small firms have been the key targets of thought and government action, with the aim of freeing them from existing protective rules and social obligations, and creating more flexibility. The effect of such labour market "deregulation" measures for the economic performance of small firms may, however, be seen as ambiguous. While they may effectively save costs and enhance the short-term flexibility of firms, they are also likely to lower the wage standard or other terms of employment. This implies that it will become more difficult for the small firm to recruit and retain skilled and motivated workers. Qualified labour, however, appears in many quarters to be a crucial asset for many small enterprises in realising their specific advantages, namely high quality and differentiated products, quick adjustment to market changes and flexible specialisation. Low wage levels often induce an exodus of managerial talent and competent workers, therefore making new-firm settlements more difficult.

Deregulation may turn out to be counter-productive in yet another way. To the extent that it actually allows for a larger differential of wages and other labour costs and enables small firms to operate with a low-labour-cost strategy of competition, it may breed complacency on the part of the entrepreneur or manager. He may rest on the cushion of the cost advantage instead of directing his efforts into innovation, new products and new markets. In other words, lower labour costs may be followed by lower performance standards and end up in higher unit labour costs, instead of the expected superior performance. Indeed, there is evidence of a close correlation in the wage gap between large, medium-sized and small enterprises and a corresponding productivity gap. In countries with large wage dispersion by enterprise size we find correspondingly large differences in efficiency levels [Sengenberger, 1987, p. 238].

Finally, widened labour-cost differentials may encourage large firms to use the small firms as "buffers" in relation to fluctuating demand, and to step up their volume of subcontracting and outsourcing because small firms can produce more cheaply. While this may create more employment in the small-firm sector, it will do so at the expense of large-firm employment; it will, therefore, not improve the overall level of employment or efficiency as long as the small firm shows no better economic performance.

2. Foster relations with large firms

In place of state support, it may be large, resourceful and politically influential enterprises, or other organisations, such as universities, that lend support to the economic existence or subsistence of small firms. These organisations can transfer various kinds of resources to small ones, such as financial capital, technical know-how, equipment, materials and human resources. To the extent that the large firm makes such "investments" it will develop an interest in the continuity and stability of the small firm, and a more long term co-operative relation may emerge.

A foster relationship is likely to generate dependence of the small firm, possibly even subordination, but domination is not an inevitable outcome for big firm/small firm relations. There exists a large array of relationships, ranging from clearly paternalistic relations to mutual dependence and symbiotic exchange on approximately equal footing. There are various hints that to a greater or lesser extent large firms do shift costs and risks - for example in testing new technology, or the risk of declining demand - to dependent firms down the line in the vertical production chain. The French report mentions that the resistance of firms to this kind of negative externalisation is the weaker, the further the firm is away from final demand, or the end producer.

Yet, as argued above, buffering is not an inescapable outcome of tight business relations between large and small firms. Outright exploitation or "milking" of the small firms often turns out to be self-defeating for the large enterprise, for if the small firm fulfils some useful function or service for the large firm, there will be a clear interest in having the small firm survive and be capable of adjustment and innovation. The counter-productive results of aggressive exploitative policies towards the small firms could be observed in the automobile and electrical appliance industry, when through widespread "second sourcing" tactics and very rough, cut-throat price competition the market of suppliers was ruined by excessive turnover.

Large corporations may also come under public pressure to use their resources to maintain or recreate employment in particular areas, especially if they have produced redundancies on a large scale. For example, British Steel is reported to have assisted a number of smaller firms in the Midlands to get off the ground; in France Renault has helped to set up 20 new firms, staffed by former employees, some of which now operate as subcontractors [see International Labour Office, 1986, pp. 46-47].

As is frequently the case, competition and co-operation exist in close proximity in the relationship between large and small firms. There is good evidence of this in Japanese manufacturing, where very often small subcontracting and supplier firms are highly dependent on large parent companies. The relationship of the small suppliers, which are typically organised in a multi-layered hierarchy, to the large customer, is characterised by vigorous competition, but also by long-term relations with those firms that perform well. Large firms have developed exclusive and sophisticated rating systems through which they continuously test, assess and control the performance of their suppliers, and rank them accordingly on the basis of criteria such as product quality, defect-rates, reliability, on-time delivery, etc. Those firms that do not satisfy the standards are squeezed out of the market while those doing well in the rating system are likely to develop long-run and stable links with the parent company.

The inter-firm relations of producers and suppliers (of parts or components, which they design and market themselves) or subcontractors (which merely manufacture parts or components predesigned and specified by the orderer) seems to have entered a new stage of development with the advent of modern *logistical concepts* of production facilitated by microprocessor-based information and communication technology. Just as with intra-plant material flow and inventories, inter-firm sourcing can be made much more efficient - i.e. inventory, storage costs, and flow periods reduced, scheduling made more precise, and personnel saved - by linking the data processing systems of the various organisations that are part of an inter-firm, vertically integrated production chain. A faster flow of inputs to the final producer requires a better and faster exchange of information, and the data processing requires compatible systems in the various units.

Computerised on-line data exchange and data-based integrated manufacturing have already progressed in a number of industries, e.g. in the automobile sector, yet large companies foresee a tremendous further potential for rationalisation in this area [Ebel and Ulrich, 1987, pp. 76-83]. Right now, it is difficult to make any reliable projections about the consequences of this process for the (smaller) supplier and subcontractor firms. What is clear, however, is that many of them, especially the hitherto independent ones, are afraid of a much greater transparency and direct access by their customers to their technical know-how. They fear the risk of becoming fully exposed to and "governed" by some external directive hand and thereby losing their managerial autonomy.

In addition to technical control there are other means of control that can become part of large firm strategies and which appear to be important for the shift to smaller units of employment in the recent past. Large firms may use smaller units for fragmenting production and services into smaller establishments within their ownership, and into small firms that are independently owned but economically dependent.

In accordance with a study by Shutt and Whittington [1984, p. 13] *fragmentation strategies* may be categorised as follows:

(i) *Decentralisation of production*

Large plants are broken up, but retained under the same ownership, by division into smaller plants or by creation of new subsidiary companies.

The reports provide evidence of this strategy in various countries. In Britain, for instance, there is evidence that firms have been growing larger in this century, but plant sizes have grown more slowly. Between 1973 and 1981, amongst the top 100 manufacturing firms, average employment per establishment has fallen faster than average employment by enterprise. The number of establishments in this group has increased greatly.

There have also been important decentralisation moves in Italy during the 1970s, after the trade unions had been unusually successful in influencing the labour process in the large industrial companies in northern and central Italy. Decentralisation by relocation or break-up was seen by management as a counter-measure to evade trade union power and to enlarge opportunities to adjust production capacities more easily by closures or workforce reduction [see, for example, Murray, 1983].

(ii) *Devolvement*

Large firms cease to own units directly, but retain revenue links with them, such as licensing or franchising. This fragmentation strategy allows the large enterprise to transfer responsibilities of ownership to smaller firms while still benefiting from a guaranteed income stream for themselves. Franchising was originally developed in the motor trades and brewing industry but spread quickly to other areas, like retail, fast food chains, printing, cleaning, repair and maintenance services, etc.

(iii) *Disintegration*

Fragmentation into separate units of ownership. Again, there exists a variety of forms (like subcontracting and managements' and workers' buy-outs) the common element of which is the shifting of responsibilities of ownership on to small firms while large firms retain ultimate control either through market or contractual power. For example, subcontracting takes work out of the stable and expensive internal labour markets of large firms and reallocates it into insecure, low-wage and non-union employment of small firms. It also gives large firms flexibility in the face of fluctuating demand. Another form of fragmentation along ownership lines has been the splitting of enterprises into separate legal units. This type has recently gained momentum in the Federal Republic of Germany (following a reform of the profit tax law in 1977) through the division of companies into separate legal entities comprising an "ownership" and a "production" unit. This division allows tax savings, reduces responsibilities and liabilities (in case of insolvency or mass dismissal) and weakens or evades obligations of employers under the German system of co-determination and worker participation. (In the Federal Republic of Germany, the 1968 reform of the turnover tax law - the introduction of the net turnover tax - provided incentives for a greater degree of subcontracting. It eliminated the promotion of corporate concentrations resulting from the previous cumulative taxes). In Japan, the abolition of cumulative sales taxes and the introduction of value added tax also created incentives for more subcontracting.

These fragmentation strategies naturally carry with them the likely effect of (greater) dependence and subordination of the small units and their use as "buffers" for costs and risks. Whether they do in fact produce satellite-type relations depends essentially on a number of institutional background factors which are discussed below. Large firms may use the small unit to externalise costs and risks, such as the risk of fluctuating demand or testing new technology but there are also occasions in which the small firm benefits. Licensing of maintenance and repair by large automobile manufacturers to small craft firms in the Federal Republic of Germany, for example, often amounts to a loss of autonomy in organising the business (including work organisation and payment methods). But at the same time, the licensed firm benefits from some protection through the large firm, when, for example, the producer firm limits the number of competitors in an area.

3. Communal support structures

As an alternative to protection and resource transfer from the state or large enterprises, small firms can look for other small firms to build a joint support system. By forming communities or congregations, small firms can overcome the kind of deficiencies which they face as individual market agents acting entirely on their own. Again there is a wide variety of historical and modern communal support structures, ranging from co-operatives to industrial districts, science parks, craft combines, and ad hoc co-operations. What makes this type of supportive institutions especially interesting is the thesis that they have been spreading in recent years. Piore and Sabel [1984] list examples of communal organisation of small business in various countries which provide the social underpinning of "flexible specialisation".

In the literature as well as in the country reports one finds two interconnected kinds of rationales by which communal organisation can resolve the resource deficiency problem of small firms: namely economic and socio-political.

The *economic rationale* essentially says that by grouping together, small firms can obtain economies of scale similar to those of large enterprises. In the Italian report, which elaborates a great deal on the resurgence of industrial districts over the past two decades, the scaling up effect in these districts is described as "Marshallian", referring to Alfred Marshall's analysis of external economies of scale. Higher efficiencies can be gained by joint design of products, purchase of raw materials and energy, joint use of equipment, office space, and transport vehicles, joint production, financing, marketing, advertising, distribution, organisation of exports, research and development, training, and so forth. In addition to joint purchase and joint utilisation of resources there may also be efficiency gains through bunching and spatial agglomeration of firms, which reduces transport costs and facilitates various sorts of inter-enterprise exchanges of information and other resources. The spatial conglomeration of small firms, at the extreme, may come close to the spatial concentration exhibited by big integrated plants. Sometimes entrepreneurial networks develop spontaneously but frequently they are built into existing social networks. In some cases there is public support given, as for example in some of the Italian provinces which provided a public infrastructure for small business development; or under the two successive pieces of legislation of 1982 and 1983 in France which provide a legal frame for decentralisation coupled with various kinds of local logistic assistance, such as buildings, real services and counselling.

Concentration in a locality may not merely be significant for the pooling of resources and for their exchange, but also for the process of diffusion of innovation and new technology. The industrial districts (just like occupational markets) do live on an egalitarian principle that in this case requires a rapid assimilation of all firms in the group.

Density of demand and supply is also an important functional requirement of occupational labour markets that rest on the easy substitution and mobility of workers with the same skills across firms. There must be enough employers and workers in the local market to enforce the "law of large numbers", which forms the basis for quantitative and qualitative adjustment in this labour market structure. Further, the work sites must be close enough geographically to avoid undue mobility costs.

The economies flowing from communal relations pertain to both co-operating firms in the same industry or product area and firms operating in different branches. In other words, the efficiency gains of small firm communities can be built on the principles of industrial and spatial grouping. Some of the best known examples of industrial communities can be found in the shoe, textile, leather and clothing industries in Italy, France and the United States.

Firms with different products, product market affiliations and technologies may profit less from exchange relations and transfer, as far as the specific product is concerned, but may still benefit from co-operation and co-ordination; e.g. through joint procurement or use of resources, such as energy supply, office capacity, and various services.

The second principal rationale for communal organisation is more *social* or *political* in nature. Joint organisation and representation of firms may strengthen their "voice" vis-à-vis various levels of government. For example, for the industrial districts in Sweden, their bargaining power vis-à-vis the local public authorities is said be at least as important for their economic welfare as the benefits accruing from the efficiency gains of grouping together.

There are often less tangible resources of communal organisation that stem from existing residential ties, kinship, religious affiliation, political parties, social class, ethnic group and other sorts of coherent and socially integrated structures. These resources provide a "sense of belonging" (Becattini) as well as trust, which again form the basis for mutual exchange and co-operation. If people are bound to live together for a long time, there is little space for the opportunistic behaviour typical of short-lived, casual market relations. Both the Italian report, which analyses the social fabric of industrial districts, and the United States report, which investigates cases of effective communal organisation in garments and construction in New York City based on ethnic or religious ties or on immigration links, point to the close interplay of social and business organisation. Becattini defines an industrial district as the "thickening" of inter-dependencies among several firms, and between this group and a population of workers or other people within a common and relatively circumscribed location.

In fact it may ultimately be the social control feature of organisation, in particular the power of sanctioning "unsocial" economic behaviour through a tight social group which constitutes the common thread to all kinds of success stories of large as well as small firms. Still, by far not all well-integrated social organisations produce effective economic organisation, and a key question for research may be under what circumstances "social resources" are tapped and mobilised for economic ends.

Obviously, one of the effective mechanisms of social organisation lies in the reduction or even elimination of short-run competition. This appears to be required for dynamic efficiency to materialise, for generating resources and making good use of them, both within firms as well as across firms. One may even speak of "internal product markets" within which competition is not absent but is regulated in a way that is compatible with the collective interests and ends of the community.

The country reports furnish various kinds of evidence that curtailing competition is an essential organisational feature in the small firm sector. The Swiss report, for example, speaks of a long-standing tradition of collective organisations in Switzerland to cope with the challenges of adjustment. Protection and cartels are explicitly seen as legal, and a very high cartel density has emerged grounded in associational rather than collective concentration of economic responsibilities. The law is intended merely to prevent abuses in the reduction of competition, not to prevent its curtailment as such.

The law may not be everywhere as explicit about the desirability of organised co-operation or collusion, but these forms are often tolerated. In the Federal Republic of Germany, the Federal Cartel Office and the courts responsible for acting in anti-trust cases have viewed inter-firm co-operation with a critical eye, especially where it begins to lead to the fusion of the co-operating firms and toward corporate concentration. But in fact, a lot of spontaneous and organised types of co-operation have taken place, especially among small industrial firms and in the craft sector.

VII. Conclusions

Public debate about small and medium-sized enterprises today is marked by a wide spectrum of viewpoints and attitudes. Many predict a great future for these enterprises, while others see them on the road to decline. Assessments of their performance vary from "highly flexible and efficient" to "backward and exploitative".

Neither unbridled enthusiasm nor complete scepticism is appropriate when considering the future development of SMEs. It is argued in this study that the size of enterprises or establishments does not crucially determine business performance measured either in economic or social terms. Instead, business performance depends decisively on organisational structure and on the public and private policies which influence their development. This is evident in the international comparisons presented above, which demonstrated clearly the effect of institutional structures on the size distribution of employment and size-related earnings differentials.

There are many reasons to examine SME development. First, after many decades of decline, the employment share of SMEs began to increase in the 1970s, though at different rates in different countries and sectors. But even in the absence of this job growth, it is important to look into the SME sector simply because the large majority of business units are small, and they employ significant, although internationally widely varying, proportions of workers.

From the empirical evidence gathered in the various countries under review in this volume it appears that the employment gains in the SME sector are neither merely the results of sectoral change toward the service sector, nor the effects of the business cycle. Rather, they are to a significant extent a function of industrial restructuring of two kinds: one is the decentralisation and vertical disintegration of large companies; the other is the formation of small new business communities, as exemplified by industrial districts and other local or regional small firm agglomerations. The two types of development represent different, but possibly inter-related, responses to changes in product and labour markets during the past two decades. These changes include increasing consumer demand for more differentiated, or customised, goods and services; heightened product market competition for standardised goods; the spread of micro-electronic production and communication technology, and changing labour force composition.

Both public and private policies have an important role to play in promoting the SME sector. However, deregulation of the labour market and wage cutting are not promising routes. What small firms need most of all are some kind of support systems to compensate for the inadequate resources available to individual small business. In this respect, there are two principal choices: first, small firms may benefit from the power and resources of large companies, a solution which is likely also to generate the unilateral dependence of the small firm in a hierarchically structured relationship. The other main solution is a communal organisation under which the small firm looks for other small firms to associate with and to build a more permanent, mutually constructive network of joint support and resource sharing, possibly with the co-ordinated specialisation of each firm in the network. This model is likely to produce more egalitarian relations among autonomous firms. The choice, then, is one between "top down" versus "bottom up" control of inter-firm relations, or between "kingdom" and "republic".

Bibliography

Armington, Catherine; Odle, Marjorie. 1982. "Small business - How many jobs?", in *Brookings Review*, Winter, pp. 14-17.

Bade, F.J. 1983. "Large corporations and regional development", in *Regional Studies*, Vol. 17, No. 5.

Bagnasco, A. 1977. *Tre Italie. La problematica territoriale dello sviluppo italiano*, Bologna, Il Mulino.

Becattini, G. 1987. *Mercato e forze locali: Il distretto industriale*, Bologna, Il Mulino.

Birch, David L. 1979. *The job generation process*, Final report to Economic Development Administration, Cambridge, MA, MIT Program on Neighborhood and Regional Change (mimeo).

---. 1987. *Job creation in America*, New York, Free Press.

Bluestone, Barry; Harrison, Bennett. 1982. *The deindustrialization of America*, New York, Basic Books.

Boltho, Andrea. 1975. *Japan - An economic survey 1953-73*, London, Oxford University Press.

Brown, Charles; Medoff, James. 1989. *The employer size wage effect*, National Bureau of Economic Research Working Paper 2870, Cambridge, MA.

Brüderl, Josef; Preisendörfer, Peter. 1986. "Betriebsgrösse als Determinante beruflicher Gratifikationen", in *Wirtschaft und Gesellschaft*, No. 4.

Brusco, Sebastiano. 1982. "The Emilian model: Productive decentralisation and social integration", in *Cambridge Journal of Economics*, Vol. 6, No. 2.

Contini, Bruno; Revelli, Riccardo. 1987. "The process of job destruction and job creation in the Italian economy", in *Labour*, Vol. 1, No. 3.

Cramer, U. 1987. "Klein- und Mittelbetriebe: Hoffnungsträger der Beschäftigungspolitik?", in *MittAB*, No. 1.

Dunne, Timothy et al. 1987. *Plant failure and employment growth in the U.S. manufacturing sector*, Pennsylvania State University, December (mimeo).

Ebel, Karl-H.; Ulrich, Erhard. 1987. *The computer in design and manufacturing - Servant or master? Social and labour effects of computer-aided design/computer-aided manufacturing (CAD/CAM)*, Geneva, International Labour Office, Draft Report.

Evans, David S. 1987. "Tests of alternative theories of firm growth", in *Journal of Political Economy*, Vol. 95, No. 4, August.

Fritsch, Michael. 1989. "Einzelwirtschaftliche Analyse der Arbeitsplatzdynamik - Theoretische Ansätze und empirische Befunde", in *SAMF-Arbeitspapier*, No. 4.

Fritsch, M.; Hull, C. (eds.). 1987. *Arbeitsplatzdynamik und Regionalentwicklungbeiträge zur beschäftigungspolitischen Bedeutung von Gross- und Klein-unternehmen, WZB Forschungsschwerpunkt Arbeitsmarkt und Beschäftigung*, Berlin, Editions Sigma.

Gallagher, C.; Stewart, H. 1984. *Jobs and the business life cycle in the U.K.*, Research Report No. 2, University of Newcastle upon Tyne, Department of Industrial Management.

Gibbons, Robert; Katz, Lawrence. 1989. *Layoffs and lemons*, Cambridge, MA, MIT, Department of Economics, April (mimeo).

Hall, Bronwyn. 1986. *The relationship between firm size and firm growth in the U.S. manufacturing sector*, Working Paper No. 1965, Cambridge, MA, National Bureau of Economic Research, Inc., June.

Hull, Christopher J. 1986. *Job generation in the Federal Republic of Germany: A review*, Discussion Paper, Berlin, Wissenschaftszentrum, Labour Market Policy, Research Unit, September. (ISSN 0722-673X)

International Labour Office. 1986. *Report VI: The promotion of small and medium-sized enterprises*, International Labour Office, Report to the International Labour Conference, 72nd Session.

Kerr et al. 1960. *Industrialism and industrial man. The problems of labor and management in economic growth*, Cambridge, MA, Harvard University Press.

Kleber, W.; Stockmann, R. 1986. "Wachstum und Strukturwandel des Beschäftigungssystems - Eine Analyse der historischen Berufs- und Arbeitsstättenzählungen in Deutschland", in *Soziale Welt*, No. 1.

Kubota, H. 1983. "A statistical survey of the situation of small and medium subcontracting firms in the Federal Republic of Germany" (Part I-III), in *Journal of Industry and Management of Kyushu Sangyo University*, No. 16.

Laroche, Gabriel. 1989. *Petites et moyennes entreprises au Quebec: Organisation économique, croissance de l'emploi et qualité du travail*, Geneva, Institut international d'études sociales, No. 91.

Leonard, Jonothan S. 1986. *On the size distribution of employment and establishments*, Working Paper No. 1951, Cambridge, MA, National Bureau of Economic Research Inc., June.

Loveman, Gary W. 1989. *Changes in the organisation of production and the skill composition of employment*, Unpublished Ph.D. dissertation, Cambridge, MA, MIT, Department of Economics, September.

Marshall, A. 1919. *Industry and trade*, London, Macmillan.

Marx, Karl. 1934. *Capital*, Volume 1, London, Lawrence and Wishart.

Mendius, B.-G. et al. 1987. *Arbeitskräfteprobleme und Humanisierungspotentiale in Kleinbetrieben*, Schriftenreihe "Humanisierung des Arbeitslebens", Volume 82. Frankfurt/New York, Campus Verlag.

Murray, F. 1983. "Production decentralisation and the decline of the mass worker", in *Capital and Class*, Vol. 19.

OECD. 1985. "Employment in small and large firms: Where have the jobs come from?", in *Employment Outlook*, Paris, September.

---. 1986. "Self-employment in OECD countries", in *Employment Outlook*, Paris, September.

Paleczek, O. 1986. *Interfirm co-operation: An instrument to improve small business competition*, Paper presented to the 16th European Small Business Seminar, Sweden, 9-12 September.

Piore, Michael. 1988. *Corporate reform in American manufacturing and the challenge to economic theory*, Cambridge, MA, MIT, Department of Economics (mimeo).

Piore, Michael; Sabel, Charles. 1984. *The second industrial divide*, New York, Basic Books.

Prais, S. et al. 1981. *Productivity and industrial structure*, Cambridge, Cambridge University Press.

Pyke, Frank et al. 1990. *Industrial districts and inter-firm co-operation in Italy*, Geneva, International Institute for Labour Studies.

Raveyre, M.-F.; Saglio, J. 1984. "Les systèmes industriels localisés: Eléments pour une analyse sociologique des ensembles de PME industriels", in *Sociologie du Travail*, April-June.

Rubery, J. 1987. "Flexibility of labour costs in non-union firms", in Tarling, R. (ed.): *Flexibility in labour markets*, London, Academic Press.

Sabel, Charles. 1981. *Work and politics - The division of labor in industry*, Cambridge, Cambridge University Press.

Sengenberger, Werner. 1987. *Struktur und Funktionsweise von Arbeitsmärkten - Die Bundesrepublik Deutschland im internationalen Vergleich*, Frankfurt/Main-New York, Campus-Verlag.

Shutt, J.; Whittington, R. 1984. *Large firm strategies and the rise of small units: The illusion of small firm job generation*, Working Paper Series No. 15, University of Manchester, School of Geography, December.

Storey, D.J.; Johnson, S. 1987. *Small and medium-sized enterprises and employment creation in the EEC countries: Summary report*, Commission of the European Communities, Programme of Research and Actions on the Development of the Labour Market, Study No. 85/407.

Teitz, Michael B. et al. 1981. *Small business and employment growth in California*, Working Paper No. 348, Berkeley, University of California, Institute of Urban and Regional Development, March.

United States Small Business Administration. 1985. *The state of small business: A report of the President*, Washington, D.C. US Government Printing Office, May.

2   France

Jean-François Amadieu

I.   Introduction

The relative importance of small and medium-sized enterprises[1] in the economy is beginning to attract attention. In 1985, enterprises with fewer than 500 employees employed 64.5 per cent of the labour force and accounted (in 1981) for 50.9 per cent of valued added, 50.7 per cent of investment and 58.7 per cent of turnover. Moreover, the smallest of these enterprises (those with between 0 and 19 employees) made a significant contribution to these figures.[2] These figures alone would be sufficient to encourage investigation into the world of small and medium-sized enterprises, but it is obviously the dynamism that these enterprises have shown during the recession that explains the renewal of interest on the part of analysts. This renewal of interest is a recent phenomenon and can be attributed largely to the fact that the development of small enterprises and their relative performance seem, after 12 years, to be sufficiently well established. The international nature of this development is certainly also a factor to be noted.

It is important to recall that the revival of small and medium-sized enterprises is absolutely contrary to the predictions of economists in the 1960s. In view of this, every effort is now being made to assess the full significance of the phenomenon: is it simply a temporary reaction to an economic crisis similar to that of the 1930s? Does the development of small and medium-sized enterprises not indicate the emergence of a dualist system of industrial organisation and segmentation of the labour market? Are small enterprises not rising from the ashes of a disorganised industrial framework? Is the vitality of small enterprises not an indication that a stable form of industrial organisation is emerging in which they will be the driving force?

The last hypothesis, which runs counter to the long-established arguments that concentration and mass production are the only effective routes to progress, is advanced, in particular, by Piore and Sabel [1984].

---

1.   If not otherwise stated, the following general definitions will be used: enterprises with fewer than 20 employees will be called "small", those with between 20 and 499 employees "medium-sized", and those with more than 500 employees "large".

2.   The information on the proportions of the labour force employed is provided by INSEE (*Institut national de la statistique et des études économiques*) in its SIRENE index (*Système informatique pour le répertoire des entreprises et établissements*). Data relative to value added, investments and turnover are obtained by INSEE through fiscal declarations of industrial and commercial benefits (BIC).   In the latter index, the number of small enteprises is underestimated (i.e. enterprises which do not pay tax on commercial benefits do not appear: co-operatives, associations, civil companies).

The efficacy of this argument depends on indicators taken from several different areas: small enterprises would have to prove themselves more productive by virtue of their qualities (flexible specialisation, innovation, etc.) rather than their faults (drastic reduction of labour costs, for example). Furthermore, the industrial framework must be undergoing a restructuring, not on the basis of the dependency of small enterprises on large ones, but rather on the basis of relationships of a "contractual" nature. Co-operation between firms should be developing, for example, on the local level. New rules should be governing commercial life. And finally, the rules governing industrial relations should be evolving and the state of industrial relations in small enterprises should be reaching normalisation.

We shall attempt to answer these questions in stages. In the first stage, data are presented on the classification of enterprises, and questions are raised as to the value of a typology based on the number of employees in an enterprise. The second stage summarises briefly the historical development of small enterprises. Next, the changes that have affected small enterprises since 1974 are investigated.

The fourth and final stage consists of a more qualitative analysis of the development of small enterprises. This section includes an examination of the evolution of the institutional framework within which small and medium-sized enterprises are asserting themselves; and analysis of the extent of the phenomenon and its stability.

II. Volume, structure and characteristics of the small enterprise sector

The diverging assessments of the vitality (growth and job creation, for example) of small enterprises in France are due, no doubt, to the diversity of small and medium-sized enterprises themselves, as well as the relevance of the criteria used for classification.

1. Some basic data

This study employs a standard method of enterprise classification by size based simply on the number of employees (average for the year or the number at the end of the year, as the case may be). On this basis, Table 1 shows the distribution of enterprises by number of employees in 1980.

Similarly, it is possible to classify establishments by number of employees, as shown in Table 2. Finally, Table 3 gives employment share by enterprise size in 1985.

Nevertheless, this division of enterprises by number of employees (and by sector) may not be most appropriate for this study. Other variables which would more accurately reflect the industrial framework, the changes that have taken place within it and the behaviour of firms might be preferable.

Table 1: Number of enterprises by sector and size category (1), January 1980

	0 employees	1 to 19	20 to 499	More than 500	Total
Agricultural and food industries	20 426	37 364	2 913	130	61 333
Energy	398	718	170	25	1 311
Intermediate goods	17 740	22 209	7 970	390	48 309
Capital goods	13 135	15 145	5 800	450	34 530
Consumer goods	44 786	40 921	10 290	360	96 357
Manufacturing industry	**96 485**	**116 857**	**27 143**	**1 335**	**241 950**
Construction/civ. eng. agriculture	130 718	161 500	12 446	204	304 868
Commerce	233 835	275 138	14 779	265	524 017
Transport	38 340	23 488	3 732	118	65 678
Services	435 574	359 022	14 467	333	809 396
Insurance and finance	1 020	2 794	607	143	4 564
Total	**935 972**	**938 799**	**73 174**	**2 418**	**1 950 363**

Note: (1) The limits of the classifications used in this table define spheres of statistical work: detailed verification of the data for firms with more than 500 employees, standard usage of surveys for firms with fewer than 20 employees.
Source: Quelennec, M. 1986. *Les statistiques d'entreprises*, Document Series E, June.

Table 2: Distribution of establishments by sector and size categories, 1980

	0 employees	1 to 19	20 to 499	More than 500	Total
Agricultural and food industries	22 069	40 734	3 940	101	66 844
Energy	533	1 126	620	130	2 409
Intermediate goods	19 869	28 149	9 950	441	58 409
Capital goods	14 833	18 677	7 840	661	49 011
Consumer goods	46 963	47 157	12 460	216	106 796
Manufacturing industry	**104 267**	**135 843**	**34 810**	**1 549**	**276 469**
Building and public works	133 718	167 055	14 779	102	315 654
Commerce	252 649	395 500	22 701	104	670 954
Transport and telecommunications(1)	40 731	30 581	5 516	112	76 940
Services	446 673	400 417	18 598	256	865 944
Insurance and finance	1 632	7 124	1 894	127	10 777
Total	**979 670**	**1 136 520**	**98 298**	**2 250**	**2 216 738**

Note: (1) Excluding GPO.
Source: Quelennec [1986].

France

Table 3: Number of enterprises + employment shares by size, 1985

	Firms		Employees	
	Number	Per cent	Number	Per cent
Without employees	1 661 834	58.7	0	0.0
1 - 9 employees	998 660	35.3	2 646 303	18.5
10 - 19 employees	78 222	2.9	1 051 618	7.3
Total small firms	**2 738 716**	**96.8**	**3 697 921**	**25.8**
20 - 99 employees	73 344	2.6	2 920 795	20.4
100 - 499 employees	13 073	0.5	2 625 817	18.3
Total small and medium firms	**2 825 233**	**99.9**	**9 244 533**	**64.5**
Large firms	2 671	0.1	5 083 378	35.5
Total all firms	**2 827 804**	**100.0**	**14 332 911**	**100.0**

Source: INSEE. Table compiled from data in enterprise index or SIRENE (*Système informatique pour le répertoire des entreprises et établissements*), in INSEE, Series 92E, No. 482, March 1985.

2. Other relevant typologies

Alternative typologies may be useful. These could include:

A. *Legal form*

The classification of enterprises by legal form provides some interesting data, and Table 4 shows a few examples. Many different circumstances are faced by enterprises in which the wealth of the individual entity (artisans, shopkeepers) and the business capital are one and the same, versus enterprises in which individual and company wealth are distinct and liability in the case of failure does not extend to the private property of the owner of the firm. The prospects for development, the freedom to increase the number of employees (there are limits, for example, on artisanal firms), the opportunities for raising finance (from public funds for large companies, in the bond market, etc.) all depend on the legal form of the company in question. Thus, classification schemes that group these two very different forms together may be misleading.

Similarly, it is important to distinguish profit-making activities from those whose aim is not to generate profits (friendly societies, associations, etc.). The latter ("the social economy") have benefited in recent years from particular state interest; prior to March 1986, there was even a secretary of state for the social economy. It has sometimes been claimed that these non-profit making activities provide a genuine alternative to enterprises in the competitive sector. In 1982, there were 238,000 employees in co-operatives,

155,000 in friendly societies and 710,000 in associations (on the institutionalisation and development of the social economy, see for example Dupuis et al. [1984], from which these figures are taken). Finally, this method of classification makes it possible to distinguish between public and private activities.

It is also interesting to measure the development of various kinds of co-operation between enterprises or individuals. This co-operation may take the form of "economic interest groups", whose aim is to pool resources and services (research departments, publicity, import-export offices, sales counters, management, etc.) or co-operatives. The current trend is toward further development of economic interest groups.

Table 4: Number of firms by sector and legal forms, January 1980

Sector	Individual entities	Limited liability companies	Public companies	General or limited partnerships	Others	Total
Agricultural and food industries	51 513	4 427	3 679	403	1 311	61 333
Energy	250	221	470	67	302	1 311
Intermediate goods	25 718	11 718	9 692	428	753	48 309
Capital goods	18 193	8 563	6 959	293	522	34 530
Consumer goods	62 402	20 835	11 703	595	1 272	96 357
Total for Manufacturing	**163 976**	**45 434**	**32 503**	**1 806**	**5 421**	**241 940**
Building and public works	251 045	33 928	10 679	1 501	7 715	304 868
Commerce	405 034	74 569	33 388	4 619	6 407	524 017
Transport	50 234	8 763	4 772	479	1 430	65 678
Services	633 700	67 886	32 892	5 695	69 223	809 396
Insurance and finance	150	440	2 231	68	1 675	4 564
Total	**1 498 239**	**230 900**	**116 465**	**14 148**	**90 611**	**1 950 363**

Source: Quelennec [1986].

The French Government Statistical Service recently drew up a typology based on the nature of the "decision-makers/capital holders" derived from the above data [Quelennec, 1986].

- family sector, with merging of company and household of director;
- autonomous small and medium-sized firms or family firms that have expanded;
- large private companies and subsidiaries;
- public sector;
- social sector (non-profit);
- companies under foreign control.

"Secret" or "hidden" companies should also be included in a typology based on legal form. It is obviously extremely awkward to measure the scale of the underground economy (the black economy, criminal activities). At the end of the 1970s, the black economy was estimated to be worth between 10 and 90 billion francs, to employ between 800,000 and 1.5 million people and to account for 6.5 per cent of GNP [Gaudin and Schiray, 1984].

B. The integration of enterprises

It is advantageous to classify enterprises according to the extent to which their activities are integrated. Indeed, might not the explanation for the development of small and medium-sized enterprises lie in the trend away from integration towards specialisation? There are several aspects to the dispersal of a company's functions to which we shall return later. A few of them will be mentioned here.

Some enterprises - obviously small and medium-sized enterprises are the most important - can be subcontractors for other firms. This phenomenon, which emerged as early as the 1950s, has increased since the recession. In 1981, 40 per cent of small and medium-sized enterprises were engaged in subcontracting, which accounted for 60 per cent of their total turnover. In 1983, subcontracting accounted for 6.4 per cent of sales in manufacturing industry [Bizaguet, 1985].

Many enterprises also provide services to other enterprises which are relinquishing an increasing proportion of the functions hitherto carried out in-house. The externalisation of activities such as cleaning, catering, caretaking, packaging and warehousing, together with engineering, accounting and data processing services, led to a 2.6-fold increase in the number of people (1 million in 1981) employed in the supply of services to enterprises [Bizaguet, 1985].

Finally, certain functions (marketing, product design) may lie outside the scope of some enterprises, while others may hire directly all or some of the technical and human capital that these functions require. In a study of the clothing industry in Provence-Côte d'Azur, Anselme and Weisz [1981] stressed that one of the major changes of the 1970s was the splitting-up of the enterprises, which is a precondition for reacting rapidly to demand and the requirements of distributors. In this industry, the integration of functions has become a "luxury".

C. Factors of production

Delattre and Eymard-Duvernay [1984] have put forward a different typology, based on the factors of production: value of assets per employee; proportion of engineers and technicians; share of tertiary jobs; percentage of male employees; and size of enterprises. According to this typology, the interaction of these variables produces seven different categories of enterprises which are shown in Figure 1.

Figure 1: Classification tree for enterprises, based on production characteristics

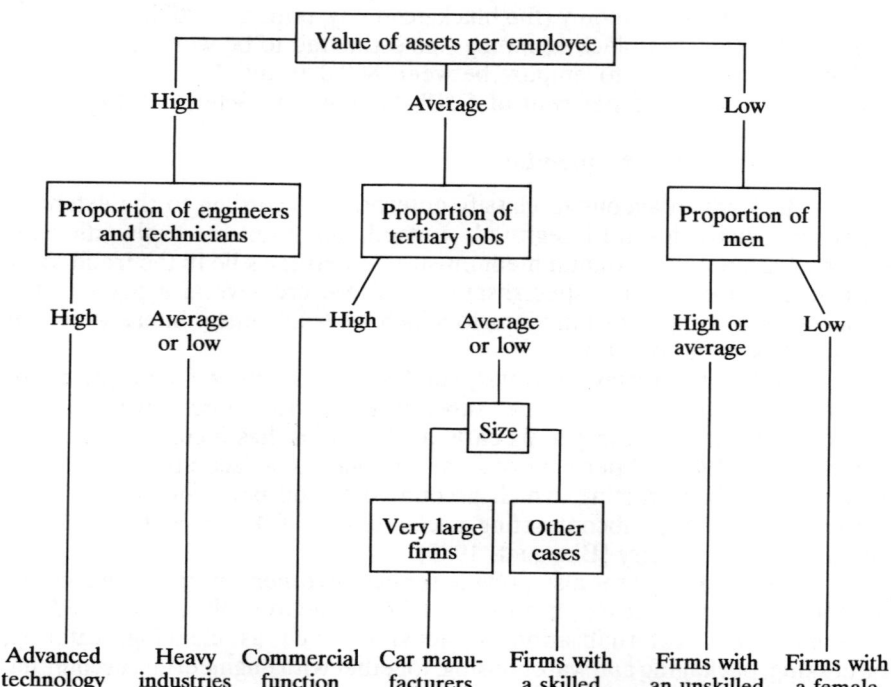

Source: Delattre and Eymard-Duvernay [1983], p. 74.

This typology seems to have real value in comparison with those based on size, particularly because it takes account of several considerations not used to construct the other typologies. The 2,471 enterprises included in the sample were manufacturing companies with 50 or more employees.

The concept of the small enterprises is obviously fairly vague, and the use of the size of workforce as a criterion for classifying enterprises has its limits. However, it is not without value. Table 5 shows, for example, that size provides a good explanation for the relatively favourable evolution of employment in small and medium-sized enterprises between 1974 and 1980 and attempts could be made to identify those characteristics for which variations in size provide an explanation (proportion of engineers and technicians, performance, etc.).

France

Table 5: Value of the F statistic for the different tests

	Effect of activity	Effect of size	Effect of category	Effect of introduction of size + activity	Effect of introduction of category + activity	Effect of introduction of category + activity + size
Gross fixed assets/ employee (1)	39	27	260	16	79	76
Value added/employee	18	5	58	2	23	22
Net fixed assets/Total assets	20	2	44	1	10	10
Other fixed assets/ Total assets	15	49	134	26	93	88
Debts/liabilities	14	1	14	1	3	3
Short and medium-term debts/total debts	17	21	97	9	34	33
Apparent rate of interest	23	6	63	1	5	5
Financial proceeds/ value added	9	25	62	9	35	33
Wage costs/employee	70	70	344	58	148	136
Unskilled workers/ workforce (1)	50	9	657	7	317	312
Exports/turnover	19	56	159	26	34	32
Gross operating surplus/ Total assets	10	20	22	12	9	8
Rate of growth of value added between 1974 and 1980	9	9	35	13	7	6
Rate of growth of workforce between 1974 and 1980	8	36	21	35	9	9
Rate of increase in productivity (Value added/employee between 1974 and 1980)	9	1	22	1	1	1

Note: (1) These variables were used for the automatic classification of the firms, and thus for defining the categories.
Source: Delattre and Eymard-Duvernay [1983], p. 83.

Let us just take two illustrations:
- "The desire for growth (to become a large firm) is highly correlated with the increasing size of the enterprise". The desire of firms to establish "clusters" of firms (financial links between firms) undergoes a very marked "threshold effect" when the workforce reaches 50 and becomes even more marked as the 100, 200 and 300 marks are reached. These "successive threshold effects" reveal the psychological significance of these stages of growth for the director of the enterprise [Huppert, 1981].
- The distribution of enterprises by size is characterised by breaks which can be explained by the effects of social legislation: the crossing of certain thresholds (10, 11, 20, 50 employees, etc.) leads to extra costs for firms, or requires the establishment of representative bodies for the workforce. Employers are thus hesitant about crossing the thresholds which can be seen in the data on exact enterprise size given in Figure 2.

III. The quantitative development of small firms

1. Historical evolution

The long-term trend towards concentration in French industry appeared so well established as to be irreversible. Sustained by government intervention, it was presented in economic analyses, official reports and planning studies as the path to progress. International comparisons lent additional weight to this view, and validated the argument that large firms made possible economies of scale and had greater capacity to predict and react to variations in demand. The increase in the size of firms, the gradual disappearance of the artisanal sector, and the transition to very large-scale production mobilising large volumes of capital seemed inevitable. These economic changes were associated with changes in the organisation of work (Taylorism), in skills (disappearance of the traditional trades and the rise of maintenance and supervisory workers), in industrial relations systems and in the forms of economic and social regulation (Fordism).

The evolution of thought on this point dates from the end of the 1960s [Douard, 1986], while the reversal of the secular trend towards concentration began in the mid-1970s. Tables 6 and 7 show the extent of the phenomenon of concentration since 1906, and reveal that there have been two reversals in the long-term trend: one corresponding to the Great Depression of the 1930s, and the other to the recession of 1974.

France 71

Figure 2: Number of enterprises by exact size

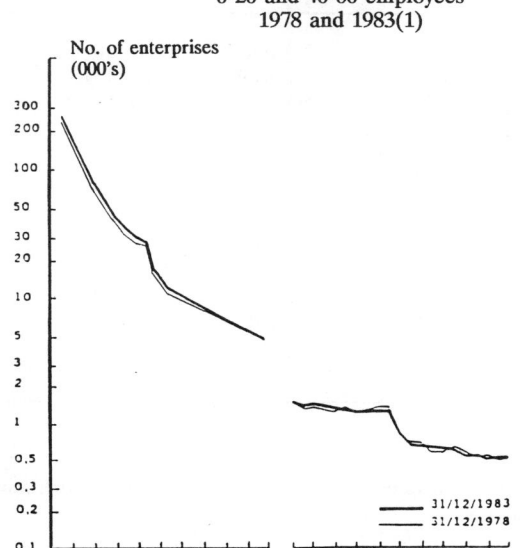

Note: (1) Number is that for all sectors (excluding agriculture, energy, post and telecommunications, and non-market services).
Source: UNEDIC.

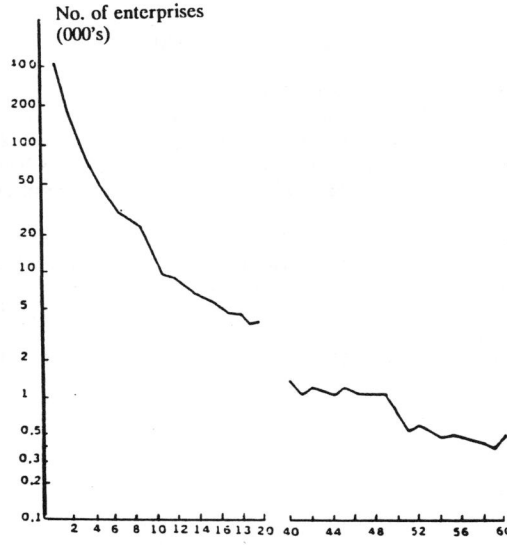

Source: SIRENE.

Table 6: Size distribution of employment in French industrial establishments in selected years between 1906 and 1981 (in per cent)

Year	0 employees	1 to 9 employees	Total 0 to 9 employees	10 employees or more	Total
1906	27	31	58	42	100
1926	14	27	41	59	100
1931	12	22	34	66	100
1936	17	22	39	61	100
1954	6	19	25	75	100
1962	5	16	21	79	100
1966	4	16	20	80	100
1974	3	13	16	84	100
1981	4	14	18	82	100

Table 7: Size distribution of employment in industrial establishments with more than 10 employees (in per cent)

Number of employees in establishment	1906	1926	1931	1936	1954	1966	1974	1981
11 to 20	12	10	10	10	8	8	7	8
21 to 100	28	27	27	27	28	28	27	27
101 to 500	31	30	30	30	31	32	32	32
500 +	29	33	33	33	33	32	34	33
Total	100	100	100	100	100	100	100	100

Note: These figures cover active employment. For the years 1954, 1966, 1974 and 1981 it is assumed that each firm has only one non-wage-earning employee.

The activities listed in groups 06 to 08 and 10 to 61 in the French Government Statistical Service's industrial classification are used for the years to 1966, and those listed in groups 04 to 55 are used for 1974 and 1981 (classification of activities and products).

For 1966, the distribution published in [2] below has been adjusted to include the state-owned electricity and gas companies and the French National Coal Board, which were not included in the SIRENE index. These organisations are large concerns, which means that the relative importance of the large size group is increase (500+ employees).

Source: (Tables 6 and 7) Didier (INSEE), [1] *Economie et Statistique*, No 144, May 1982 and [2], No.2, 1969.

Nevertheless, can this secular trend be explained by the increase in the number of people employed in large enterprises, or by the disappearance of small enterprises and the decline of the artisanal sector? As far as very small establishments are concerned, Table 8 shows that there was an increase in the number of production units employing one to five wage-earners between 1896 and 1978, and a slow reduction in the percentage of such establishments in the total number of establishments employing wage-earners.

Table 8: Number and proportion of production units with between 1 and 5 employees (1), 1896-1978

Year	Establishments		Enterprises	
	Number in thousands	% relative to total number of establishments employing wage-earners	Number in thousands	% relative to total number of firms employing wage-earners
1896	765	89	-	-
1901	804	89	-	-
1906 (87 departments)	843	89	-	-
1921 (90 departments)	723	85	-	-
1926	779	83	-	-
1931	719	81	-	-
1936	701	84	-	-
1978	860	74	762	76

Note: (1) All market activities, excluding railways.
Sources: 1896 to 1936: Ms. Cahen: "La concentration des établissements en France de 1896 à 1936," in *Etudes et Conjoncture*, INSEE, 1957. 1978: Calculations based on the SIRENE index (INSEE).

As far as the percentage of non-wage-earners outside agriculture relative to the economically active population is concerned, it fell from 18.8 per cent in 1954 to 11.2 per cent in 1975. Taking into account the tax incentives that exist to choose certain commercial forms, this represents virtual stability, and there has been an increase since 1975. Legislation introduced in 1985 made it possible to set up a limited liability company with only one member. Very small and artisanal firms would thus appear to be remarkably resilient and dynamic in a period of crisis [Madinier, 1983].

Some analyses reject the notion of a long-term reversal of the trend towards concentration, if employment size is not the only factor taken into account. One study, conducted by the *Direction générale de l'industrie* during the period 1974-1980, concluded that, on the contrary, the trend was continuing. However, it should be pointed out that this study related to the manufacturing industry (i.e. did not include agriculture and food) and non-artisanal enterprises with more than 10 employees. Manufacturing is significantly more concentrated than agriculture and food [Saunier, 1985] or the service sector, and the very small enterprises with fewer than ten employees are very dynamic. Taking these limitations into account, the study shows that the sectors in which concentration has taken place represent 76 per cent of total employment. Concentration has been most sustained in the consumer goods sector, with the capital goods sector in second place. The increase in the number of small enterprises and the fall in total employment do not indicate a reduction in the level of concentration. However, they may conceal a process of redistribution within the group of larger enterprises which has led to a greater degree of asymmetry in market shares, investment, etc.

In 1975, one of the central recommendations of the Sudreau report on the reform of the enterprise was that the establishment of new enterprises and the development of small and medium-sized enterprises should be encouraged [Sudreau, 1975]. In 1979, the Mignot report examined the prospects for the development of artisanal and small enterprises [Mignot, 1979].

Since 1974, circumstances have changed, but there is no doubt that the worsening of the economic crisis and the transformation of the ideological context have facilitated the changes. The period between 1981 and 1986, when the left was in power, has had its effect. There has been a shift in ideology: the enterprise has been rehabilitated, along with the entrepreneur and the profit motive. A "new realism" has emerged, both within the political parties and the trade unions of the left, together with the new creed of "company creation" propagated by both private and public initiatives (legislation and public agencies, such as the National Agency for the Creation of Companies). Thus, what has changed is not only economic doctrine, observed reality (concentration, performance of firms, etc.) and government policies, but also, and more particularly, a whole set of convictions and values relating to the place of the enterprise and the entrepreneur (autonomy, the taking of responsibility, individualism), its organisation and its size. This ideological transformation, which has undoubtedly been accelerated by economic circumstances, makes it possible to assess the scale of the swing since 1974. The adaptation of both the doctrine and the practice of the left has, in a way, made permanent the trend that emerged from the first oil shock.

2. Recent changes: The relative performance of small and medium-sized enterprises between 1974 and 1985

Since the first oil shock, small and medium-sized enterprises have developed differently from large firms. The trend towards concentration has been reversed and small enterprises have performed better in terms of employment, profitability, growth and investment. It should be stressed at the outset that it is not only enterprises in the service sector that are involved here; the shift towards the service sector is not the only explanation for the dynamism of small and medium-sized enterprises and the decline of the large manufacturing firms. This judgement also needs

France

qualification, particularly by focusing attention on the various phases in this process. Have small and medium-sized enterprises found it possible in the more recent period (1980-1984) to sustain both the trend away from concentration and the greater ability to cope with recession that were observed at the end of the 1970s?

A. Evolution of the number of firms

Between 1967 and 1973, the number of industrial and commercial enterprises declined considerably and one manufacturing enterprise in four had disappeared after increasing since 1950. This reversed a trend towards an increasing number of enterprises that began as early as 1950. The year 1973 marks a distinct break [Didier, 1982], since from that point onwards, the number of firms increased, rapidly at first and then more slowly (see Figure 3).

Figure 3: Number of industrial and commercial firms, 1950 to 1977

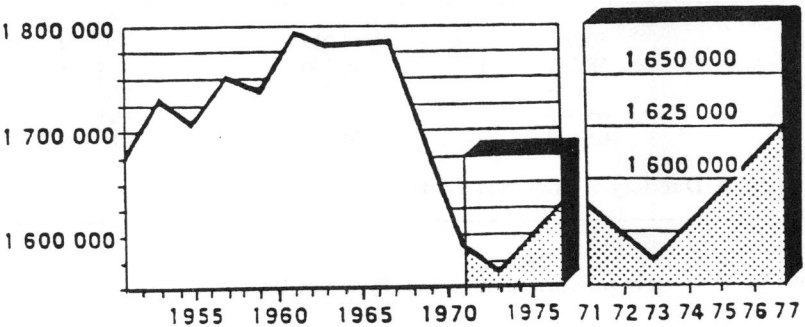

Source: BIC in Didier [1982].

The increasing number of enterprises may be explained by the number of small enterprises established, but this is counterbalanced by an increase in the number of failures. In any case, the rate of increase has slowed since the beginning of the 1980s. The number of small and medium-sized enterprises increased at 0.8 per cent per annum between 1977 and 1981, but began to fall in 1982, and the decline persisted until 1984. During the similar period of 1977 to 1980, the number of large firms fell by 1.9 per cent per annum.

The situation is rather divergent. These aggregate statistics, however, mask rather divergent developments at more detailed levels.

First, it is the very small enterprises (up to 50 employees) that have increased in number. For companies larger than this, the evolution of large and medium-sized enterprises is comparable. In certain cases such as construction and civil engineering, it is even artisanal firms that have increased in number. In the craft sector, the balance of set-ups and failures increased sharply between 1975 and 1979 (see Table 9). In addition, the number of enterprises with up to five employees increased from 1,464,000 in 1971 to 1,597,000 in 1983.

Second, it was the service sector that served as the breeding ground for small enterprises. The number of small and medium-sized enterprises in services increased by 3.3 per cent per annum between 1977 and 1982. In the sub-sector of enterprises providing services to other enterprises, the comparable growth rate was 4.4 per cent. In the same period, the number of small manufacturing enterprises (up to 500 employees) fell by 1 per cent from 1980 to 1982, after having been stable since 1974. There were 1,300 manufacturing firms with more than 500 employees in 1979, compared with 1,500 in 1974. Table 10 shows the share of various sectors in the creation of enterprises in 1980, 1982 and 1983 [*Crédit d'Equipement des PME*, 1985].

Table 9: **Evolution of the number of firms in the craft sector, 1975-1979**

Year	Registrations	Failures	Balance
1975	50 090	46 036	+ 454
1976	58 761	48 550	+10 021
1977	65 988	47 967	+18 021
1978	63 308	48 837	+13 471
1979	65 500	50 500	+15 000

Source: APCM, Directory of Crafts and Trades in Zarca [1984].

Table 10: **Distribution of enterprise foundations by sector, 1980, 1982, 1983**

	1980	1982	1983
Services	15.6	17.5	20.6
Manufacturing	6.8	9.0	9.3
Hotel/Catering	6.1	6.6	6.7
Construction/ civil engineering	8.5	8.5	7.8
Commerce	63.0	58.4	55.6
Total	**100.0**	**100.0**	**100.0**

Source: Crédit d'Equipement des PME (CEPME) [1985].

France

B. The evolution of employment

In the same way as the first oil shock brought a reversal of the trend in the number of small and medium-sized enterprises, there was also a reversal in terms of employment, since from that point onwards the share of wage earners employed in smaller enterprises began to increase. Table 11 gives the employment shares of small and medium-sized enterprises relative to that of large enterprises.

The reversal in employment shares since 1974 is clearly attributable to the fall in the number of people employed in large enterprises, and the greater durability of smaller enterprises, particularly very small ones, to the recession. Table 12 shows the change in employment by establishment size from 1969-1973 and 1974-1980. In manufacturing, for example, the number of wage earners in large enterprises fell by 300,000, or 10 per cent of the workforce; between 1974 and 1979 the corresponding figures for medium-sized, small, and very small enterprises were only 100,000, 30,000 and 40,000, respectively [Delattre, 1982].

Table 11: **Employment shares of small and medium-sized enterprises relative to that of large enterprises, 1971, 1979, 1985**

Size of enterprise	Total Economy 1971	1979	1985	Manufacturing 1971	1979
Fewer than 20	20.5	23.3	25.8	9.7	10.7
20 to 100	18.5	20.1	20.4	16.7	17.9
100 to 500	18.4	17.3	18.3	23.1	22.0
Fewer than 500	57.4	60.7	64.5	49.5	50.6
500 +	42.6	39.3	35.5	50.5	49.4
Total	**100.0**	**100.0**	**100.0**	**100.0**	**100.0**

Source: Bizaguet from BIC (INSEE).

Table 12: **Changes in employment by establishment size**

Establishment size	Changes in thousands 1969-1973	1974-1980	as % 1969-1973	1974-1980
Small (0 to 19 employees)	+ 166	+555	+ 5	+16
Medium (20 to 199 employees)	+ 712	+150	+17	+ 3
Large (200+ employees)	+ 863	-557	+22	-12
Total	**+1741**	**+148**	**+15**	**+ 1**

Source: UNEDIC, in Didier [1982].

The important point is that the phenomenon is substantiated: between 1977 and 1982, small and medium-sized enterprises cut their workforce by 0.5 per cent per annum, while the corresponding figures for large enterprises were 1.3 per cent up to 1980, and 2.7 per cent subsequently. For the period 1982-1984, Amar [1986], using two samples of 11,000 and 12,000 industrial enterprises, finds that this development was sustained. According to Amar, employment in small and medium-sized enterprises fell by 0.4 per cent during this period, while large enterprise employment fell by 4.3 per cent. Between 1977 and 1984, the enterprise employment fell by 630,000, compared with 130,000 in smaller enterprises. Table 13 shows the evolution over a ten-year period of the number of industrial establishments with more than 500 employees by geographic region. It is clear from the table that job losses vary from region to region.

Table 13: **Number of industrial firms with 500 or more employees by region (1), 1974, 1983**

Regions	1974	1983
Alsace	69	53
Aquitaine	44	43
Auvergne	33	28
Burgundy	60	48
Brittany	32	32
Centre	81	57
Champagne-Ardenne	66	40
Corsica	0	0
Franche-Comté	35	22
Ile-de-France	317	258
Languedoc-Roussillon	14	16
Limousin	13	11
Lorraine	98	69
Midi-Pyrénées	33	36
Nord-Pas-de-Calais	154	102
Lower Normandy	32	27
Upper Normandy	93	61
Loire	69	63
Picardy	89	61
Provence-Alpes-Côte d'Azur	40	41
Rhône-Alpes	177	134
France	**1,582**	**1,230**

Note: (1) Data exclude the energy and agro-food industries (Data presented in map form in original article).
Source: SESSI, in Gloaquen [1986].

In 1985, the number of people employed in large manufacturing enterprises was still falling, while employment in small and medium-sized enterprises was holding up better. There was, however, a new development: medium-sized enterprises with between 100 and 500 employees were

France

experiencing job losses similar in proportion to those in small enterprises [Mathieu, 1986].

Unfortunately, these data have several methodological problems that impair their usefulness in gauging the actual performance of the enterprises themselves. Because of the fall in employment, large firms may change status, and take-overs and mergers can affect the composition of the size categories. These structural changes, however interesting they may be, do not provide much information on the performance of small and medium-sized enterprises, yet they do affect measures based on employment size groups. In order to control these problems, a constant sample of firms must be used. Two studies carried out by the Company Research Department of INSEE, the French Government Statistical Service, used this methodology. The first one, which covers the period 1974 to 1979 [Delattre, 1982], confirms that small and medium-sized manufacturing enterprises did indeed create jobs. The results are summarised in Table 14.

Table 14: **Employment growth by enterprise size for manufacturing firms between 1974 and 1979** (1)

	Size of firm in 1974		
	Fewer than 100 employees	100 to 500 employees	More than 500 employees
Meat and dairy products	4.1	2.9	0.0
Other agricultural and food products	0.4	1.1	-0.7
Minerals and ferrous metals	1.0	-3.0	-5.5
Minerals and non-ferrous metals	5.8	-3.0	-1.7
Building materials	1.3	-1.5	-1.9
Glass	0.3	1.5	-2.5
Basic chemicals, man-made fibres	0.5	-4.1	-2.4
Parachemicals, pharmaceuticals	3.4	2.5	-0.9
Casting and metal working	1.1	-1.4	-2.3
Mechanical engineering	2.1	-0.7	-2.0
Industrial and domestic electrical equipment	1.0	0.6	-0.4
Motor vehicles and other land transport	5.5	1.7	0.7
Shipbuilding, aeronautics and armament	0.9	0.8	-1.3
Textiles and clothing	4.8	-0.5	-2.9
Leather and footwear	5.2	0.2	0.8
Wood, furniture, various industries	1.6	1.6	-0.2
Paper and box makers	3.8	-1.5	-3.8
Printing and publishing	1.0	-0.3	-1.6
Rubber and plastics	5.3	0.4	0.4
Total manufacturing (including agro-food industries)	**2.5**	**-0.1**	**-1.2**

Note: (1) The percentages are average annual rates of growth during the period 1974-79. They are the results obtained from the INSEE constant sample of firms. The sample includes only those which were in existence from the beginning to the end of the period without having been affected by restructuring.

Source: Delattre [1982].

The second study, which covers the years 1978 to 1982, produced similar results [Amar, 1986].

Another study of a constant sample of industrial enterprises largely confirmed these results obtained for all enterprises. Between 1974 and 1984, the employment situation in small and medium-sized enterprises was more favourable than in large enterprises, even in the case of a comparable group of firms; this was particularly true of small, very small and artisanal firms. Industrial firms with between 10 and 49 employees created jobs, even after 1980, while the evolution of employment between 1977 and 1982 in firms with between 20 and 499 employees was similar to that in large firms. In the construction industry, only very small firms recorded increases in the number of employees, and this occurred only until 1980. In the service sector, on the other hand, large firms took on more people than small ones as a result of sustained growth.

C. The growth of value added

Growth in value added by enterprise size shows that the improved employment performance of small and medium-sized enterprises has not been just factor substitution. Value added increased more rapidly in small and medium-sized enterprises than in large firms between 1974 and 1984, reversing a trend favouring large enterprises in earlier periods: between 1971 and 1974, value added rose more rapidly in large firms. The better performance of smaller firms in this respect was true for virtually all sectors of manufacturing between 1974 and 1979, as shown in Table 15.

Moreover, evidence from constant samples of enterprises for the period 1974-1982 confirms the superior performance in terms of value added of small and medium-sized enterprises. Finally, it is the smaller firms which again show particular dynamism in this respect, as was also the case in terms of employment and number of firms.

The subsequent tables present the results obtained with constant samples.

At the beginning of the 1980s there emerged differences in value added growth rates by enterprise size in the various sectors, even though the general trend remained unchanged (see, for example, agriculture and food, capital goods and consumer goods). Table 16 shows that while value added grew more rapidly in small and medium-sized enterprises, there was considerable variance across sectors and time periods.

D. Profitability and wage and profit shares

Small and medium-sized enterprises, whose financial situation tends to be precarious, have, in contrast, proved to be more economically profitable than large enterprises. From this point of view, there is a negative relationship between profitability and size (and between profitability and dependency on a group) [Vassille, 1982]. Similarly, the least concentrated sectors are the most profitable. Monfort and Vassille [1985] show that, contrary to the period before 1974, there is a negative relationship between

France

Table 15: Value added growth of firms in existence between 1974 and 1979

	Size of firm in 1974		
	Fewer than 100 employees	100 to 500 employees	More than 500 employees
Meat and dairy products	6.2	3.9	2.2
Other agricultural and food products	-2.3	2.4	-2.4
Minerals and ferrous metals	-0.5	2.6	-0.4
Minerals and non-ferrous metals	13.2	7.1	9.0
Building materials	4.7	0.5	-1.0
Glass	5.6	4.5	2.0
Basic chemicals, man-made fibres	1.0	-2.1	-5.5
Parachemicals, pharmaceuticals	5.1	6.2	1.3
Casting and metal working	-0.1	-1.8	-1.7
Mechanical engineering	3.5	1.2	0.0
Industrial and domestic electrical equipment	5.5	7.4	6.7
Motor vehicles and other land transport	0.9	-0.7	0.6
Shipbuilding, aeronautics and armament	1.5	11.3	1.7
Textiles and clothing	3.4	-0.2	-2.9
Leather and footwear	-0.2	-2.1	0.4
Wood, furniture, various industries	3.2	4.7	2.6
Paper and box makers	7.0	1.1	-1.3
Printing and publishing	2.0	2.6	2.2
Rubber and plastics	6.7	2.9	1.8
Total manufacturing (including agro-food industries)	**2.6**	**2.0**	**1.0**

Note: In each sector, the changes in value added taken from the constant sample of enterprises were reduced by the value added price index for the sector in question. The sums thus calculated were then aggregated at the level of manufacturing as a whole.

Source: Delattre [1982].

Table 16: Value added growth in volume terms of firms in existence between 1978 and 1982

	Small and medium-sized firms			Large firms		
	78-80	80-82	78-82	78-80	80-82	78-82
Agricultural and food industries	+ 2.2	+1.0	+1.6	+0.9	+5.8	+3.3
Intermediate goods	+ 3.6	-2.2	+0.6	+2.0	-5.1	-1.6
Capital goods	+ 5.4	-0.4	+2.5	+2.6	+2.4	+2.5
Consumer goods	+ 5.8	+2.1	+4.0	+4.9	+3.2	+4.0
Total for manufacturing industry	+ 4.5	+0.2	+2.3	+2.5	+0.8	+1.6
Construction/civ.eng./agriculture	+ 0.1	-1.3	-0.6	-2.8	+2.1	-0.4
Commerce	+ 6.9	+1.9	+4.4	+3.0	+2.7	+2.8
Transport	+ 0.3	+0.8	+0.5	+1.3	-1.7	-0.2
Market services	+10.7	-2.2	+4.1	+2.1	+0.7	+1.4
Total	**+ 5.6**	**+0.0**	**+2.8**	**+2.1**	**+0.7**	**+1.4**

Source: Amar [1986].

profitability and concentration, and that the relationship between market share and the profitability of the enterprise is now weak.

Between 1974 and 1979, the disparity in profitability - or, more precisely, in the rate of return on fixed assets - between large and small enterprises grew even wider, increasing from 6 to 10 per cent. The reduction in the profitability of firms since 1979 has affected large enterprises more than small ones, and this remains true even if a constant sample of firms is used [Amar, 1986]. Table 17 shows that small and medium-sized enterprises in manufacturing, building and public works and services enjoyed higher profit rates than large enterprises in every year from 1977 to 1984, and the differential widened as profit levels fell.

Table 17: Rate of economic return in the manufacturing, building and public works and service sectors (1), 1977-1984

	1977	1978	1979	1980	1981	1982	1983	1984
Small and medium-sized enterprises	12.9	13.4	14	14.1	13.8	13.6	13.3	12.1
Large enterprises	11.9	10.6	11.7	11.3	11	9.6	9.1	8.9

Note: (1) Gross operating surplus as a percentage of own capital and non- trade debt.
Source: Amar [1986].

These performances can be explained by the level and favourable evolution of the profit margins of small and medium-sized enterprises, and by the low level of capitalisation of small enterprises. With respect to the first point, profit margins of large and small enterprises did not begin to converge until 1973. Table 18 shows that the profit margins of small and medium-sized enterprises deteriorated less than those of large enterprises from 1979 to 1982, but the differential narrowed between 1982 and 1984 [Amar, 1986].

With respect to capitalisation, it should be pointed out that large enterprises have a higher level of capitalisation than smaller ones (twice as high in 1979) regardless of sector; in 1979, large firms had capital stocks twice those of smaller enterprises. However, Table 19 shows that the productivity of capital is higher for small and medium-sized enterprises and the differential widened as capital productivity in small and medium-sized enterprises rose from 1977-82 while that of large enterprises fell.

France

Table 18: Profit margins and manufacturing industry, construction and services, 1977-1984

	1977	1978	1979	1980	1981	1982	1983	1984
Small and medium-sized enterprises	22.1	22.4	23.4	23.4	22.7	22.4	22.1	20.9
Large enterprises	19.9	19.9	21.5	19.9	19.3	17.0	16.9	16.8

Source: Amar [1986].

Table 19: Productivity of capital, 1977-1984

	1977-78	1979-80	1981-81	1983-84
Small and medium-sized enterprises	76.6	78.4	81.0	75.5
Large enterprises	57.7	56.2	55.3	52.9

Source: Amar [1986].

The favourable results recorded by small and medium-sized enterprises in terms of economic profitability are parallelled by the superior performance in terms of financial profitability. Measured by the quotient of gross operating surplus borrowing and own capital, the financial profitability of small and medium-sized enterprises fell from 28.2 in 1977 to 25.6 in 1984, while the corresponding figures for large enterprises were 19.2 and 7.8. Smaller enterprises had already been more profitable financially than large firms, but as these figures show, the gap widened considerably between 1977 and 1984. In 1985, smaller enterprises were still significantly more profitable than large ones.

IV. Recent changes: A qualitative analysis

Does the performance of small and medium-sized enterprises reflect the dynamism of autonomous enterprises, which are producing new products, exporting, achieving increases in productivity, using the latest technologies and an increasingly skilled workforce enjoying favourable working conditions and salaries, or does it reflect the opposite?

1. Deregulation and destructuring

Are the good results achieved by small and medium-sized enterprises in fact a statistical illusion, the result of factors which tend rather to point to a breakdown in the industrial fabric and a worsening of the position of large enterprises and of the employment conditions of the workforce? The answer to this question requires consideration of several issues. First, small and medium-sized enterprises have a high failure rate, in contrast to large firms, both public and private. Only the fittest survive. A study by the CEPME [*Crédit d'Equipement des PME*, June 1986] shows that 40 per cent of bankruptcy petitions relate to enterprises less than ten years old, whereas such enterprises represent only 10 per cent of all small and medium-sized enterprises. The variable which best accounts for the failure of enterprises is the rate at which new enterprises are established, with a time lag of three years [Marco and Rainelli, 1986]. The CEPME study also shows that one new enterprise in three closes down within five years. Of all the enterprises set up in 1984, 17 per cent had ceased trading by 1 January 1985, and the equivalent figure for those established in 1983 was 28 per cent. Those which continue trading have particular characteristics.

Is the good performance of small and medium-sized enterprises in the recession explained by sector of activity, production system and type of product? The sector of activity is not a decisive factor.[3] On the other hand, the position occupied by an enterprise upstream or downstream of a production system, or its position in a specific system, is significant. Delattre and Eymard-Duvernay [1984] observed that it was those small and medium-sized enterprises closest to final demand that were best able to survive the recession years from 1974-1980. The enterprises in these categories were those in the traditional consumer goods sectors (clothing, etc.) and the commercial sector and small and medium-sized mechanical engineering and advanced technology enterprises (these latter are often dependent on a large firm).

Is it not the proximity to final demand which has enabled small enterprises to vary their prices (they are, for example, less exposed to international competition) and thus compensate for their relatively modest productivity gains and return on investment between 1977 and 1984 by price increases? Or to be more exact, is analysis in terms of "category" [Delattre and Eymard-Duvernay, 1983] not more helpful when it comes to explaining labour productivity, unit wage costs and skill levels, level of capitalisation, the rate of increase of value added, etc., than analysis in terms of employment size?

Can the development of small and medium-sized firms be explained by low wages and poor employment conditions? Wage costs per employee in small and medium-sized industrial enterprises as a whole are lower. The gap between wage costs per employee in small and medium-sized enterprises

---

3. However, it does explain export performances. Studies show that export results are one of the key factors in the growth of SMEs [Roncin, 1982].

France

and those in large enterprises was 23 per cent in 1977; in 1984, the difference had increased to 34 per cent.

These low wage costs are primarily the result of two factors: the skill level in smaller enterprises tends to be lower; and lower wages are paid for equal skills, particularly because of increased labour mobility. Wages have risen less in small and medium-sized enterprises since 1975-76, which suggests that the adjustment of smaller enterprises to economic crisis was based, at least in part, on a strategy of reducing wage costs. It should not be forgotten that in certain sectors (clothing), small and medium-sized enterprises use workers from the black economy and exploit their labour force. As Figure 4 shows, working hours are longer in smaller firms. Furthermore, working conditions are poorer in smaller enterprises.

Figure 4: Comparative evolution of the average annual working hours/employee between 1981 and 1984 by size of firm

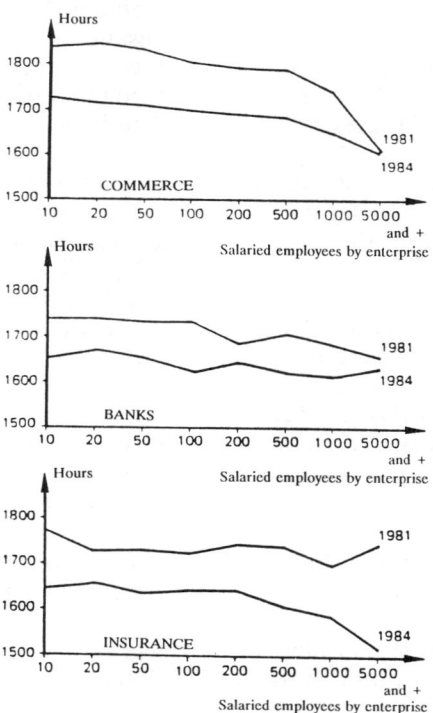
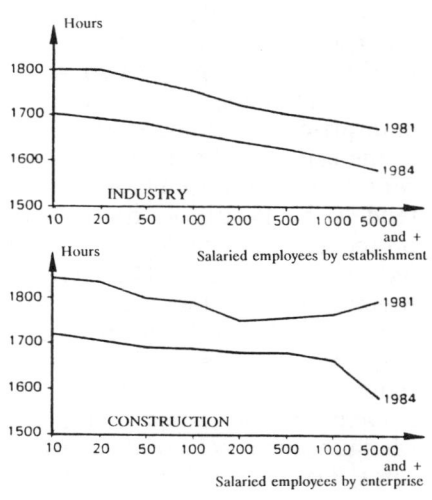

Source: INSEE.

The low level of trade union representation and the relative lack of collective agreements in small and medium-sized enterprises certainly make it easier to implement a flexible labour policy. In 1981, 18.9 per cent of employees in enterprises with between 11 and 49 employees and 11.3 per cent of those in enterprises with between 50 and 200 employees were covered neither by a sector-level nor a company agreement. It is not compulsory to establish works committees in companies with fewer than 50 employees. In enterprises with more than 11 employees, the election of employee representatives is required, although even this level of representation is dependent on candidates coming forward. In fact, in 1985, only 10 per cent of companies held such elections and only just over half of those enterprises with between 50 and 100 employees had employee representatives. Moreover, in enterprises with fewer than 50 employees, almost 69 per cent of the elected representatives are not members of a trade union organisation. This reflects the low level of unionisation in small firms. It is true that, on a more general level, this is a French characteristic, since the rate of unionisation today (including the public sector) has settled down at between 10 and 15 per cent of all employees.

The number of union branches established, which has traditionally been low, particularly in the private sector and in small and medium-sized enterprises, has fallen in line with the general reduction in unionisation rates in France. The proportion of elected representatives who are not trade union members, which was already high in small and medium-sized enterprises, is tending to rise. Labour disputes, which may be an indicator of the capacity of employees to resist, are less frequent in small enterprises. Moreover, certain employers' organisations representing small enterprises tend to be hostile to trade unions and to legal constraints that provide protection for employees, or which lay down certain rules governing industrial relations. The CGPME (General Confederation of Small and Medium-sized Firms) sometimes demonstrates its independence of the CNPF (National Council of French Employers) in national inter-sectoral negotiations. This was recently the case when a national agreement on redundancy was signed by the CNPF and several trade union organisations in October 1986. Since 1981, the SNPMI (National Association of Small and Medium-sized Industrial Firms), an independent organisation, has scored some successes, which reflect the support that anti-statism and vigorous anti-trade-unionism can find among some employers in small enterprises (the SNPMI received almost 15 per cent of the votes in 1982 in the elections to the conciliation boards). For the same reasons, the CNPF has suffered from its own internal wranglings. The voice of the small employer is making itself heard.

Small enterprises have thus made considerable progress in having their interests represented. Yvon Gattaz, president of the CNPF throughout the period of socialist government, had been a member of a group which called itself "Industrial and Commercial Enterprise on a Human Scale". The ideas put forward by some of these organisations are not at all reactionary; on the contrary, they tend to recognise trade unionism as a fact and to welcome negotiation and inter-firm co-operation. This is the case, for

France

example, with a particularly dynamic employers' organisation, the Centre for Young Managers. However, the same is not always true of organisations such as the CGPME and, especially, the SNPMI.

In the view of Delattre and Eymard-Duvernay [1984], small and medium-sized enterprises have also profited from and contributed to the loosening of conventions which regulated commercial relationships before the crisis. Inter-firm relationships and the rules governing the relationships between the enterprises and the final consumer have undergone radical change. By making mass production unfeasible, the rapid change in the nature of products and the length of their commercial life has led to a reduction in investment and a considerable shortening of commercial contracts. Business life in many sectors was organised on the basis of rules, super-rules and formal investment, which guaranteed enterprises an adequate degree of stability.

It is these conventions that small and medium-sized enterprises, located downstream of production systems, are said to have overturned. The study of the clothing industry in Provence-Côte d'Azur conducted by Anselme and Weisz [1981] describes this "collapse of the rules", brought about largely by the increasingly volatile nature of demand. This strategy of overturning commercial practices and the rules of industrial relations is said to have contributed to the success of small enterprises, but to have inhibited the pursuit of innovation. It may be true that there is a relatively low level of research and development in small and medium-sized enterprises, although the evidence varies for different indicators. Table 20 shows the number of research staff employed in manufacturing by enterprise size. The smaller enterprises have larger research staffs, in percentage terms, than do larger enterprises.

On the other hand, Table 21, which shows the percentage of engineers and technicians by enterprise size, suggests relatively less employment of research and development personnel in small enterprises.

Table 20: **Number of research staff employed by size category in manufacturing, 1981**

Size of firm	Number of research staff	Total employees	% employees in research
Fewer than 500 employees	4 948	15 000	33
500 to 999	3 589	11 953	30
1,000 to 1,999	2 945	10 615	28
2,000 to 4,999	5 999	21 980	27
5,000 +	17 614	68 092	26
Total	**35 095**	**127 460**	

Source: Quelennec [1986].

Table 21: **Fixed assets per capita and percentage of engineers and technicians by size category, 1981**

Size of firm	Gross fixed assets per employee (in thousands of francs)	% of engineers and technicians
50 to 99 employees	101.4	5.0
100 to 199	96.8	5.3
200 to 299	110.3	6.5
300 to 399	119.6	6.1
400 to 499	116.3	7.3
500 to 599	133.5	7.9
600 to 699	124.3	7.0
700 to 799	129.4	8.4
800 to 899	133.2	8.4
900 to 999	134.3	9.4
1,000 to 1,999	143.2	9.1
2,000 and over	172.3	12.1

Source: Quelennec [1986].

2. The nature and extent of the recent changes: The paths of regulation

This section presents a few indicators which would appear to show that the recent development and performance of small and medium-sized enterprises represent the early stages of an evolution in industrial organisation. In particular, certain changes in the institutional framework and in inter-firm relationships, initiatives taken by both local and central governments, and the development of the system of industrial relations in small and medium-sized enterprises, point in this direction.

A. *Industrial relations*

Certain legal initiatives and achievements indicate that a genuine system of industrial relations, which has traditionally been lacking in smaller enterprises, is now being developed.

The number of employees in small and medium-sized enterprises covered by a collective agreement increased considerably between 1981 and 1985, as is indicated in Table 22.

Moreover, enterprise-level negotiation has spread to smaller enterprises, even though contractual activity at the enterprise level used to be very limited in France. Table 23 presents what is, in truth, a profound

France

change in the French system of industrial relations, as the penetration of company or plant-level agreements reached more than one-third of total employment in 1985.

Table 22: **Proportion of employees not covered by either a sectoral, company or plant agreement, 1981, 1985**

	11-49 employees 1981	11-49 employees 1985	50-199 employees 1981	50-199 employees 1985	300-499 employees 1981	300-499 employees 1985	500+ employees 1981	500+ employees 1985	All sizes 1981	All sizes 1985
Manufacturing industry	12.4	5.2	4.6	1.7	2.9	0.5	2.4	0.0	5.0	1.7
Construction, civil eng. and agriculture	17.9	5.8	7.9	1.2	5.2	0.8	6.2	0.0	12.0	3.4
Services	22.5	11.9	18.7	6.2	13.4	3.5	6.7	0.0	18.0	7.6
All sectors	18.9	9.1	11.3	3.7	6.3	1.6	3.6	0.0	11.0	4.4

Source: Annual accounts of the collective agreement, 1986, Ministry of Labour.

Table 23: **Proportion of enterprises implementing at least one company or plant agreement and the proportion of employees covered, 1981, 1985**

Size of firm	Firms 1981	Firms 1985	Employees 1981	Employees 1985
10-49 employees	7.7	14.8	8.0	15.4
50-199 employees	15.8	25.9	15.7	27.8
200-499 employees	29.5	45.0	29.1	46.1
500+ employees	44.7	63.8	51.5	68.7
All sizes	9.9	17.7	24.2	35.4
of which: firms with 50+ employees	19.1	30.7	32.2	46.0

Source: Annual accounts of the collective agreement, 1986, Ministry of Labour.

In service activities, such as cleaning or temporary employment agencies, a series of collective agreements have been concluded since 1982. Temporary employment, which had expanded considerably up until 1981 and had been the subject of serious reservations, has been "rehabilitated" and given a sounder moral basis, as a result of both legal measures (the decrees of 1982) and the introduction of collective negotiation. The sector has, as a result of these "cleaning up" measures, been able to safeguard its existence.

The Ministry of Labour reported in 1981 that 39.5 per cent of employees in organisations offering market services to firms, and 16.2 per cent of those in the non-food retail trade, were not covered by a sectoral or company agreement; in 1985, the figures were 11.7 per cent and 4.5 per cent, respectively. The increase in coverage is particularly marked in those sectors which had been lagging significantly behind.

Although still limited, worker representation has increased in small and medium-sized enterprises. On the one hand, legislation has continually increased the number of worker representatives and their responsibilities. On the other hand, actual achievements have followed the lead given by the legislature. In 1982, the threshold of 50 employees, above which a trade union branch could be granted recognition within the firm, was abolished.

However, a more important indication of recent trends in legislation is a measure introduced in 1982 involving the right to representation of workers employed by several small enterprises. It is now possible to elect "site delegates" to represent the interests of employees of enterprises located in a given geographical area (shopping centre, office block, industrial park, etc.). The law of November 1982 was also intended to encourage agreements covering enterprises with fewer than 11 employees on a local or departmental, sectoral or inter-sectoral level. This law set up joint sectoral or inter-sectoral committees whose function is to assist in the drawing-up and implementation of collective labour agreements, and also, should the need arise, to investigate individual or collective complaints. The two sides of industry have been involved in initiatives in this direction, which have led to local agreements [Murcier, 1984]. In 1984, workers and management almost concluded an agreement under which the opportunity to develop inter-company representation would offset the relaxation of the obligation on small enterprises to set up representative bodies [Amadieu and Mercier, 1985]. This development was made possible by the expansion of contractual arrangements and by a significant shift in the thinking of certain trade union organisations, notably the CFDT [Boulin et al., 1984]. Some legal writers are advocating a simplification of the legislation, the extension of contractual arrangements and the creation of inter-company representative bodies [Savatier, 1986].

These attempts to provide small and medium-sized enterprises with a system of negotiation and employee representation are also supported by certain employers' organisations, such as the Centre for Young Managers.

B. Employment conditions

Amar [1986], in his study of 2,712 small and medium-sized enterprises over the period 1978-82, observed 1,420 enterprises which had experienced strong growth. Two-thirds of these enterprises had achieved greater than average productivity gains and had seen their wage costs increase by 16.4 per cent (compared with 14.7 per cent for the large firms in the sample). This increase, which was probably the result of a rise in skill level, was thus associated with growth, investment and increases in productivity.

Several surveys have highlighted trends towards higher skill levels, due to technological changes, the organisation of work (versatility) and the pursuit of quality. This was the conclusion, for example, of Livian and

France

Thomas [1985] who studied ten firms (including five medium-sized firms) in the Rhône-Alpes region in 1984. These trends are far from always reflected in wage levels.

It should be noted that distortions can be observed not only in the employment structure of small and medium-sized enterprises, but in that of large enterprises as well. Table 24 shows the occupational distribution of employment by enterprise size in 1979 and 1983. In view of the indications of a trend towards normalisation, however limited, in the small enterprise sector - notably among those in the service sector - should the hypotheses of a dualist segmentation of the industrial fabric and the labour market not be re-examined?

Table 24: Distribution of employment by occupation and size of firm

	11 to 49 employees	50 to 199 employees	200 to 499 employees	500+ employees	Total
			1979		
Production engineers	1.15	1.57	1.98	2.81	1.89
Middle managers/services	8.85	6.64	5.59	4.90	6.53
Production technicians	2.54	3.33	4.60	8.38	4.78
Technicians/services	5.11	4.65	4.06	3.34	4.29
Supervisors/production	2.91	3.92	4.10	4.49	3.86
Skilled manual workers	26.30	27.85	27.81	27.27	27.41
Unskilled manual workers	15.04	20.12	27.31	23.73	20.23
Managerial staff/services	2.55	2.91	3.17	3.50	3.03
Skilled non-manual employees	25.32	20.28	19.32	16.20	20.25
Unskilled non-manual employees	8.42	7.75	6.65	4.77	6.83
Various	1.25	1.10	0.35	0.57	0.85
Total	**100.00**	**100.00**	**100.00**	**100.00**	**100.00**
			1983		
Production engineers	1.24	1.70	2.21	3.53	2.12
Middle managers/services	9.30	7.40	6.35	5.89	7.36
Production technicians	2.64	3.48	4.93	10.01	5.13
Technicians/services	5.43	5.15	5.23	3.88	4.93
Supervisors/production	2.86	3.92	3.80	4.48	3.75
Skilled manual workers	26.50	26.73	26.32	27.40	27.76
Unskilled manual workers	12.78	17.67	19.53	19.14	17.03
Managerial staff/services	2.76	3.23	3.41	3.73	3.26
Skilled non-manual employees	25.97	20.95	20.27	16.94	21.21
Unskilled non-manual employees	8.92	8.46	7.42	4.59	7.43
Various	1.54	1.25	0.48	0.36	0.97
Total	**100.00**	**100.00**	**100.00**	**100.00**	**100.00**

Source: INSEE, *Enquiry into the costs of manpower*, Document Series M, 1984.

C. Inter-firm co-operation

The relationships between firms are changing in several ways. First the relationships between large and small enterprises are changing. Enterprises engaged in subcontracting, and small enterprises in general, are tending to achieve a higher level of autonomy, through mastery of particular technologies and through product and client diversification. Observers and analysts agree on this point [e.g. Theiss, 1986; Coue, 1986; Martinaud-Deplat, 1983; Camus and Rousset, 1980].

A study carried out by the *Centre d'Etudes de l'Emploi* [Courault and Rerat, July 1986] showed how shoe manufacturers in the Cholet region had solved the problems posed by a stagnating market. A key element in their strategy was the decision to diversify their product range (while retaining standardised products), to take control of the distribution network and operate simply as a supplier, and to adapt their products more rapidly. What is described here is the transition from mass production to flexible specialisation. Increased autonomy for small and medium-sized enterprises vis-à-vis distributors is part of this process of transition, in the same way that small clothing firms in Provence [Anselme and Weisz, 1981] diversified their distribution channels. Another study carried out by the *Centre d'Etudes de l'Emploi* [Gorgeu and Mathieu, May 1986] of 93 suppliers to manufacturing enterprises in three regions in central France confirmed the trend towards product and client diversification, and showed that firms were not abandoning the pursuit of technological proficiency or quality.

Two surveys [OREAM, 1986] carried out in small and medium-sized enterprises in the coalmining and iron and steel-producing region of Lorraine show that, despite the proportion of large enterprises in the area, between 51 and 73 per cent of the enterprises produce their own products, either in whole or in part. Moreover, these surveys showed that between 55 and 38 per cent of small and medium-sized enterprises have attempted, either successfully or otherwise, to diversify, and that about 30 per cent plan to diversify within the same general area of activity.

The study conducted by the CEPME on the reasons for the failure of enterprises [*Crédit d'Equipement des PME*, 1986] highlighted the inadequate level of diversification: 80 per cent of the small and medium-sized enterprises established are subcontractors. However, one possible source of misunderstanding should be cleared up; 69 per cent of subcontractors stated in 1981 that their client was another small firm.

Large firms are encouraging spin-offs. The employment creation effect of spin-offs is probably small, even though it is much discussed [Archier and Serieyx, 1986]. Mention is often made of the Lesieur company, which offers a year's half-time training to employees wishing to set up a company [see also Beaunez and Pietri, 1982]. In addition, it should be noted that the law of 1984 set up a scheme whereby employees can buy out their employer and thus ensure that the firm's activity continues. Large enterprises are also taking on smaller enterprises as partners to whom they supply services without becoming a major participant in their activities.

Large enterprises have facilitated job creation in areas in which they have reduced their own activities. To this end, they have often set up retraining companies. Companies which have followed this path include the French Coal Board, which since 1984 has been supporting enterprises with fewer than 50 employees; *St-Gobain Développement*; the various steel companies (e.g. Sodilor, Solodev); *Creusot-Loire*, etc. Venture capital companies have been set up by large companies and banks, and projects of this nature are increasing in number. Finally, local inter-firm clubs have been established. Beaunez and Pietri [1982] describe this relatively novel development.

Second, networks of co-operation and mutual assistance are being developed, which are a rediscovery and extension of the local professional associations, some of which have survived until the present day. Ganne [1983] discusses such local networks in the leather and paper industries in Annonay, and Raveyre and Saglio [1984] have done the same thing for the plastics industry in Oyonnax. Anselme and Weisz [1981] point out that clothing manufacturers in the Provence-Côte d'Azur region have become aware of the benefits to be gained from going beyond individualism to develop joint services on the model of the clothing firms in the Cholet region. Boisard and Letablier-Zelter [1986] of the *Centre d'Etudes de l'Emploi* have shown the vitality of the local industrial system built up by the producers of Camembert. Beaunez and Pietri [1982] give examples of local inter-firm clubs in cases dominated hitherto by a degree of individualism that excluded all forms of co-operation.

A survey by the CEPME [Huppert, 1981] shows that small and medium-sized enterprises with between 75 and 225 employees appear to have a fairly novel strategy of developing in what might be termed as clusters. They make a conscious decision to remain small or medium-sized, to diversify while still specialising in one particular area, and to invest financially in other companies.

There have been many co-operative initiatives in areas such as technology, training, research, exporting, finance and promotion. This trend has been encouraged by the laws on decentralisation introduced by the socialist government in 1982 and 1983. This legislation increased the responsibilities of and resources available to local government (at regional, departmental and commune levels) relative to those of central government. The administrative supervision exercised by central government over local authorities was abolished. Thus, for example, local authorities may directly take over enterprises about to collapse, or give them financial support. In January 1983, responsibility for continuing vocational training and the apprenticeship system was transferred to the regions.

The 1983 law on the democratisation of the public sector, although much less ambitious, did provide for the establishment of joint committees with members drawn from local enterprises and elected representatives of the local community. Despite its very limited practical significance, the spirit behind the legislation is interesting, since it was a somewhat half-hearted attempt to link a sort of communalism with a more decentralised system of company management, both of which are foreign to the private sector. Local representatives and both sides of industry have increased the number of initiatives, most notably through bodies like the Local Employment Pool

Committees (set up at the instigation of central government in 1982). There were 300 such committees in existence in 1985.

Efforts are being made to forge links between enterprises and teaching and research institutions. The following are a few illustrations of these trends. Transfers of technology are organised locally, as in Picardy, where the university, research laboratories and enterprises lend support to the polymer industry. Several regional centres for technological innovation have been set up for this purpose.

In the Burgundy region, local products are promoted and exported. The regional authorities have taken responsibility for image creation, assist with the transfer of technology to small and medium-sized enterprises and investigate sales outlets. They have funds available to finance consultancy, modernisation and innovation. They encourage the creation of new enterprises, and administer a company analysis and diagnosis centre to which enterprises in the region have access. And finally, through its institute for economic development, the region is able to encourage exports and to provide finance for small and medium-sized enterprises. Frequent contributions are made to the capital resources of small enterprises; the funds are sometimes provided solely from public money, and sometimes from private funds or a mixture of the two. Before the legislation on decentralisation, local authorities were not legally empowered to intervene directly in the establishment and management of private companies.

A survey of 160 local employment pool committees conducted in 1985 reveals the nature of the programmes implemented by these joint bodies (with members from industry and politics). They have been involved in vocational training, career guidance for young people, observation of employment trends, promotion of aid to enterprises, sectoral economic programmes, liaison between enterprises and schools, individual economic initiatives, promotion of local employment pools, aid for workers wishing to be regraded or to re-enter the labour market, direct aid to firms, economic planning and urban development.

In 1986, the Deposit and Consignment Office carried out an evaluation of the increasing number of "breeding-grounds" for new enterprises; i.e. the public and private logistical support systems (land, services, advice, etc.) that are intended to encourage the establishment and development of new firms.

It is not possible to examine in detail the diversity of local programmes, but it is essential to stress the extent and importance of what would appear to be new local industrial systems.

V. Conclusion

It has been shown that the trend towards concentration of employment in large enterprises and an increase in the size of firms began to be reversed from the time of the first oil shock onwards. Furthermore, small and medium-sized enterprises weathered the years of crisis better than larger ones. Several indicators reveal the dynamism shown by smaller enterprises during the period 1974 to 1984. It remains only to account for these relative performances and to ask whether the effect of the size of enterprises is an adequate explanation; that is, to ask whether small is indeed beautiful.

Researchers have argued that small and medium-sized enterprises tend to be located downstream of production systems and that their dynamism is due to their ability to adapt rapidly to fluctuations in demand. Delattre and Eymard-Duvernay, in particular, see the development of small and medium-sized enterprises as an indication of a breakdown of the industrial fabric, and they emphasise the danger of such a process. In their view, small and medium-sized enterprises, by brushing aside the rules and conventions governing inter-firm and firm-client relationships and industrial relations, are preventing the development of collective wealth. By opting for unbridled competition, smaller enterprises are erecting an obstacle to the co-operation that is required. The burden of research, training and large-scale investment programmes weighs heavily on large enterprises and the public sector. The "private pole" (small and medium-sized enterprises) would like to do away with the constraints that produce collective wealth. Thus, the demands for flexibility made by the employers' organisations include a lessening of the "burden" that enterprises are required to shoulder (training, transport, housing, union representation, etc.).

Alongside these trends towards deregulation and a lack of social or moral standards within the industrial fabric, in employment conditions and in industrial relations, is it not possible to detect signs of a process of re-regulation? Some of the directions such a process might take have been identified above, including the rediscovery of local industrial systems. Piore and Sabel [1984] stress the remarkable resilience and efficiency of these industrial fabrics, and suggest that they offer a promising path for the process of re-regulation that involves linking co-operation and competition. There have been many public and private initiatives in this direction. The period of socialist government was characterised by the increased value attached both to the enterprise and to local government.

The efforts that have been made to normalise working relations within small enterprises and to improve and adapt the system of industrial relations have also been highlighted. This involves reconciling the retreat of the State (deregulation, privatisation), the lifting of constraints imposed by the State, and the implementation of agreements negotiated by workers and management.

Several studies, referred to above, provide data and put forward the hypothesis that the restructuring of the industrial fabric is taking place in accordance with new principles. Future studies should focus on these new regulations and combine the industrial economics approach with that of industrial relations. Local sectoral surveys would certainly shed light on the restructuring currently taking place, if they were to adopt a multidisciplinary approach.

Bibliography

Anselme, M.; Weisz, R. 1981. *L'industrie de l'habillement en région Provence-Alpes - Stratégies d'entreprise et organisation de la production*, Cerfise, October.

Amadieu, N.-F.; Mercier, N. 1985. *Négociation sur la flexibilité de l'emploi 1984*, Report for the EC, Paris.

Amar, M. 1986. *La place des PME dans le système productif*, INSEE, Company Research Department, 22 October.

Archier, G.; Serieyx, H. 1986. *Pilotes du 3e type*, Paris, Seuil.

Barge, P. et al. 1983. *L'intervention économique de la commune*, Paris, Syros.

Beaunez, R.; Pietri, J. 1982. *Les communes et l'emploi*, Paris, Les Editions Ouvrières.

Bizaguet, A. 1985. "L'impact économique des petites et moyennes entreprises", in *La Revue du Trésor*, November, pp. 597-606 and December, pp. 661-672.

Boisard, P.; Letablier-Zelter, M.-Th. 1986. *Liens locaux de production et standards industriels - Le cas du camembert*, Centre d'Etudes de l'Emploi, June.

Boulin, J.-Y. et al. 1984. "Les relations sociales dans les PME", in *Les PME créent-elles des emplois?*, Paris, Economica, pp. 89-106.

Caisse des Dépôts et Consignations. 1986. *Des pépinières pour les entreprises de demain*, Colloque Economique et Térritoire, October.

Camus, B.; Rousset, M. 1980. "La polyvalence des entreprises", in *Economie et Statistiques*, No. 125, September, pp. 3-14.

Comité de Liaison des Comités de Bassin de l'Emploi. 1985. *Actes du colloque "Territoire pour l'emploi"*, Conference held from 25-26 October 1985, December.

Coue, D. 1986. "Les sous-traitants deviennent ensembliers", in *L'usine nouvelle*, No. 42, 16 October, pp. 74-81.

Courault, B.; Rerat, F. 1986. *Les stratégies des producteurs face à la distribution - Le cas des entreprises de chaussure du Choletais*, Centre d'Etudes de l'Emploi, July.

Crédit d'Equipement des PME (CEPME). 1985. *La démographie des entreprises en 1984*, March.

---. 1986. *Les causes de défaillance des entreprises industrielles*, Detailed Report, June.

Deck, J.-P. 1986. *Creusot-Loire: Une reconversion réussie*, Editions ERES.

Delattre, M. 1982. "Les PME face aux grandes entreprises", in *Economie et Statistiques*, No. 148, October, pp. 3-19.

Delattre, M.; Eymard-Duvernay, F. 1983. "Sept catégories d'entreprises pour analyser le tissu industriel", in *Economie et Statistiques*, No. 159, October, pp. 71-87.

---. 1984. "Les progrès des PME dans la crise: Signe d'un relâchement du tissu industriel", in *Critique de l'Economie Politique*, Nos. 26-27, January-June, pp. 119-132.

Didier, M. 1982. "Crise et concentration du secteur productif", in *Economie et Statistiques*, No. 144, May, pp. 3-12.

Douard, H. 1986. *La taille des établissements industriels*, Doctoral thesis, Paris, February.

Dupuis, X. et al. 1984. "Quel mode de développement pour l'économie sociale?", in *Consommation*, No. 2, pp. 3-21.

Ganne, B. 1983. *Gens du cuir, gens du papier* (bibliography), Paris, CNRS.

Gaudin, J.; Schiray, M. 1984. "L'économie cachée en France: Etat du débat et bilan des travaux", in *Revue Economique*, No. 4, Vol. 35, July, pp. 691-731.

Gloaquen, J. 1986. "La fin des grandes usines", in *Le nouvel économiste*, 5 September.

Gorgeu, A.; Mathieu, R. 1986. *Marchés, investissement, emploi chez les fournisseurs de l'industrie*, Centre d'Etudes de l'Emploi, May.

Greffe, X. et al. 1984. *Les PME créent-elles des emplois?*, Paris, Economica.

Huppert, R. 1981. "Stratégies de développement des PME françaises", in *Revue d'Economie Industrielle*, No. 17, 3rd quarter, CEPME, pp. 26-41.

Jaeger, C. et al. 1985. "L'artisanat en évolution: L'exemple de 3 métiers", in *Revue d'Economie Industrielle*, No. 36, 4th quarter, pp. 58-70.

Livian, Y.-F.; Thomas, J. 1985. "Taille des établissements et effets de seuil", in *Economie et Statistique*, No. 173, January.

Madinier, Ph. 1983. "La persistance des très petites entreprises dans les activités non agricoles", in *Travail et Emploi*, No. 16, pp. 67-81.

Marco, L.; Rainelli, M. 1986. "Les disparitions de firmes industrielles en France: Un modèle économétrique", in *Revue d'Economie Industrielle*, No. 36, 2nd quarter, pp. 1-13.

Martinaud-Deplat, D. 1983. "Ardennes l'Etat d'urgence", in *L'usine nouvelle*, No. 31-33, August.

Mathieu, E. 1986. "Les résultats des entreprises industrielles en 1985", in *Economie et Statistiques*, No. 192, October, pp. 13-16.

Mignot, G. 1979. *Perspectives de développement de l'artisanat et de la petite entreprise*, Paris, La Documentation Française.

Monfort, J.-A.; Vasille, L. 1985. "La concentration des activités économiques, les établissements, les entreprises et les groupes", in *Les collections de l'INSEE*, E98, October.

Murcier, J.-P. 1984. "L'application du droit syndical et des institutions représentatives dans les entreprises de moins de 50 salariés", in *Droit social*, No. 2, February, pp. 107-119.

Muret, J.-P. et al. 1983. *L'économie et les emplois*, Paris, Syros.

OREAM. 1986. *Etude PMI bassin houiller-lorrain*, September.

---. 1986. *Les relations entre les H.B.L. et le tissu économique*, September.

Piore, M.J.; Sabel, Ch.F. 1984. *The second industrial divide*, New York, Basic Books.

Quelennec, M. 1986. *Les statistiques d'entreprises*, INSEE Series E, June.

Raveyre, M.-F.; Saglio, J. 1984. "Les systèmes industriels localisés: Eléments pour une analyse sociologique des ensembles de PME industriels", in *Sociologie du Travail*, No. 2.

Roncin, A. 1982. "L'engagement des PMI dans l'exportation", in *Economie et Statistiques*, No. 148, October, pp. 39-51.

Saunier, P. 1985. "L'industrie française des viandes de volailles: Les raisons de la faible rentabilité et de la tendance à la déconcentration dans le secteur", in *Revue d'Economie Industrielle*, No. 34, 4th quarter, pp. 101-116.

Savatier, J. 1986. "Etablissement ou entreprise: Quel cadre pour l'évaluation des seuils d'effectifs?", in *Droit social*, No. 9-10, September-October, pp. 703-708.

Schmitt, D. et al. 1984. *La région à l'heure de la décentralisation*, La Documentation Française.

Sudreau, P. 1975. *Reforme de l'entreprise*, Report of Comité d'Etude pour la reforme de l'entreprise, Paris, La Documentation Française.

Theiss, U. 1986. *Les théories de la segmentation: Un examen*, Paper given at the GRECO Conference on The Labour Market, CNAM, Paris.

Vassille, L. 1982. "Les PME fragilité financière, forte rentabilité", in *Economie et Statistiques*, No. 148, October, pp. 21-37.

Zarca, B. 1984. *Survivance et transformation de l'artisanat dans la France d'aujourd'hui*, Doctoral Thesis, University of Dauphiné.

3 Federal Republic of Germany

Stephanie Weimer

I. The size, structure and characteristics of the small firm sector

1. Size and principal characteristics

In order to determine the employment share of the small firm sector in the economy of the Federal Republic of Germany as a whole, it is necessary to refer back to the 1970 workplace census. This census shows that in 1970, 98.9 per cent of all enterprises (Table 1) and 98.8 per cent of all establishments (Table 2) were small firms, where small is defined to be fewer than 100 employees. Although the share of the small firm sector in total employment was considerably lower, it was still very significant: 44.2 per cent of all employees were working in small enterprises, while about half of all employees (53.3 per cent) were employed in small establishments.

Craft firms constitute a significant proportion of the small firm sector in the Federal Republic of Germany: it is estimated that in 1970 enterprises of this kind accounted for about 31 per cent of all enterprises and 42 per cent of employees in the small firm sector. The share of craft enterprises among small manufacturing enterprises is even higher: here it is estimated that craft enterprises account for 77 per cent of all enterprises and 54 per cent of all employees.

More recent data on the size of the small firm sector are available only for manufacturing. These data show that in 1984, 71.2 per cent of all enterprises in the manufacturing sector were small enterprises. These small manufacturing enterprises employed 15.6 per cent of total manufacturing employment (Table 3). To these figures should be added very small manufacturing enterprises with fewer than 20 employees, which accounted for 51,873 enterprises and 327,079 employees in 1984 (Table 4).

Which sectors of manufacturing are dominated by small firms? If "small firm dominance" is defined to be those sectors in which at least 95 per cent of establishments have fewer than 100 employees, the largest (in terms of employment) manufacturing sectors dominated by small firms are clothing, woodworking, the extraction and processing of stone and earth, steel and metal construction, printing and duplication, and the bakery and meat products industries.

According to the last craft census in 1977, the craft segment of the small firm sector comprised 494,243 enterprises with a total of almost 4 million employees (Table 5). Craft firms are usually small. In 1977, 93.4 per cent of craft enterprises had fewer than 20 employees, while only 0.5 per cent had more than 100 employees. The craft segment can thus be

Federal Republic of Germany

Table 1: Number of enterprises and employment shares by enterprise size, 1970 (1) (per cent distribution)

	\multicolumn{8}{c}{Enterprise size (number of employees)}
	1-2	3-9	10-49	50-99	100-199	200-499	500+	Total
Number of enterprises	52.0	36.5	9.3	1.1	0.6	0.4	0.2	100.0
Employment share	6.7	15.0	15.6	6.9	7.2	9.7	39.0	100.0

Notes: (1) All non-agricultural enterprises.
Source: Statistisches Bundesamt (Federal Statistical Office).

Table 2: Number of establishments and employment shares by establishment size, 1970 (1) (per cent distribution)

	\multicolumn{9}{c}{Establishment size (number of employees)}
	1	2-4	5-9	10-19	20-49	50-99	100-199	200-499	500+	Total
Number of establishments	27.9	44.0	15.6	6.3	3.7	1.3	0.7	0.4	0.1	100.0
Employment share	2.8	11.8	10.0	8.4	11.2	9.1	9.2	12.0	25.5	100.0

Notes: (1) All non-agricultural establishments, excluding non-profit organizations, regional authorities and social security.
Source: Statistisches Bundesamt (Federal Statistical Office).

Table 3: Number of enterprises and employment shares in manufacturing by enterprise size, 1984 (per cent distribution)

	\multicolumn{7}{c}{Enterprise size (number of employees)}
	20-49	50-99	100-199	200-499	500-999	1000+	Total
Number of enterprises	47.4	23.8	14.3	9.5	3.0	2.4	100.0
Employment share	7.5	8.1	9.8	14.3	10.1	50.2	100.0

Source: Statistisches Bundesamt (Federal Statistical Office).

included in its entirety in the small firm sector in accordance with the definition used in this paper.

There are no strict regulations in the Federal Republic of Germany governing the classification of a firm as a craft enterprise. There are no clear criteria, such as number of employees, turnover or the existence of a particular production structure. The classification of a firm as a craft enterprise is the result of a legal-normative definition. The craft regulations lay down which businesses may be operated as craft firms. If a firm wishes to be classified as a craft enterprise, a master craftsman's certificate is required in order to manage the firm. The classification of a firm depends also on economic considerations; e.g. differences in agreed wage scales between the craft sector and manufacturing industry. It is possible, therefore, that two basically identical firms may be classified differently.

Table 6 shows the breakdown of the craft sector by industry. The largest manufacturing industries within the craft sector are the metal and food industries. The building trades and certain services are also important sectors. The construction, food and the wood processing industries are among the sectors in which craft firms can claim a relatively strong position.

One outstanding characteristic of the small firm sector in the Federal Republic of Germany is its heterogeneity. There is no single dominant type of small firm which can be distinguished from large firms on the basis of certain characteristics - e.g. wage levels - and which would make it possible to speak of a dualistic business structure based on firm size. There is a wide spectrum of businesses in the small firm sector. At one end are small companies with a strong market position, which employ highly qualified personnel to produce high quality goods, which are themselves innovative, and in which working conditions match or even exceed those in large firms. At the other end are small firms which mass produce a relatively simple, substitutable product, which operate in a market with sharp fluctuations in demand, and in which the jobs require few qualifications and are low-paid and unpleasant. Even the craft sector is by no means homogeneous: in addition to those firms in which traditional craft processes are still used, there are also craft firms which have specialised to a very high degree (e.g. as suppliers), which mass produce, and which have changed over to quasi-industrial production methods.

This heterogeneity makes it more difficult to analyse the small firm sector in terms of a typology of small firms. The first attempts at drawing up a typology of this kind were made by Mendius et al. [1987] and were based on various combinations of external operating conditions.

One external condition by which small firms can be distinguished is, for example, the nature of the relationships with large firms: do they compete with large firms in the same product market, or do they operate in a niche of their own? Do they operate as suppliers to large firms? Are they dependent on large firms for the purchase of primary products or raw materials? Alternatively, what is the structure of demand for their products? Is it very sensitive to economic fluctuations, is it seasonal, highly concentrated or atomistic?

Federal Republic of Germany

Table 4: Number and employment shares of very small enterprises by enterprise size, 1984 (per cent distribution)

	\multicolumn{5}{c}{Enterprise size (number of employees)}
	1	2-4	5-9	10-19	Total
Number of enterprises	18.7	31.5	24.1	25.7	100.0
Employment share	3.0	13.9	25.7	57.5	100.0

Source: Statistisches Bundesamt (Federal Statistical Office).

Table 5: Number of enterprises and employment share in the craft sector by enterprise size, 1977

	1	2-4	5-9	10-19	20-49	50-99	100+	Total
Number of enterprises	87 377	192 130	126 304	55 806	24 261	5 707	2 658	494 243
(per cent)	17.7	38.9	25.5	11.3	4.9	1.2	0.5	100.0
Employment	87 377	552 377	817 821	736 959	709 847	387 710	614 441	3 906 532
(per cent)	2.2	14.1	20.9	18.9	18.2	9.9	15.7	100.0

Source: Statistisches Bundesamt (Federal Statistical Office).

Table 6: Number of enterprises and employment shares in the craft sector by industry, 1977

	Wood	Construction	Metal	Textile/leather	Food	Services in health, hygiene and cleaning
Number of enterprises	44 515	103 163	147 974	50 743	74 263	57 371
(per cent)	9.0	20.9	29.9	10.3	15.0	11.6
Employment	242 514	1 162 270	1 224 476	150 640	476 437	554 303
(per cent)	6.2	29.8	31.3	3.9	12.2	14.2

Source: Statistisches Bundesamt (Federal Statistical Office).

2. The institutional background to the small firm sector

A. Legislation

Firms conduct their activities within an institutional framework moulded by the traditions of the country in which they operate. These institutional-legal conditions are part of the external environment with which firms have to grapple strategically. The question is whether these conditions are the same for all firms or whether there are differences depending on the size of the firm. What have been the effects of the existence (or non-existence) of such special regulations on the development of the small firm sectors?

The regulations that impinge most directly on the activities of firms are the system of wage determination, the regulations governing labour law and social security and the system of taxation.

In the Federal Republic of Germany, wage agreements in the different sectors are concluded centrally for regional wage zones. Within these wage zones, which often cover a wide geographical area, the same contractual wage applies to all firms covered by the agreement. No allowances are made for the profitability of individual firms or for companies of different sizes. The wage agreement is binding on all firms which are members of the employers' associations, as well as on all trade union members. It is common practice, however, for companies to extend the agreed-upon wage rates to employees who are not members of trade unions.

Even companies that are not members of the employers' association cannot simply evade the contractual wage rate. As a result of the legal provisions that exist for declaring the agreed-upon rates to be generally binding, wage agreements can be extended to those firms that are not members of the employers' association. The aim of declaring an agreed-upon rate to be generally binding is to prevent firms from obtaining competitive advantages by paying wages lower than the contractual rate [*Sozialpolitische Informationen*, 1983]. Although the proportion of wage agreements declared to be generally binding is very low (only 7.8 per cent of all agreements in 1978 - Boedler and Keiser [1979]), it is above average in those sectors in which smaller firms predominate. This follows from the fact that membership in employers' associations is often very low in the sectors with many small firms; for example, textiles and clothing, food and luxury goods and the extraction and processing of stone and earth [Schatz, 1984].

It is thus true to say that in the area of the contractual remuneration of labour - i.e. wages and salaries, capital-forming payments under the employees' saving scheme, holiday entitlement and holiday pay - small firms in the Federal Republic of Germany are subject to the same initial conditions as other firms. Nor are there exceptions for any particular group of firms with respect to employees' social security contributions, a proportion of which are paid by firms and which are classified as incidental labour costs. Social security contributions must, in principle, be paid for all employees, provided that their income exceeds a certain low threshold.

Figure 1 shows the most important provisions of labour and social security law in the Federal Republic of Germany, and the special regulations applying to firms in particular size categories. In the case of important regulations that restrict employers' room for manoeuvre when taking personnel decisions (e.g. the law on protection against summary or unfair dismissal, the works councils' right to consultation), there are special regulations for small firms. The same is true for laws that might, under some circumstances, involve high costs for a firm (e.g. the laws on the continued payment of wages and safety at work). Figure 1 shows that firms with up to 20 employees seem to constitute the threshold up to which firms are exempt from many of the legal provisions. Only firms with up to five or six employees are exempt from the obligation to establish a works council and from the provisions of the law on dismissal. Thus, the special regulations apply basically only to the very smallest firms.

No study has yet been conducted on the effects of such special regulations on the development of the distribution of firms by size, on the decision to split off parts of firms, or to contract-out certain functions. According to a study of small and medium-sized firms carried out by the *Institut für Mittelstandsforschung* (Institute for Research on Small Businesses), it is the laws on the continued payment of wages, on dismissal and on the employment of handicapped people that have a particular influence on firms' calculations [Keyser and Friede, 1984].

As far as the most important forms of taxation for firms (turnover, income, corporation, trade and property tax) are concerned, there is no significant differentiation by size of firm. However, they are not always size-neutral in their effects; for example, it is easier for large firms to benefit from tax relief, and high tax allowances mean that small firms are, in fact, exempt from certain forms of taxation.

If all the parameters relevant to economic activity are taken into account, it becomes clear that small firms in the Federal Republic of Germany are not basically subject to any special initial conditions. This is not true of the very smallest firms with fewer than 20 employees, to which a whole range of legal provisions do not apply. However, formal equal treatment for small firms does not prevent the actual effects of existing legal provisions from discriminating against or favouring small firms.

B. Collective organisations and forms of co-operation

Compared with large firms, small firms are at a disadvantage in many respects: for example, in terms of financial and human resources, and of access to sources of capital and suppliers. The amalgamation of several small firms - whether in the form of a temporary, ad hoc alliance set up to solve a particular problem or of a permanent organisation - is one route by which small firms can offset their competitive disadvantages. Where and in what form can co-operative structures of this kind be found in the small firm sector in the Federal Republic of Germany?

The craft sector in the Federal Republic of Germany provides examples of particularly highly-developed forms of co-operation. Indeed, the economic success of the craft sector could even be attributed to the fact that

Figure 1: Social security, labour laws and the special regulations for small firms

Law on continued payment of wages ("Lohnfortzahlungsgesetz")	If an employee is absent from work due to illness, the employer must continue to pay his wages and social security contributions for a period of six weeks.	For small firms with fewer than 20 employees, there is a contribution procedure: they pay a monthly contribution to a fund which pays back to the firm 8 per cent of the cost of continuing to pay an employee's wages in the event of sickness.
Law on handicapped people ("Schwerbehindertengesetz")	Regulates firms' obligations to employ physically and mentally handicapped people, and the arrangements for the employment of such people (equipping of workplace, special holiday entitlement, exemption from overtime).	Firms with more than 16 employees must make at least 6 per cent of their jobs available to handicapped people. Otherwise an equalisation payment of 100 DM per month must be paid for each handicapped person not employed.
Law protecting mothers-to-be and nursing mothers ("Mutterschutzgesetz")	Regulates the employment of pregnant women (working hours, protection from dismissal and prohibition of certain activities) and provides periods of protection before and after the birth when women must not, or are permitted not to, work.	None.
Law on employment of young people ("Jugendarbeitsschutzgesetz")	Contains protective regulations which must be observed when employing young people.	None.
Law on protection against summary and unfair dismissal ("Kündigungsschutzgesetz")	Regulates employers' scope for action in the case of redundancies (observance of certain time limits, opportunity for employees to appeal, redundancy payments, etc.).	Applies only to firms with more than five employees, excluding trainees.
Protection against mass dismissals in the labour promotion law ("Arbeitsförderungsgesetz")	In the event of large-scale redundancies, the employer has an obligation to give certain information to the employment office; the employment office must be given 30 days' notice of the redundancies.	Applies to firms with more than 20 employees. Firms with between 20 and 59 employees must give notice if more than five employees are to be made redundant.

Labour Management Act ("Betriebsverfassungsgesetz")	Regulates the employment relationship between employer and the workforce on the basis of the collective representation of the employees' interests through a works council.	Only in firms with at least five permanent employees do employees have the opportunity to elect a works council. The rights of codetermination with respect to the suspension, classification or reclassification, or transfer of employees do not apply to firms with fewer than 20 employees.
Social Plan ("Sozialplan" im Betriebsverfassungsgesetz)	In the event of operational changes (e.g. closure or transfer of parts of the firm), the works council has the right to demand that a social plan be drafted to compensate for the economic hardship suffered by the affected workers. The employer has an obligation to give the works council early notice of any planned changes and to discuss them with the council.	The right of the works council to be involved in the event of operational changes applies only to firms with more than 20 employees.
Economic Committee ("Wirtschaftsausschuss" im Betriebsverfassungsgesetz).	Appointed by the works council and has the task of advising the employer on economic matters.	Exists only in firms with more than 100 employees.
Law on safety at work ("Arbeitssicherheitsgesetz")	Governs the employment of and obligation to appoint doctors and safety specialists at the workplace. The trade associations administer the obligation to appoint for their own sector.	Taking an average of all trade associations, firms with between 20 and 50 employees have an obligation to appoint safety specialists. Firms with 20 or more employees have an obligation to appoint a person responsible for safety at work. On average, only firms with more than 50 employees have an obligation to appoint a doctor at the workplace.
Workplace regulations ("Arbeitsstättenverordnung")	Govern the organisation of work and the workplace (e.g. noise protection, dimensions).	None.
Regulations on working hours ("Arbeitszeitordnung")	Govern the length and status of working hours (breaks, overtime, etc.).	None.

firms in the sector succeeded at an early stage in setting up powerful self-help organisations and interest groups, the guilds and trade corporations. These organisations have a central umbrella organisation, but are structured on the local level and encompass every single craft firm. The objectives of these organisations go far beyond those of an employers' association and include, in addition to the operation of the entire training and examination system, further training, business consultancy, specialist and expert departments and much more. The collective organisation of the craft sector did not, of course, take place without the aid of the state, which created the essential preconditions by authorising compulsory membership and the transfer of state functions to self-governing organisations in the craft sector.

Against the background of this organisational structure, additional forms of collective self-help have developed. Thus several craft sectors - e.g. the food sector - have established strong co-operative organisations. These organisations, which were originally set up in order to obtain more favourable terms with suppliers through collective purchasing, have in the course of time considerably increased the scope of their activities. They now organise further training courses, carry out business consultancy and conduct sector-specific research. Another form of co-operation in the craft sector was developed in order to offer workers welfare benefits in excess of those normally provided by individual small firms; by this means, it is hoped to improve the position of small firms in the labour market when competing for skilled labour. Thus, several craft sectors have set up joint pension funds.

In the construction segment of the craft sector, the so-called building co-operatives are increasing in importance. These co-operatives are local affiliations of, for the most part, small and medium-sized construction companies in the same or different trades. The purpose of co-operation of this kind is the joint acceptance and carrying out of contracts. By bringing together different capacities and services, a certain degree of rationalisation can be achieved which makes it possible to offer lower prices (joint purchasing of raw materials, joint advertising, etc.); in this way small firms can also participate in large projects which would be beyond the scope of individual small firms.

However, outside of the craft sector, co-operative solutions in the small firm sector appear to be less well developed. Where they do exist, they tend to be organised informally, so that little information about their activities becomes public. There have been no empirical studies of co-operative relationships between small firms; e.g. investigations of the networks of co-operation that very probably exist within regional small firm centres. At best, isolated empirical indications can be found of the existence of such co-operative structures. One example is a study of innovation in small and medium-sized firms, which showed that in the area of research and development various forms of co-operation between innovative small and medium-sized firms were developing. They ranged from occasional informal contacts, via loose affiliations of several small firms, to the joint implementation of a particular development plan involving two firms from different sectors [Meyer-Krahmer et al., 1984a].

The state has recognised the importance of co-operative solutions for the competitiveness of small firms. Thus, in the latest amendment to the law against restraint of competition, those forms of co-operation which serve to improve the performance of small and medium-sized firms are expressly excluded from the provisions banning cartels. However, only a few firms are making use of the lifting of the constraints on co-operation between small and medium-sized firms (Law against restraint of competition, paragraph 5).

With the exception of the craft sector, co-operative structures in the small firm sector of the Federal Republic of Germany are very rudimentary. The example of the collective structures developed in the craft sector shows the fundamental importance of state initiatives in mobilising the existing potential for co-operation. It also shows that the presence of an infrastructure set up to organise co-operation facilitates the application of co-operative solutions to other problem areas.

3. Employment and work in the small firm sector

There is a close correlation between the way in which the small firm sector develops in an economy and the working conditions that small firms offer their employees relative to large firms. The greater the difference between wages and working conditions in firms in different size categories, the more difficult it is for small firms to hire better, more highly-qualified personnel and the more difficult it is for them to compete with large firms in markets which make high demands on product quality, innovative capacity and company flexibility.

Looking first at wages and salaries, a study conducted in 1983 shows that the gross annual income of employees rises considerably with firm size. According to this study, full-time male workers in firms with more than 1,000 employees earned 17 per cent more than their counterparts in firms with fewer than 100 employees, while male white-collar employees earned 23 per cent more than the same group in small firms. In the case of female workers, the differences were even more marked [Weimer, 1983]. Significant differentials remain after controlling for qualifications.

The study also shows that there is no difference in agreed-upon wage scales between firms in different size categories. In addition to the more widespread use of piece-work, which offers opportunities for higher earnings, it was mainly voluntary special allowances that were responsible for most of the differences in earnings. On the other hand, there were only small differences between size categories in collectively-negotiated special allowances.

Even if there is an earnings gap between large and small firms in the Federal Republic of Germany, an international comparison shows that, compared with other countries such as the United States of America or Japan, this gap is relatively narrow. Average earnings in small firms in the Federal Republic of Germany are 90 per cent of those in firms with more than 500 employees. The figures for Japan and the United States of America are only 77 per cent and 57 per cent respectively [OECD, 1985].

A fundamental cause of this relatively small gap, in international terms, lies in the German system of central, sector-wide collective bargaining. This is confirmed by the small differences in the collectively-negotiated wage components between firms of different sizes mentioned above. As far as working conditions in small firms are concerned, it could be expected, given the heterogeneity of this sector, that there would be a multiplicity of different working situations within it. The spectrum ranges from small firms with extremely unfavourable working conditions, such as short-cycle, repetitive and physically demanding work, unstable employment and excessively long working hours, to small firms in which skilled jobs predominate. In the latter case, small firm jobs may offer a great deal of scope for planning and creativity, stable employment, enhanced safety at work and ergonomics in the design of the work stations.

There are indications that the small firm sector in the Federal Republic of Germany still contains a relatively high proportion of jobs with favourable working conditions, i.e. working conditions that in terms of the scope and skill-level of the jobs, the opportunities for co-operation and autonomy, could be described as even more favourable than those in large firms. The great importance of the craft industries in the small firm sector should be noted here: even today, craft work is still mainly skilled work. Data on the qualification structure of employees in firms in different size categories show that in the case of male workers, for example, the proportion of skilled workers increases as the size of firm falls, from 60 per cent in firms with more than 100 employees to 76 per cent in small firms with fewer than 20 employees. On the other hand, the share of semi-skilled workers rises as the size of firm increases, while the proportion of unskilled workers remains relatively constant in all size categories [Weimer, 1983]. However, there are quite definite sector-specific differences within this general trend: in the mechanical engineering industry, for example, it is only in firms with more than 50 workers that the proportion of skilled workers begins to decrease. It is true that smaller firms in this sector have a higher proportion of skilled workers than the average for the sector, but as a whole that proportion is lower than in firms with 50-99 employees.

The intensification of work processes is still much less far advanced in small firms than in large firms. If the existence of incentive payment schemes is taken as an indicator, the fact that such schemes are not very common in the small firm sector suggests a lower degree of intensification of work processes in small firms. On the other hand, there do appear to be strains and burdens that are quite definitely specific to the small firm sector. Statistical inquiries and employee surveys repeatedly confirm that overtime is both longer and more frequent in small firms. Flexible working hours appear to constitute a significant element of small firms' overall potential for flexibility. On the other hand, the collectively agreed upon weekly working hours have, to a large extent, been brought into line with those in larger firms. However, there is still a considerable gap between large and small firms in the length of the period of holiday entitlement [Weimer, 1983].

The vast majority of small firms in the Federal Republic of Germany have no works council. Although it is possible for a works council to be elected in firms with six or more employees, a representative survey conducted in 1980 showed that only 25 per cent of small firms in the manufacturing and construction sectors had set up works councils. The proportion in the economy as a whole must be even lower, since the survey did not include the commerce and service sectors, which have a very low level of organisation [Bosch, 1983]. Employers in small firms repeatedly attempt to obstruct the election of works councils.

The cause of the often strongly emotional rejection of trade unions and works councils in small firms lies in the specific social structure of these firms: one owner/entrepreneur, who often still works himself; the paternalism of many employers; and close social contact between employees and employers. Even when works councils are established in small firms, their opportunities for looking after employees' interests are very limited. It is rare for time to be made available for works council business, there are only limited material and personnel resources available and only limited opportunities to make use of the further training courses offered by trade unions.

The rate of trade union organisation is 7 per cent in small firms with up to ten employees, 26 per cent in small firms with between 11 and 100 employees and 56 per cent in large firms with more than 2,000 employees [Bosch, 1983]. In contrast to the United Kingdom and the United States of America, there is no difference in the frequency of strikes between firms of different sizes [Prais et. al., 1981]. The main reason for this is probably the centralised system of collective bargaining and the consequently small - in international terms - differences between working conditions in large and small firms.

II. Quantitative evolution of the small firm sector

1. The historical development of the small firm sector

What are the long-term trends in the development of the small firm sector in the Federal Republic of Germany? Are the number and structure of small firms the result of an extended process of contraction? Has the development of small firms proceeded in a discontinuous or consistent manner?

There has been virtually no investigation into the historical development of the size distribution of enterprises and establishments in Germany. Only very recently has an attempt been made to use the various workplace, industry and company censuses that are available for the years from 1875 onwards for an historical, empirical investigation of this question [Stockmann et al., 1985; Stockmann et al., 1983]. These data make it possible to trace the development of the size structure of companies as far back as the first phase of industrialisation in Germany.

Table 7 clearly shows a long-term shift in the share of employment towards larger establishments. In 1882, almost two-thirds of all people included in the company census were working in one-man businesses or very small establishments with fewer than five employees; by 1907, this proportion had fallen dramatically. In 1970, only 13 per cent of workers were employed in very small establishments. On the other hand, the share of employment in all other size categories - particularly very small establishments with between five and ten employees - has risen slightly but continuously over the period of 100 years. Large establishments with more than 1,000 employees have expanded very considerably: by 1970, they had increased their share of total employment from 3 per cent to more than 16 per cent, a rise of more than 500 per cent. The evolution of the number of establishments reveals the same trends (Table 8): a drastic reduction in the number of one-man workplaces, a sharp decrease in the number of very small establishments with fewer than five employees, and a significant increase - particularly from 1950 onwards - in small and medium-sized establishments with up to 200 employees.

Table 7: Employment shares by establishment size: Total economy, 1882-1970

	One self-employed person	1-5	6-10	11-50	51-200	201-1000
1882	-	61.2	4.7	12.1	10.1	9.0
1895	-	46.5	8.1	15.8	14.0	11.3
1907	12.4	24.9	7.7	17.9	16.8	13.8
1925	8.1	21.2	7.4	16.6	16.6	17.0
1933	12.3	27.4	7.9	14.4	14.4	15.2
1950	6.4	18.7	11.7	20.0	16.2	14.8
1970	2.5	10.8	9.5	20.8	19.6	20.6

Source: Stockmann and Kleber [1985].

Table 8: Number of establishments by size: Total economy, 1875-1970

	One self-employed person	1-5	6-10	11-50	51-200	201-1000
1875	-	97.6	0.9	1.2	0.2	0.05
1882	-	96.8	1.4	1.5	0.3	0.2
1895	59.8	33.5	3.6	2.5	0.5	0.2
1907	51.9	39.3	4.3	3.5	0.8	0.2
1925	43.5	45.6	5.4	4.2	1.0	0.2
1933	50.5	41.4	4.4	2.9	0.6	0.2
1950	38.2	43.0	11.2	6.3	1.1	0.2
1970	27.0	43.1	15.8	11.1	2.3	0.6

Source: Stockmann and Kleber [1985].

Thus, it can be ascertained that there has been a long-term trend in Germany towards an increase in the size of establishments. However, this trend can be attributed largely to the dramatic decline in one-man businesses and very small establishments and the simultaneous sharp increase in the share of large establishments in total employment. On the other hand, the small and medium-sized firms sector as a whole has remained stable throughout the 100-year period, or has even tended to grow slightly. The displacement of small and medium-sized firms by large ones predicted by the proponents of the concentration theory has not therefore occurred. The concentration and expansion of the German economy have taken place not through the absorption of small and medium-sized firms, but rather through the growth of such firms and, at the same time, the constant creation of new small firms [Rieker, 1960].

The general trend towards larger firms has not been continuous; it was interrupted by a reversal in 1933, during the Great Depression, when the proportion of very small firms rose and the proportion of small and medium-sized firms contracted. This interruption of the trend can be attributed largely to the "escape into self-sufficiency" triggered by the economic crisis and the simultaneous shedding of jobs by larger firms. The years that followed saw a rapid return to the general trend toward large firms.

It is also possible to identify phases in which the rate of development varied, as well as differences between sectors. The present firm size structure emerged very early: the main phase of concentration had finished before 1925. Thereafter, the process of concentration proceeded much more slowly. Whereas the capital goods sectors had reached their peak level of concentration as early as 1925, the consumer goods sectors did not embark on the process of concentration until the years following the Second World War, and did not reach their peak level of concentration until 1970.

How can we explain the fact that in Germany a stable small and medium-sized firms sector has survived all the processes of change and concentration? Just as the resilience of the small firm sector has only recently been recognised - much to the surprise of some people - systematic investigation of the reasons for this structural stability is still in its infancy [Siegrist, 1983]. Economic and socio-historical research in the Federal Republic of Germany has not yet explicitly tackled this question. Only a few isolated indications of an explanation exist, and they may be summarised as follows:

- One explanation for the survival of the small firm sector in the Federal Republic of Germany lies in the "late conquest" of large areas of the economy by the industrial sector [Lutz, 1984]. Thus, until after the Second World War it was possible for a dual economic structure to exist in Germany, comprising an industrial/market economy sector and a traditional craft sector. Within this dual structure, it was the function of the craft sector to meet most of the population's need for everyday goods. A specific mechanism, based on the terms of exchange in product and labour markets between the two sectors, together with

the existence of an industrial reserve army, prevented the advance of industrial production methods into these areas. It was only the welfare state policy introduced after the Second World War and the associated increase in and stability of incomes that ousted the everyday goods and services produced in the craft sector, and led to the developoment of a manufacturing sector producing goods for mass consumption [Lutz, 1984].
As a result of the delayed "industrial conquest", the traditional small firm sector had sufficient time to modernise itself, both in terms of production techniques and industrial management methods. Certain areas of the small firm sector were thus able to strengthen themselves to such an extent that they were able to not only survive but even maintain their ascendancy over the industrial sector.

- Even the technology of mass production was late developing in Germany. Unlike in England, for example, the railway industry was the motor of industrialisation, rather than a sector of the consumer goods industry such as the textile industry. The mechanical engineering industry experienced a particularly sharp upturn as a result of supplying the railway industry [Henning, 1973]. The skills and know-how of the mechanical engineering industry were thus directed, for the most part, towards the capital goods sector and not towards equipping the mass production goods industry. Later on, the decision to rearm brought the mechanical engineering industry into even closer association with the non-consumer goods industry.

- A vocational training system of the formal, off-the-job type, coupled with the existence of an occupational labour market, provides Germany with the right preconditions for a production structure based on small firms and a craft sector [Sorge, 1983]. The transmission of vocational skills while work is actually going on, which is a typical characteristic of training within the firm, is in many respects dysfunctional for small firms: it is (a) too protracted and (b) the gradual acquisition of skills requires the division of labour to be much more highly developed than is the case in many small firms. An off-the-job vocational training system provides training with a standardised content, which is not firm-specific and which produces relatively rapidly skills which can be fully implemented. Since a large proportion of industrial training takes place in the craft sector - it used to be the case that all training of industrial recruits was carried out in the craft sector - craft firms have never had much problem in gaining access to skilled workers, despite the migration of skilled labour from the craft to the industrial sector.

- Although the process of industrialisation ousted craft firms from some of their traditional spheres of activity, it also opened up new areas of activity, such as the repair, installation and sometimes even the sale of the goods produced by manufacturers. Completely new craft industries emerged, which today account for a considerable proportion of the sector as a whole; e.g. vehicle repair and the electrical trade.

Thus, the craft sector has experienced not so much a process of displacement as one of restructuring [Aubin and Zorn, 1976; Abel, 1978].

2. The more recent development of the small firm sector

It has been shown above that a small firm sector of considerable size and economic vitality has been maintained in the Federal Republic of Germany. This section examines the development of this small firm sector in the fundamentally different economic conditions of the 1970s. Has there been an increase in the relative share of employment in small firms, as there has been in the United States of America [Birch, 1979]? If this is not the case, why has there not been comparable growth in employment in the small firm sector in the Federal Republic of Germany? Is it simply a question of a time-lag, or are there factors - e.g. in the specific institutional conditions - which lead small firms to develop in a different direction?

A. The evolution of the share of employment: the official statistics

The official statistics available in the Federal Republic of Germany provide only very limited data on the development of the size structure of enterprises and establishments. The last comprehensive investigation of enterprises and establishments was the workplace census of 1970, which is obviously very much out of date. Since 1970, only isolated statistical investigations, restricted to certain segments of the economy and sometimes overlapping one another, have been carried out.

The most important source of official data on industrial firms is the annual report on manufacturing. However, these data are available only up to 1976. There is no comparability with the data for subsequent years because of changes in the economic systematisation and the inclusion of manufacturing firms in the craft sector with more than 20 employees. For the years since 1976, pure industrial statistics are no longer available.

Table 9 shows the evolution of the enterprise size structure in manufacturing in the 1970s and 1980s. In the 1960s, small and medium-sized enterprises with fewer than 500 employees lost employment share, particularly to large enterprises with more than 1,000 employees. This trend was reversed in the first half of the 1970s, as enterprises with up to 200 employees expanded, while the employment share of all other size groups fell. Even for the enterprises included in the statistics since 1977 (manufacturing enterprises with more than 20 employees and manufacturing enterprises in the craft sector with more than 20 employees), this new trend toward higher employment shares in small enterprises was strongly sustained until 1984. However, the new trend was not without interruptions: between 1977 and 1980, the employment share of the two smallest sizes of enterprises fell temporarily, while that of the two largest size categories increased.

Table 10 shows that the evolution of employment by establishment size ran very largely parallel to that of employment by enterprise size. After considerable losses in the 1960s, employment in small and medium-sized

Table 9: Employment shares by enterprise size: Manufacturing (1), 1963-1984

	\multicolumn{6}{c}{Enterprise size (number of employees)}
	20-49	50-99	100-199	200-499	500-999	1000+
1963	6.1	7.4	9.6	15.2	10.8	50.9
1970	5.4	6.6	9.0	15.0	10.8	53.2
1976	5.6	7.1	9.2	14.9	10.6	52.6
1977	7.4	7.9	9.3	14.4	10.3	50.6
1980	7.1	7.9	9.4	14.4	10.5	50.7
1984	7.5	8.1	9.8	14.3	10.1	50.2

Note: (1) Enterprises with fewer than 20 employees are excluded. Data for the period 1977-1984 are not comparable with the preceding data due to methodological changes and inclusion of craft firms in the latter period.

Source: *Statistisches Bundesamt* (Federal Statistical Office).

Table 10: Employment shares by establishment size: Manufacturing (1), 1963- 1984

	\multicolumn{7}{c}{Establishment size (number of employees)}
	1-19	20-49	50-99	100-199	200-299	300-399	400-499
1963	4.3	7.1	8.6	11.0	7.4	5.3	4.5
1970	3.9	6.5	8.1	10.8	7.2	5.6	4.4
1976	4.4	6.8	8.4	10.9	7.6	5.5	4.7
1977	0.9	8.4	9.4	11.3	7.7	5.7	4.5
1980	0.9	8.0	9.4	11.4	7.7	5.7	4.6
1984	0.9	8.2	9.5	11.7	7.9	5.5	4.8

Note: (1) Establishments with fewer than 20 employees are excluded. Data for the period 1977-1984 are not comparable with the preceding data due to methodological changes and inclusion of craft firms in the latter period.

Source: *Statistisches Bundesamt* (Federal Statistical Office).

establishments with fewer than 200 employees showed a considerable increase in the 1970s. This trend has been sustained in the 1980s for the establishments included in the statistics since 1977 (establishments belonging to enterprises with more than 20 employees). However, employment in very small establishments with up to 50 employees has stagnated or even fallen very slightly (see Table 11).

How has the craft segment of the small firm sector grown in recent years? In the period between the two craft sector censuses of 1968 and 1977, the number of craft enterprises fell by almost 20 per cent (see Table 12). The sharpest reductions were in the number of one-man businesses and very small enterprises with up to four employees. On the other hand, the fall in the number of employees was considerably smaller, so that the employment losses caused by the reduction in the number of enterprises were offset to a certain extent by a trend towards larger enterprises.

Table 13 shows that developments in the individual industrial groupings in the craft sector have varied considerably. Thus, contrary to the general trend, firms in the metal industry and particularly those in the service segment of the craft sector have recorded increases in their share of employment. Food firms in the craft sector also recorded employment losses significantly lower than the general trend. There has been no comprehensive statistical investigation of the service sector in the Federal Republic of Germany. No statement can thus be made about the development of the enterprise and establishment size structure in this sector of the economy, which, for the most part, belongs to the craft sector.

Even if the official statistics for manufacturing industry show employment gains for small and medium-sized enterprises and establishments, it would nevertheless appear premature to talk of a "reversal of the trend" [Klodt, 1980] in the development of the enterprise and establishment size structure. The problem in interpreting the official data is that they are only snapshots which do not reflect the processes of job creation and loss which occur between the survey dates. Thus, the growth of employment in the small firm sector may be attributable to very different processes, e.g. to a build-up of employment in the existing small firms in the observed size categories, but also to the shedding of jobs in the next largest category. Similarly, newly-created firms, which expand into the observed size categories between the survey dates, may be responsible for the growth in employment. An enterprise-based longitudinal study would be required to break down this dynamic process of job creation and loss into its individual components.

B. Job generation investigations

There has never been a comprehensive investigation of the evolution of employment in the Federal Republic of Germany along the lines of the Birch study. However, several attempts have been made, using a considerably narrower empirical base, to test the applicability of the results of Birch's study to the Federal Republic of Germany. Figure 2 provides an

Table 11: Employment changes in very small manufacturing establishments, 1977-1984

Size of Establishment (number of employees)	1977-80 (%)	1980-84 (%)
1	- 0.4	+ 15.6
2 - 4	+ 2.9	+ 5.9
5 - 9	- 0.5	+ 2.2
10 - 19	+ 3.9	+ 0.2
Total	**+ 2.5**	**+ 1.9**

Source: Statistisches Bundesamt (Federal Statistical Office).

Table 12: Changes in the number of enterprises and employment in the craft sector by enterprise size, 1968-1977 (per cent change)

Size of Enterprise (number of employees)	Enterprises	Employment
1	- 41.9	- 41.9
2 - 4	- 21.4	- 19.9
5 - 9	- 9.1	- 9.3
10 - 19	+ 17.8	+ 16.2
20 - 49	- 1.7	- 2.6
50 - 99	- 11.7	- 11.9
100 +	- 6.3	+ 13.1
Total	**- 19.6**	**- 4.4**

Source: Statistisches Bundesamt (Federal Statistical Office).

Table 13: Changes in the number of enterprises and employment in the craft sector by industry, 1968-1977 (per cent change)

Industry	Enterprises	Employment
Construction	- 12.4	- 16.0
Metal	+ 0.2	+ 5.1
Wood	- 29.0	- 10.7
Clothing, textile and leather	- 51.6	- 40.0
Food	- 24.0	- 5.4
Health and beauty, dry-cleaning	- 11.6	+ 37.5
Glass, paper, ceramics and others	- 15.8	- 12.2

Source: Statistiches Bundesamt (Federal Statistical Office), Craft Sector Censuses.

overview of the most important of these studies. If the results of all the studies conducted hitherto are combined, Birch's findings would seem to be confirmed. All the studies show that in the 1970s employment generation in small and medium-sized firms exceeded that in large ones, and some of the latter shed massive numbers of jobs. The critical firm size above which the number of jobs tended to fall most turned out to be 200 [Fritsch, 1984]. The very smallest firms, those with up to 10 or 50 employees, emerged as a particularly successful group [Fritsch, 1984; Dahrenmöller, 1985 and Hull, 1985]. There are also indications that it was in young [Hull, 1985], expanding [Irsch, 1985] firms that employment tended to grow most rapidly.

Despite the uniformity of the empirical findings, the thesis that employment in small firms in the Federal Republic has grown disproportionally and that there has been an associated change in the size structure of firms has not gone unchallenged [Irsch, 1985; Eckart et al., 1985; Bade, 1985]. The criticisms are aimed at methodological weaknesses in the available studies: the samples used are not sufficiently representative or accurate since they are all restricted to regional or sectoral samples. Moreover, one important component of the process of job creation and restructuring is not taken into account: since all the studies are ex-post analyses, the samples only include those firms which survived until the time at which the study was conducted. Failures due to liquidation or closure are not included. However, since these fates very often befall small firms, this omission may well give rise to a considerable distortion effect in favour of small firms.

Further criticisms have been directed against the conclusion, made on the basis of the empirical findings, that employment in small firms has grown and that small firms experienced particular economic success in the 1970s [Irsch, 1985; Bade, 1985]. According to these critics, growth in employment is not in itself a sufficient indicator of the economic success and growth of a firm. In their view, account should also be taken of more performance-oriented indicators, such as the evolution of value added, turnover and profitability. However, during the period in question, the evolution of these indicators for small firms in the Federal Republic of Germany was, without exception, negative. Thus, between 1977 and 1982, large manufacturing firms increased their share of both sales and investment and also recorded above-average increases in turnover [Bade, 1985; Irsch, 1985]. Even the statistics on turnover tax for the period between 1970 and 1982 show no shift in the share of turnover towards small and medium-sized firms [Bade, 1985]. A study conducted by the *Kreditanstalt für Wiederaufbau* (Reconstruction Credit Bank) shows that, between 1981 and 1985, changes in the profitability of small firms were also significantly less favourable than those of large firms [Irsch, 1985].

The second fundamental criticism is directed against the assumption that the small and medium-sized firms in the samples are economically independent; as a result, the influence of large firms on the evolution of employment observed in the small firm sector may well have been underestimated [Bade, 1985; Irsch, 1985]. It is true that most of the studies are based on firms that are independent legal entities, but, argue the critics,

Figure 2: Job generation surveys in the Federal Republic of Germany (as of 1986)

Title	Wolfgang Steinle: "Der Beitrag kleiner und mittlerer Unternehmen zur Beschäftigungsentwicklung", in: *Mitteilungen aus der Arbeitsmarkt- und Berufsforschung* Nuremberg, Vol. 2, 1984, p. 257.	C.J. Hull: "Job generation among independent West German manufacturing firms 1974-1980, Evidence from four regions", in: *Environment and planning: Government and policy*, Vol. 3, 1985, p. 215.	Michael Fritsch: "Die Arbeitsplatzentwicklung in kleinen und mittleren Betrieben bzw. Unternehmen", in *Information zur Raumentwicklung*, Vol. 9, 1984, p. 921.
Result	Jobs have been lost in manufacturing firms of all sizes; only in firms with 20-49 employees was employment jobs static. In the service sector, the highest rate of growth in employment is in firms with 20-49 and 500-999 employees.	Small firms, particularly young firms, were more successful in job creation. In firms with 10-19 and 20-49 employees, the number of jobs rose by 34 per cent and by 21 per cent, respectively. In firms with 50-59 employees, employment was static, while it fell in larger firms.	The share of expanding companies was greatest in firms with 1-9 employees, and it fell as firms rose in size. The "critical" size was around 200. Much of the size-specific employment effect can be attributed to large-scale job-shedding by large companies.
Period	1973-1980	1974-1980	a) 1974-1983 b) 1970-1980
Remarks	Data include closures, but there is considerable doubt about the validity of the data, since the sources used are not usually updated; sample not representative: small firms with fewer than 100 employees are under-represented; distortion effects caused by rounding up figures to nearest 100.	Includes only surviving firms; very limited representation of full population of firms.	Includes only surviving firms; limited representation of full population of firms; includes only applicants to the Credit Bank for Reconstruction; selectivity unknown; (b) mechanical engineering only; cohort analysis with regional differentiation.

Federal Republic of Germany

Title	Norbert Irsch: "Kleine und mittlere Unternehmen im Strukturwandel", in Kreditanstalt für Wiederaufbau, Analysen - Meinungen - Perspektiven, Frankfurt, no date.	Axel Dahrenmöller: *Der Beitrag mittelständischer Unternehmen zur Beschäftigung und zum Wachstum unter Berücksichtigung der Unternehmensfluktuation*, Interim report, IFM, Bonn, 1985.	Kurt Bock: *Unterschiede im Beschäftigungsverhalten zwischen kleinen und grossen Unternehmen*, IFM, Bonn, 1985.
Result	Only in expanding firms was the rise in employment in small and medium-sized firms greater than in large ones. In recession, employment falls equally in large and small firms. Small, expanding firms create more jobs than large expanding ones, even with the same evolution of turnover and labour productivity.	The number of jobs lost rises continuously with size of firm. Only small manufacturing firms with fewer than 10 employees showed a net gain.	The smaller the firm, the greater the rise in employment. Expanding small firms (100-199) had considerably higher employment growth rates than expanding large firms. In the case of contracting firms, size made little difference.
Period	1978-1984	1978-1984	1978-1982
Remarks	For discussion of sample see Fritsch [1984]; adjustment for possible indivisibility effects; takes into account liquidations by means of mathematical correction factor.	"Component-specific analysis" of employment, i.e. takes account of migration between size categories; includes closures and new firms from the statistical collection zone, although not the causes.	Includes only surviving firms.

a not insignificant proportion of these legally independent firms are "... within the direct sphere of influence of large concerns as a result of economic interdependence and capital involvement" [Bade, 1985, p. 13]. No direct investigations have been conducted on the financial relationships between large and small firms in the Federal Republicof Germany. However, critics argue that, according to empirical studies carried out in the 1970s, larger industrial firms have virtually doubled the number of subsidiaries [Bade, 1985], and since the middle of the 1970s there has been increased penetration by large firms into small-business markets through takeovers or the acquisition of financial interests [Irsch, 1985]. Reference is also made to the results of an investigation carried out by the Monopolies Commission, which in their principal report for 1982 came to the conclusion that between 1975 and 1982 the process of concentration in the Federal Republic of Germany had not slowed down and that there had been no observable movement towards deconcentration [Bade, 1985; Irsch, 1985].

The most recent study of the growth of employment in small firms is an investigation carried out by the *Institut für Arbeitsmarkt- und Berufsforschung* (Institute for Labour Market and Vocational Research) at the Federal Labour Institute [Cramer, 1987]. It is based on the employment statistics collected on a regular basis by the Institute. The use of these hitherto unevaluated statistics makes available for the first time representative, firm-based longitudinal data.

This study confirms for the period 1977 to 1985 the trend that emerged from the other studies cited above; namely, an increase in employment in small firms, particularly in the smallest firms with up to 20 employees. In the period in question, the number of employees in these firms increased by 13 per cent (580,000), while large firms with 500+ employees recorded job losses totalling 4.2 per cent (225,000). This trend is, of course, attributable basically to the structural change from the secondary to the tertiary sector. Within several manufacturing sectors, however, a trend towards smaller firms does emerge: this is the case in plastics processing, foundries and metalworking, steel and light steel construction, mechanical and electrical engineering, precision engineering, woodworking, printing and food and luxury goods. However, these increases in employment in small firms were not enough to offset the job losses that occurred during the same period in large firms.

C. Attempts at explanation

The development of theoretical explanations for the observed trend in the evolution of employment in the Federal Republic of Germany is still in its early stages [Eckart et al., 1985]. The only real debate that has emerged so far has centred on the cause of the suspected rise in employment in small firms. The following reasons are put forward for the increase in employment in small firms:

- the change in economic conditions in the 1970s (change in the structure of demand towards individual, more highly-differentiated products; increased competition from imports for standardised mass-produced goods; technologically determined decreases in the importance of economies of scale) has favoured small firms, because it corresponds to their specific advantages such as flexibility, creativity and closeness to markets and customers [Klodt, 1980; Schatz, 1984];

- the particular flexibility and adaptability of smaller firms, which have exploited fully the opportunities offered by this structural change [Klodt, 1980; Schatz, 1984];

- a sectoral, or compositional effect: as incomes have risen, domestic demand has shifted towards services, which has, of course, favoured firms in the tertiary sector, which tend to be smaller firms [Klodt, 1980; Schatz, 1984]. The influence of the change in sectoral composition on the recent evolution of the firm size structure is confirmed in the study carried out by the Institute for Labour Market and Vocational Research [Cramer, 1987];

- an increased trend towards self-employment, associated with consistently high levels of unemployment [Schatz, 1984]; after falling continuously for many years, the number of self-employed people began to rise again in the 1970s. The year 1976 can be identified as the turning point. "In other words, in precisely those years in which poor economic growth and high unemployment became the central problems, the downward trend in the number of self-employed was interrupted and a new upward trend began to emerge" [Schatz, 1984, p.10]. There had already been a similar, short-lived increase in the number of self-employed in the recession of 1966-67. If this argument is followed through, the growth in employment in the small firm sector is a temporary phenomenon. No empirical studies of the connection between the situation in the labour market and self-employment have been carried out in the Federal Republic of Germany. However, a study conducted by the *Institut für Wirtschaftsforschung* (IFO) of new firms founded in 1981 and 1983 concluded that the number of people founding firms who had been unemployed before setting up on their own, or who had described their last job as insecure, was considerably higher in 1983 than in 1981. An above-average share of the newly-founded firms in the craft sector were set up by unemployed people [Weitzel, 1986];

- employment in large firms has been particularly affected by the structural change. According to this hypothesis, a number of indicators show that "the reversal of the trend in the evolution of the firm size structure probably reflects not so much the great flexibility of small and medium-sized firms but rather the special problems experienced by large industrial companies in achieving growth under changed domestic and international conditions" [Ewers et al., 1984, p.14]. According to this argument, the reaction of large firms to an adverse change in economic conditions has been to shed jobs, especially since labour-saving rationalisations are more easily achieved in mass-production industries. The apparent expansion of employment in the small firm sector is, therefore, simply relative growth. In support of their thesis that small and medium-sized firms are not especially flexible in their response to structural change, these commentators cite the results of studies which seem to show that, in terms of innovation in the area of microprocessor technology (i.e. the technology which, according to the long wave theory, ought to be the basis of the next upturn), small and medium-sized firms have not been particularly successful [Ewers, 1986]. In sum, the expansion of employment in small firms is a reflection less of a particular strength of small firms than of a particular weakness of large ones. However, as is shown by the indicators of economic performance, which are running in the opposite direction to the evolution of employment, this could, in the long term, also be interpreted as an economic strength.

The first two explanations, in particular, have become part of the public debate on the development of small firms in the Federal Republic of Germany.

III. The qualitative evolution of the small firm sector

As the quantitative analysis showed, the small firm sector in the Federal Republic of Germany has begun to grow. This section attempts to identify a few of the qualitative trends in this process of evolution which might lead to considerable changes and shifts in the near future. On the one hand, these trends are leading to an expansion of employment in small firms, but, on the other hand, they constitute a threat to that employment and are bound to have an effect on the quality of jobs in such firms.

1. Changes in traditional small firm sectors

A. The power of large firms in determining demand levels

A massive threat to firms and jobs is currently emerging in a few sectors of the economy whose structure has traditionally been based on small firms, and in which a large number of small and medium-sized firms find themselves confronting a few highly-concentrated customers in their product markets. Overcapacity in the producer firms, combined with stagnant demand, have led to an extremely sharp rise in the power of these large customer groups to determine the level of demand. As a consequence, firms in the affected sectors are fighting each other to avoid being squeezed out of the market, which has, in turn, led to closures and a process of concentration [Mendius et al., 1987].

A situation of this kind can currently be found in the food industry, particularly in the industrial bakery and meat products sectors. These are two of the sectors in which a significant industrial segment developed, relatively late, in the 1950s and 1960s. This industrial segment is still dominated by small firms, many of which were formerly craft firms. The retail sector, in contrast, is very highly concentrated and its power in the market is increased still further by the emergence of so-called purchasing cooperatives. Faced with idle capacity and often dependent on only one large customer, the producers are forced to accept the terms of trade offered by their customers. One result of this has been a massive deterioration in working conditions reflected, for example, in the payment of wages below the collectively agreed rates. Commentators are also predicting that firms will continue to shut down [Mendius et al., 1987].

Even the craft segment of the food industry is being affected by this development. Craft firms in the bakery and butchery trade, even those that market their own products, are facing increasing competition from large suppliers such as discount stores and cut-price supermarkets. Because of their combined purchasing and the other cost advantages available to large-scale retail firms, these stores are in a position to sell their products much more cheaply than the craft firms.

B. *The split-up of companies*

Another practice which is leading to a shift in the firm size structure in traditional small firm sectors is the so-called "split-up" of companies which, according to the calculations of experts, is a phenomenon which has spread in recent years "like an epidemic" through the small and medium-sized firm sectors of the economy [Merson, 1982]. The splitting-up of companies must be understood in the context of the German system of tax and company law.

Put very simply, the operating principle behind company split-ups is that companies are divided into a holding company and a production or operating company constituted in legal terms as a limited liability company. The holding company retains ownership of all land and production plant, while the operating company has virtually no property apart from the minimal capital of 50,000 Deutschmarks legally required in order to set up a limited liability company. The operating company rents buildings and plant from the holding company. However, it is the operating company that employs the personnel. Even the owner/entrepreneur and his partners are employed as directors by the operating company. Significant tax savings can be made if the owner of a company who is employed by the company as its managing director can have his salary and the company pension provisions declared as tax-deductible operating expenses. The limited liability arises out of the fact that the two companies, which in legal terms are independent limited liability companies, are liable only for their own debts and only with their own capital. Thus, if the operating company, which usually has virtually no assets, closes down, becomes insolvent or makes large numbers of employees redundant, there can be no claim on the operating capital of the holding company. In particular, this arrangement precludes the drafting of a costly social plan for those employees affected by the closure, since there is no capital available. In accordance with the same principle, the production unit itself can be further divided; legally independent companies under the central management of a holding company can be formed from individual departments, divisions or technical production units. It is possible by this means to split up a strong works council into several smaller, weaker works councils with fewer rights (e.g. release from work). And if the individual companies thus formed have fewer than 20 employees, it would even be possible to avoid the formation of a works council altogether.

In the textile and clothing industries, which are traditionally small firm sectors, the practice of splitting up companies is very far advanced and represents an attempt by companies to cope with the increased uncertainties in product markets [Krüer-Buchholz, 1983]. The same process is taking place in the woodworking sector.

This practice of splitting up companies conceals the process of concentration and centralisation that is taking place in the sectors in question. A type of small firm is emerging which, although independent in strictly legal terms and thus classified as such in the statistics, is in fact economically "incomplete", a sort of "rump firm" which offers below average job security for its employees.

C. The change in competitive strategies

For some small firms, there has recently been a shift in competitive strategy which could have serious effects on the quality and, in the long term, the quantity of jobs in those firms. There are increasing signs that small firms are attempting to maintain their positions in tight markets by competing with each other in lowering labour costs. This is also becoming apparent in the trend that is emerging in various small firm sectors towards the abandonment of both wage payments higher than the agreed rates, and company social welfare payments [Mendius et al., 1987]. These rates are not guaranteed by contract in many small firms. It is also significant that there has been an increase of smaller firms resigning from employers' associations in order to avoid being bound by wage agreements.

There are further aspects to the serious deterioration in working conditions in these small firms; for example, the attempts by some craft firms to obtain a competitive advantage by adjusting their opening hours to accommodate customers' wishes [Mendius et al., 1987]. With the introduction of stand-by duties at weekends, the reintroduction or expansion of Saturday working and the introduction of shift work, firms are attempting to turn the clock back on standards of working hours that were, at least in part, already established practice and enshrined in agreements. This erosion of personal standards of living is made easier by the absence of any representation of employees' interests in most small firms and by high unemployment and the consequent increased willingness of workers to accept a deterioration in their working conditions.

The pattern of development that is emerging in some small firms could well cause problems in the long term. The resilience of the small firm sector in the Federal Republic is based largely on the ability of many small firms to introduce high quality, individualised products or services and to adapt quickly to changes in product markets. It was in part the uniform basic conditions created by generally binding wage agreements and industrial safety regulations that had, in the past, encouraged small firms to seek their market opportunities less in lower prices than in higher quality. The precondition for this route was the availability of skilled labour. A serious decline in working conditions relative to large firms could, in the future, make it considerably more difficult for small firms - particularly in a changing labour market - to recruit and retain qualified, innovative and adaptable personnel. This would seriously threaten one of the fundamental elements of their success to date, and very probably lead to a further deterioration in their competitive situation through the loss of innovativeness and adaptability. The small firms most affected by these negative feedback effects would be those offering technologically advanced and innovative products in specialised markets, for which constant technical innovation is a precondition of their competitiveness.

D.   Penetration of new manufacturing technologies

In some small firm sectors, such as woodworking, new technologies based on microelectronics are currently being introduced on an increasingly wide scale. Computer numerically controlled (CNC) turning machines are able to make both small and medium-sized runs profitable, while simultaneously considerably reducing set-up times. It is true that these technologies offer small firms new opportunities for rationalisation - not only by shedding jobs but also by reducing the number of rejects and raising the quality and accuracy of machining - but they also make it possible for large firms to offer a highly differentiated and very flexible programme. As a result, large firms may make further inroads into those niches of the market that have hitherto been the preserve of smaller firms.

Information is not yet available as to whether and in what way a squeezing out process of this kind is taking place in the Federal Republic of Germany. However, the diffusion of advanced automatic control technologies is still very much in its infancy in many small firm sectors. The studies available on the diffusion of numerically controlled and CNC technologies in firms of different sizes show that small firms tend to lag behind. A study of the mechanical engineering industry shows that it was mainly the large establishments and firms that invested early and heavily in flexible automation and control technologies [Ewers and Kleine, 1983; Kleine, 1983].

In addition to the rapid adaptation to technological innovations, the ability of small firms to make innovative changes to their own products and manufacturing processes is of special importance for their competitiveness. For a long time, the innovative ability of small firms was underestimated [Gielow, 1986], but there has recently been a "rediscovery" of the innovative potential of small and medium-sized firms. Research into innovation in the Federal Republic of Germany has, in the meantime, made available an extensive range of empirical material on the ability of its small firms to implement technological innovation.

According to these data, the proportion of small and medium-sized manufacturing firms (those with fewer than 500 employees) which could be classified as innovatory, i.e. which carry out some form of research and development, is about one-third [Gielow, 1986]. Moreover, there are wide regional variations in the innovative potential of firms [Meyer-Krahmer et al., 1984a]. The results of the expert evaluation of the personnel costs subsidy programme for research and development (R & D) staff show that the proportion of fairly small firms (fewer than 50 employees) in the Federal Republic of Germany which carry out their own R & D is very small [Meyer-Krahmer et al., 1984b]. However, those small firms that do undertake R & D activities often belong to the elite of innovative firms, and their expenditure on R & D is relatively high. Continuous product development, i.e. innovation, is a central element of their market strategy. These firms often produce technologically advanced specialist products for a particular market niche [Meyer-Krahmer et al., 1984a].

However, even the innovative activity of the majority of "normal" innovative small firms has specific characteristics. Their innovatory activity is directed more towards product innovation than towards innovations in the manufacturing process. The R & D activities of small firms usually follow closely the current product programme and consist for the most part of further development of existing products - often in reaction to or anticipation of specific customer requests. The innovative activity of the normal small firm is thus more akin to development than to research [Meyer-Krahmer et al., 1984a]. Moreover, R & D activities in small firms are much less planned and formalised. They are often carried out within the design department, and in many firms there are no employees engaged solely in R & D. Instead, staff is made available for R & D work on a case-by-case basis. For normal innovatory small firms, technological innovation is of lesser importance in firms' competitive and market strategies than qualities such as meeting deadlines, short delivery times and flexibility in adapting to special requests from customers [Meyer-Krahmer et al., 1984b].

Thus, there is no evidence that small and medium-sized firms are more innovative, but rather that their innovatory activity is different from that of larger firms. On the other hand, research on innovation has confirmed the thesis that innovatory small and medium-sized firms experience above-average growth in employment. Thus, in innovative small and medium-sized firms, employment growth has been significantly more favourable than the average for the sector in question [Meyer-Krahmer et al., 1984a]. However, since it has already been shown that only a small proportion of small firms have any potential for innovation, a firm's innovatory capacity can be only one of several factors that might explain the growth in employment in the small firm sector.

2. Changes in the relationships between large and small firms

A. *Contracting-out*

One of the fundamental characteristics of many small firms in the Federal Republic of Germany is that, in one form or another, they have a collaborative relationship with one or more large firms; they may act as a supplier or be responsible for functions such as the sale, repair or maintenance of the products of one or more large firms. It has recently become apparent that the division of labour between large and small firms is in a state of flux. It would appear that large firms, in the face of changed economic conditions, have begun to restructure their relationships with small firms. Thus, large firms looking for opportunities to cut costs are increasingly contracting-out services or manufacturing functions previously performed internally. This strategy may be implemented both by placing orders with small firms and by splitting-off the relevant sections in the form of new companies.

A representative study of the new companies set up in 1981 and 1983 shows that most of the new manufacturing companies were set up in order to take over production functions which had been contracted-out from existing firms [Weitzel, 1986]. The new firms included repair and assembly companies, printers, and photocopying and duplication firms. At the same time, this was the group of new firms which even in their early stages had relatively high numbers of employees. The study does not show whether the founders of the new companies were former employees of the large companies that were purchasers of the subcontracted products, or whether the new companies received any form of assistance from the existing firms.

As far as the Federal Republic of Germany is concerned, it would appear to be mainly service functions, such as repair and maintenance or cleaning, that are contracted-out. In several areas, however, the contracting-out of various stages of the manufacturing process can also be observed. In the motor vehicle industry, for example, where the number of suppliers is estimated to total around 10,000 [Hess and Holz, 1987], the manufacturers are clearly making a concerted effort to reduce their own production commitment [*Beschaffung-aktuell*, 12/83]. In the face of the increasing technological and qualitative demands made on their products, the acceleration in the rate of innovation and increased price competition in international product markets, the vehicle manufacturers are adopting the strategy of concentrating on their principal activities, and thus their strengths, and using the know-how and experience of specialist suppliers in other product areas. As a result of this strategy, there has emerged a trend towards the supply and fitting of complete components rather than individual parts and thus towards the contracting-out of assembly stages to suppliers. In addition to exploiting the greater know-how of specialist suppliers, the increased use of subcontracting is also intended to reduce costs (e.g. through a gradual decrease in suppliers' unit costs and the opportunity to exert pressure on suppliers to lower their prices) and to take advantage of the greater flexibility of suppliers relative to in-house production. It can generally be assumed that the subcontracting market will tend to grow in the future.

One precondition for the increase in subcontracting by large manufacturers is the availability of an adequate pool of efficient, flexible and innovative small and medium-sized subcontractors. In the Federal Republic of Germany, this precondition is satisfied. Because of the increased pressure of competition in their own product markets, at the moment craft firms are also making increasing inroads into the subcontracting market. This trend is being actively supported by the central craft associations, which are assisting in the organisation of stands at trade fairs and attaching so-called subcontracting consultants to the regional craft associations.

Not only the quantity but also the quality of subcontracting networks and relationships is currently going through a process of change which will have potentially enormous consequences for the small firms involved. The reduction in the production commitment of large firms makes new demands on subcontractors, and makes them more dependent than ever on their customers. Even in these new areas the motor vehicle industry is taking a lead. The vehicle manufacturers are now tending to reduce their stock levels. Instead of ordering large quantities at long intervals, they are now ordering small quantities from subcontractors with shorter intervals between orders. These new logistical plans end in the "just-in-time" delivery of components directly into the manufactuer's production process. At the same time, responsibility for controlling the quality of subcontracted products is delegated to the subcontractor at his cost and in accordance with standards laid down by the customer. Modern logistics, with their demands for short and variable delivery times, together with the increased range of products being subcontracted and ever shorter re-tooling times for new products, make it necessary to expedite and rationalise communication between subcontractor and client. The vehicle manufacturers are thus making every effort to use modern communications technologies in order to establish data-processing links with their subcontractors. These computer link-ups may in some cases go so far as to involve the subcontractors' manufacturing and development processes. According to a recent study, BMW had data exchange or transfer links with 35 of its subcontractors; the figures for Daimler-Benz and Volkswagen were 160 and 200, respectively. It is the manufacturers' intention to triple these figures by 1990 [*Beschaffung-aktuell*, 6/86]. In the long term, no subcontractor will be able to avoid installing such communications systems.

According to the manufacturers, a sort of "industrial combine" will develop in the future between subcontractors and clients, in which the subcontractor will become a close "associate" [*Beschaffung-aktuell*, 1/85] from whom increased collaboration in the development phase will be expected, with a corresponding transfer of a proportion of the risk associated with innovation. The use of long-term contracts is intended to ease the considerable investment burden associated with the new demands on subcontractors [*Beschaffung-aktuell*, 12/86].

However, it is questionable whether all subcontractors - particularly the small firms - could raise the finances necessary to implement the changes made necessary by the new demands. Their earnings position is worsened by the new order systems, since they require smaller, less economic batch sizes, or alternatively, increased stock levels. And it is precisely small subcontractors who have fewer opportunities to pass on these increased costs in their own prices. As a consequence, small subcontracting firms could be squeezed from the market, or forced down on to the third or fourth rung of the supply chain. The vehicle manufacturers themselves start from the assumption that there will be a "drastic reduction in the number of subcontractors" [*Handelsblatt*, 53/86].

However, even for the subcontractors who survive, the integration strategies implemented by the large firms may have serious consequences. As a result of the data-processing links, the client may gain an insight into the know-how and indeed the whole production process of the subcontracting firm. This would obviously threaten the autonomy of the subcontracting firms and weaken their market position.

B. Decentralisation

Currently, decentralisation or fragmentation strategies - i.e. the splitting off of divisions or departments of a company in order to make them into independent firms - are not playing a very significant role in large firms in the Federal Republic of Germany. At least, there is little empirical evidence of any such trend towards decentralisation.

The studies carried out in the Federal Republic of Germany of the evolution of employment in various sizes of firm distinguish neither between single and multi-establishment enterprises, nor between branches (see section II). It is thus impossible to establish to what extent the increase in employment in small firms is attributable to decentralisation strategies on the part of large firms; i.e. to the establishment or expansion of subsidiaries [Eckart et al., 1985]. One study of changes in the fragmentation of companies in the Federal Republic in the period 1970-1977 concluded that the degree of fragmentation remained relatively constant throughout the period [Schwalback, 1983].

At the moment, even fragmentation strategies such as buy-outs and spin-offs are of minimal significance in large firms in the Federal Republic of Germany. A survey of German companies, banks and management consultancies conducted recently by the *Frankfurter Allgemeine* newspaper concluded that only very few salaried managers founded their own firms, and that only very few companies have any sympathy for such strategies or encourage their managers to embark on such ventures [*Frankfurter Allgemeine*, 24.9.1986]. Most companies have not even begun to tackle the issue. One of the few German companies that has already begun to implement spin-offs, and continues actively to encourage them, is Siemens AG. Among the few examples of buy-outs in large German companies is the buy-out plan implemented by Loewe Opta GmbH (entertainment electronics).

The reasons for the scarcity of buy-outs and spin-offs lie, in the opinion of experts, in the non-transferability of the plans implemented in the United States of America and the United Kingdom to the institutional conditions that exist in the Federal Republic of Germany (differently structured financial markets, and legal obstacles), in the lack of experience in implementing such plans and, last but not least, in differences of mentality between German and American and British managers.

The explanation for the scarcity of the various forms of external decentralisation in large firms in the Federal Republic of Germany might also lie in the motives behind firms' decisions to implement such fragmentation strategies. There is very little incentive to subcontract production and to move into low-wage areas, since the central wage agreement structures mean that there are only slight differences in wage levels between different companies and regions. An empirical survey carried out by Bade shows that most of the transfers and foundations of new companies occurred in the boom years of the 1960s and early 1970s, and that the main motive for this kind of decentralisation was not wage differences but rather the supply of labour. In view of the extreme shortage of labour in the urban conglomerations, companies were seeking in this way to tap new pools of labour, particularly in rural areas [Bade, 1981].

Even the opportunity to place an obstacle in the way of worker representation is of little importance in those cases where large sections of firms are to be split off. A works council can be elected as soon as a firm has 20 or more employees (see section I). Of course, other employee participation rights can be circumvented by the decentralisation of a large firm; for example, the establishment of an economic committee (in companies with more than 100 employees) or the participation of worker representatives on the supervisory board of limited companies with more than 500 employees. The introduction of codetermination in 1976 for the supervisory boards of companies and concerns with more than 2,000 employees was cause for several large firms to circumvent the provisions of the law on codetermination by implementing a policy of fragmentation and/or changing the legal form of the company.

Tax considerations also influence the propensity of large firms to decentralise. Thus, the reform of the law on turnover tax in 1968 made vertical decentralisation more attractive for firms. Until that date, cumulative turnover tax, which taxed all preliminary work purchased from outside several times, had been an incentive to keep all stages of the production process within the company. The VAT system, which has been in force in the Federal Republic since 1968, has largely put customer and inter-company sales on the same tax footing, so that there is no longer any tax advantage to be gained from contracting out stages of the production process.

What is true of external forms of decentralisation is also true of internal decentralisation. Thus, in the view of a leading management consultant, a relatively centralist style of management still prevails in large German firms.

C. Subcontracting of innovation

There is, however, a new form of relationship between large and small companies which is currently being built up in a completely different way. In recent years, large firms have become increasingly committed to encouraging young, innovative firms active in the area of new technologies, a trend which amounts to the subcontracting of innovation. Large firms are acquiring an increasing stake in independent venture capital companies which both make available start-up capital for young expanding firms and provide professional support in the areas of marketing and management.

However, the venture capital market in the Federal Republic of Germany is still in its infancy. It was only in 1983, with the discovery of the so-called technological gap between the Federal Republic of Germany and the United States of America and Japan and repeated complaints about the level of risk capital available through the established financing system, that a venture capital infrastructure began to emerge, although with some difficulty. There are now about 25 active venture capital companies, which have invested about 250 million Deutschmarks in 140 projects [*Fraunhofer Institut für Systemtechnik und Innovationsforschung*, 1986]. German companies were relatively late in committing themselves to the venture capital market. In the meantime, however, several venture capital funds have been set up in which large companies have invested considerably.

In addition to holding interests in venture capital funds, however, large companies have also taken a direct interest in innovative young companies. The pharmaceuticals company Boehringer Mannheim GmbH, for example, has acquired shares in several companies in the Heidelberg Technology Park, which specialise in biotechnology and medical technology [*Handelsblatt*, 13.3.1985].

The motives of large companies in externalising innovation in this way lie, on the one hand, in the use of the specific creative and motivational potential of smaller firms and of young, committed founders of companies for the processes of innovation. On the other hand, they lie in the pursuit of new technological developments and the securing of potential access to innovations of interest to the company. Shifting the burden of the risks inherent in the process of innovation may also play a role, depending on the stake held by the lender of capital.

Since it is such a recent development, the direction that this commitment on the part of large firms will take cannot yet be predicted. To what extent, and in what way, will successful small firms be taken over by the large firms that fostered them? Will they be incorporated into the organisational structure of the large company, or will looser forms of association be chosen (securing of distribution rights, licence rights, participation)? At what stage will such a takeover occur (perhaps at the particularly costly phase of translating the innovations into marketable products)? Are there already examples of innovations from small firms fostered by larger ones leading to the development of new product lines in the larger company? To what extent is a new sector of innovative, technology-oriented and autonomous small firms emerging, or is this rather a temporary phenomenon created by the strategic consideration of large firms?

3. The development of new small firms

A. *New foundings*

Recent years have seen the foundation of an increasing number of new firms in the Federal Republic of Germany. What contribution these newly-founded firms have made to the increase in employment in the small firm sector depends not least on the extent to which they are offset by the simultaneous sharp increase in the number of functions carried out by such firms.

There are no nation-wide statistics on the founding of new firms in the Federal Republic of Germany. Estimations of the evolution of the number of new firms established are based for the most part on two sources: the trade register compiled by the district courts in which, however, only qualified businessmen are obliged to register; and the trading registrations compiled by local authorities which record each foundation and closure, but which are compiled and evaluated statistically in only four of the federal states. Both sources contain specific distortion effects. The entries in the trade register, which are regularly evaluated by the Association of Credit Companies, tend to underestimate the number of new firms, since by no means all firms are run by qualified businessmen. It has been estimated that only 20 per cent of all new firms are entered in the trade register [Weitzel, 1986]. On the other hand, the trading registrations, on which the studies conducted by the *Institut für Mittelstandsforschung* and the University of Cologne [Szyperski and Kirschbaum, 1981; Clemens et al., 1986] are based, tend to overestimate the number of new firms, since they include not only newly-founded firms but also changes in the legal form of a company and takeovers of existing firms. The data also include the growing number of newly-founded subsidiaries [Weitzel, 1986]. The influence of these factors can only be estimated.

Nor is there a comprehensive statistical database for the number of firms that disappear each year. It is true that bankruptcies are included in the official statistics of the Federal Republic of Germany, but only about 4 per cent of firms are closed each year because of bankruptcy [Hunsdiek, 1985]. Closures due, for example, to the death of the owner, the transfer of ownership or liquidation are contained partly in the trading registrations and partly in the cancellation entries of the trade register.

The most comprehensive attempt to date to measure the extent of fluctuations in the number of firms in the Federal Republic of Germany was conducted by the *Institut für Mittelstandsforschung* in collaboration with the University of Cologne [Szyperski and Kirschbaum, 1981 and Clemens et al., 1986]. These studies project the commercial registrations in the state of North Rhine-Westphalia to the country as a whole. They conclude that, on average, in the period between 1973 and 1979, 150,000 new firms were founded each year in the Federal Republic of Germany, and 144,000 were closed. From 1974 onwards, there was a continuous increase in the number of new firms set up and from 1976 onwards the balance between new foundings and liquidations became positive, i.e. the number of new firms set up exceeded the number closed [Szyperski and Kirschbaum, 1981]. The follow-up study of the period between 1980 and 1984 shows that a sharp increase in the number of new firms was accompanied by a similar rise in the number of liquidations: almost double the number of new firms (298,000) were established in 1984, while the number of liquidations rose to 254,000. Thus, for 1984 alone, the number of new firms established exceeded the number of liquidations by 45,000 [Clemens et al., 1986].

The figures published by the *Institut für Mittelstandsforschung* are without doubt excessively high as a result of the distortion effects inherent in the database. Bearing this in mind, however, the empirical evidence does, nevertheless, show a sharp rise in the number of new firms established in recent years in the Federal Republic of Germany and that, at least in the 1980s, this figure exceeds the number of closures.

What sort of empirical data exist on the quality of the new firms? A representative study conducted by the IFO Institute and commissioned by the Federal Ministry of Economics shows the distribution by sector of firms established in 1981 and 1983. According to this survey, most of the new firms were in the craft sector; of these, the majority were vehicle repair firms, followed by construction and services. The fourth highest proportion of new firms was in the retail trade, and the fifth highest was in the category of "other services", which includes advertising, software houses, economic consultants, office services and technical services such as engineering consultants [Weitzel, 1986]. Only 5 per cent of the new firms were in the manufacturing sector.

As far as the question of the growth of employment in the small firm sector is concerned, the main interest lies in the job potential created by the newly-founded firms, i.e. in their size structure. Only the IFO and the *Institut für Mittelstandsforschung* studies provide data relevant to the question. According to the IFO survey, the majority of the newly-founded firms (60 to 70 per cent) were one-man firms. Only a small proportion, mainly in the manufacturing and craft sectors, employed two or more people right from the beginning. Significant employment effects did not begin to emerge until the second and third years of trading, when employment in new firms in the craft and wholesale sectors rose by a factor of 2.7 and 2.5 respectively [Weitzel, 1986]. The *Institut für Mittelstandsforschung* starts from the assumption that the average employment effect was 2.9 to 3.4 jobs, including that of the founder; according to this survey, the most significant employment effects were in the new craft and manufacturing firms [Hunsdiek, 1985].

What sort of empirical data exist on the stability of newly-founded small firms? The increase in the number of insolvencies indicates that the mortality rate for newly-founded firms is high. According to the analysis of insolvency carried out by the *Creditreform*, the number of liquidations in 1985 (13,700) was the highest level ever recorded in the Federal Republic of Germany [*Verband der Vereine Creditreform e.V.*, 1985]. More than a third of the insolvencies (37 per cent) involved firms that had been in existence for less than four years, while another third involved firms that had been trading for between five and ten years. Eighty-five per cent of all liquidations involved firms with fewer than 50 employees, and a very high proportion affected very small firms with no more than five employees [*Verband der Vereine Creditreform e.V.*, 1985]. Of the newly-founded small firms, those in the service sector (software houses, firms active in transport and communications, and catering and retail firms) were particularly vulnerable to insolvency. On the other hand, firms in the craft and manufacturing sectors were particularly resistant to crisis [Hunsdiek, 1985].

Analysis of the trade registrations confirms this sectoral mortality rate. According to the observations of *Creditreform*, the high number of closures is due to the high number of new firms established without a sound economic basis; they tended to be under-capitalised and the founders tended to lack the necessary commercial and technical skills [*Verband der Vereine Creditreform e.V.*, 1985].

B. New firms in the high-tech sector

In addition to job creation, much public interest has been focused on the contribution of new firms to the process of modernisation in the economy as a whole. This raises the question of what proportion of the new companies are technologically innovative firms operating in the so-called technological growth sectors. There is very little data available on high technology based new firms (HTBNFs) in the Federal Republic of Germany, either on the share of HTBNFs in small and medium-sized firms as a whole or on the proportion of HTBNFs among new companies. Any estimates have to be based on very fragmentary empirical material.

An evaluation of the new entries in the 1983 trade register by the Fraunhofer Institute for Systems Technology and Research on Innovation produced a maximum figure of 1,030 HTBNFs among the newly-founded firms, which is just 3 per cent of all new entries [Segal Quince et al., forthcoming]. A separate analysis of trade register entries in selected regions of the country in the period 1973-1983 concluded that a total of 1,008 HTBNFs were founded during that decade [Kulike, 1986]. Thus the available data would appear to indicate that the proportion of HTBNFs among recently-founded firms is very low. Experts estimate that they account for no more than 2 per cent of all manufacturing firms established in any one year. However, the available empirical studies show a sharp increase in the number of new HTBNFs set up since the end of the 1970s. Moreover, a North-South divide appears to be opening up: 42 per cent of the new HTBNFs recorded in the 1983 trade register were located in Bavaria and Baden-Württemberg [Segal Quince et al., forthcoming].

There are several empirical clues as to the origin of the founders of HTBNFs. More than 50 per cent of the founders of advanced technology firms had been employed in manufacturing, mainly in the R & D departments of large firms, and to a lesser extent in management. A further large proportion came from the research institutions of universities and other public research institutes [*Fraunhofer Institut für Systemtechnik und Innovationsforschung*, 1986].

No empirical investigations have yet been conducted of the economic performance of new firms in the hi-tech sector in the Federal Republic of Germany, which is a reflection of the recent nature of the development (the founding of most of these firms did not start until the end of the 1970s). The level of employment in the newly-founded hi-tech companies tends to be fairly low, since they are mostly small firms. There is no empirical evidence that employment in this category of firms is growing by more than the average for the Federal Republic of Germany as a whole [Segal Quince et al., forthcoming].

IV. Attitudes and policies towards small firms

1. Government

In considering the way that government policy has reacted to the developments outlined above, the truly astonishing fact is that, despite the absence of any spectacular changes or indeed successes in the small firm sector, there has been a clearly detectable "change of mood" [Bade, 1985] in the Federal Republic of Germany: earlier scepticism about the future opportunities for small firms has given way to an almost euphoric rediscovery of the small firm. This is reflected both in articles in the economic pages of newspapers and in the public statements of politicians.

The rediscovery of small and medium-sized firms has many causes, only very few of which, however, lie in observable developments in this sector of the economy. The first is the persistently high level of unemployment that has prevailed for several years in the Federal Republic. In this context, small firms have been seen as the hope for the future, and are expected to make an important contribution to the creation of new jobs. In this respect, Birch's study has played a role that should not be underestimated, and the rapturous welcome it has received in political circles in the Federal Republic of Germany is itself confirmation of its impact.

A second explanatory factor lies in the debate surrounding the so-called gap that exists in several key technological sectors, particularly with respect to Japan and the United States of America. This debate made a significant contribution to the rediscovery of the innovative potential of small and medium-sized firms. A third, and possibly most important, cause is a shift in the balance of power in the Federal Republic of Germany, which has led in turn to a change in the prevailing economic and political climate. With the election of a new government in 1982, two parties came to power whose programmes and leaders had always given strong support to the economic interests of the small business sector.

One important characteristic of the Federal Republic of Germany which is of crucial importance to an understanding of the political support for small firms is that small business policy has always been a special policy area. Small and medium-sized firms have always played a particular role in political and policy declarations. The small business sector in the Federal Republic of Germany is an organised political lobby whose interests are represented by the small business alliance of the CDU (Christian Democratic Union), and the discussion group on small business policy within the CDU parliamentary group. The constituency to which small business policy is addressed is, of course, very heterogeneous, and embraces manufacturing and the craft sector, commerce and the liberal professions. The content of small business policy is correspondingly diffuse.

Against this background, a number of amendments to laws, individual measures and special programmes aimed explicitly at the small business constituency have been introduced in the Federal Republic. One important area of the policy measures aimed at the small firm sector that have been taken by the Federal Government is that of research and technology policy, which fits with the role that has been ascribed to small firms in the modernisation of the economy. Since about the middle of the 1970s, policy in this area has been increasingly directed at small and medium-sized firms, and most of the policy measures introduced recently have been aimed at these categories of firms. The Federal Republic is one of the few countries to have an overall research and technology plan for small and medium-sized firms, and the federal government has implemented an unusually wide range of measures targetted at precisely these firms [Bräunling et al., 1982].

According to a report published recently by the Federal Ministry for Research and Technology, 25-30 per cent of total federal expenditure on civil R & D is channelled to small and medium-sized firms with fewer than 500 employees. However, small and medium-sized firms contribute only 13-16 per cent of total research expenditures in the economy as a whole; in other words, smaller firms are currently being supported at a level that far exceeds their actual importance to the research process in the economy.

Support measures for newly-founded companies are one of the other main planks of the Federal Government's current policy towards small firms, and these activities have increased considerably in recent years. In 1975, loans from the ERP business set-up programme totalled 142 million Deutschmarks; by 1984, this had risen to 807 million Deutschmarks. Under the capital aid programme set up in 1979, a total of 467 million Deutschmarks had been loaned by 1984. These two programmes currently provide assistance for 17,000 new firms each year [*Trade Gazette*, 29.7.1986]. If it is assumed that in 1984 the number of new firms established exceeded liquidations by about 45,000 (see section III.3), about 37 per cent of the surviving companies founded in any one year would have received financial assistance from the Federal Government. These federal programmes are supplemented by the various programmes introduced by the individual states. Experts have calculated that a person founding a company in the Federal Republic can currently seek assistance from about 100 different support programmes, which is why there has been much public discussion of this "confusing proliferation" and the "urgent need for harmonisation".

Current government policy towards small firms also includes a number of fiscal measures which were adopted after the change of government, with the express aim of easing the burden on small and medium-sized firms [Bangemann in *Bundesverband der Deutschen Industrie* (BDI), 1985]. These measures include the reduction of trade tax in 1982 and the 1984 law on tax relief which reduced property tax and introduced the special depreciation allowance of 10 per cent for small and medium-sized firms.

According to an estimate by the Federation of German Manufacturing Industries (BDI), more than half of the company-related tax relief granted between 1983 and 1985 - almost 3.8 billion Deutschmarks - benefited small and medium-sized firms. Further tax relief measures for small and medium-sized firms are planned. One of the complaints made in the current debate on economic policy in the Federal Republic of Germany is that small and medium-sized companies are under-capitalised, which, it is claimed, limits their scope for investment and thus innovation. The claim that these firms are under-capitalised is very debatable, since studies of the question have produced widely divergent results. Equally controversial are the fiscal measures introduced as a consequence (see, for example, the debate on the tax-free investment allowance in the *Trade Gazette* of 4/5.4.1986 and 20.5.1986).

In accordance with its liberal economic policy plans, the Federal Government is currently pursuing a policy of deregulation with respect to tax and building regulations and, in particular, the provisions of labour and social legislation. It is true that this policy of deregulation affects all companies; however, small firms have been explicitly exempted from several existing regulations on the grounds that the burden on small firms is disproportionately high. An initial step in the direction of deregulation was taken with the Employment Promotion Law of 1985. The new law contains the following special provisions for small firms:

- the period within which newly-founded firms with fewer than 20 employees may conclude fixed-term employment contracts was extended from 18 to 24 months;

- in determining the level of employment up to which small firms are exempt from the law on protection against unfair or summary dismissal, part-time workers working up to 10 hours a week (45 hours a month) are no longer included;

- the obligation to draw up a social plan in the event of operational changes involving job losses is now restricted to cases in which at least 10 to 29 per cent of the workforce are to be dismissed (the minimum level at which the social plan becomes compulsory varies on a sliding scale according to the size of firm). In small firms with between 20 and 60 employees, at least 20 per cent of the workforce, or six employees, must lose their jobs before the firm is obliged to draw up a social plan to assist those made redundant; the previous figure was 5 per cent;

- small firms with up to 30 employees are now able to benefit from the compensation scheme for the costs of continued wage payments in cases of sickness (the previous maximum was 20). In determining the size of firms, part-time workers are now accounted for in proportion to their hours of work. The compensation scheme was changed to include the costs of continuing to pay trainees' wages in case of sickness and of maternity provisions. These considerable savings in the costs incurred by small firms and the relaxing of protective regulations which, it is claimed, are a constraint on employment, are intended to introduce greater flexibility into the labour market and, in particular, to break down barriers to employment.

In addition, demands are being made for sweeping changes to the wage bargaining system, which would also have a considerable effect on small firms. One of the proposed changes is to do away with the provision for making wage agreements generally binding, since, it is argued, this acts as a particular constraint on the growth of small and newly-founded firms [see, for example, Schatz, 1984]. The Federal Government's demands for "greater flexibility in bargaining rights" are a step in the same direction [Bangemann in *Bundesverband der Deutschen Industrie*, 1985]. Further decentralisation of the wage bargaining system is intended to make wages more responsive to the different levels of profitability of companies in different regions, sectors and size categories.

2. Trade unions

From the trade unions' point of view, these developments in the small firm sector require action on two fronts:

- if the growth in employment is indeed going to shift in favour of smaller firms, this will mean an increase in the importance of those areas of employment to which the unions have hitherto had difficulty in gaining access, and in which the workforce - e.g. in the service or hi-tech sectors - tend to have reservations about union membership;

- as a direct result of government policy, a forced process of technological modernisation is currently taking place in small and medium-sized firms, which is likely to have serious effects on the working conditions of employees in those companies. This modernisation drive stands in sharp contrast to the wholly inadequate opportunities for employees and the bodies representing their interests in small firms to have any influence on the development of the new technologies.

Decisive evaluations by the trade unions of these trends in the development of the small firm sector are few and far between. However, the discernible change in mood in favour of small and medium-sized firms in political circles and in the media, together with the massive amount of support being given by the present government, has begun to bring forth reactions from the unions. The notion that small firms are increasing in importance is treated with a great deal of scepticism in the trade union movement. The connection between the increase in the number of new firms and the high level of unemployment is emphasised, as are the weak employment effects and high instability of the newly-founded firms. In the unions' view, the new firms are partly the result of decentralisation and cost-cutting strategies implemented by large firms, which will have serious consequences for the employment situation of workers in those areas of activity. The current level of support being afforded small and medium-sized firms, both in terms of tax advantages and of assistance in conducting research, is rejected as an exercise in redistribution which will have little effect on employment.

In general terms - which is how the unions' views on the "small firms issue" are summarised - an increase in the importance of small and medium-sized firms could be very much in the interests of employees and their trade unions, since the existence of a large number of small and medium-sized firms potentially offers employees greater opportunities for influencing economic life than monopolistic economic structures. However, the precondition for this - and it is here that the unions' main demand in this area lies - is an improvement in the opportunities for codetermination available to employees in small firms.

The trade union movement is currently giving little consideration to fundamentally new forms of organisation and strategies within the small firm sector. The question of trade union organisation in small firms is less a problem of inappropriate organisational forms and strategies than of a lack of personnel. Campaigns carried out by regional offices, e.g. in the craft sector, show that it is indeed possible to organise workers in small firms, but that this requires considerable commitment of both effort and time on the part of senior officials in the regional union offices. In a situation in which the trade unions, in the Federal Republic of Germany as in many other countries, are being forced on to the defensive, such resources are already committed to other tasks.

The following quote from a speech given at the last craft conference held by *IG Metall* (the metalworkers' union) illustrates this position: "We can have no influence on the firm size structure. We must put up with the structures that exist, possibly for decades. ... It is to be feared that the burdens on senior officials in regional offices will increase. This statement is not intended to awaken expectations that in many offices there will in the future be officials solely responsible for the craft sector." [*Industriegewerkschaft Metall* 1985, p.13]. *IG Metall* is concentrating its recruitment drives on those companies where a works council can be elected.

One central, and long-standing, demand made by the unions in the craft sector is that the opportunities for employees in the sector to exercise codetermination at a level higher than that of the firm should be improved by the introduction of joint codetermination in the self-governing bodies of the craft sector, the guilds and trade corporations. In accordance with the craft regulations of 1953, employees have only one-third of the votes in these bodies. Moreover, any contribution to the work of these organisations requires the contributor to have journeyman status; i.e. to have completed a relevant course of craft training.

Nevertheless, there are isolated signs of innovations within the German trade union movement, which might be interpreted as an attempt to react to developments in the small firm sector. One such attempt is the establishment in recent years of so-called Technology Information Centres. The purpose of these centres is to provide information on technical questions to works councils, shop stewards and employees so that technical rationalisation measures and their social consequences can be identified quickly. In this way, it is hoped both to make full use of existing rights to influence technological developments and to put forward possible alternative routes for such developments. The information centres are intended to provide a counterbalance to the government-subsidised advice received by small firms on implementing their modernisation programme. The information provided is aimed particularly at employee representatives in small and medium-sized firms [*Deutscher Gewerkschaftbund*, 1986]. The centres are a means of compensating for the specific deficiencies and disadvantages of employee representatives in small firms by making available external know-how. The first Technology Information Centre was set up by *IG Metall* in 1979 in Hamburg, with assistance from the Federal Ministry for Research and Technology. Further information centres have since been set up throughout the Federal Republic of Germany.

V. Summary

In recent years, small firms in the Federal Republic of Germany have, as in other countries, increased their share in total employment. However, it is still unclear whether this will lead in the long term to a strengthening of the small firm sector: a high proportion of the growth in employment in small firms can be attributed to the structural change in the economy in favour of the tertiary sector. In view of the instability of the new firms and the close association between their founding and the current high levels of unemployment, the recent wave of new companies being founded must be placed in context. Even the trends towards decentralisation emanating from large firms are not as yet particularly marked in the Federal Republic of Germany. On the other hand, the qualitative analysis showed that there are certainly trends within the small firm sector which could in the long term threaten the existence and autonomy of parts of the small firm sector.

The reasons why the expansion of the small firm sector in the Federal Republic of Germany has tended to be somewhat restrained lie, on the one hand, in the specific institutional conditions which do not particularly favour small firms over large ones. On the other hand, further growth may have been limited by the fact that an extensive substructure of efficient small and medium-sized firms, developed over time, already exists in the Federal Republic of Germany.

Government policy towards small firms has also become quite active in recent years. This is reflected in a multiplicity of government measures in support of small and medium-sized firms. These measures are less a reaction to real changes in the small firm sector than a reflection of the country's long-standing small business policy. Nevertheless, they could have very real consequences for the small firm sector. For example, the policy of deregulation which is currently planned and has indeed been partially implemented, can be expected to lead to a greater divide between working conditions in small and large firms than has hitherto been normal. This could, in the long term, lead to the small firm sector in the Federal Republic of Germany developing in new directions.

Bibliography

Abel, W. (ed.). 1978. "Handwerksgeschichte in neuer Sicht", in *Göttinger Beiträge zur Wirtschafts- une Sozialgeschichte*, Vol. 1, Göttingen.

Aubin, H.; Zorn, W. 1976. *Handbuch der Deutschen Wirtschafts- und Sozialgeschichte*, Stuttgart, Röhrscheid Verlag.

Bade, F.-J. 1981. *Survey on industrial choice of location in the Federal Republic of Germany*, Berlin, Wissenschaftszentrum Berlin, IMM/IP 81-18.

---. 1985. *Die wachstumspolitische Bedeutung kleiner und mittlerer Unternehmen*, Berlin, Technische Universität Berlin, Wirtschaftswissenschaftliche Dokumentation 1985, Discussion Paper 100.

Birch, D.L. 1979. *The job generation process*, Cambridge, MA, MIT Program on Neighborhood and Regional Change.

Bleicher, S. n.d. *Kleinere und mittlere Unternehmen - Hoffnungsträger bei der Bekämpfung der Arbeitslosigkeit und Zentren der Innovation?*, Düsseldorf, Unpublished manuscript.

Boedler, S.; Keiser, H. 1979. "30 Jahre Tarifregister", in *Bundesarbeitsblatt*, No. 9, pp. 22-29.

Bosch, G. 1983. "Interessenvertretung in Mittel- und Kleinbetrieben", in *Die Mitbestimmung*, p. 322.

Braunling, G. et al. 1982. *Internationaler Vergleich der Technologie- und Innovationspolitik für kleine und mittlere Unternehmen in ausgewählten Industrieländern*, Karlsruhe, Fraunhofer Institut für Systemtechnik und Innovationsforschung.

Bundesregierung (Federal Government). 1983; 1984; 1985. *Jahreswirtschaftsbericht* (Annual Economic Report), Bonn.

---. (pub.). n.d. *Der Mittelstand - Motor der Wirtschaft*, Bonn.

Bundesverband der Deutschen Industrie (BDI) (Confederation of German Industry). 1985. *Wende in der Mittelstandspolitik?*, Cologne.

Clemens, R. et al. 1986. *Existenzgründungen in der Bundesrepublik Deutschland, Grundlagen einer Existenzgründungsstatistik*, Stuttgart.

Cramer, U. 1987. "Klein- und Mittelbetriebe: Hoffnungsträger der Beschäftigungspolitik?", in *Mitteilungen aus der Arbeitsmarkt- und Berufsforschung*, No. 1.

Dabrowski, H. et al. 1981. *Klein- und Mittelbetriebe in der sozialwissenschaftlichen Forschung*, Eschborn, Rationalisierungskuratorium der Deutschen Wirtschaft.

---. 1984. *Humanisierungsprobleme und Belegeschaftsvertretung in Klein- und Mittelbetrieben*, Göttingen, Sozialwissenschaftliches Forschungsinstitut.

Dahrenmöller, A. 1985. *Der Beitrag mittelständischer Unternehmen zur Beschäftigung und zum Wachstum unter Berücksichtigung der Unternehmensfluktuation*, Bonn, Institut für Mittelstandsforschung, IFM-Materialen No. 32.

Deutscher Gewerkschaftbund (German Trade Union Federation). Technology Advice Centre, North Rhine-Westphalia (pub.). 1986. *Gründer- und Technologiezentren: Bewertung und alternative Konzepte, Technologiepolitik in Nordrhein-Westfalen*, Oberhausen.

Deutsches Institut für Wirtschaftsforschung (German Institute for Economic Research). 1982. "Insolvenzen - Nur geringe Auswirkungen auf Produktionspotential und Arbeitsmarkt", in *DIW Weekly Report*, No. 45.

Eckart, W. et al. 1985. *Dynamik der Beschäftigungsentwicklung - Stand der empirischen Forschung*, Dortmund, University of Dortmund, Department of Economics and Social Sciences, Working Paper 3501.

Ewers, H.-J. 1986. *Strukturwandel und Wirtschaftsförderung in alten Industriestädten*, State and City Development Series published by the state of North Rhine-Westphalia, Vol. 2.051, Dortmund.

Ewers, H.-J.; Kleine, J. 1983. *The interregional diffusion of new processes in the German mechanical engineering industry*, Berlin, Wissenschaftszentrum Berlin, Discussion Paper IIM/IP 83-2.

Ewers, H.-J. et al. 1984. *Bildungs- und qualifikationsorientierte Strategien der Regionalförderung unter besonderer Berücksichtigung kleiner und mittlerer Unternehmen*, Regional Development Series of the Federal Ministry for Regional Development, Construction and Town Planning, Vol. 06.053, Bonn.

Fraunhofer Institut für Systemtechnik und Innovationsforschung (pub.). 1986. *Förderung technologieorientierter Unternehmensgründungen - Eine Zwischenbilanz des Modellversuch des Bundesministers für Forschung und Technologie*, Karlsruhe.

Fritsch, M. 1984. "Die Arbeitsplatzentwicklung in kleinen und mittleren Betrieben bzw. Unternehmen", in *Informationen zur Raumentwicklung*, p. 921.

Gielow, R.-D. 1986. *Unterschiede im Innovationsverhalten zwischen kleinen und grossen Unternehmen*, Karlsruhe, Fraunhofer Institut für Systemtechnik und Innovationsforschung Karlsruhe, Unpublished manuscript.

Henning, F.-W. 1973. *Die Industrialisierung in Deutschland 1800 bis 1914*, Paderborn, Ferdinand Schöningh Verlag.

Hess, H.-J.; Holz, B. 1987. *Entwicklung von Hilfsmitteln und Methoden zur Marktsicherung und Markterweiterung von Zulieferunternehmen*, Aachen, Gesellschaft für Produktionstechnik und Organization.

Hull, C.J. 1985. "Job generation among independent West German manufacturing firms 1974-1980, evidence from four regions", in *Environment and Planning C: Government and Policy*, Vol. 3, p. 215.

Hundsiek, D. 1985. "Beschäftigungspolitische Wirkungen von Unternehmensgründungen und -aufgaben", Bonn, Institut für Mittelstandsforschung, *IFM-Materialen*, No. 28.

Industriegewerkschaft Metall (IG-Metall). 1985. *Protokoll der 8 Bundeshandwerkskonferenz*, Frankfurt, October.

Irsch, H. 1985. "Kleine und mittlere Unternehmen im Strukturwandel", in *Kreditanstalt für Wiederaufbau, Analysen - Meinungen - Perspektiven*, Frankfurt.

Keyser, G.; Friede, C. 1984. *Wirkungsanalyse der Sozialgesetzgebung*, Bonn, Institut für Mittelstandsforschung.

Kleine, J. 1983. *Investitionsverhalten bei Prozessinnovationen*, Frankfurt-New York, Campus Verlag.

Klodt, R. 1980. "Kleine und grosse Unternehmen im Strukturwandel, Zur Entwicklung der sektoralen Unternehmenskonzentration", in *Weltwirtschaft*, No. 1, p. 79.

Kruer-Buchholz, W. 1983. "Unternehmensaufspaltungen und ihre Wirtschaftlichen Hintergründe am Beispiel der Bekleidungsindustrie", in *WSI-Mitteilungen*, No. 1, p. 26.

Kulike, M. 1986. *Technologisch orientierte Unternehmensgründungen (TOU) in der Bundesrepublik Deutschland - Eine empirische Untersuchung der Strukturbildung- und Wachstumsphase von Neugründungen*, Frankfurt-Bern, Lang Verlag.

Lutz, B. 1984. *Der kurze Traum immerwährender Prosperität*, Frankfurt-New York, Campus Verlag.

Lutz, B. et al. 1987 "Das grosse Probieren, Fabrik der Zukunft, Part 6", in *Bild der Wissenschaft*, No. 9.

Mendius, H.G., et al. 1987. *Arbeitskräfteprobleme und Humanisierungspotentiale in Kleinbetrieben*, Frankfurt-New York, Campus Verlag.

Merson, G. 1982. "Betriebsaufspaltungen: Massanzug für mittelständische Unternehmen?", in *Creditreform*, Nos. 7 and 8, p. 24.

Meyer-Krahmer, F. et al. 1984a. *Erfassung regionaler Innovationsdefizite*, Regional Development Series published by the Federal Ministry for Regional Development, Construction and Town Planning, Vol. 06.054, Bonn.

---. 1984b. *Wirkungsanalyse der Zuschüsse für Personal in Forschung und Entwicklung*, Karlsruhe, Fraunhofer Institut für Systemtechnik und Innovationsforschung.

OECD. 1985. "Employment in small and large firms: Where have the jobs come from?", in *OECD Employment Outlook 1985*, Paris.

Prais, S. et al. 1981. *Productivity and industrial structure*, Cambridge, Cambridge University Press.

Rieker, K. 1960. "Die Konzentrationsentwicklung in der gewerblichen Wirtschaft", in *Tradition*, Vol. 5, p. 116.

Schatz, K.-W. 1984. *Die Bedeutung kleiner und mittlerer Unternehmen im Strukturwandel*, Kiel, Institut für Weltwirtschaft Kiel, Kiel Discussion Papers No. 103.

Schwalbach, J. 1983. *Mehrperiodische Analyse der Mehrbetrieblichkeit am Beispiel der drei grössten Unternehmen ausgewählter Industriezweige*, Berlin, Wissenschaftszentrum Berlin, Discussion Paper IIM/IP 83-13.

Segal Quince, Wicksteed and Fraunhofer Institut für Systemtechnik und Innovationsforschung. Forthcoming. *New technology based firms - A review of their recent performance and significance with special reference to the Federal Republic of Germany and United Kingdom*.

Siegrist, H. 1983. "Kommentar zu Stockmann, R.; Dahm, G.; Zeifang, K. (1983)", in Haller, M.; Müller, W. *Beschäftigungssysteme im Wandel*, Frankfurt, 1983.

Sorge, A. 1983. "Die betriebliche Erzeugung und die Nutzung beruflicher Bildung in der Bundesrepublik Deutschland, Frankreich und Grossbritannien", in Haller, M.; Müller, W.: *Beschäftigungssysteme im Wandel*, Frankfurt, 1983.

Stockmann, R.; Kleber, W. 1985. *Die Entwicklung der Betriebs- und Beschäftigtenstruktur nach Branchen 1975-1982*, Mannheim, Institut für Sozialwissenschaften der Universität Mannheim, VASMA Project, Working Paper No. 44.

Stockmann, R. et al. 1983. "Konzentration und Reorganisierung von Unternehmen und Betrieben. Empirische Analyse zur Entwicklung der nichtlandwirtschaftlichen Arbeitsstätten und Unternehmen in Deutschland 1895-1970", in Haller, M.; Müller, W.: *Beschäftigungssysteme im Wandel*, Frankfurt, 1983.

Szyperski, N.; Kirschbaum, G. 1981. "Unternehmensgründungen in Nordrhein-Westfalen", in *Beiträge zur Mittelstandsforschung*, Vol. 75, Göttingen.

Verband der Vereine Creditreform e.V. 1984, 1985 and 1986. *Unternehmensentwicklung*, Neuss.

Weimer, S. 1983. *Arbeitsbedingungen in Klein- und Mittelbetrieben*, Eschborn, Rationalisierungskuratorium der Deutschen Wirtschaft.

Weitzel, G. 1986. "Bescheidene Beschäftigungswirkungen durch Neugründungen", in *IFO-Schnelldienst*, No. 7.

4 Italy

Giacomo Becattini

I. Introduction

By any standard, Italy represents a most attractive case of a small enterprise development which is of great significance from a comparative point of view. It is not surprising, therefore, that among the countries included in this volume, Italy has aroused remarkable interest within the international scientific community and, more recently, also among politicians and practitioners.

The Italian production system is characterised by relatively small enterprises and establishments, and small-scale business organisation has become even more important during the last two decades. Also, in all economic sectors and geographical areas the small firm contribution to net job creation has been remarkable in recent years.

Equally distinctive is the regional diversity of the national economy, in which old industrialised areas in the north-western part of the country, the much less developed *Mezzogiorno*, and the "Third Italy" comprise a geographic triangle. This triangle, defined by Udine, Pisa and Ascoli Piceno, and centred on Bologna and Florence, is replete with small firm industrial districts with a renowned business culture of inter-firm competition and co-operation and remarkable economic performance, which is demonstrated, for example, by its export capacity.

There is an inter-disciplinary community in the Italian social sciences to which we owe our fairly extensive knowledge of small firm structures. Perhaps more than elsewhere empirical investigation has been linked to theoretical concerns of industrial organisation, and labour issues and labour market structures have also received much attention. Furthermore, the aforementioned community includes researchers belonging to a whole set of public but not academic research institutions. A remarkable role in the investigation of the new phenomena has been played by several "regional" research institutes (e.g., IRPET for Tuscany, IRES for Lombardy, etc.) and by the Italian branch of the Regional Science Association.

This chapter links the structure and dynamics of small and medium-sized enterprises to the very particular Italian road to industrialisation, emphasises the relevant historical and institutional background to this development, and examines the various strands of reasoning and explanation in the contemporary debate about industrial organisation.

Italy

Table 1: Italy: Employment shares by enterprise size, total economy

Year	< 20	20-99	100-499	500+
1971	45.7	15.9	12.8	25.6
1981	53.2	16.1	12.2	18.5

Sources: Istituto Centrale di Statistica, *5° Censimento generale dell'industria e del commercio*, 25 October 1971.
Istituto Centrale di Statistica, *6° Censimento generale dell'industria, del commercio, dei servizi e dell'artigianato*, 26 October 1981.

Table 2: Italy: Employment shares by enterprise size, time series for the total economy

	1951	1961	1971	1981
- Small (1)	60.2	63.5	61.6	69.3
- Small and Medium (2)	73.0	77.1	74.4	81.5

Notes: (1) Small: fewer than 100 employees (1951 and 1961: fewer than 101).
(2) Small and medium: fewer than 500 employees (1951 and 1961: fewer than 501).

Sources: Istituto Centrale di Statistica, *3° Censimento generale dell'industria e del commercio*, 5 November 1951.
Istituto Centrale di Statistica, *4° Censimento generale dell'industria e del commercio*, 16 October 1961.
Istituto Centrale di Statistica, *5° Censimento generale dell'industria e del commercio*, 25 October 1971.
Istituto Centrale di Statistica, *6° Censimento generale dell'industria, del commercio, dei servizi e dell'artigianato*, 26 October 1981.

Table 3: Italy: Employment shares by enterprise size, manufacturing

Year	< 20	20-99	100-499	500+
1971	30.1	20.4	18.7	30.8
1981(1)	33.6	21.7	18.6	26.1

Note: (1) Manufacturing Industries: NACE Divisions 2 (not including 21 and 23 Classes), 3 and 4.

Sources: Istituto Centrale di Statistica, *5° Censimento generale dell'industria e del commercio*, 25 October 1971.
Istituto Centrale di Statistica, *6° Censimento generale dell'industria, del commercio, dei servizi e dell'artigianato*, 26 October 1981.

II. Size and development of the SME sector in postwar Italy

1. Small average firm and establishment size

Italy stands out as an economy with a very small average scale of business organisation. Table 1 shows that in 1981, the date of the most recent census, 53.2 per cent of all employees worked in very small enterprises (fewer than 20 employees). Conversely, the share of employment in large enterprises with more than 500 employees was 18.5 per cent; smaller than in any other country in this study. Italy's position at the lower end of the size distribution holds also for the manufacturing and service sectors, as well as in the data on employment shares by establishment size. Thus, in 1981, slightly more than one-half of total employment was in establishments with fewer than 20 employees. The corresponding figure for the manufacturing sector was 35.5 per cent (Table 8).

2. Changes in the size structure of employment

What is perhaps most remarkable about Italy is that despite starting from such a relatively large small firm sector in the early 1970s, the employment share of small enterprises and establishments grew quite substantially into the early 1980s. Table 2 shows that the small enterprise share of total employment reversed a decline from 1961 to 1971 with a large 7.7 percentage point increase from 1971 to 1981. The employment share of medium-sized enterprises fell only slightly, so the share of large enterprises declined significantly.

Table 4 shows a similar pattern for manufacturing enterprises, although the magnitude is slightly less: a 4.8 percentage point increase for small enterprises from 1971 to 1981 comes at the expense of a 4.7 percentage point decrease for large enterprises. Time series data are not available for services, but in the light of the relative magnitudes of the changes in manufacturing and the total economy it is unlikely that a significant concentration of employment in large enterprises occurred in the services sector. However, given the large employment shares in very small services enterprises shown in Table 5, it is clear that a shift in employment from manufacturing to services would tend to increase the total economy small enterprise employment share.

The establishment data yield very similar results: significant gains among small establishments at the expense of large establishments. Table 7 shows that the small establishment share of total employment began rising as early as 1961, while Table 9 shows that in manufacturing the more familiar V pattern of a decline and subsequent increase was observed. No establishment level data are available for services.

Finally, in addition to a large small firm sector, Italy has an atypically high proportion of self-employment. For many years, the ratio of self-employment to civilian employment has been higher in Italy than in any

Italy

Table 4: Italy: Employment shares by enterprise size, time series for manufacturing

	1951	1961	1971	1981(1)
- Small (2)	50.5	53.2	50.5	55.3
- Small and Medium (3)	67.4	72.0	69.2	73.9

Notes: (1) 1981: NACE Divisions 2 (not including 21 and 23 Classes), 3 and 4.
(2) Small: less than 100 employees (1951 and 1961: less than 101).
(3) Small and medium: less than 500 employees (1951 and 1961: less than 501).

Sources: Istituto Centrale di Statistica, *3° Censimento generale dell'industria e del commercio*, 5 November 1951.
Istituto Centrale di Statistica, *4° Censimento generale dell'industria e del commercio*, 16 October 1961.
Istituto Centrale di Statistica, *5° Censimento generale dell'industria e del commercio*, 25 October 1971.
Istituto Centrale di Statistica, *6° Censimento generale dell'industria, del commercio, dei servizi e dell'artigianato*, 26 October 1981.

Table 5: Italy: Employment shares by enterprise size, service sector

Year	< 20	20-99	100-499	500+
1981 (1)	71.1	9.2	6.1	13.6
1981 (2)	70.5	9.3	6.3	13.9

Notes: (1) Includes wholesale and retail trade
(2) Not included the following NACE Classes: 61 (Wholesale Distribution), 62 (Dealing in Scrap and Waste Materials), 64/65 (Retail Distribution), 66 (Hotels and Catering), 67 (Repair of Consumer Goods and Vehicles)

Source: Istituto Centrale di Statistica, *6° Censimento generale dell'industria, del commercio, dei servizi e dell'artigianato*, 26 October 1981.

Table 6: Italy: Employment shares by establishment size, total economy

Year	< 20	20-99	100-499	500+
1971	n.a. (1)	n.a. (1)	15.7	15.0
1981	50.7	21.7	14.9	12.7

Note: (1) n.a.: not available.

Sources: Istituto Centrale di Statistica, *5° Censimento generale dell'industria e del commercio*, 25 October 1971.
Istituto Centrale di Statistica, *6° Censimento generale dell'industria, del commercio, dei servizi e dell'artigianato*, 26 October 1981.

European OECD country [OECD, 1986]. The ratio increased significantly from 1973 to 1983, such that by 1983 over 20 per cent of civilian employment was self-employment. Thus, the share of Italians working either for themselves or for small units is quite high, at least compared to the other countries in this volume.

Table 7: Italy: Employment shares by establishment size, time series for total economy

	1951	1961	1971	1981
- Small (1)	67.2	61.6	69.3	72.4
- Small and Medium (2)	82.6	82.2	85.0	87.3

Notes: (1) Small: less than 100 employees (1951 and 1961: less than 101)
(2) Small and medium: less than 500 employees (1951 and 1961: less than 501)
Sources: Istituto Centrale di Statistica, *3° Censimento generale dell'industria e del commercio*, 5 November 1951.
Istituto Centrale di Statistica, *4° Censimento generale dell'industria e del commercio*, 16 October 1961.
Istituto Centrale di Statistica, *5° Censimento generale dell'industria e del commercio*, 25 October 1971.
Istituto Centrale di Statistica, *6° Censimento generale dell'industria, del commercio, dei servizi e dell'artigianato*, 26 October 1981.

Table 8: Italy: Employment shares by establishment size, manufacturing

Year	< 20	20-99	100-499	500+
1971	n.a. (1)	n.a. (1)	22.3	23.1
1981 (2)	35.5	23.8	21.1	19.6

Note: (1) n.a.: not available.
(2) 1981: Manufacturing Industries - NACE Divisions 2, 3 and 4.
Sources: Istituto Centrale di Statistica, *5° Censimento generale dell'industria e del commercio*, 25 October 1971.
Istituto Centrale di Statistica, *6° Censimento generale dell'industria, del commercio, dei servizi e dell'artigianato*, 26 October 1981.

Italy

Table 9: Italy: Employment shares by establishment size, time series for manufacturing

	1951 (1)	1961 (2)	1971 (3)	1981 (4)
- Small (2)	54.2	56.9	54.6	59.1
- Small and Medium (3)	74.6	78.5	76.9	80.3

Notes: (1) 1951: 1-100, 101-500, 501+.
(2) 1961: 1-20, 21-100, 101-500, 501+.
(3) 1-99.
(4) 1981: NACE Divisions 2 (not including 21 and 23 Classes), 3 and 4.

Sources: Istituto Centrale di Statistica, *3° Censimento generale dell'industria e del commercio*, 5 November 1951.
Istituto Centrale di Statistica, *4° Censimento generale dell'industria e del commercio*, 16 October 1961.
Istituto Centrale di Statistica, *5° Censimento generale dell'industria e del commercio*, 25 October 1971.
Istituto Centrale di Statistica, *6° Censimento generale dell'industria, del commercio, dei servizi e dell'artigianato*, 26 October 1981.

3. Job generation

The recent release of Italian National Institute of Social Security (INPS) data to researchers has facilitated analysis of job generation and destruction in Italy. Results of the most comprehensive study are summarised below [Contini and Revelli, 1986].

Contini and Revelli analyse employment data for the period 1978-83, and their findings are reminiscent of those of Birch [1979] in the United States. Table 10, reproduced from Contini and Revelli, breaks down employment change by sector into its component parts: *in situ* expansion and job change from new firms and closures. In each case, figures are presented to compare net job creation for very small firms with the overall average. It is quite clear that during periods of both aggregate employment growth and decline, very small firms vastly outperformed the overall average in terms of job creation; e.g., net total employment fell by 210,000 from 1981-83, while very small firms increased employment by 102,000. Very small firms did better in both sectors and by all measures, but the difference was widest with respect to *in situ* expansion ("SB" in the table). New firms and closures relate almost entirely to small firms in Italy, and they tend to cancel one another out. Thus, essentially all of the increase comes from the expansion of existing firms (roughly 85 per cent, versus 15 per cent for the net of births and deaths).

The social security data also permit analysis of job turnover. Contini and Revelli find that turnover is quite rapid in Italy, with on average one out of every four workers changing employers each year during the period 1978-83. However, the rate is much higher for very small firms: one out of 2.3, or 44 per cent, of workers change employers each year. Very small firms in Italy are thus part of a very fluid labour market.

Table 10: Jobs created and destroyed by all firms and by very small firms (0-19 employees): Yearly averages (thousands)

	Manufacturing 1978-80	Manufacturing 1981-83	Services 1978-80	Services 1981-83	Total 1978-80	Total 1981-83
In-situ expansion						
All	1 428	1 181	661	605	2 090	1 786
0-19	842	705	456	413	1 298	1 786
In-situ contraction						
All	1 376	1 380	632	593	2 009	1 973
0-19	628	643	366	362	995	1 005
New firms						
All	241	175	92	83	333	258
0-19	111	88	76	72	187	160
Closures						
All	186	189	93	91	279	280
0-19	103	101	69	70	172	171
AE						
All	106	-213	29	3	135	-210
0-19	222	49	97	53	319	102
SB (1)						
All	51	-199	33	11	84	-188
0-19	214	62	90	51	304	113
DB (2)						
All	54	-14	0	-8	54	-22
0-19	9	-13	7	2	16	-11

Notes: (1) SB: Structural Balance = jobs created by expanding firms - jobs destroyed by declining firms.
(2) DB: Demographic Balance = jobs created by new firms (hirings) - jobs destroyed by closures (layoffs).
Source: Contini and Revelli [1986].

4. Other developments in the small firm sector

Data on gross product, personnel expenses and investments in industrial, commercial, transport, and communication firms gathered by the Italian *Istituto Centrale di Statistica* permit examination of the relative performance of firms of different sizes [Borzaga, 1985]. However, it must be pointed out that, unfortunately, the data concern firms with 20 employees or more, thus leaving out the largest and most interesting group of small firms. In spite of this, some of the conclusions are sufficiently well established to shed light on the overall tendencies.

Table 11 shows, first of all, that the productivity gap, at least in terms of gross product per employee, has decreased significantly, especially since 1977. The gross product per employee of firms with 20-49 employees was 61.5 per cent of that of firms with 200 or more employees in 1972. By 1982, the proportion increased to slightly more than 90 per cent. The gap

Table 11: Gross product, personnel expenses, investments per employee

	1972	1973	1974	1975	1976	1977	1978	1979	1980	1981	1982
Gross product per employee											
20-49 employees	61.5	69.6	75.4	74.2	73.1	78.2	79.1	82.1	88.2	89.4	90.6
50-99 employees	72.0	77.5	83.4	81.0	80.3	85.9	87.2	89.6	95.6	96.3	95.4
100-199 employees	81.5	85.5	91.0	88.2	87.3	93.5	93.3	98.0	100.4	100.9	100.9
200 employees and +	100.0	100.0	100.0	100.0	100.0	100.0	100.0	100.0	100.0	100.0	100.0
Total	88.5	91.1	97.5	92.7	92.4	94.6	94.9	95.8	98.0	98.3	98.3
Personnel expenses per employee											
20-49 employees	54.8	57.7	42.6	63.3	64.6	68.9	70.0	71.3	74.4	76.3	78.9
50-99 employees	65.6	68.5	71.7	73.6	74.9	78.6	80.0	80.9	83.5	85.0	86.4
100-199 employees	74.3	77.0	79.5	81.6	82.6	85.8	86.1	86.6	89.4	90.7	91.6
200 employees and +	100.0	100.0	100.0	100.0	100.0	100.0	100.0	100.0	100.0	100.0	100.0
Total	85.8	87.2	88.9	89.5	90.6	91.6	92.0	92.3	93.4	93.9	94.5
Investment per employee											
20-49 employees	45.6	65.6	86.2	60.6	63.2	61.4	62.0	77.5	86.7	81.7	72.9
50-99 employees	55.6	64.8	70.3	62.9	70.8	72.6	71.8	89.2	93.9	87.9	73.6
100-199 employees	62.5	81.8	76.3	70.5	78.9	76.0	76.1	94.2	100.4	93.4	84.3
200 employees and +	100.0	100.0	100.0	100.0	100.0	100.0	100.0	100.0	100.0	100.0	100.0
Total	81.7	88.5	91.6	86.5	88.9	88.6	88.6				

Source: Institute of Statistics: *Monthly bulletin*, for relevant years.

in the expenses for personnel per employee between the same size groups decreased considerably during that length of time, rising from 55 per cent to 79 per cent. Investment per employee in firms with 20-99 employees went from 45.6 per cent of the corresponding level in the large category in 1972, to 72.9 per cent in 1982.

A study of export performance by size group suggests that the difference between the small (11-20 employees) and the large (500 employees and more) firms has slightly diminished between 1978 and 1984 [Carnazza and Carone, 1987].

These changes considered together reveal an overall performance of the "small" firms which has improved substantially relative to that of the "large" ones.

III. An outline of postwar Italian industrial development

1. A bird's-eye view of the Italian "miracle" and its aftermath

The war, the reconstruction, the revival of political life, and renewed participation in the international market were the main events that gave the initial spur to postwar industrial and social change in Italy.

The most rapid industrialisation occurred in the 1950s and early 1960s and ended with the 1963-1966 recession (the so-called *congiuntura*), by which time Italy had already achieved a kind of full employment. The term full employment is intended to mean a situation where several crucial industrial sectors (mechanical, chemical, transport, equipment) were experiencing labour shortages and the main industrial areas of several regions (Piedmont, Lombardy and Liguria) were sufficiently crowded with industrial plants, activities and people to begin to suffer from the external diseconomies (competition for the use of land and water, pollution and so on) and the social problems (urban immigration problems, etc.) typical of that stage of development. So the *congiuntura* can be considered the end of the so-called "Italian miracle". By the end of 1966 the face of Italy had already changed: a country with half of its active population devoted to agriculture only 20 years earlier had already become, according to the usual standards, an industrial country. The share of output from the machinery, metallurgical and chemical sectors in the gross product of manufacturing industry rose from 42 per cent to 54 per cent in the period 1952-1967, while the share of the more traditional sectors (foodstuffs, textiles, clothing, wood and furniture) fell from 42 per cent to 29 per cent.

The period 1945-63 can be split into a first sub-period (1945-1951) devoted to the material reconstruction of the country, and a second sub-period (1951-63) which saw the take-off of the Italian economy. The rates of GNP growth in the two sub-periods were 8.4 and 5.4 per cent per year, respectively, and the rates of annual increase in gross investment were, correspondingly, 7.7 and 9.3 per cent [Valli, 1986].

Italy

The following 11 years (1963-73) can be considered as a "stop-and-go" period with GNP growing at an average rate of 4.7 per cent per year and gross investment growing at the rate of only 3.5 per cent. This period, too, can be split into two sub-periods: the first devoted to an extensive restructuring of industry (1962-68), and the second (1969-73) being a period of intense social turmoil.

During the decade 1963-73 the great majority of Italian scholars saw the evolution of Italian industry as proof that Italy was destined to follow the same industrial path as that followed by the main western advanced industrial economies. The opinion still prevailed that small firms were a mere remnant of the past and that the regions squeezed between the "Industrial Triangle" and the subsidised South were a weak point, or at least a question mark, for the industrial future of the country.

The third and last period started with the 1973 rise in oil prices. The fluctuations in industrial activity became wider; the rate of increase in GNP went down to 1.9 per cent per year (1973-75), and gross investment rose by only 0.5 per cent per year. Despite the modest amount of gross investment, the replacement of capital was rather intense in this period. There was expansion in the sectors characterised by the prevalence of small firms, and consolidation in the more capital-intensive sectors.

As a result of all these developments, the economic structure of Italy changed greatly. In 1981 the distribution of total employment among the three main sectors was as follows: agriculture, 15 per cent; industry, 34 per cent; services, 50 per cent. Given that the corresponding percentages in 1951 were 48, 26 and 26 [Mazzoni, 1988], it is clear that Italy experienced in these 30 years a very real "structural evolution": a rapid and widespread socio-economic "revolution" wherein the period of predominance of industrial activity lasted only a few years.

It is during the third period that the controversy arose about the relative performances of small and large firms. As will be seen, what makes the Italian argument different from similar debates in other countries is that it is intermingled with a debate about regional economic development.

2. Some peculiar social conditions of industrial change

The social transformations which correspond to the process of economic change sketched above are many and multifarious and they cannot be addressed in this overview. But some - certainly not the most important in absolute terms - must be noted because they help to put into correct perspective the specific economic changes which will be examined in some detail. It must be emphasised, however, that the two social phenomena illustrated below were received and have been assessed differently by different observers [Bagnasco, 1988].

The first phenomenon is the disruption and disappearance of the *metayage* system of land tenure (share-cropping) that prevailed for centuries in Umbria, Marche, Tuscany, Emilia-Romagna and Veneto. The swift fading-out of this system, in less than 30 years, produced a mass of workers ready to be employed by a population of small firms requiring general rather than specific skills in order to produce (especially at the beginning of the period) technologically unsophisticated goods. This new manpower proved *ex post* more ready to acquire the necessary know-how, and more reliable on the job, than common wisdom would suggest. Even more surprisingly, against all expectations, the group of former *metayers* produced several new entrepreneurs [Paci, 1980].

These facts were taken by some observers to mean that the socialisation process that had gone on in the *metayage* system over the past centuries had not been properly understood. In addition, many commentators emphasised the culturally revolutionary effects of Italy's having been a battlefield for foreign armies for about two years, giving rise to a strong partisan movement. These circumstances can help explain the active involvement in political life of large masses of rural people after liberation. [IRPET, 1975].

A second phenomenon of importance is the very special role played by the Italian Communist Party (PCI) on the Italian political and, more particularly, the social scene. Despite its official Marxist ideology, since the Second World War the PCI has always been inclined to follow a policy of national development of a somewhat interclass character. The political formula of "class alliances" has permeated the praxis of the PCI to such an extent as to allow local administrators belonging to that party to comply with the needs of the light industrialisation in progress, without paying much attention to the Marxist or class orthodoxy of their action [D'Angelillo and Paggi, 1986; Trigilia, 1986].

Another dimension of PCI activity that has not yet been sufficiently researched is the creation of a full system of formal and informal social institutions in the geographical areas where it is well established. From the National Artisans Federation (CNA) to the Association for Recreation and Culture (ARCI), the PCI has created a continuum of institutions, more or less formal, acting as "socialising agencies" that bind people together, at work (such as unions, or CNA), at home (for example co-operatives) and in leisure time (ARCI and a whole cluster of initiatives, as, for instance the summer festival (*Feste dell'Unità*)). At those annual gatherings of the PCI members and supporters, the two processes of the political and the local identification merge into and intensify each other.

By means of what is in effect a "system" of "socialising agencies", a concept of life that puts the accent on certain values (work and family ethics, group solidarity even more than class struggle, etc.) has been transmitted from one generation to another, in a non-compulsory way. Surprisingly, some observers contend that a similar role has been played by the catholic network of institutions in regions like Veneto [Bagnasco and Trigilia, 1984 and 1985].

3. The main characteristics of postwar industrialisation

Among the peculiarities of Italy's postwar industrial development the two which have attracted the most attention and comment from foreign observers are the marked increase in the share of the small and medium-sized firms, in terms of both employment and exports, and the formation of a certain number of "industrial districts" in the central and northern part of the country. The development of small and medium-sized firms has been seen in the light of similar, or apparently similar, phenomena occurring in several other countries in Europe and elsewhere.

A careful consideration of the census data for the 30 years from 1951 to 1981 shows that the importance of small and medium-sized firms in Italian manufacturing industry has always been considerable. Table 4 shows that in 1951 firms with fewer than 100 employees accounted for 50.5 per cent of employment and those with fewer than 500 accounted for 67.4 per cent.

In the decade of the "miracle", the share of small and medium-sized firms rose almost 5 per cent, reaching the very high figure of 72 per cent of manufacturing employment. The following decade saw a change in size composition of Italian manufacturing in favour of larger firms. However, it should be noted that the decrease in employment share was greater for medium-sized firms than for small firms.

The most striking change occurred from 1971 to 1981, when the employment share of the small enterprises rose from 50.5 per cent to 55.3 per cent and that of the small and medium-sized group rose from 69.2 per cent to 73.9 per cent of total manufacturing employment measured by the census. Since the employment which escapes the census is mostly that of small businesses, it follows that, in the 1980s, more than three-quarters of Italian manufacturing employment is in firms with fewer than 500 workers. With respect to changes over time, it is important to point out that the increasing coverage and precision of the Italian censuses account for a small part of the increased employment share of small firms [Bruni, 1986].

4. Changes in the regional distribution of Italian manufacturing

The statistical data used in this section do have a severe limitation for regional analysis: the administrative boundaries separating the different regions are seldom if ever adequate from an economic point of view. This is nearly always true, the only exceptions being the Islands and perhaps the small region (or province) of Val d'Aosta. Within these limits Table 12 shows the main changes which took place in the 30 years between 1951 (end of reconstruction and first censuses) and 1981 (latest censuses) at the regional level.

The top half of the table shows changes in resident population, with the population in each region in 1951 set at 100. The second half gives changes in the degree of industrialisation, where the degree of industrialisation is defined as the ratio between employment in manufacturing (as given in the industrial census) and resident population (as given in the census of population).

At the beginning of the period two regions were well in advance of the others in terms of industrialisation: Lombardy and Piedmont (see Tables 12 and 13). Together with Liguria and Val d'Aosta, two very particular regions, although for different reasons, they constituted what came to be called the "Industrial Triangle". Their industrial take-off occurred in the last decades of the nineteenth century and, in 1951, they still represented the "core" of Italian industry. Among the other regions the only ones that were noticeable for their industrial density were Tuscany (the richest region as far as mining was concerned), Emilia-Romagna and the two frontier regions, Trentino-Alto Adige and Friuli-Venezia Giulia. All the other regions, despite some important plants and some industrial concentrations, were mainly agricultural and artisanal.

The decade 1951-1961 apparently confirms and enhances this position. Despite an increase in its population of the order of 13 per cent, Lombardy's degree of industrialisation increased to 19.50 per cent. A similar situation was seen in Piedmont, while Val d'Aosta and Liguria experienced a small decrease. Thus the gap between the "triangle" as a whole, and the regions of the South widened greatly. In fact, this was a decade of great debate about the "Southern question".

What must be noticed, and was not at the time, is the big jump in terms of degree of industrialisation of the two central regions - i.e. Tuscany and Emilia-Romagna. In the course of a decade they overtook Liguria. What is also noticeable is the fact that they had attracted much lower levels of immigration than Liguria; that is, they industrialised by turning their regional agricultural population into industrial employees.

In the same period some other North-East-Centre (NEC) regions like Veneto, Umbria, Marche and Friuli-Venezia Giulia were both increasing their level of industrialisation and losing population. At the time people were struck by the negative overall migration balance, and it was generally believed that NEC Italy [Fuà and Zacchia, 1983], despite some appearances, was losing ground.

In the decade 1961-71 the industrialisation of the "triangle" continued, albeit at a reduced rate (in fact Liguria continued to de-industrialise), but the influx of immigrants from the South was still so large that the overall "degree of industrialisation" of the "triangle" began to decline. Tuscany and Emilia-Romagna continued to progress and Veneto grew industrially, reversing a secular trend toward declining population. Umbria, Marche and Friuli, although still losing population, showed clear signs of industrialisation.

Table 12: Population and manufacturing employment in Italy by regions

	1951	1961	1971	1981
A. Index numbers - population				
Piemonte	100.00	111.26	125.98	127.31
Valle d'Aosta	100.00	107.24	115.94	119.35
Lombardia	100.00	112.79	130.11	135.42
Trentino-Alto Adige	100.00	107.87	115.55	119.87
Veneto	100.00	98.18	105.24	110.90
Friuli-Venezia Giulia	100.00	98.22	98.97	100.64
Liguria	100.00	110.75	118.29	115.38
Emilia Romagna	100.00	103.45	108.53	111.66
Toscana	100.00	104.03	109.95	113.37
Umbria	100.00	98.86	96.50	100.45
Marche	100.00	98.79	99.70	103.55
Lazio	100.00	118.50	140.37	149.72
Abruzzi	100.00	94.45	91.35	95.35
Molise	100.00	88.01	78.61	80.72
Campania	100.00	109.54	116.41	125.70
Puglia	100.00	106.23	112.25	120.22
Basilicata	100.00	102.66	96.09	97.23
Calabria	100.00	100.04	97.25	100.83
Sicilia	100.00	105.22	104.32	109.36
Sardegna	100.00	111.23	115.50	124.93
ITALY	100.00	106.54	113.93	119.03
B. Employment in manufacturing (in per cent)				
Piemonte	15.83	17.77	17.36	16.78
Valle d'Aosta	12.44	10.73	9.21	9.31
Lombardia	17.12	19.51	18.29	17.94
Trentino-Alto Adige	6.25	6.76	7.27	8.09
Veneto	6.81	9.83	11.55	14.05
Friuli-Venezia Giulia	7.49	8.91	10.60	11.18
Liguria	10.07	9.28	7.66	7.62
Emilia Romagna	5.89	9.69	11.35	13.95
Toscana	7.59	10.84	11.87	13.58
Umbria	5.62	6.27	8.37	11.23
Marche	4.59	6.51	9.24	13.76
Lazio	4.01	4.55	4.59	5.40
Abruzzi)	(	(	4.86	7.71
Molise)	(3.05	(3.51	2.34	4.39
Campania	4.01	4.47	4.37	5.24
Puglia	3.28	3.32	4.04	5.05
Basilicata	2.52	2.22	2.80	3.67
Calabria	2.59	2.38	1.80	2.09
Sicilia	2.69	2.85	2.64	2.87
Sardegna	2.51	2.56	3.05	3.82
ITALY	7.36	8.88	9.34	10.19

Note: Between the 1961 and 1971 censuses, the Abruzzo-Molise region was split into two regions: Abruzzo and Molise).

Table 13: Population and manufacturing employment in Italy by regions

	1951	1961	1971	1981
A. Population				
Piemonte	3 518 177	3 914 250	4 432 313	4 479 031
Valle d'Aosta	94 140	100 959	109 150	112 353
Lombardia	6 566 154	7 406 152	8 543 378	8 891 652
Trentino-Alto Adige	728 604	785 967	841 886	873 413
Veneto	3 918 059	3 846 562	4 123 411	4 345 047
Friuli-Venezia Giulia	1 226 121	1 204 298	1 213 532	1 233 984
Liguria	1 566 961	1 735 349	1 853 578	1 807 893
Emilia Romagna	3 544 340	3 666 680	3 846 755	3 957 513
Toscana	3 158 811	3 286 160	3 473 097	3 581 051
Umbria	803 918	794 745	775 783	807 552
Marche	1 364 030	1 347 489	1 359 907	1 412 404
Lazio	3 340 798	3 958 957	4 689 482	5 001 684
Abruzzi	1 277 207	1 206 266	1 166 694	1 217 791
Molise	406 823	358 052	319 807	328 371
Campania	4 346 264	4 760 759	5 059 348	5 463 134
Puglia	3 220 485	3 421 217	3 582 787	3 871 617
Basilicata	627 586	644 297	603 064	610 186
Calabria	2 044 287	2 045 047	1 988 051	2 061 182
Sicilia	4 486 749	4 721 001	4 680 715	4 906 878
Sardegna	1 276 023	1 419 362	1 473 800	1 594 175
ITALY	47 515 537	50 623 569	54 136 547	56 556 911
B. Employment in manufacturing				
Piemonte	556 808	695 467	769 298	751 701
Valle d'Aosta	11 707	10 830	10 054	10 458
Lombardia	1 124 371	1 445 199	1 562 797	1 594 911
Trentino-Alto Adige	45 502	53 159	61 227	70 675
Veneto	266 981	377 954	476 416	610 312
Friuli-Venezia Giulia	91 876	107 346	128 627	137 923
Liguria	157 864	161 054	141 933	137 781
Emilia Romagna	208 616	355 218	436 436	551 883
Toscana	239 903	356 277	412 165	486 357
Umbria	45 154	49 842	64 963	90 722
Marche	62 645	87 724	125 715	194 338
Lazio	133 863	180 136	215 134	269 934
Abruzzi)	(	(	56 688	93 899
Molise)	(51 337	(54 882	7 481	14 400
Campania	174 190	212 828	221 294	286 211
Puglia	105 657	113 710	144 573	195 481
Basilicata	15 798	14 330	16 899	22 386
Calabria	52 987	48 672	35 762	43 075
Sicilia	120 889	134 566	123 416	140 698
Sardegna	32 032	36 369	44 944	60 843
ITALY	3 498 220	4 495 563	5 055 822	5 763 988

The decade 1971-81 witnessed the industrialisation of the Marche, Friuli-Venezia Giulia and Umbria regions and interesting changes even in some southern regions (Abruzzi and Molise). The "Triangle" experienced a general tendency towards deindustrialisation, and a simultaneous decline in population levels. However, since this decade saw a great expansion of the tertiary sectors related to industry, at least part of the fall of the index is due to a different statistical classification of tertiary activities previously performed inside industrial firms [Momigliano and Siniscalco, 1982]. The rest of Italy did not show signs of industrial growth. This does not mean that local phenomena of industrialisation, heavy and light, concentrated and dispersed, were altogether absent, only that they were not strong enough to offset, in terms of employment, the increase in population.

At the beginning of the 1970s, discussions were still in terms of a "Third Italy" lagging behind the industrialised North [VV.AA., 1970]. At the end of the decade the tone was partially different. Several observers started to speak of the extraordinary, albeit temporary, performance of the NEC regions: a performance attributable mainly to a very peculiar international conjuncture (high dollar rates and high returns for oil countries) that allowed Italian small firms, although operating in mature sectors, to win sections of the widening international market.

As a result of 30 years of industrial change the situation has greatly changed from the one depicted at the beginning of the chapter. By 1981 there was a group of eight regions with a high "degree of industrialisation", indicated by a share of manufacturing employment above 11.0 per cent, another group of eight regions with a share below 5.40 per cent, and four regions (Val d'Aosta, Trentino-Alto Adige, Liguria, Abruzzo) somewhere in the middle. The gap between the first and the second group was still wide. More importantly, it would appear that the passage of 30 years has produced nothing, in terms of industrialisation, in at least two regions: Sicily and Calabria [Becattini and Bianchi, 1982].

IV. The new industrial districts

Research in Florence by a research fellow of IRPET (Tuscan Institute for Planning) Fabio Sforzi, permits the location of the industrial districts, produced by the post-war wave of industrialisation in Italy [Sforzi, 1987]. As can be seen from Map 1 they belong mainly to NEC regions. Some of them belong also to the older industrial regions (Lombardy and Piedmont). Apparently there are no industrial districts in the South.

160 · *The re-emergence of small enterprises*

Map 1: Marshallian Industrial Districts in Italy

Source: Sforzi, F. "L'identificazione spaziale", in Becattini, G. (ed.): *Mercato e forze locali: Il distretto industriale*, Bologna, Il Mulino, 1987.

To understand this territorial distribution, one must pause to consider the concept of industrial district adopted here. The industrial district (ID) is a "thickening" of industrial and social interdependencies in a certain place. This thickening appears in at least three ways: as a relatively self-contained labour market; as a matrix of localised technical interrelationships; and as a web of socio-cultural connections. Following this idea Sforzi builds up a technique for identifying IDs. He begins by identifying self-contained labour market areas using the 1981 census data on commuting. By means of an appropriate algorithm, he isolates groups of agents bound together by a network of daily movements for work or for other reasons.

The result of this first step is a complete classification of every community in Italy, each belonging to one and only one "local system". Thus the map of the local systems (i.e., self-contained labour markets) is the starting point for all successive elaborations.[1]

The second step is an embryonic analysis of the social structure of the local systems. The Census of Population data provide a great deal of information on the activities of respondents on the structure of their families, and on other socio-economic aspects of their lives. Thus a typology of social situations can be constructed. Among the different cases, one is better adapted than others to the requirements of the new industrial districts.

Roughly speaking, it is a situation where the presence of workers, small entrepreneurs and working wives is superior to the average and where the extended family, including both old people who are still active and young people starting work early, prevails. If the local systems are sorted to isolate those with this particular social structure, a sub-set of candidates is identified to be considered as "industrial districts". The results are given in Map 2.

Map 2 shows clearly the regional systems of Marche, Emilia-Romagna, Tuscany, Veneto and Friuli. There are also some areas in Lombardy and Piedmont, a few traces in Trentino and Umbria, and nothing at all in the remaining regions. It is worth noting that the Tuscan block (which corresponds to what has been called the "urbanised countryside") is interrupted by the "urban system" of Florence, where the cosmopolitan character of the city interferes with the social structure typical of the ID.

The next step consists of an attempt to select the "local systems" which present the production characteristics of an ID. Here Sforzi puts the accent on productive specialisation: that is, the prevalence of just one sector or a cluster of strictly related sub-sectors. The new sub-set may appear disappointingly poor (see Map 1), since it does not contain several well-known industrial areas. The reasons for this lie in the method. If the method imposes on a predetermined set of units (the self-contained labour markets) a double set of conditions on the social and productive structures, the result will be a small final sub-set. But there is a logic to the method. The new IDs include neither the areas of very recent industrialisation which are not yet organised around a leading sector, nor the older industrial areas which are already mature and crystallised in terms of social structure. In addition, the way in which the "elementary units" were formed taking

---

1. For details of the technique used, see Sforzi [1987].

The re-emergence of small enterprises

Map 2: Location of social structures in Italy which are favourable to the emergence of Industrial Districts

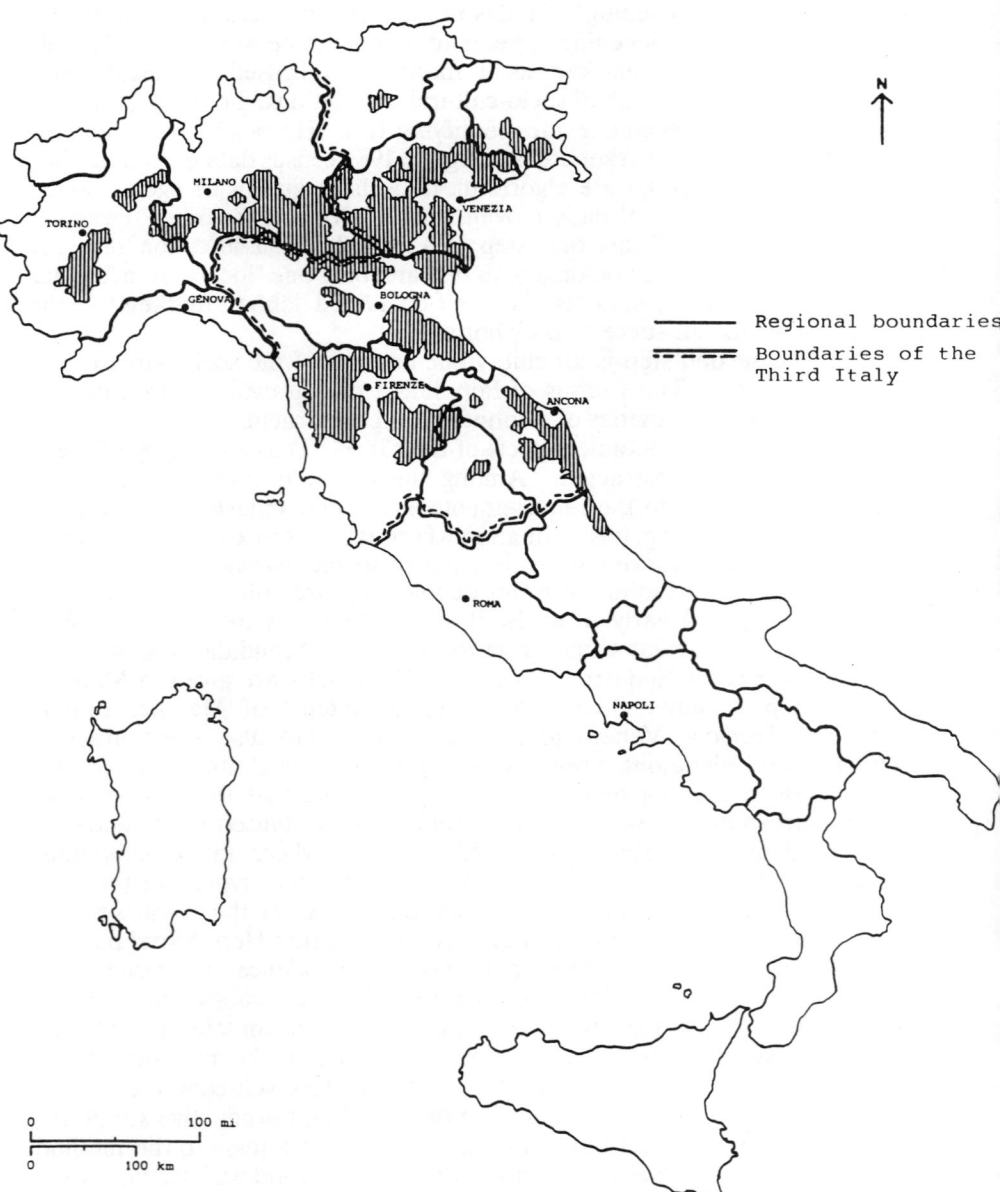

Source: Sforzi, F. "L'identificazione spaziale", in Becattini, G. (ed.): *Mercato e forze locali: Il distretto industriale*, Bologna, Il Mulino, 1987.

together all kinds of commuting movements) undermines the identification of some complex or embryonic industrial districts.

Putting together the result of this attempt at spatially identifying the industrial districts with considerations of a more theoretical character, a general hypothesis may be formulated: the ID can be thought of as a stage in one of the possible paths towards the industrialisation of a country or of a region.

The path of the NEC Italy - which may possibly be replicable - leads from an artisan-agricultural stage to an industrial one, through intermediate stages characterised by high territorial short-range mobility of population, high social mobility of the population, the subdivision of production tasks between firms grouped territorially, and their gradual organisation around a particular sector. But there is a point beyond which the ID as such, with its characteristics of productive flexibility, of bottom-up innovation processes, and of capacity for social integration, starts to change. It then either yields to a mature specialised industrial area, merges into a more complex urban organism (e.g. a conurbation or a metropolitan area), or peters out.

V. The debate: Smallness versus agglomeration

1. The two main options for debate

Several different lines of argument could be pursued to explain the phenomena discussed above. And indeed, several lines have been followed by the scholars who tried to decipher the Italian data, and more generally the empirical evidence of the post-war period. However, this discussion concentrates on two options which, in fact, played the main parts in the Italian controversy over the role played by small firms and the unexpected regional distribution of industrial activities.

The first line of reasoning starts with the "strange" explosion of small firms in recent years. According to some commentators this "strange" result can be explained by a peculiar evolution of final demand, at the level of the world market, and by some technological changes on the side of industrial production. The demand for standardised goods had already reached its limits at the end of the 1960s (at least in the more advanced countries, which comprise the largest part of the world market in consumer durables), so the 1970s were characterised by an explosion of demand for differentiated, even personalised, consumer goods. In this new situation the main advantage of large firms, working on long production series, disappears, and correspondingly the share of the market open to small firms increases. On the production side, technological and other developments take place which allow small firms to increase their utilisation of modern technology without giving up the advantages of their moderate size.

The commentators who stressed these two new developments tended to explain the "strange" growth in NEC regions by the fact that a light industry, in existence there at the beginning of the 1970s, allowed those regions to capitalise on the specific advantages of the new situation. A "neo-artisan" way of production (an alternative to Fordism) which had been considered for many decades, rightly or wrongly, uneconomical and obsolete, started to flourish again in those places where appropriate historical conditions had survived the long-lasting Fordist supremacy [Sabel and Zeitlin, 1985; Sabel and Piore, 1984].

A second line of reasoning orthogonal, so to speak, to the one just outlined, starts from the geo-historical peculiarities of the North-East and Centre Regions. Some commentators noticed that there were important elements common to the NEC regions: e.g. the "core" of them (Tuscany, Marche, Umbria, and to a lesser extent Emilia-Romagna and Veneto) had for centuries been *metayage* regions. The *metayage* system, they said, has an impact on the character of the populations involved that is different from the capitalistic, or other kinds of land tenure systems prevailing elsewhere. The former sharecropper is relatively more apt to become either an autonomous worker developing into a small entrepreneur, or a life-long worker in a small firm, than a dehumanised "hand" in a large factory. This peculiar reservoir of workers and initiative represented, for the central regions, the fuel for an industrialisation that, at least at the beginning, had to rely on low wages and poor working conditions.

Another peculiarity, much emphasised by this group of commentators, is the previous existence in most of NEC regions of formal and informal links with foreign markets. The "culture-tourism-external trade" complex, already well established at the end of the 1960s for these regions and less complete or non-existent for other underdeveloped Italian regions, can explain the rapid build-up of trade connections between their systems of small firms and the foreign, distant, markets for the goods of the district.

In a sense, those commentators put the accent more on the endogenous cultural resources of a population and an area than on technological or demand conditions. They seemed to think that this sort of industrialisation was to be considered more as the outcome of conducive localised phenomena, based on historical heritages, than a temporary switch to a way of production induced by some changes in the external conditions of demand or of technology.

If we take the first view, the accent is on the size of the firms, while the second emphasises the territorial network. In this second case, a qualification is in order. If we take account of the fact that each small firm which belongs to an industrial district operates in one or just a few phases of the production process, it follows that such units of production are different from the small manufacturing firms which operate elsewhere. We are dealing in fact with: (a) units which sell to more than one buyer; (b) units which operate mostly in intermediate and final markets; (c) firms which in whole or in part turn to the outside (buyers, *impannatori* and similar figures) for such crucial functions as product design; (d) units which are "components", in essence, of a system and would lose much of their competitiveness if they were taken out of that system. What holds this population of firms together is then a network of economies which are external to the individual firm, but internal to the district. This network lives on the dynamic interaction between an increasing division of labour and a progressive opening up of new markets for the district as a whole [Bellandi, 1986].

As a consequence of these considerations the data concerning small firms included in this report should be subdivided according to whether or not they refer to small firms grouped in a district. The hypothesis which derives from the interpretation offered here is that the performance of small firms grouped in a district should be, *ceteris paribus*, better than the average of the firms of the same size bracket.

2. Control of the workforce

There is a central line of reasoning that constitutes the "core" of many works on the issues considered in this study. It can be summarised as follows. Around 1963 the Italian economy started to experience bottlenecks due to scarcity (local and/or sectoral) of labour. The economic situation, together with political and cultural factors originating outside Italy, gave more and more power to the workers' unions and to the left-wing parties. This shifting of the balance of social forces produced an increase in wages (which some said was out of proportion with the increase in productivity) and, what matters most, a new climate in the factories wherein the rights attached to property were reduced in favour of a more civilised - and relaxed - way of working.

These two factors - higher wages and a new industrial climate - were perceived by employers as attacks not only on profits but also on property rights. This started a reaction, the main target of which was the strength of the unions and the unity of the working class. Among the several weapons used by the employers to achieve these aims was a widespread fragmentation of the industrial structure and, consequently, of the industrial workforce. The disintegration of some of the industrial processes (textile, furniture, boots and shoes, etc.) examined in this paper was accordingly considered a side-effect of this "great design" of the industrialists, which was aimed at regaining full control over their firms and factories [Graziani, 1976]. In the end they succeeded, as is shown clearly by the recent divisions among the unions, by the general decline of the same unions and by the erosion of real wages in the past five years.

This explanation is now common wisdom in Italy and nobody rejects it entirely. It certainly contains more than an element of truth, but it would be an oversimplification to use it to explain a whole host of different phenomena. Some commentators, in fact, stressed the element of genuine entrepreneurship incorporated into the growth of many new firms. Even if, and when, these projects have been "tutored" by major firms, they cannot be reduced to the mechanical result of a decision taken at a higher level. The growth of a population of small firms seems to be a manifestation of an outburst of entrepreneurship no less than the result of some industrial asperities felt at the level of the major enterprises [Brusco, 1986].

These are the two main positions on the problem and they are less divided by statistical findings than by theoretical paradigms: one takes for granted that the basic aim of private enterprise is to guarantee the social reproduction of the capitalistic mode of production and accumulation, and the other places a heavy accent on human entrepreneurship as the major source of change.

3. From agglomeration economies to "industrial districts"

One lateral issue to the argument over small firms that came to occupy an ever more central position in the Italian debate is the "regional" one. In general terms it scales up the argument from the single firm to the territorial system of firms. The problem is no longer the comparison of a small firm, or several small firms, with a large firm producing the same products. Now the focus is on a "system" of small firms operating together to produce a full range of varieties of a certain basic commodity.

Traditional economic theory makes use of agglomeration economies in order to explain why and when the territorial grouping of firms can reduce their individual production costs. But this common wisdom of economists and geographers alike remains unfruitful from the viewpoint considered here until it is applied simply to a generic population of "close firms". The main points are not their smallness as an instrument of production or their territorial proximity as such, but rather their smallness as a link with the everyday life of a certain population and the specific pattern of the localised division of labour.

On one side the small firms and the intermediaries (buying offices and *impannatori*) are a kind of converter of potentialities embodied in the culture of a community into goods and services that can be sold in the market. The smallness of the firms in a district creates a particular atmosphere inside the individual firm and among the firms. Relationships between members of the small firm do not reach the degree of abstractness that is required by the neoclassical concepts of market and firm. For instance, they remain personalised enough to discourage the spread of "opportunistic behaviour" in the district and in the firms. Social sanctions reinforce and occasionally replace purely economic sanctions against opportunism. This does not mean that there is no competition in the district. On the contrary there is a great deal of it, but competition and co-operation (between participants) are intimately intermingled [Dei Ottati, 1987].

With the industrial district the "small-large" argument is somewhat by-passed, because, if taken together, the small firms of a district act as a large producing entity enjoying analogous economies of scale. Its peculiar strength (and weakness) lies in the fact that it is not the result of a man-made plan, with the rigidities that any abstract plan implies, but the result of a continuous process of adaptation of individual aims and means.

With the introduction of this theme the Italian debate became more complex, shifting from industrial economics to somewhere at the intersection among industrial, regional, labour and development economics. But it would perhaps be more accurate to say that it shifted to a meeting ground between economics and the other social sciences.

4. The problem of the "size of a firm"

The "final" stage of the Italian debate was reached with two lines of reasoning, both aiming to undermine the concept of "firm size". The first line of reasoning is the direct result of the importation into Italy of the literature on transaction costs. When the activity of the firm is seen as a continuous series of transactions, each one of which poses the problem of whether to produce or to buy outside, the frontier between what is internal and what is external to the firm becomes very hazy and unstable. So much so that it becomes legitimate to ask whether it makes sense to speak of the firm as something distinct from (and opposed to) the market in which it is immersed. This literature does not stretch the idea to its limit, but its thrust is - to use a well-known metaphor [Coase, 1937] - towards the melting of the piece of butter into the surrounding milk.

Some scholars say that this line of reasoning, although an improvement on the older approach, is a blind alley without much constructive value. Instead, they take a different approach, based on the idea that the traditional emphasis on the firm's size was justified by the conditions prevailing up to 15 years ago. Those conditions were created by a demand for mass, standardised goods, with the possibility of dominating the well-defined markets for those goods by means of an enlargement of the space of control of a single central managerial entity, and by the differential research and development capabilities possessed by the larger organisations over the smaller ones.

The current situation is very different. The demand for many final goods is now much more diversified and even personalised, so the advantages of long production runs are mainly gone. On the other hand, the character of technological progress has radically changed in recent years. The dynamic source of technological improvement is no longer R & D, but the scientific research carried on outside the firms, in the universities and other public institutions. Every firm, small or large, is small if compared with the new tasks. Consequently, the decisive factor becomes the ability of each firm to "fish" innovations from the common scientific "pond". From this point of view a relatively small, well-organised firm can be the right size for this kind of fishing activity, while a big concern may be less well suited to it [Vaccà, 1986].

In addition to these factors it is important to point out the tendencies always at work in the bigger organisations, whether public or private, towards bureaucratisation. Territorial grouping of firms and decentralisation of decision-making in the big firms have come to be considered as two different manifestations of one tendency.

All things considered, this group of industrial economists says there is more room than ever for modern, small or medium-sized firms, provided they find some form of co-operation for the mutual exchange of information and the sharing of marketing expenses among themselves. Chains or networks of small or medium-sized firms, spread possibly over the entire world market, and operating on a set of related markets (i.e. selling related goods) are, they think, the future winners of the race. This leaves to the older multinationals - expressions of the traditional way to conquer mass markets - the role of dinosaurs on the way to extinction.

5. Other problems

A related problem is that of exploitation and self-exploitation of workers and small entrepreneurs. There has been a lot of discussion about this, particularly in the 1970s, when Marxist ideas were prominent in the scientific arena and in common discourse alike.

The statistical evidence produced is, as usual, not decisive. What has been proved beyond any doubt is: (a) the rate of wages per hour worked is lower in small firms than in large ones in the same sectors; (b) the length of the working day is longer in small firms than in large ones; (c) the working conditions (mainly health) are worse in small firms than in large ones; (d) the level of unionisation is lower in small firms than in large ones. As far as human relations within the firm are concerned, no clear conclusion is apparent. On the one hand, the closer relationships between managers and workers can foster some subtle forms of exploitation. But on the other hand, the fact that both share the same working conditions and, more frequently than not, even the same (or similar) living conditions, makes for a better understanding and less strife.

All in all, one could infer that there is more exploitation in small firms than in large firms, and several commentators come to that conclusion. But others observed that working conditions are only a part of living conditions, and the overall living conditions in an industrial district, for instance, are more frequently as good as, if not better than, those in many highly industrialised areas. This would not mean much if the working conditions were independent of the living conditions. But if the whole system is considered as a dynamic process, it may be concluded that an industrial district made up of small firms is the result of a mutual adaptation between the contrasting requirements of the accumulation process, which is of necessity competitive, and of a population that wishes to preserve its values and to live in its homeland. Following this line of reasoning, many statistical findings lose their power. Working conditions and the length of the working day have to be judged in the context of a 24-hour day or 365-day year time span, taking into account, too, the living conditions (educational facilities, entertainment, social relationships and so on) of the other members of the worker's family.

The level of wages is a crucial point because it determines the income constraint. But for a member of a non-nuclear family, living in the "urbanised countryside" with concrete possibilities for several ways of supplementing his wage (several allowances of different kinds, social help for children and the elderly, some agricultural products from the cultivation of a remnant piece of land, and so on), the difference between the rate of wages in a small firm and that of a large firm becomes, in the end, much less relevant. There is, however, the additional problem of the very low earnings coming from moonlighting activities and part-time jobs that form the basis of this system. This is a real problem, but the situations in which moonlighting activities and part-time jobs go together with heavy and chronic unemployment must be distinguished from those in which they provide cash for youngsters or extra earnings for a family which is already relatively well-off. In these latter cases it can safely be assumed that there has been a fine marginal adaptation between means and ends, and it would be preposterous to impose our academic judgement upon the judgement of the actors involved. There are several signs that these last situations arise rather frequently in the industrial districts of NEC. A symptom of this is the high rate of savings by families. A second symptom is the strange fact that in the NEC the total number of strikes corresponds, more or less, to that which prevails in other parts of the country, but they are *shorter*. This very peculiar behaviour suggests a kind of mixed feelings towards strikes: they have a political meaning and an economic effect. To strike means to show solidarity with fellow workers all over the country, but to prolong the strike means to specifically damage the firm where one works. The solution seems to be shorter strikes.

Finally, there is the problem of self-exploitation of small entrepreneurs. There are many sides to this problem, and they will not all be considered here. In very general terms, the idea of self-exploitation is a puzzling one. It is based, in the final analysis, on the supposition that the small entrepreneurs are hidden dependent workers. They - like the hawthorn seedlings that believe they are acorns in Robertson's famous metaphor [Robertson, 1927] - live under a delusion, and in the end all their efforts will be harvested by big business. So they are extracting from their human creativity something that, in due time, will push them back to their true position as wage-earners. This construction is derived from the same simplistic approach which viewed share-croppers as imperfect day labourers. As in that case, the approach hinders an understanding of the specific evolution under consideration.

VI. Conclusions

The overall meaning of this chapter lies in demonstrating that the substantial development of small industrial firms which has occurred in Italy during the last 15 years, is not the outcome of a superiority of the small size as such, not even with regard to those goods which have characterised the recent successes of Italian export. What determined the expansion of the Italian population of small firms was the co-operation of two factors: (a) a world-wide tendency towards the decentralisation and disintegration of the firm, which was especially strong in Italy due to special circumstances in the labour market; (b) an explosion of small entrepreneurship, which was fostered by historical cultural inheritance, by a very stable local political environment that was not hostile to an industrialsation of "lowly" origin, by a polycentric urban structure, and last but not least, by a habit of contacts and exchanges with foreign countries.

One part of this complex and unexpected transformation is most striking, namely the fact that the formation of the territorial systems of small firms has not involved - other than marginally - the area of the earliest industrialisation and has not touched - despite all efforts of public intervention - the regions of the South and the islands. Explanations for this resistance to the rise of new industrial districts are far from complete. However, the research carried out so far seems to point to the role of the social, political and cultural environment. In the North, the social and political milieu was, at the beginning of the period, characterised by the classical direct confrontation between large industrial firms and their masses of employees. With such a climate there was no room for the self-help ideology which at one and the same time with the strengthening of the "local identities", is needed for the development of industrial districts.

The conditions for a strengthening of "local identities" would indeed have existed - theoretically speaking - in the South; yet the system of values and institutions which had been formed in the course of the centuries, developed after the war along lines which were seemingly incompatible with the rise of industrial districts. A recent study of the interplay between Mafia activities and economic development in southern Italy has concluded that the growth of family business based on illegal economic activities and on close relations with local government officers is a strong obstacle to the development of entrepreneurial attitudes on the market and to the genesis of a large set of small and medium-sized enterprises in the industrial sector [Catanzaro, 1988; Trigilia, 1988].

One feature of the industrial district which is linked with those previously mentioned but which has not been extensively studied is the network of specialised connections with foreign markets. The hints on the role of buyers and *impannatori* that have been offered here are just the starting point of an inquiry, the relevance of which for the future of the districts cannot be over-emphasised [IRPET, 1980; Becattini, 1986].

From the point of view of an evolution of ideas on socio-economic development, the Italian debate may have a relevance which goes beyond the Italian scene. On the one hand, very schematic and aggregate interpretations (e.g. the dualistic ones) of the Italian experience have been abandoned in favour of interpretations which are more complex and disaggregated (e.g the multiregionality of the Italian development). On the other hand the hegemony of interpretations, *à la Kuznets*, maintaining that essentially only one path towards industrialisation existed, has been challenged. One cannot deny that this approach is still rather popular with Italian economists, yet some greater open-mindedness now exists towards an effort to discover genuinely novel elements in the evidence, statistical or otherwise.

Bibliography

Bagnasco, A. 1988. *La costruzione sociale del mercato*, Bologna, Il Mulino.

Bagnasco, A.; Trigilia, C. (eds.). 1984. *Società e politica nelle aree di piccola impresa. Il caso di Bassano*, Venezia, Arsenale.

---. 1985. *Società e politica nelle aree di piccola impresa. Il caso della Valdelsa*, Milano, Angeli and IRPET.

Becattini, G., 1986. "Riflessioni sullo sviluppo economico della Toscana in Questo dopoguerra", in: Mori, G. (ed.) *Storia d'Italia. Le regioni dall'Unità ad oggi. La Toscana*, Turin, Einaudi.

Becattini, G.; Bianchi, G. 1982. "Sulla multiregionalità dello sviluppo economico italiano" in *Note Economiche*, No. 5-6.

Bellandi, M. 1986. "The Marshallian industrial district", in *Dipartimento di Scienze Economiche, Collana Studi e discussioni*. No. 42, Florence.

Birch, A. 1979. *The job generation process*, Final Report to the Economic Development Administration, Cambridge, MIT Program on Neighborhood and Regional Change (mimeo).

Borzaga, C. 1985. "Il ruolo della piccola impresa nelle regioni italiane", in Innocenti, R. (ed.): *Piccola città e piccola impresa*, Milan, Angeli.

Bruni, L. 1986. "Documentazione. Dinamica strutturale dell'industria italiana nel trentennio 1951-81", in *L'Industria*, April-June.

Brusco, S. 1986. "Small firms and industrial districts: The experience of Italy", in *Economia Internazionale*, No.2-3-4.

Carnazza, P.; Carone, G. 1987. "Piccole imprese ed esportazioni nell'economia italiana" in *Rivista di Politica Economica*, November.

Catanzaro, R. 1988. "Il governo violento del mercato. Mafia, imprese e sistema politico", in *Stato e Mercato*, No. 23.

Coase, R.H. 1937. "The nature of the firm", in *Economica*, No. 4.

Contini, B.; Revelli, R. 1986. "Natalità e mortalità delle imprese italiane: Risultati preliminari e nuove prospettive di ricerca", in *L'Industria*, April-June.

D'Angelillo, M.; Paggi, L. 1986. *I comunisti italiani e il riformismo*, Turin, Einaudi.

Dei Ottati, G. 1987. "Il mercato comunitario" in Becattini, G.: *Mercato e forze locali. Il distretto industriale*, Bologna, Il Mulino.

Fuà, G.; Zacchia, C. 1983. *Industrializzazione senza fratture*, Bologna, Il Mulino.

Graziani, A. (ed.). 1976. *Crisi e ristrutturazione nell'economia italiana*, Turin, Einaudi.

IRPET. 1975. *Lo sviluppo economico della Toscana, con particolare riguardo all'industrializzazione leggera* (ed. Becattini, G.), Florence, Guaraldi.

---. 1980. *Il buyer in Toscana. Contributo allo studio dell'intermediazione mercantile*, Florence.

Mazzoni, R. 1988. "Le tendenze localizzative delle attività terziarie nel periodo 1951-81", in *L'Industria*, January-March.

Momigliano, F.; Siniscalco, D. 1982. "Note in tema di terziarizzazione e deindustrializzazione", in *Moneta e Credito*, No. 138.

Organisation for Economic Co-operation and Development (OECD). 1986. *Employment Outlook*, Paris.

Paci, M. (ed.), 1980. *Famigilia e mercato del lavoro in un'economia periferica*, Milan, Angeli.

Robertson, D.H. 1927. "The Colwyn Committee, the income tax, and the price level", in *Economic Journal*, December.

Sabel C.; Piore, M.J. 1984. *The second industrial divide*, New York, Basic Books.

Sabel, C.; Zeitlin, J. 1985. "Historical alternatives to mass production: Politics, markets and technology in nineteenth-century industrialisation", in *Past and Present*, No. 108.

Sforzi, F. 1987. "L'Identificazione spaziale", in Becattini, G. (ed.): *Mercato e forze locali. Il distretto industriale*, Bologna, Il Mulino.

Trigilia, C. 1986. *Grandi partiti e piccole imprese*, Bologna, Il Mulino.

---. 1988. "Le condizioni non economiche dello sviluppo:problemi di ricerca sul Mezzogiorno di oggi", in *Meridiana*, January.

Vaccà, S. 1986. "Internazionalizzazione delle imprese. Passaggio obbligato per lo sviluppo tecnologico o veicolo di dipendenza?" in *Economia e politica industriale*, No. 49.

Valli, V. 1986. *Politica economica. Il modelli, gli strumenti, l'economia italiana*, Rome, Nuova Italia Scientifica.

VV.AA: 1970. *La terza Italia*. Atti del Convegno economico per un indirizzo di sviluppo dell'Italia centrale nel quadro della politica nazionale, Florence.

5 Japan

Kazutoshi Koshiro

I. Introduction

Before commencing a more formal description and analysis of the development of small enterprises in Japan, it would be helpful to provide readers with two sets of background information relating to changes in Japan's labour market conditions after the Second World War. The first set deals with major changes in the labour market up to 1960, while the second covers more recent developments.

After the Second World War, Japan suffered from a large excess supply of labour due to: (a) a net inflow of 5 million immigrants and disbanded forces returning from overseas; (b) 3.6 million demobilised members of the domestic armed forces; and (c) 1.6 million demobilised war production workers. Altogether these three groups constituted a surplus workforce of roughly 10 million people [Uemura, 1964, pp. 64-67]. On the other hand, because of war devastation and an extremely deficient supply of raw materials [Kosai, 1981, pp. 40-46], Japan was unable to provide enough job opportunities for the excess labour force, most of whom found temporary employment on farms[1] and in small, urban-based businesses. This excess supply of labour continued until at least the middle of the 1950s, when economic growth accelerated and demand for labour began to increase.

Reflecting such a labour market situation, the Economic White Paper of 1957 characterised the Japanese economy as being a "dual economy" which depended heavily upon employment in small businesses:

> The decreasing proportion of the farming population does not necessarily mean that the dual structure of our country has been mitigated, because the proportion of persons employed by large firms decreased whereas those employed by small firms increased compared with the pre-war days. That is to say, the lower parts of employment have just shifted from the agrarian sector to small businesses, the latter still remaining as the pre-modern sector [Keizai Kikaku Cho (Economic Planning Agency), 1957, p. 39].

Despite a continuing obsession with the idea of a dual economy, some economists also recognised and stressed the emergence since the 1960s of highly prosperous and independent middle-sized firms [Nakamura, 1964; Kiyonari, 1967]. They further proceeded to emphasise the more recent development since the 1970s of "venture businesses" which succeeded in

---

1. In 1947, 51 per cent of employment was in agriculture and forestry, but the percentage decreased to 36 per cent in 1955, 22 per cent in 1965, 11.6 per cent in 1975, and 8.9 per cent in 1984. (For 1947, *Census of Population*; for others, Prime Minister's Office, *Labour Force Survey*).

developing new products and extending their own markets through the intensive use of new technology and R & D activities [Kiyonari et al., 1972].

Side by side with these new views concerning small businesses, government economists were emphasising the necessity of continuous economic growth in order to overcome the dual economic structure. Beginning in 1963, the Medium- and Small-sized Enterprises (SMEs) Agency of the Ministry of International Trade and Industry began to publish annual reports on medium-sized and small firms which emphasised the modernisation and improvement of productivity taking place within these underdeveloped firms.

On the other hand, the majority of scholars who specialised in this field continued to stress the oppression and exploitation of small businesses by large "monopolistic capitalists", who take advantage of low wages and the inferior bargaining position of subcontractors. Most of these studies were strongly influenced by Marxist thought, although a few of them demonstrated empirical objectivity and proficiency in their research [Ikeda, 1972, 1982; M. Watanabe, 1972; Y. Watanabe, 1982].

II. Volume, structure and characteristics of the small enterprise sector

1. The definition of small and medium-sized enterprises

The Basic Law for Small and Medium-Sized Enterprises of 1963 first officially defined small and medium-sized enterprises (SMEs) as follows: "in manufacturing, those firms with fewer than 300 employees and capitalisation less than 50 million yen; but in wholesale and retail trade and services, those with fewer than 50 employees and capitalisation less than 10 million yen".

These definitions were revised by an amendment of the law in 1973 which remains in effect today. It states: "In manufacturing, those firms employing fewer than 300 persons and capitalised with less than 100 million yen; in the wholesale trade, those employing fewer than 100 persons and capitalised with less than 30 million yen; in the retail trade and service industry, those employing fewer than 50 persons and capitalised with less than 10 million yen". This definition is applied to all of the official statistics and regulations relating to SMEs.

In view of this detailed official definition of SMEs, the usual research practice is to define SMEs in terms of employment using 300 employees as the upper limit of classification. Unfortunately, the coverage is not always complete because many official statistics often exclude very small firms below 30 employees (VSFs) or extremely small firms below five persons (EXSFs).

Japan 175

2. Volume and employment share of the small firm sector

A. *Enterprises*

The latest available Labour Force Survey of 1986 shows that 7.8 per cent of the total (43,500,000) employees in non-agricultural industries were employed in EXSFs, 33.5 per cent in VSFs and 49.4 per cent in enterprises employing fewer than 100 persons (Table 1). Unfortunately, this survey does not include a classification of enterprises employing up to 300 persons. However, it is possible to suggest that a majority (64.9 per cent) of workers is still employed in the small and medium-sized firm sector employing fewer than 500 persons.

Table 1: Employment status of the labour force in 1986 (10 000s)

Total population 15 years and over	**9,587** (1)	
Labour force	**6 020**	
Employed persons	5 853	
Agriculture and forestry	450	
Non-agricultural industries	5 403 (2)	
Self-employed workers	699	
Family workers	338	
Employees	4 350	(100)
Size of enterprise		
1-4 persons	341	(7.8)
5-29 persons	1 116	(25.7)
30 - 99 persons	687	(15.8)
100 - 499 persons	674	(15.5)
500 - 999 persons	202	(4.6)
1 000 and over	817	(18.8)
Government	500	(11.5)
Unclassifiable	13	(0.3)
Unemployed	**167**	
Not in labour force	**3 513**	

Notes: (1) Including the unclassifiable (54).
(2) Including the unclassifiable (16).
Source: Statistics Bureau, Management and Co-ordination Agency: *Annual report on the labor force survey* [1986], p. 100.

Table 2 shows the employment of working persons (including self-employed and family workers) by size of enterprise and by industry for 1982, the year of the latest available Employment Status Survey.[2] A majority (51.4 per cent) of the total working population was employed by VSFs, whereas the proportion employed in non-agricultural industries was 46.8 per cent. The corresponding percentages for manufacturing, the wholesale and retail trades, and services were 39.6, 65.5, and 45.8 per cent, respectively.

On the other hand, the employment share of SMEs defined in accordance with the comprehensive official classification noted above shows that such firms account for 67.5 per cent of employment in manufacturing, 76.3 per cent of employment in the wholesale and retail trade, and 50.7 per cent in services. If government employees are excluded from the service sector statistics, 65.0 per cent of total private service workers were in SMEs. Altogether, 25,108,000 persons out of total 47,387,000 persons in the non-agricultural industries excluding government employees, or 53.0 per cent of the total, were employed in SMEs in 1982.[3]

B. Establishments

Up to 1981 the government undertook a census of establishments every three years, but due to financial considerations the interval has been extended to five years. The latest Census of Establishments for 1986 is currently being processed so that the aggregate figures from this source are not yet available. Therefore, the distribution of employment by size of establishment shown in Table 3 is for the year 1981. The majority (53.7 per cent) of all employees were employed by very small establishments (VSEs) engaging fewer than 30 persons. However, the situation differs significantly across industries, with the highest concentration of VSEs being observed in the catering industry (89.7 per cent), followed by real estate (83.9 per cent), the retail trade (79.2 per cent), the wholesale trade (62.7 per cent), the construction industry (62.6 per cent) and the service sector (54.2 per cent). On the other hand, the lowest concentration of employment in VSEs is observed in the public service (12.4 per cent), public utilities (21.0) per cent, the transport and communications industry (27.4 per cent), finance (35.1 per cent), manufacturing (38.0 per cent) and mining (44.4 per cent).

---

2. The source for this table is the Employment Status Survey (ESS) which has usually been undertaken every three years since 1956 and is based on the *usual* status of employment on a specific date, whereas the Labour Force Survey is undertaken every month based on the *current* status of employment in the survey week. The "current status" means the kind of gainful work he(she) was *actually* engaged in during the survey week, irrespective of his(her) *ordinary* status of employment in other weeks. On the other hand, the *usual* status refers to the kind of gainful work he(she) is *ordinarily* engaged in on the survey date (1 October). For example, students or wives who happened to be engaged in gainful work for more than one hour during the survey week are classified as "employed" by the LFS although their *usual* status is technically "outside labour force".

3. These figures are based solely on the classification standard defined in terms of the amount of capital. Official employment statistics combining these two standards are not available.

Table 2: Working persons by size of enterprise (number of persons engaged) by industry in 1982 (thousand persons)

Size of enterprise	Total	Agriculture and forestry	Non-agricultural industries Total	Manufacturing (1)	Wholesale and retail trade (2)	Services (3)
Total	57 888 (100.0)	5 264	52 506 (100.0)	14 255 (100.0)	12 886 (100.0)	11 193 (100.0)
1-4 persons	17 719 (30.6)	4 930	12 778 (24.3)	2 521 (17.7)	4 990 (38.7)	2 839 (25.4)
5-29 persons	12 027 (20.8)	200	11 805 (22.5)	3 117 (21.9)	3 454 (26.8)	2 283 (20.4)
30-49 persons	2 838 (4.9)	17	2 814 (5.4)	949 (6.7)	642 (5.0)	545 (4.9)
50-99 persons	3 619 (6.3)	16	3 597 (6.9)	1 293 (9.1)	742 (5.8)	781 (7.0)
100-299 persons	4 744 (8.2)	16	4 721 (9.0)	1 733 (12.1)	1 000 (7.8)	1 040 (9.3)
300-499 persons	1 815 (3.1)	4	1 809 (3.4)	696 (4.9)	418 (3.2)	324 (2.9)
500-999 persons	1 961 (3.4)	3	1 954 (3.7)	777 (5.4)	454 (3.5)	292 (2.6)
1000 and over	7 906 (13.7)	3	7 893 (15.0)	3 158 (22.2)	1 142 (8.9)	615 (5.5)
Government	5 197 (9.0)	75	5 119 (9.7)	10 (0.0)	41 (0.3)	2 470 (22.0)
Not reported	61 (0.1)	1	16 (0.0)	2 (0.0)	3 (0.0)	4 (0.0)

Notes: (1) and (3) The line in the table indicates the upper limit of SMEs in terms of employment.
(2) The dotted line in the table indicates the upper limit of SMEs in terms of employment in the wholesale trade. Because of simultaneous inclusion of retail trade, the size classification here is not precise.

Source: Statistics Bureau, Prime Minister's Office: 1982 Employment status survey, whole Japan, 1984, p. 48.

Table 3: Number and distribution of employed persons by industry and by size of establishment, 1981

Industry	Total persons engaged (000s)	Total persons	1-4 persons	5-9 persons	10-29 persons	30-49 persons	50-99 persons	100-299 and over	300
Total non-agricultural	51 237	100.0	18.6	13.7	21.4	9.7	11.0	12.2	13.4
Mining	129	100.0	4.0	9.3	31.1	11.7	9.9	9.9	24.0
Construction	4 969	100.0	13.2	17.9	31.5	11.7	11.5	9.3	4.9
Manufacturing	12 896	100.0	8.5	10.1	19.4	9.5	11.6	15.1	25.9
Wholesale trade	4 350	100.0	12.7	19.0	30.7	11.5	11.6	9.2	5.3
Retail trade	7 396	100.0	42.5	19.1	17.6	6.1	5.7	5.3	3.7
Catering	3 123	100.0	45.9	24.4	19.4	5.1	3.3	1.6	0.3
Finance	1 711	100.0	4.3	4.4	26.4	18.5	17.5	13.9	14.9
Real estate	629	100.0	54.1	16.7	13.1	4.1	4.8	4.8	2.4
Transport and communication	3 401	100.0	4.4	4.8	18.2	10.8	15.6	26.5	19.6
Public utilities	322	100.0	2.6	4.3	14.1	8.7	15.7	30.9	23.7
Services	10 548	100.0	19.3	13.3	21.6	11.2	12.9	12.3	9.4
Public service	1 735	100.0	2.3	2.4	7.7	6.2	14.0	24.0	43.4

Source: Prime Minister's Office, Statistics Bureau: *Census of Establishments*, 1981, Vol. 5, pp. 52-65.

Japan

A more detailed analysis of employment (and other aspects) by size of establishment is given by the Census of Manufacturers. According to the 1981 census, the share of employment in VSEs was 35.2 per cent, which was comparable with the Census of Establishments mentioned above. The latest available Census of Manufacturers for 1985 shows that 34.2 per cent of employed persons were working in VSEs (Table 4).

Table 4: Percentage and total number of employed persons in the manufacturing industry by the size of establishments, 1957-1984

Year	Fewer than 30 persons	30 - 99 persons	100 - 299 persons	300 and over	Total number (000s)
1957	38.8	19.8	13.6	27.7	6 604.6
1958	38.3	20.1	13.9	27.7	6 664.3
1959	35.3	20.4	14.7	29.6	7 293.6
1960	34.0	20.4	15.1	30.5	8 169.5
1961	32.8	19.9	15.3	32.0	8 751.0
1962	32.1	20.1	15.7	32.1	8 998.4
1963	33.8	20.2	15.4	30.6	9 727.9
1964	32.8	19.9	15.7	31.5	9 900.8
1965	33.1	20.1	15.6	31.2	9 921.0
1966	34.0	20.0	15.7	30.3	10 291.6
1967	33.5	19.7	15.7	31.2	10 554.1
1968	33.0	19.1	15.9	32.0	10 862.7
1969	33.3	18.9	15.7	32.1	11 412.1
1970	32.7	18.9	15.9	32.5	11 679.7
1971	32.6	19.2	16.1	32.1	11 463.7
1972	34.3	19.3	15.9	30.5	11 783.4
1973	34.1	18.9	16.0	31.0	11 961.1
1974	34.5	19.0	15.7	30.8	11 486.8
1975	36.5	19.1	15.1	29.3	11 296.2
1976	36.8	19.2	15.3	28.7	11 173.8
1977	37.2	19.2	15.3	28.3	10 874.8
1978	38.7	19.3	15.2	26.8	10 890.1
1979	38.9	19.4	15.3	26.5	10 859.8
1980	38.8	19.1	15.5	26.6	10 932.0
1981	35.2	20.4	16.3	28.1	10 567.6
1982	35.0	20.5	16.4	28.1	10 481.0
1983	35.4	20.3	16.5	27.8	10 651.0
1984	34.4	20.4	17.0	28.2	10 733.4
1985	34.2	20.5	17.0	28.3	10 889.9

Note: The classification of the size is regrouped due to discontinuity in some years.
Source: Ministry of International Trade and Industry: *Census of manufacture* for each year.

Table 5: Total number and percentage of employed persons by size of establishment in commerce and industry in 1985

Employed persons	Total	Total commerce Incorporated	Unincorporated	Total	Wholesale trade Incorporated	Unincorporated	Total	Retail trade Incorporated	Unincorporated
Total number (000s)	10 327	7 023	3 304	3 998	3 622	376	6 329	3 401	2 928
Percentage									
1-2 persons	16.3	3.4	43.9	4.1	1.6	28.4	24.1	5.3	45.9
3-4 persons	16.8	10.6	30.0	9.1	6.5	34.0	21.7	14.9	29.5
5-9 persons	18.7	20.8	14.2	18.7	17.9	26.8	18.7	23.9	12.5
10-19 persons	15.0	19.3	5.7	19.7	20.9	8.0	12.0	17.7	5.4
20-29 persons	7.7	10.2	2.3	10.9	11.8	1.6	5.7	8.5	2.4
30-49 persons	8.1	10.9	2.2	11.7	12.8	0.8	5.9	8.9	2.4
50-99 persons	7.5	10.4	1.5	11.6	12.8	0.2	4.9	7.8	1.6
100 and over	9.9	14.4	0.2	14.3	15.7	0.2	7.0	12.9	0.2

Source: Ministry of International Trade and Industry: Census of Commerce, 1985, Vol. 1, pp. 76-77 and 106-107.

Japan

With respect to commerce, the Ministry of International Trade and Industry undertook a Census of Commerce every two years between 1952 and 1976. Subsequently, the Census has been available every three years and a summary of the latest results for 1985 is shown in Table 5. If the official definition of SMEs noted above is extended to establishments, their employment share was 85.7 per cent in wholesale trade and 88.1 per cent in retail trade. The employment share of EXSEs (below five persons) in the unincorporated sector of the retail trade is an enormous 75.4 per cent, accounting for 2.2 million persons. In the unincorporated wholesale trade, EXSEs account for 62.4 per cent of total workers, or 235,000 people. Finally, in commerce as a whole, two-thirds (74.5 per cent) of the total, or 7.7 million persons, were employed in VSEs.

3. Main structural features of the small firm sector

A. Typology of small businesses

Considering only manufacturing, SMEs were responsible for 50.8 per cent of total shipments and 71.8 per cent of total employment in 1984.[4] Kiyonari [1972] classified SMEs into the following four categories:

(a) Incorporated small firms, which amounted to 680,000 or 11 per cent of the total SMEs in 1966;

(b) Quasi-incorporated small firms that present official financial reports to the tax office, which amounted to 960,000 or 16 per cent of the total;

(c) Poor self-employed firms which are running at the subsistence level. Their number is calculated by deducting category (b) from the total number of private firms, and they amounted to 2,190,000 or 26 per cent of the total.

(d) Subsidiary homework not involving independent offices, which amounted to 2,220,000 or 37 per cent of the total.

This classification was used by many scholars (Table 6). By 1981, the share of category (b) had increased to 33 per cent and that of category (a) to 19.6 per cent, whereas category (d) reduced its share to 31.8 per cent and category (c) declined most remarkably to 15.6 per cent.

---

4. See Ministry of International Trade and Industry, *Census of manufacturers*, 1984.

Table 6: Categories of SMEs

Category	1966 (a)	1975	1981 (b)	(b/a) x 100
1. Incorporated SMEs (1)	68 (11.2)	117 (15.9)	166 (19.6)	224.1%
Unincorporated SMEs	537 (88.8)	621 (84.1)	680 (80.4)	
Establishment based (2)	315 (52.1)	376 (50.9)	411 (48.6)	130.5
2. Quasi-incorporated	96 (15.9)	217 (29.4)	279 (33.0)	290.6
3. Subsistence-related	219 (36.1)	159 (21.5)	132 (15.6)	60.3
4. Non-establishment based (3)	222 (36.7)	245 (33.2)	269 (31.8)	121.2
Total	605 (100.0)	738 (100.0)	846 (100.0)	139.8

Note: (1) Capitalised with less than 50 million yen.
(2) "establishment based" is where the owner of the firm works in separate premises from his own home.
(3) "non-establishment based" is where the owner's workplace and home are located in the same premises.

Source: Compiled by Nakamura [1985], p. 25, based on various previous studies.

B. Independence and subordination

Another way of classifying SMEs is the dichotomy between independent and subordinate firms. The dominance of subcontracting has characterised Japan's industrial structure from the very beginning of her industrialisation, for the following reasons: (a) an abundant supply of cheap labour; (b) limited employment opportunities in modern industry, which preferred to borrow labour-saving modern technology from the West; (c) competition among several industrial/financial groups (*Zaibatsu*) which resulted in increased vertical integration in Japanese industry. This tradition has been continued through time by the reorganised industrial groups that emerged after the dissolution of *Zaibatsu* groups in the late 1940s; (d) high concentration of a large population in a limited geographical area, with a particularly high percentage of the population concentrated in metropolitan areas.

It has been a long established view that the intensive use of subcontracting has helped parent companies to save on fixed capital, to mitigate the adverse effects of business cycles, and to exploit cheap labour. As will be discussed later, some commentators argue that such a situation seems to have undergone a dramatic change since the 1960s. The exploitive nature of the subcontracting system has been significantly transformed into a more co-operative relationship on an equal footing, representing a kind of highly developed system of the division of labour [Nakamura, 1985, p. 90].

One of the easiest ways of classifying subcontracting firms is the proportion of subcontracted sales in total shipments. If the proportion exceeds 80 per cent, then those firms are classified as "totally subcontracted firms". Table 7 shows that 65.5 per cent of the total number of firms surveyed by the Agency of Small- and Medium-sized Firms in 1981 were subcontract firms, and 54.0 per cent were "totally subcontracted firms". (In manufacturing, the proportion of subcontract firms increased from 60.7 per cent in 1976 to 65.5 per cent by 1981.) The proportion of subcontract firms was higher than average in the textile industry and various machinery industries.[5]

Table 7: Percentage composition of subcontracted SMEs (1) in 1981

Industry	Total number of firms in the population	of which: Subcontracted	Totally subcontracted	Partly subcontracted	Independent
Manufacturing	710,476	65.5	54.0	11.5	34.5
Textile	98,474	84.9	80.0	4.9	15.1
General machinery	62,304	84.2	70.7	13.5	15.8
Electric appliance and machinery	31,959	85.3	75.6	9.7	14.7
Transportation equipment	21 428	87.7	78.7	9.0	12.3
Precision instrument and machinery	12,073	80.9	71.4	9.5	19.1

Note: (1) Totally subcontracted firms mean those firms whose amount of sales depends heavily upon a single customer (80-100 per cent).
Source: Nakamura [1985], p. 92, based on the Agency of SMEs: *The sixth basic report on the conditions of industry*, 31 December 1981.

---

5. A graphic example of the extensive use of suppliers by a major automobile company is given in Koshiro [1983a].

C. *Firms of medium standing and "venture businesses"*

Some researchers emphasised the development of profitable firms of medium standing in the 1960s [Nakamura, 1964; Kiyonari, 1967]. Nakamura defined the "firms of medium standing" as those capitalised with 50 million-1 billion yen, exclusive of subsidiaries of large companies. He estimated that about 10,000 companies could be classified under this category, and that these companies comprised about 20 per cent of total corporate profit. He also estimated that about 225 out of a total 1,409 companies whose stocks are listed in stock exchanges originated from SMEs, the best examples of which are Sony, Honda, Tokyo Kogyo (Matsuda) and Daiei [Nakamura, 1964, pp. 30-31].

According to Nakamura, the basic characteristics of "medium standing" are as follows: (a) independence - subsidiaries are excluded from this definition; (b) capital is raised beyond the limit available from owners. The best examples are those companies whose stocks are listed in the Second Class Stock Exchange Market; (c) despite outside capital, owners or their families may still maintain a strong influence on the management of the company. However, the separation of management from ownership is a prerequisite; (d) the firms serve their own markets, have self-developed products or a unique technology; (e) high profitability; and (f) high wages comparable to large companies [Ibid., pp. 35-36]. Nakamura estimates that the firms of medium standing make up 1.5 per cent of the total number of companies, 16.6 per cent of total corporate capital, and 19.3 per cent of total corporate profit [Ibid., p. 37].

In addition to medium standing firms, a group of new small businesses called "venture businesses" has emerged during the past two decades. Most of them are smaller than the medium standing firms, but have similar characteristics; in particular, they have their own products or technology based on intensive R & D activities and have innovative management. They specialise in certain areas of new technology and maintain profitability. The Agency of Small- and Medium-sized Firms selected and surveyed about 1,500 venture businesses. Its major findings were as follows: most venture businesses are capitalised with 10-30 million yen, and the proportion of large firms with capitalisation in excess of 100 million yen is less than a fifth of the total. Almost nine out of ten venture businesses employ fewer than 300 persons. The majority of them have sales of less than 1 billion yen a year. The profit rate in terms of sales for the most successful one-fifth of these businesses was more than 10 per cent. They suffer from a shortage of engineers, research staff members, supervisors, salesmen, and skilled workers [Agency of SMEs, 1984a].

Koshiro [1986] undertook a questionnaire survey of some 1,800 "venture business" firms and 1,000 ordinary SMEs in 1985, and estimated that about 257,000 workers were employed by these venture business firms. By using a simple quantitative analysis of the relationship between the rate of sales growth (S) and the rate of employment growth (L), based upon the Verdoon Law, he found that the venture business firms (VBFs) have stronger demand for labour than ordinary SMEs in the sense that VBFs absorb more labour than ordinary SMEs at the same growth rate of sales and the actual growth rate of sales is much higher in VBFs than in SMEs. Therefore, if the growth rate of sales is 10 per cent, VBFs employment grows at the rate of 9.7 per cent, while that of ordinary SMEs grows at only 4.3 per cent. Koshiro also surveyed 648 workers in 28 VBFs, and found that about six out of ten workers employed by VBFs changed jobs and came to the VBFs after quitting a job elsewhere. Furthermore, about three-quarters of these job changers were previously employed in SMEs. The main reason for their quitting previous jobs was dissatisfaction with wages and other conditions of work. On the other hand, they were mostly satisfied with the conditions of employment at their present firms and did not want to quit their present jobs in the near future. The average annual separation rate among these VBFs was only 5.8 per cent and the absentee rate was minimal.[6]

D. Traditional local small businesses specialised in particular products

There are many localised areas where large numbers of small businesses specialise in a particular kind of product. According to a survey by the Agency of SMEs, there were 427 such areas in 1980. To cite just a few famous examples, the metal industry in the city of Tsubame, Niigata, consisting of 280 small firms; 2,899 bag producers in the city of Toyooka, Hyogo; footwear in Shizuoka; kimono-belt weaving in Nishijin, Kyoto; foundries in Kawaguchi, Saitama; and ceramics in Mashiko, Tochigi, etc. According to another survey by the Agency of SMEs in 1978, there were 334 specialised local industrial areas comprising 75,839 firms, employing about 891,000 persons and with sales totalling 7.8 trillion yen. This was equivalent to 9.6 per cent of total production by SMEs [Nakamura, 1985, p. 115].

Many of these traditional local small businesses have been suffering from falling demand, increasing labour costs, labour shortages, and competition from less developed countries. However, new technology is penetrating this area as well. For example, computer graphics and a direct jacquard weaving system with electronic punching have been introduced by some innovative small firms in Nishijin. Similar innovations can also be observed in new wood lathes for lacquer products in Kawazura, Akita, and Aizu-Wakamatsu, Fukushima, and finally, a painting robot was introduced in mosaic wooden food container production in Hakone, Kanagawa [Koshiro, 1985a, 1985b].

E. Employment and work in small firms

a. The institutional setting: terms of employment and working conditions

(i) the Labour Standards Law

The Labour Standards Law of 1947 is uniformly applied to all employers irrespective of firm size. Therefore, SMEs are also covered by the provisions concerning various aspects of labour protection under this law.

---

6. Koshiro [1985a] and [1986, mimeo]. Only 6.8 per cent of workers surveyed were absent from work for more than 10 days per year including paid vacations.

For example, the principle of equal footing between employer and employee; equal treatment of individual workers regardless of nationality, religion, or social status; equal pay for men and women; prohibition of compulsory labour; and prohibition of exploitation of labour by an intermediary. With regard to labour contracts, the law stipulates the prohibition of employment contracts over one year; explicit notification of employment conditions; prohibition of compulsory savings; restriction of dismissal; and notification of dismissal. Concerning wages, the law requires full direct payment of wages in cash, payment at least once a month, payment at the fixed date, and a minimum wage. Working hours are limited to eight hours a day, 48 hours a week, and the law also regulates overtime, rest time, holidays (at least once a week), premiums for overtime work (25 per cent) and night work (50 per cent), paid vacations, etc.[7]

(ii) unemployment insurance and workmen's compensation

Unemployment insurance and workmen's compensation cover all employees except for seasonal workers employed for a period of less than four months. Employers and employees are required to share the unemployment insurance premium, which is equivalent to 1.5 per cent of monthly wages. Employers are solely responsible for contributing workmen's compensation premiums.

(iii) medical care

Workers employed by very small firms employing fewer than five persons are covered by the National Health Insurance. Workers employed by firms employing five or more but fewer than 300 persons are covered by the government-controlled health insurance plan. Workers employed by large firms employing 300 or more persons are covered by an autonomous health insurance plan at each enterprise which can provide member workers with more generous benefits than other plans. Health insurance plans of large firms often reduce the proportion of premiums paid by workers. Instead of a fifty-fifty contribution under the government-controlled health insurance plan, employers of large firms often contribute 70 per cent of the premium. In this sense, workers in SMEs have fewer benefits than those employed by large firms.

(iv) old-age pension plans

Old-age pension plans are separated into eight systems according to the status of the employees. However, the majority of workers in the private sector are covered either by the Welfare Pension Fund or by the

---

7. The Labour Standards Law was amended in September 1987 to shorten the maximum hours of work to 46 hours a week. However, small and medium-sized firms are exempt from this new requirement for a further three years. The amended law also declares that 40 hours a week should be adopted in the near future, although the date for the introduction has not been stipulated specifically. These provisions concerning working hours are not applied to agriculture, forestry, and aquaculture industries.

National Pension Plan. An independent Welfare Pension Fund can be established by any firm employing 1,000 or more employees. It can provide workers with benefits in excess of those provided by the nationally uniform basic pension. Workers employed by firms employing fewer than 1,000 persons are covered by the national welfare pension plan. Workers employed by very small firms employing fewer than five persons are covered by the National Pension Plan, which also covers self-employed persons, family workers, and wives who are not covered by other plans. In this respect, workers in small firms are again less favourably treated than those employed by large firms.

(v) the SME's mutual aid fund for retirement allowances

Large firms usually have a system of retirement allowances stipulated by collective bargaining agreements at each enterprise. For example, the 336 large companies surveyed by the Central Labour Relations Commission in June 1985 paid an average of 38.7 months' pay for a university graduate at the time of the retirement at age 55 with 33 years of service; 42.9 months' pay for a senior-high school graduate production worker at age 55 with 37 years of service; 45.0 months' pay, or 15,129,000 yen for a junior-high school graduate production worker at age 55 with 40 years' service.[8]

It is difficult for SMEs to pay comparable lump sum benefits at the time of retirement without special financial preparation. Therefore, the government enacted a law in 1959 establishing a special programme to assist the mutual aid funds of SMEs in accumulating financial resources for retirement allowances by a law in 1959. Contributions to the mutual fund specified by the law are tax deductible, and the government subsidises a part of the retirement allowance. The SMEs covered by this law are: (a) those which employ fewer than 300 regular employees and whose authorised capital is less than 100 million yen; (b) wholesale trade firms which employ fewer than 100 regular employees and whose authorised capital is less than 30 million yen; (c) retail trade companies which employ fewer than 50 regular employees and whose authorised capital is less than 10 million yen.

As of March 1986, the Fund covered about 255,000 SMEs and roughly 2 million workers. The average amount of retirement allowance paid to 165,368 workers by the Fund in the 1985 fiscal year was 434,000 yen. The rest of SMEs and self-employed small businesses are not covered even by this Fund. Therefore, less than 10 per cent of workers in SMEs benefit from this system.

---

8. Central Labour Relations Commission, *Survey of lump-sum retirement allowance and retirement system for 1985*, quoted in Japan Productivity Center's *Handbook of labour statistics for 1986*, pp. 94-95.

(vi) minimum wages

Local minimum wages are set in each prefecture by a tripartite wage board. The original Labour Standards Law stipulated minimum wages, but they were not effective until 1959 when a separate law was enacted. For the first 20 years, the law was not sufficiently effective, but in 1978 a local across-the-board minimum wage system was introduced in each prefecture. The minimum hourly wage rates as of 1 October 1986 range from the highest (488 yen per hour) in Tokyo to the lowest (407 yen per hour) in the southern (Kyushu) and northern (Tohoku) areas. The national average minimum hourly wage rate is now 451 yen, which is equivalent to 40 per cent of the average hourly earnings of all industries. The rate has been revised every year following the recommendation by the Central Wage Board.

The actual wages and hours of work in small firms have been the subject of serious social concern among academics since the pre-war days. The differentials in wages and other conditions of work between large and small firms are discussed in detail in Section V.

b. The institutional setting: industrial relations

Labour unions in Japan concentrate mostly on large firms and public employees. Union activity is very low among SMEs. Currently, only 6.7 per cent of workers in small businesses employing fewer than 100 workers and 0.5 per cent of those employed by very small firms with fewer than 30 are organised into labour unions (Table 8). In terms of industries, the wholesale and retail trades are less organised than others.

In the unorganised sector, some firms have informal employee organisations (usually called *Shinboku Kai*, a friendly society) or profit-sharing plans. Among 605 venture business firms surveyed by Koshiro [1986], only 18.8 per cent had labour unions but about one-half of unorganised firms had friendly societies. In addition, roughly one-third of the venture businesses had profit-sharing plans.

Collective bargaining agreements in Japan are usually negotiated between individual firms and enterprise unions. But in some localities, workers of small firms are organised into a local branch of an industrial union and covered by a regional agreement. Also, some workers in small firms are organised by amalgamated unions covering miscellaneous industries. In the country as a whole, the number of labour disputes has decreased considerably since the oil crisis. There are, however, a few serious industrial conflicts in some small firms, most of which tend to be influenced by new left wing political forces.

Japan

Table 8: Union activity by size of firm and by industry, 1960-1985

Sector, size and industry	1960	1970	1980	1985
Private sector	-	28.5	24.5	24.3
Public sector	-	82.2	74.5	61.7
Private sector				
500 employees and over	67.1	63.9	61.1	59.9
100 - 499	36.4	30.7	27.8	24.3
30 - 99	8.0	8.9	7.4	6.7
1-29	0.6	0.6	0.5	0.5
Construction	30.0	25.0	16.2	19.3
Manufacturing	32.6	38.0	34.7	32.9
Wholesale and retail trades	15.0	9.7	10.4	10.6
Financial and real estate		68.5	56.8	49.9
Transportation and communication	69.9	63.9	61.5	56.9
Public utilities		76.9	79.7	67.9
Service	27.6	26.2	23.0	20.1
Public service	59.7	65.6	69.1	71.0

Source: Ministry of Labor: *Labor in the year 2000* (March 1986), p. 79, based on Ministry of Labor: *Basic survey of labor unions*, and Prime Minister's Office: *Labor force survey*. Figures are as of June each year.

III. Quantitative development of the small firm sector

1. Increasing employment in small business

The trend since the late 1960s is seen clearly in Table 9. According to the Employment Status Survey,[9] the relative share of employment in small businesses in the non-agricultural industries has increased sharply since 1971. The number of employees employed by large firms (with more than 300 employees) amounted to 10.7 million (32.1 per cent) in 1971 and increased to 11.7 million by 1982, but its relative share dropped to 27.7 per cent. On the other hand, the middle-sized firms, employing more than 30 but fewer than 300, increased their share from 23.9 per cent in 1959 to 26.4 per cent by 1982. Small firms, employing fewer than 30, experienced a decrease in employment share from 1959 (33.5 per cent) to 1965 (29 per cent), but it subsequently rose to 33.6 per cent by 1982.

---

9. This survey is conducted by the Prime Minister's Office every third year, except for the 1979 survey which was one year early in order to avoid overlapping with the population census of 1980.

Table 9: Percentage and total number of employees by size of firm in the non-agricultural industries, 1959-1982

	Fewer than 4 persons	5-9 persons	10-29 persons	30-99 persons	100-299 persons	300-999 persons	1000 and over	Governments	Total number (000s)
1959	8.5	9.9	15.1	13.2	7.9	23.9		21.4	19 654
1962	6.7	8.6	14.1	14.4	9.5	7.8	23.8	14.8	23 740
1965	5.8	7.9	15.3	14.8	9.9	8.4	23.1	14.2	26 484
1968	7.0	9.3	14.0	14.7	10.0	8.6	23.5	12.7	30 197
1971	6.9	9.2	14.2	14.8	10.4	9.0	23.1	12.3	33 360
1974	7.8	9.6	14.1	15.0	10.5	8.7	21.7	12.2	35 622
1977	7.8	25.0		15.5	10.6	8.4	20.2	12.5	37 517
1979	8.1	26.0		15.2	10.9	8.2	19.4	12.2	39 091
1982	8.2	25.4		15.2	11.2	8.9	18.8	12.2	42 056

Note: Those who are employed by public corporations and institutions are included in "Governments".

Source: Prime Minister's Office: *Employment status survey*, 1974 and 1982 volumes for commentary. The latest figures for 1985 are not yet available.

Japan

Table 10: Percentage and total number (in 10,000s) of employees in non-agricultural industries by size of enterprise (number of persons engaged)

	1970(1)	1971(1)	1972(1)	1973(1)	1973	1974	1975	1976	1977	1978	1979	1980	1981	1982	1983	1984	1985
Total (2)	3 277 (3.4)	3 387 (3.4)	3 438 (1.5)	3 562 (3.6)	3 585	3 607 (0.6)	3 617 (0.3)	3 682 (1.8)	3 738 (1.5)	3 770 (0.9)	3 846 (2.0)	3 941 (2.5)	4 008 (1.7)	4 068 (1.5)	4 176 (2.7)	4 236 (1.4)	4 285 (1.2)
Size of enterprise																	
1-29 persons	[32.4]	(2.4) [32.2]	(2.7) [32.5]	(4.1) [32.7]	[32.7]	(0.3) [32.6]	(2.0) [33.1]	(3.2) [33.6]	(4.1) [34.5]	(2.3) [35.0]	(0.8) [34.6]	(1.5) [34.2]	(1.9) [34.3]	(1.1) [34.2]	(1.9) [33.9]	(▼0.2) [33.4]	(0.9) [33.6]
30-99 persons	[14.7]	(3.7) [14.8]	(1.4) [14.7]	(5.7) [15.0]	[15.0]	(0.0) [14.9]	(0.6) [15.0]	(5.5) [15.5]	(0.2) [15.3]	(1.6) [15.4]	(2.4) [15.5]	(3.4) [15.6]	(0.6) [15.5]	(1.3) [15.4]	(2.7) [15.4]	(2.6) [15.6]	(1.7) [15.7]
100-499 persons	[14.2]	(7.1) [14.7]	(▼2.8) [14.0]	(4.8) [14.2]	[14.1]	(▼0.4) [14.0]	(0.0) [14.0]	(1.4) [13.9]	(1.2) [13.9]	(0.2) [13.8]	(4.8) [14.2]	(3.7) [14.3]	(3.2) [14.5]	(1.0) [14.5]	(3.6) [14.6]	(2.6) [14.8]	(4.5) [15.3]
500 persons and over	[26.5]	(3.3) [26.5]	(1.3) [26.4]	(1.4) [25.9]	[25.7]	(1.2) [25.9]	(▼2.4) [25.2]	(▼1.0) [24.5]	(▼1.1) [23.9]	(▼2.2) [23.1]	(1.8) [23.1]	(3.2) [23.2]	(1.7) [23.3]	(3.1) [23.6]	(4.3) [24.0]	(2.4) [24.2]	(0.9) [23.7]
Government employees	[12.0]	[11.8]	[12.1]	[12.0]	[12.1]	[12.3]	[12.5]	[12.2]	[12.3]	[12.5]	[12.6]	[12.4]	[12.3]	[12.1]	[11.9]	[11.8]	[11.7]

Notes:
(1) Excluding Okinawa.
(2) The total number includes those who cannot be classified or whose classes are unknown.
( ) shows percentage changes compared with the previous year.
[ ] shows the percentage of the total in every year.
▼ indicates a decrease.

Source: Prime Minister's Office: Annual report of the labor force survey, 1977 and 1985

2. The recent trend

A similar trend since 1970, based on different size classifications and another source (Labour Force Survey), is shown in Table 10. Here the share of employment in large firms with more than 500 employees declined between 1970 and 1978, but the slow recovery between 1978 and 1984 can also be seen clearly. It should also be noted that the middle-sized firms have been stable or have slightly increased their share throughout this period.

The employment figures by enterprise size for both manufacturing and services are given in Tables 11 and 12.[10] The share of employment in SMEs (employing fewer than 300) in manufacturing remained around 55-57 per cent until 1971, but increased to 61.4 per cent by 1979. The increasing employment share of SMEs, or the decreasing employment share in large enterprises (employing more than 500) is also observed in Table 13. Large enterprises lost a substantial employment share between 1974 and 1979, recovered it slightly until 1984, and then lost it again in 1985 and 1986. Conversely, in the service sector, very small firms (employing fewer than 30) lost employment share from 1959 to 1979, while middle-sized firms (employing between 30 and 1000) have been increasing their share.

Table 11: Percentage and total number of employees by size of firm in the manufacturing industry, 1959-1979

	Fewer than 4 persons	5-9 persons	30-99 persons	100-299 persons	300-999 persons	1000 and over	Government	Total number
1959	4.0	26.6	19.0	13.0	36.5		0.8	6 855
1962	2.9	21.7	18.3	13.7	12.4	30.5	0.3	9 041
1965	2.6	21.6	17.8	13.9	12.9	30.6	0.2	9 837
1968	3.5	21.6	17.5	13.5	12.8	30.9	0.2	10 750
1971	3.6	21.2	17.0	13.5	12.7	31.9	0.1	11 743
1974	4.0	21.3	17.9	13.6	12.5	30.3	0.1	11 861
1977	4.0	23.2	19.2	13.8	11.7	28.0	0.1	11 640
1979	4.2	24.3	18.6	14.3	11.3	27.3	0.1	11 403

Note: Figures for 1982 are not available due to changed tabulation.
Source: Statistics Bureau, Prime Minister's Office: *1979 Employment status survey, Statistical tables (Time series)*, p. 75.

---

10. However, Tables 11 and 12 do not contain figures for 1982 which are not available due to changed tabulation caused by financial constraints. Table 13 gives an alternative statistical series for employees by enterprise size in manufacturing, but it differs slightly from the figures in Table 12 because of different statistical methods.

Japan

Table 12: Percentage and total number of employees by size of firm in the service industry, 1959-1979

	Fewer than 4 persons	5-9 persons	30-99 persons	100-299 persons	300-999 persons	1000 and over	Government	Total number
1959	16.5	24.1	8.1	3.9	5.0		42.1	3 290
1962	14.6	23.8	9.9	5.0	2.9	5.9	37.6	3 541
1965	11.4	25.6	12.4	6.1	3.4	6.1	35.3	4 052
1968	11.9	23.2	13.0	8.3	4.7	6.7	31.9	4 907
1971	9.4	22.6	13.9	8.7	5.4	6.8	33.1	5 637
1974	10.0	22.1	13.9	9.6	5.5	7.2	31.4	6 274
1977	8.8	22.9	14.3	10.3	5.9	6.6	31.0	7 154
1979	8.9	23.3	14.5	11.0	6.0	6.9	29.3	7 789

Note: Figures for 1982 are not available due to changed tabulation.
Source: Statistics Bureau, Prime Minister's Office: *1979 Employment status survey, Statistical tables (Time series)*, p. 75.

Table 13: Percentage and total number of employees in the manufacturing industry by size of enterprise

	1-4 persons	5-29 persons	30-99 persons	100-499 persons	500-999 persons	1 000 and over	Government employees	Total number (10 000s)
1970	26.6	17.7	19.6	36.1			0.1	1 144
1971	26.0	17.1	20.2	36.4			0.1	1 156
1972	26.5	17.2	19.4	36.8			0.1	1 155
1973	25.1	17.6	19.5	35.7			0.1	1 203
1974	26.4	17.7	19.0	36.8			0.2	1 201
1975	27.2	18.3	19.1	35.3			0.1	1 138
1976	27.9	19.1	19.1	33.8			0.1	1 133
1977	29.0	19.2	18.8	32.9			0.1	1 126
1978	29.3	19.4	18.8	32.4			0.1	1 109
1979	29.4	19.4	19.4	31.6			0.2	1 107
1980	28.8	19.3	19.5	32.2			0.2	1 135
1981	28.2	19.1	19.9	32.7			0.1	1 152
1982	28.1	19.1	19.6	32.8			0.1	1 151
1983	27.7	19.2	19.6	33.3			0.1	1 175
1984	27.2	19.2	19.8	33.5			0.1	1 212
1985	27.3	19.4	20.5	33.1			0.1	1 229
1986	27.3	19.5	20.3	32.2			0.1	1 235

Note: The total number includes those who cannot be classified by size of enterprise.
Source: Statistics Bureau, Management and Co-ordination Agency, Japan: *Annual report of the labour force survey*.

A third source, the Census of Establishments, gives employment shares by establishment size for employed persons, including self-employed and family workers, in non-agricultural industries for every third year since 1969 (Table 14). The declining share of large establishments and the increasing share of small establishments is quite striking.

Table 14: Total number and percentage of employed persons by size of establishment

	1969	1972	1975	1978	1981
Total number	38 177 026	38 793 883	39 641 176	42 295 443	45 720 190
		Percentage of the total each year			
Size of establishment					
1-4 persons	18.4	19.5	20.1	20.5	20.5
5-9 persons	12.0	12.6	13.5	14.5	14.8
10-19 persons)		12.4	13.3	13.9	14.1
)	19.5				
20-29 persons)		7.4	7.6	7.9	8.0
30-49 persons)		9.0	9.1	9.1	9.3
)	20.2				
50-99 persons)		10.6	10.3	10.3	10.3
Subtotal of less than 100	70.1	71.5	73.8	76.1	77.1
100-299 persons	13.0	12.7	11.8	11.4	11.2
300 and over	16.9	15.8	14.4	12.5	11.7

Note: For 1969 including those who are employed by the public sector - others excluding them.
Source: Prime Minister's Office: *Census of establishments, Commentary volumes for 1972*, p. 15, and *for 1981*, p. 19.

A similar tendency can be observed within manufacturing. While the relative share of output of large establishments was more than 50 per cent in the 1960s and about 47-49 per cent even after the oil crisis, their employment share was only 33 per cent in the early 1970s and declined continuously to below 30 per cent in the following decade (Table 4). On the other hand, the relative share of both output and employment of very small establishments (employing fewer than 30) increased sharply during the 1970s, but declined in the 1980s. The employment share of medium-sized establishments remained almost constant through the 1970s, and then increased gradually in the 1980s.

3. The job creation process

Birth and mortality rates of business establishments are exhibited by industry in Table 15. The birth rate was 6.1 per cent and the mortality rate 3.7 per cent between June 1978 and June 1981, resulting in a net increase of 2.4 per cent in the number of non-agricultural establishments. It is safe to say that most of these establishments were small and medium-sized firms. The birth rate as well as the rate of net increase were highest in the catering industry, followed by the services sector. Retail trade had higher birth and mortality rates than manufacturing, but the net increase was larger among the latter.

Table 15: Birth and mortality rates of private establishments

Period		July 1966-June 1969	July 1969-Aug. 1972	Sept. 1972-May 1975	May 1975-June 1978	June 1978-June 1981
Total of	(A)	6.5	7.0	6.1	6.2	6.1
Non-agricultural	(B)	3.2	3.8	4.2	3.4	3.7
Private industry	(C)	3.3	3.2	1.9	2.8	2.4
	A	5.4	6.4	5.4	4.6	4.7
Construction	B	▼0.8	0.5	2.2	1.1	1.1
	C	6.2	5.9	3.2	3.5	3.6
	A	6.0	5.6	4.3	3.4	3.7
Manufacturing	B	2.5	3.2	3.4	2.3	2.5
	C	3.5	2.4	0.9	1.1	1.2
	A	6.2	7.7	7.9	6.6	6.3
Wholesale trade	B	6.5	4.1	5.3	3.8	3.9
	C	▼0.3	3.6	2.6	2.8	2.4
	A	5.0	4.8	4.3	4.9	4.4
Retail trade	B	2.1	3.6	3.6	3.3	4.0
	C	2.9	1.2	0.7	1.6	0.4
	A	15.8	17.0	13.3	15.1	14.1
Catering	B	6.7	8.6	9.3	8.6	8.9
	C	9.1	8.4	4.0	6.5	5.2
	A	6.3	6.7	6.1	6.1	6.4
Service	B	3.9	4.0	3.8	3.3	3.1
	C	2.4	2.7	2.3	2.8	3.3

Note: (A) = birth rate; (B) = mortality rate; (C) = net increase. ▼ indicates a decrease.
Source: National Financing Corporation: *Chosa Geppo* (Monthly research), No. 301, May 1986, p. 16, based on the Prime Minister's Office: *Census of establishments*. The birth rate and the mortality rate of enterprises are calculated by comparing the results of the latest census with those of the previous one.

Table 16: Changes in the number of employed persons by private industries, 1972-1981

Industry	Year	Small establishments Employed persons	Small establishments Per cent	Large establishments Employed persons	Large establishments Per cent	Total Employed persons	Total Per cent
Mining	1972	118 518	63.5	68 090	36.5	186 608	100.0
	1975	101 449	69.4	44 749	30.6	146 198	100.0
	1978	93 841	70.4	39 501	29.6	133 342	100.0
	1981	97 590	75.9	30 938	24.1	128 528	100.0
Construction	1972	3 594 476	90.3	386 636	9.7	3 981 112	100.0
	1975	3 865 989	92.9	294 738	7.1	4 160 727	100.0
	1978	4 349 173	94.2	267 176	5.8	4 616 349	100.0
	1981	4 714 388	95.3	234 366	4.7	4 948 754	100.0
Manufacturing	1972	9 209 146	69.2	4 088 508	30.8	13 297 654	100.0
	1975	8 929 279	70.5	3 734 632	29.5	12 663 911	100.0
	1978	9 194 642	73.5	3 314 464	26.5	12 509 106	100.0
	1981	9 551 914	74.3	3 311 003	25.7	12 862 917	100.0
Wholesale and retail trades	1972	10 056 035	86.0	1 634 808	14.0	11 690 843	100.0
	1975	10 703 352	86.8	1 625 283	13.2	12 328 635	100.0
	1978	11 868 673	87.6	1 686 972	12.4	13 555 645	100.0
	1981	12 978 043	87.4	1 872 195	12.6	14 850 238	100.0
Finance and insurance	1972	1 160 649	83.3	232 318	16.7	1 392 967	100.0
	1975	1 238 605	82.6	260 858	17.4	1 499 463	100.0
	1978	1 356 899	83.6	267 017	16.4	1 623 916	100.0
	1981	1 453 073	85.9	237 624	14.1	1 690 697	100.0

Real estate	1972	384 242	96.0	15 849	4.0	400 091	100.0
	1975	453 726	97.6	11 133	2.4	464 859	100.0
	1978	516 843	98.0	10 517	2.0	527 360	100.0
	1981	609 574	97.6	15 127	2.4	624 701	100.0
Transport and communication	1972	1 716 437	83.9	329 055	16.1	2 045 492	100.0
	1975	1 750 712	85.6	293 879	14.4	2 044 591	100.0
	1978	1 877 206	86.5	293 592	13.5	2 170 798	100.0
	1981	2 083 364	88.8	263 894	11.2	2 347 258	100.0
Public utilities	1972	121 839	66.1	62 592	33.9	184 431	100.0
	1975	125 433	63.3	72 864	36.7	198 297	100.0
	1978	132 621	65.9	68 698	34.1	201 319	100.0
	1981	138 361	66.5	69 731	33.5	208 092	100.0
Service	1972	4 039 149	71.9	1 575 536	28.1	5 614 685	100.0
	1975	4 361 494	71.1	1 773 001	28.9	6 134 495	100.0
	1978	4 899 257	70.4	2 058 351	29.6	6 957 608	100.0
	1981	5 579 852	69.2	2 479 153	30.8	8 059 005	100.0
Total of the secondary and tertiary industries	1972	30 400 491	78.4	8 393 392	21.6	38 793 883	100.0
	1975	31 530 039	79.5	8 111 137	20.5	39 641 176	100.0
	1978	34 289 155	81.1	8 006 288	18.9	42 295 443	100.0
	1981	37 206 159	81.4	8 514 031	18.6	45 720 190	100.0

Note: SMEs are those establishments employing fewer than 300, but fewer than 100 for the wholesale trade, and fewer than 50 for the retail trade and services. The establishments of government enterprises and public corporations are excluded.

Source: Agency of SMEs: *White paper for 1987*, Appendix, p. 3; the original source is *Census of establishments*.

Employment can be generated either by expansion of existing firms or by a net increase in the number of firms. To what extent employment has been generated by either of these two factors is the subject of an OECD study [see country report from Japan by Kuwahara, 1987]. More generally, the Census of Establishments shows that SMEs accounted for the majority of new jobs in the private sector between 1972 and 1981, and 72.2 per cent of these jobs were generated in the retail trade and service industry (Table 16).

IV. Qualitative development of the small firm sector

1. Economic, social and institutional background to recent changes

As shown in Table 9, employment expanded more rapidly in large firms during the period of high economic growth until the early 1970s. The labour market in this period was characterised by the following three aspects: a labour shortage, increased wages, and intensified competition among large firms in order to prepare for the open economy beginning in the 1960s. This labour shortage first became evident in the labour market for students graduating after nine years of compulsory education. They were paid minimum wages under the traditional *nenko* (seniority-oriented) wage system. The job offers/job seekers ratio in this category of workers became 1.0 in 1956, increased to 1.2 by the late 1950s, jumped to between 2.6 and 2.9 in the 1960s and climbed further to 6.8 by 1971. Similarly, the comparable ratio for the senior high school graduates with 12 years of education became 1.0 in 1957, doubled to 2.0 by 1961 and rose to 8.4 by 1971.[11]

Reflecting the tightening labour market, the starting monthly wages for male junior high school graduates increased from 6,020 yen (US$16.72) in 1960 to 25,500 yen (US$70.83) in 1970, 81,100 yen (US$398.33) in 1980, and 96,200 yen (US$479.56) by 1985. Similarly, the comparable rates for male senior high school graduates as well as university graduates increased as shown in Table 17. In terms of US dollars (which reflects the appreciation of yen), the starting wage rate for junior and senior high school graduates increased at an annual rate of 14.4 per cent and 13.6 per cent, respectively, during the past 25 years.

At the same time, labour unions of major industries took advantage of the tightening labour market conditions and organised a concerted wage negotiation (spring offensive) beginning in 1955. The rate of wage increase continued to rise throughout the 1960s and amounted to more than 14 per cent after 1969, when the foreign currency reserves of Japan for the first time exceeded the long-planned 2 billion dollar ceiling. Under the fixed exchange rate system, this meant that the money supply began to increase

---

11. Ministry of Labour, *Labour exchange operating statistics*, quoted in *Handbook of Labour Statistics for 1968* (p. 54) and *1979* (p. 35).

side by side with increasing foreign reserves, thus creating inflationary pressure.

On the other hand, during these decades Japan gradually moved towards being a more open economy. In 1955, the country joined the General Agreement on Tariff and Trade (GATT), and in 1960 began the liberalisation of trade and capital transfers. Japan also acquired the status of an Article 8 country of the International Monetary Fund and joined OECD in 1964. These changes meant that Japanese companies had to compete in the world market on an equal footing with the gigantic corporations of other advanced countries. Pushed by such international competitive pressure, as well as by increasing labour costs, major companies introduced new technologies and invested in establishing efficient, modern plants which were labour saving. Thus, many large manufacturing companies began to reduce the number of employees even several years before the oil crisis.

The labour market situation changed dramatically after the first oil crisis in 1973. First, large companies whose stocks were listed on the Tokyo First Class Stock Exchange were obliged to reduce their employment quite significantly. Table 18 shows that the employment reduction was more severe in manufacturing than in non-manufacturing: employment fell nearly 12 per cent between 1973 and 1978 in the former, whereas employment fell only 5 per cent in the latter during the same period.

Second, new business opportunities for small firms have expanded dramatically since the 1960s. The increased per capita income during the period of high economic growth provided ambitious entrepreneurs with good opportunities to expand their businesses. For the first time in the history of Japan, a huge domestic market emerged for durable goods such as electric appliances and cars. These metal fabricating industries needed to have an extensive network of suppliers and subcontractors. In addition, the development of these mass-production industries also demanded an expansion of the machinery industry, which generated a large number of small manufacturing companies. Furthermore, demand expanded for other related industries ranging from steel to transportation, wholesale and retail trades, as well as services. The very fact that a huge reservoir of surplus labour existed until the 1950s made it possible to expand small, labour-intensive businesses in the following decades.

Third, new technology such as microelectronics and biochemistry gave a strong impetus to small businesses development. The very nature of new technology allowed entrepreneurs to establish their own businesses with a fairly small amount of capital. In addition, the supply of capital became abundant after the oil crisis due to decreased economic growth, so that small businesses which once suffered from serious capital shortage had easier access to the necessary financial resources. At the same time, consumer tastes changed dramatically after the oil crisis, favouring differentiated rather than homogeneous mass-production goods. The demand for differentiated products intensified the incentive for the development of flexible small businesses. New businesses emerged not only in manufacturing, but also in the trade, distribution and service sectors.

Table 17: Starting monthly wage rates for school graduates by education level (male)

	Junior high school	Senior high school	University
1960	¥ 6 020 ($16.72)	¥ 8 220 ($22.83)	
1965	13 210 (36.69)	16 670 (46.31)	¥ 23 265 ($64.63)
1970	25 500 (70.83)	31 700 (88.06)	39 900 (110.83)
1975	59 800 (195.97)	74 900 (245.45)	89 300 (292.64)
1980	81 100 (398.33)	92 800 (455.80)	114 500 (562.38)
1985	96 200 (479.56)	112 200 (559.32)	140 000 (697.91)
Average annual rate of increase	11.7% (14.4%)	11.0% (13.6%)	9.4% (12.6%)

Note: The exchange rate of the yen currency against US dollar changed as follows: 360 yen until August 1971 and 308 yen in December 1971; under the floating exchange rate system, 305.15 yen in 1975, 203.60 yen in 1980, and 200.60 yen in 1985.

Source: Ministry of Labor: *Handbook of labor statistics*, 1968 (pp. 136-7); 1977 (p. 142); 1986 (p. 128). For 1960 and 1965, the manufacturing industry; for 1970-85, the average of total industries.

For exchange rates, Bank of Japan: *Economic statistics monthly*, September 1986, p. 6 (Inter-Bank Rates US Dollar Spot Closing at the end of the year).

Table 18: Declining number of employees among major firms, 1973-1983 (thousand persons)

Fiscal year	Total industry 863 companies	Manufacturing industry	Non-manufacturing industry
1973	3 765.9 99.4 (1)	2 757.9 100.0 (1)	1 008.0 97.6 (1)
1974	3 786.8 100.0	2 753.6 99.8	1 033.2 100.0
1975	3 719.5 98.2	2 693.6 97.7	1 025.9 99.3
1976	3 592.3 94.9	2 585.5 93.7	1 006.7 97.4
1977	2 510.6 92.7	2 518.2 91.3	992.5 96.1
1978	3 412.2 90.1	2 430.8 88.1	981.4 95.0
1979	3 368.3 88.9	2 391.6 86.7	976.7 94.5
1980	3 395.2 89.7	2 411.9 87.5	983.3 95.2
1981	3 431.6 90.6	2 443.7 88.6	988.0 95.6
1982	3 461.0 91.4	2 469.5 89.5	991.5 96.0
1983	3 452.5 91.2	2 465.7 89.4	986.7 95.5

Note: (1) The indexes show the change in employment from the peak year (100) in each category.

Source: Koshiro [1984], p. 26 based on NEEDS data bank.

Finally, a negative aspect of increased employment among small businesses after the oil crisis must be mentioned. Major companies tried to decrease their labour force after the oil crisis in response to decreased demands for their products, and increased labour and energy costs.[12] In particular, those industries which had depended heavily upon an abundant supply of cheap oil, such as petrochemicals, shipbuilding, ferroalloy, and aluminium refining, were the first to decrease their labour force. Then other industries that suffered during the world depression were also obliged to make reductions. The automobile and electric appliance industries (excluding the heavy electric machinery industry) were the only exceptions, as they expanded employment almost continuously even after the oil crisis.

For example, as stated earlier, major manufacturing companies listed on the Tokyo First Class Stock Exchange Market reduced their employment by 13.3 per cent between 1973 and 1979 (Table 18), whereas total employment and dependent employment increased by 4.5 per cent and 7.5 per cent, respectively, during the same period. This meant that employment increased almost exclusively in the small and medium-sized firms, most of which were in the tertiary sector.

Although it is evident that prosperous and innovative independent small businesses have flourished in the past two decades, it is also undeniable that employment was forced to increase almost exclusively among small firms due to the decreased job generation ability of large firms.

2. The nature and characteristics of change: Alternative views of the subcontracting system

Studies in the field of small businesses in Japan have been dominated by Marxist-oriented scholars since the prewar period. The latest comprehensive bibliographical study in this field, edited by Takizawa [1985], contains about 5,000 books and papers, most of which have a strong inclination toward a Marxist interpretation of the problem; they tend to stress exploitation of small firms by "monopolistic capital" and the misery of poorly paid workers in these firms. It would appear that these studies have been strongly motivated by the political and ideological desire that some day in the future these exploited workers, as well as some owners of these oppressed firms, will become part of the "revolutionary mass" which will overthrow the capitalist system. Although their desire has so far been proved wishful thinking, a few of them have undertaken empirical research which merits mention here.

The development of studies in this field since the pre-war period is summarised by Watanabe [1985] as follows. In the pre-war period, three types of studies existed in this field. One was a microeconomic approach, advanced by Tasugi [1941] and based on the theory of optimum firm size. His studies did not gain widespread support among the experts, who tended

---

12. Wages rose 33 per cent in 1974, reflecting inflation and social instability following the first oil crisis.

to have strong sympathies with the misery of workers in small businesses. Another approach was that of competing views developed by two Marxist economists: Komiyama [1941] and Fujita [1943]. Both stressed the backwardness of Japanese manufacturing, the subordination of sub-contract firms to large firms, and the exploitation of the former by the latter. However, they differed in their evaluation of the nature or growth possibility of a particular type of small business. In particular, they disagreed over whether subordinated subcontract firms, developing under the militaristic expansion of industry, could realise sufficient technological progress to be free from parent firms. Komiyama looked at the possibility of technological progress among subordinated subcontract firms and stressed the existence of an "equivalent exchange" between parent firms and subcontractors, which denied the exploitive nature of the system. Fujita, on the other hand, emphasised the continuous exploitive nature of the system and denied the possibility of technological catch-up by small businesses.

The controversy between Komiyama and Fujita was continued after the Second World War in the work of different scholars. The technology gap between large and small firms was also an issue tackled in the postwar period. The urgency of this issue was widely acknowledged, not only by scholars in this field but also by government officials. When large firms began to introduce new technology from the West, they faced the necessity of closing the technological gap between themselves and their subcontractors. The latter were required to process new materials supplied by large companies (e.g. in the synthetic chemical fibres) and maintain high quality, or to supply reliable parts to large companies (e.g. in the electric appliance and automobile industries).

This time Fujita developed a positive view, whereas Kobayashi [1958] and Ichikawa [1957] criticised his view and stressed the exploitive nature of the new relationship between large companies and subcontractors. Nakamura [1962] intervened in this controversy and clarified the problem using a more sophisticated theory in which there is competition both among large monopolistic firms for control of efficient suppliers, and among small firms themselves.

The debate became more diversified in the decades after high economic growth. It became evident, even for doctrinaire Marxist economists, that the advanced manufacturing sector, with improved technology, had been able to compete internationally by the 1970s. A 1981 survey conducted by the Central Bank for Commerce and Industry revealed that 51.5 per cent of the 1,592 subcontracting SMEs claimed that their technological competence was equal to or even superior to their parent companies. Nakamura and Kiyonari pointed out such progress and changes among small firms since the 1960s. They insisted that the traditional subordination of subcontractors to large companies had faded away due to increased technological independence of subcontractors and, moreover, that the relationship between large companies and subcontractors had become more or less a co-operative division of labour. On the other hand, many other analysts still concentrate on the traditional view, using extensive case studies that emphasise the subordinate and exploitive nature of the subcontract system.

3. Explanations for the changes in the 1970s

Among the Marxist economists, some conducted sound, empirically based case studies and recognised the different relationships between large companies and subcontractors. For example, Ikeda [1972] states:

> Particularly since 1965, the conditions surrounding SMEs changed dramatically due to an intensified labour shortage and increased wages. These changes forced subcontractors to invest in labour saving machinery and equipment and to improve productivity in order to meet increased wages. Thus, even subcontractors have become modernised in their business management. The development of a productive force (*productivkraft*) of subcontractors reduced the subordinate nature of the system, and the vertical relationship between large companies and subcontractors has been transformed into more of a horizontal relationship with all parties on an equal footing. ... Generally, the degree of monopsony by large companies was reduced and the excessive competition among subcontractors has been reduced considerably. The control-subordination relationship between large companies and subcontractors has faded away to a considerable extent, reflecting the changed demand and supply conditions.... It is obvious that the rapid expansion of the machinery industry during the boom period affected the traditional subcontract system to a considerable extent, and even very small subcontractors became relatively independent from the control of large companies [Ikeda, 1972, pp. 160-162].

After examining developments following the 1971 depression that resulted from the re-evaluation of the yen, Ikeda concluded that the changed relationship described above would continue in the 1970s; he foresaw no possibility of a reversal. Furthermore, he anticipated an increasing number of independent subcontractors [Ibid., p. 171]. His study covers the machinery, automobile, electric appliance, and precision machinery industries. Ikeda, among others, admits that the first-tier subcontractors in the automobile industry have already acquired the superior technological ability necessary to meet the severe demands of large companies. In addition, by the early 1970s, many large suppliers, such as Nihon Springs and Nihon Oil Seal, were trying to reduce their dependency on the automobile industry through increasing sales to other industries. Ikeda also emphasises that major large companies in the machinery and electric appliance industries have reduced the number of subcontractors they work with by reallocating their business to a select few of the most competent subcontractors. For example, Hitachi selected only 27 per cent of their existing subcontractors and ceased doing business with the remainder. Many efficient SMEs succeeded in reducing their dependency upon sole customers in order to achieve a better bargaining position [Ibid., pp. 172-202].

The research division of the Central Bank for Commerce and Industry published its report on the status of subcontracting SMEs in June 1971. It classifies the total 4,364 subcontracting firms surveyed into the following five categories:

(a) Subcontractors relying exclusively on a single customer for 75 per cent or more of their sales (26 per cent of the total subcontractors surveyed). Their products are of a high quality, and can be produced only with high technology and specialised modern capital equipment.

(b) Independent subcontractors whose products are as in (a), but depend on a single customer for only 25 per cent or less of their sales (19.5 per cent of the total).

(c) Subordinate subcontractors who produce ordinary parts without having any specialised high technology, and depend on a single customer for 75 per cent or more of their sales (8 per cent of the total).

(d) Floating subcontractors who produce products as in (c), but depend on a single customer for 25 per cent or less of their sales (3.7 per cent of the total).

(e) Intermediate subcontractors who cannot be classified in any of the above categories (42.3 per cent of the total) [Ikeda, 1972, p. 207].

4. Relations between large and small firms: technology and structural changes in the 1980s

During the period between the late 1970s and the 1980s, Japanese industries suffered from a series of structural changes, in addition to increased oil prices. These include an appreciation of the yen once in 1978 (by 70 per cent) and again since late 1985 (by 80 per cent). Such a tremendous appreciation of the yen forced export industries to reduce costs. Cost reduction has been achieved through the introduction of microelectronic technology, automation of the production process, and reductions in the labour force. At the same time, demands for improved quality have been intensified by fierce international competition. Furthermore, in the late 1970s major electric appliance companies were obliged to shift their colour TV production into the advanced countries, instead of exporting, in order to avoid trade conflicts. Similarly, in the 1980s automobile manufacturers were obliged to invest abroad, particularly in the United States.

Subcontractors in these export industries suffered from such changes, and struggled to survive. The introduction of integrated circuits and other microelectronic technology reduced the number of parts to be assembled. Increased overseas TV production reduced the demand for domestic parts, and more flexibility to meet the changing tastes of customers became imperative for survival. Some large automobile parts producers established co-operative relationships with foreign producers such as Akebono Brakes and Bendix (USA), Nihon Spring and Hesch (the Federal Republic of Germany), and Atsugi Automobile and Karl Schmidt (the Federal Republic of Germany). Others increased their supply of automobile parts to American producers, who prefered to increase their use of international outsourcing. Major automobile parts and electric appliances producers proceeded further to select efficient subcontractors and to drop less efficient ones in order to meet these challenges [Ikeda, 1982, pp. 81-128].

Koshiro undertook field research in the Japanese automobile industry under the Massachusetts Institute of Technology's Future of Automobile Project in the 1980s. The results suggest that even one of the most competitive automobile producers in the world still depends upon a multi-tiered hierarchy of subcontractors, which includes handwork by women at home. The use of homework is more extensive in the electric appliance and apparel industries. More generally, the percentage of subcontract firms in the total number of firms exceeds 80 per cent in such industries as textile, apparel, general machinery, electric appliance and machinery, transportation equipment, and precision machinery.

Nakamura points out the diversity of these subcontractors, and emphasises the positive aspect of the subcontract system as a system of social division of labour. He criticises as over-simplified a view which concentrates on the exploitive nature of a multi-tiered hierarchy. As explained earlier, he underlines the simultaneous development of medium standing R & D firms and small venture businesses. According to Nakamura, the international competitive advantages from outsourcing are based on a subcontracting system which developed mostly after the middle 1960s. Now, the competitiveness rests not upon the exploitation of cheap labour, but mainly on an accumulation of technical knowledge which supports high productivity in each specific engineering area. Nakamura examines a number of exciting cases in this field to support his arguments, and concludes: "If the high productivity of Japan's 'mechatronics' (a compound of mechanics and electronics) still depends heavily on the existence of changing subcontractors, there remain a number of problems to be re-examined relating to the role of subcontracting as an economic system" [Nakamura, 1985, p. 112].

In contrast to Nakamura, Mitsui presents an orthodox Marxist view criticising "the positive argument for the Japanese-style division of labour". He emphasises the intensive competition among and exploitation of subcontractors through reorganisation by "monopolists" at the international level. The exploitive nature of the subcontract system still remains unchanged, which is reflected in wide profit and wage differentials. Subcontractors are still exploited as effective buffers for business cycles, in spite of the seemingly modern appearance of a technical division of labour [Mitsui, 1985, pp. 128 and 153].

V. The extent of the remaining labour market duality

The dual structure of the Japanese economy has long been a subject of heated discussions among experts such as Ohkawa and Rosovsky [1965], Fei and Ranis [1964], Minami [1970], and Taira [1970]. As stated earlier, the Economic Planning Agency's White Paper in 1957 paid special attention

Figure 1: The rate of current profit against the amount of sales by capital size of firm in all industries

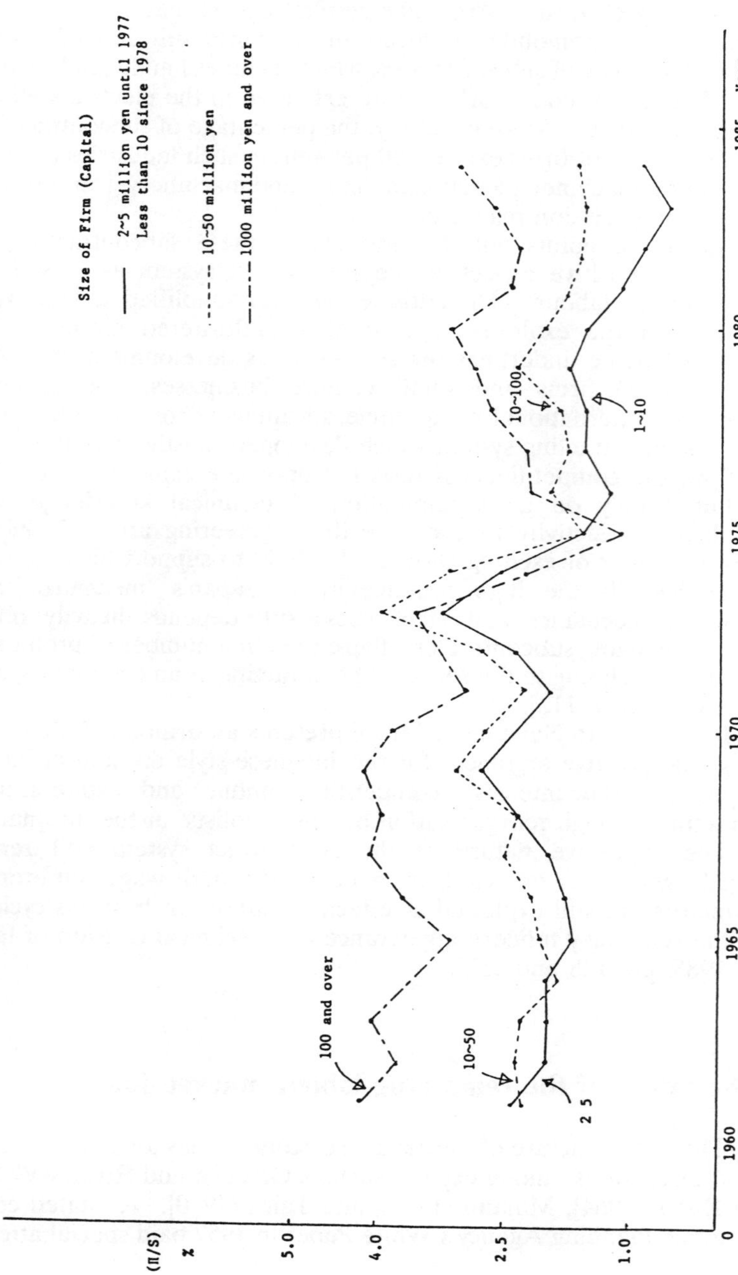

Source: Ministry of Finance, *Hojin Kigyo Tokei* (Statistics of Incorporated Firms).

to this subject. The wage differential between small and large firms decreased remarkably between 1955 and the 1960s but has increased gradually since around 1970, particularly after the oil crisis. Some experts stress the resurgence of the dual economy whereas others point out that simple average wage differentials tend to overstate any true duality in the economy.

1. Profit differentials

Figure 1 shows the difference in profit rates between large and small firms for the total economy. Here the profit rate is defined as the ratio of current profits to sales, and firm size is defined in terms of capital. With the exception of the oil shock period of 1973-75, there have been clear differences in profitability between large and small firms since at least 1960, and the differentials have widened since 1975. A similar tendency can be observed in manufacturing. However, the picture for wholesale and retail trade is different, with large firms experiencing lower profit rates than smaller ones, at least up to a few years ago.

The situation is different when the profit rate is measured as a percentage of capital in use (including borrowed capital). Comparing these profit rates at the total industry level, large firms recorded roughly equal, lower, and then higher profit rates than smaller firms in the 1960s, 1970s and 1980s, respectively (Figure 2). In manufacturing, large firms had a lower profit rate than smaller firms almost throughout the period until the early 1980s. It is noteworthy that smaller manufacturing firms earned considerably higher profits between the late 1960s and the early 1970s. In wholesale and retail trade (as in the earlier case), larger firms continuously earned less than smaller firms until the early 1980s.

The discussion so far has been limited to the average profit rate by firm size. However, Nakamura and Kiyonari stress that a wide range of profit rates exists within each size group. For example, Kiyonari [1980] shows that there are many profitable and growing small firms. Therefore, arguments concentrating on duality tend to overlook the emergence and existence of profitable "medium standing" firms and venture businesses. Unfortunately, in 1975 the Bank of Japan stopped publishing the survey showing the distribution of profit rates by firm size, and no similar data are available for the 1980s.

2. Wages, working hours and hourly wage differentials

In analysing wage differentials, a distinction must be made between regularly paid wages and salaries (including overtime allowances), and total cash earnings (including bonus payments and retroactive payments of increased pay). With regard to the former, significant average wage differentials between large firms and smaller firms have existed since at least 1965 (Table 19). The differentials were fairly stable between 1965 and 1975,

Figure 2: Rate of current profit against the amount of capital used by capital size of firm in all industries

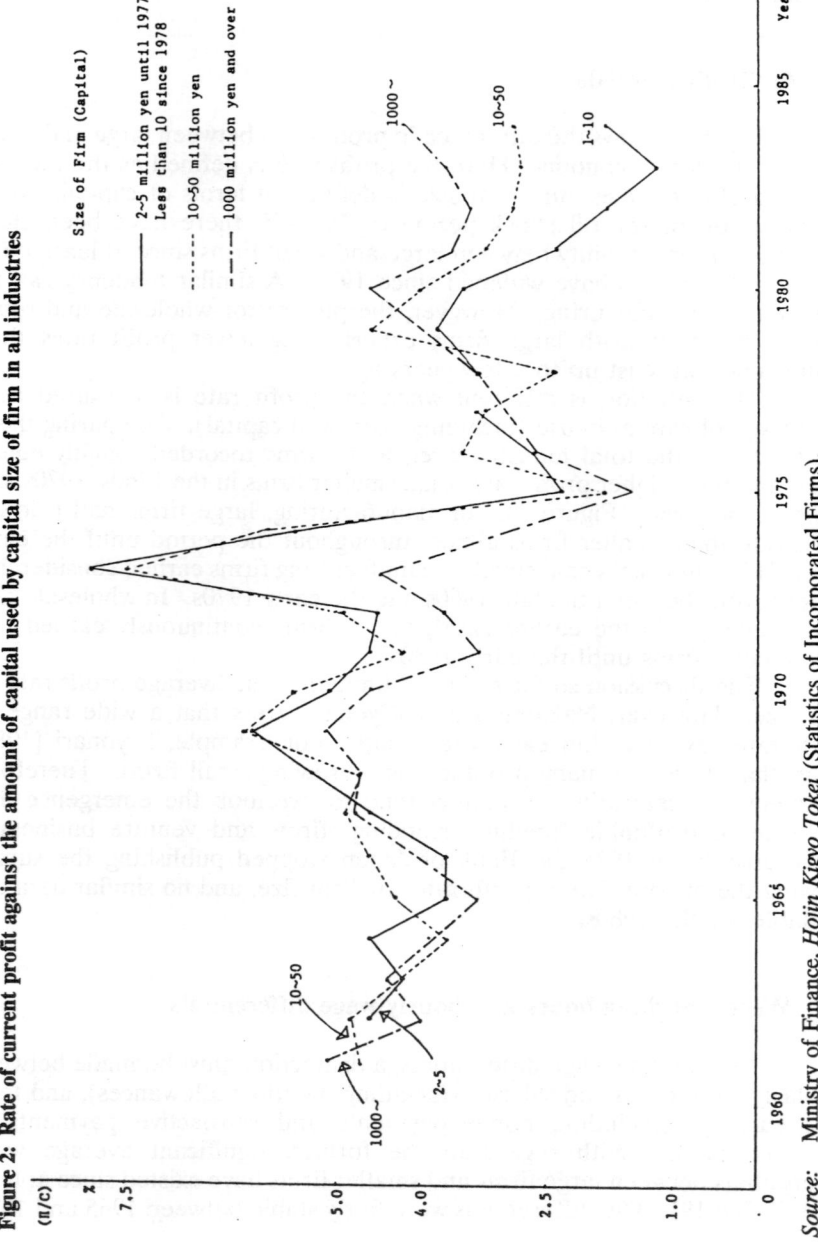

Source: Ministry of Finance, *Hojin Kigyo Tokei* (Statistics of Incorporated Firms).

Japan

but began to increase thereafter. By 1984, average wages in firms with fewer than 100 employees were no more than 75 per cent those in firms with 500 or more employees. Looking at these differentials it seems obvious that labour market duality in terms of wage differentials re-emerged after 1975. The expansion of differentials was most significant for companies with 30-99 employees.

Table 19: Average monthly regular pay of regular employees by size of firm in all industries excluding the service industry, 1965-1984

Relative wage index taking large firms (employing 500 or more) = 100
Size of firm

Year	100-499 persons	30-99 persons	5-29 persons
1965	89.5	84.3	74.6
1966	88.6	82.5	72.4
1967	87.4	81.5	71.0
1968	87.9	81.8	73.7
1969	88.3	82.3	73.8
1970	88.7	82.5	74.2
1971	89.1	83.1	75.0
1972	88.7	82.3	73.6
1973	88.6	83.5	73.4
1974	86.7	82.7	74.0
1975	90.1	82.4	75.1
1976	88.2	81.3	72.1
1977	88.1	80.8	72.1
1978	88.1	81.2	72.0
1979	86.3	78.4	70.9
1980	85.7	77.1	70.1
1982	85.1	76.3	69.5
1983	85.4	75.4	68.9
1984	85.2	74.8	68.3

Source: Ministry of Labor: *Yearbook of monthly labor statistics*, 1971, 1976, 1979, 1984.

Wage differentials by size of firm are even greater with respect to cash earnings including bonus payments than in the case of regular pay (Table 20). In addition, the pattern of stable and then increasing differentials is apparent also for total cash earnings. The combination of wider and increasing differentials resulted in earnings in firms with 5-29 employees dropping below 60 per cent of those in large firms since 1983.

It is not easy to conclude from these statistics alone whether labour market duality exists or was revived. At least two points must be considered in this respect: the *average* wage differentials by firm size may not reflect the true differentials because the quality of labour (education, skill, age, years of service, and gender, etc.) is not controlled for. This point is particularly important in Japan because wages are usually strongly related to age, years of service, education, and gender; workers' career patterns are very different in large versus small firms. As Koike [1981] points out, in Japan many blue collar workers in small businesses can be promoted to white collar status, and may even become independent owners of small businesses mostly by their late thirties or early forties.[13]

Table 20: Average monthly cash earnings of regular employees by size of firm in all industries excluding the service industry, 1965-1984

Relative wage index taking large firms (employing 500 or more) = 100

Size of firm

Year	100-499 persons	30-99 persons	5-29 persons
1965	78.3	65.9	74.6
1966	86.4	76.7	63.6
1967	85.2	76.0	63.1
1968	85.4	76.0	65.1
1969	85.3	76.3	64.5
1970	85.8	76.2	64.9
1971	85.8	76.8	65.7
1972	85.9	77.0	65.1
1973	85.4	76.3	64.5
1974	86.0	76.4	64.2
1975	86.2	75.6	64.9
1976	85.9	75.7	62.6
1977	86.1	76.1	63.4
1978	86.1	77.0	63.3
1979	84.3	74.3	62.1
1980	83.6	72.7	61.7
1981	83.8	72.2	60.1
1982	83.1	71.9	60.0
1983	83.1	70.4	59.1
1984	73.4	70.0	59.3

Source: Ministry of Labor: *Yearbook of monthly labor statistics*, 1971, 1976, 1979, 1984.

In order to estimate true wage differentials by firm size, it is necessary to control for such essential factors as age, education, job content (blue- and white-collar), and years of service. Figure 3 shows monthly regular pay differentials between large (employing 1,000 workers and over) and small (employing 10-99 workers) firms for *male* employees by *age* group in manufacturing in 1961, 1972, and 1984. Here other essential factors (*blue- and white-collar, education,* and *years of service*) are controlled for using the Laspeyres formula. It is noteworthy that, first, pay differentials are reduced remarkably by controlling for these factors and, second, the differentials have

---

13. Koike [1981], pp. 75, 79-97. He contends that the real wage differentials between large and small firms could be halved if these two elements were taken into account.

decreased during the past 23 years for the standard male workers. However, the differentials are still significant for workers in their forties and fifties.

Significant differences by firm size also exist with respect to hours of work. Hours of work are longer in small firms than in large firms for the following reasons: (a) the five-day week is less prevalent among small firms; (b) the standard hours of work are longer among small firms. Labour and management in large firms have reduced their standard hours of work by collective bargaining agreements to almost 40 hours a week, whereas small firms are mostly unorganised and are still bound only by the Labour Standards Law; (c) many small firms operate even on national holidays (only 8 days out of the total 12 national holidays are observed); (d) the number of days of paid vacation is fewer among small firms, because the average worker there has fewer years of service. The Labour Standards Law requires an additional paid vacation day for each additional year of service, up to a maximum of 20 days a year. Therefore, workers in small firms whose turnover rate is greater and who have fewer years of service have fewer days of paid vacation than workers in large firms. Furthermore, workers in small firms tend to leave more days of vacation unused; (e) on the other hand, overtime hours are shorter on average in small firms than in large firms, although small subcontracted firms may be forced by their customers to do overtime work.

Table 21 shows that the total monthly hours worked including overtime have, with the exception of a few years, been lowest in large firms. Small firms (employing fewer than 30 employees) have worked the longest hours throughout the period from 1970 to 1984.

Table 21: Total monthly hours worked in all industries by size of firm, 1970-1984

Year	500 and over	100-499 employees	30-99 employees	5-29 employees
1970	185.4	186.3	187.8	195.9
1971	181.7	184.7	187.0	193.5
1972	180.3	183.5	186.4	192.6
1973	179.8	182.0	183.3	190.1
1974	172.1	175.5	177.6	184.4
1975	166.6	171.9	175.5	182.7
1976	170.6	174.2	177.3	183.9
1977	171.7	174.0	177.3	184.3
1978	171.8	174.5	178.2	183.8
1979	173.8	175.1	178.2	183.8
1980	174.4	174.2	177.8	184.5
1981	174.1	173.6	177.0	182.7
1982	173.0	174.3	175.9	182.3
1983	173.5	174.3	175.8	182.6
1984	176.1	175.2	177.5	182.9

Source: The Ministry of Labor: *Monthly labor statistics.*

Figure 3: Wage differentials for the standardised workers in 1961, 1972 and 1984 (male workers in the manufacturing industry

(1) 1961

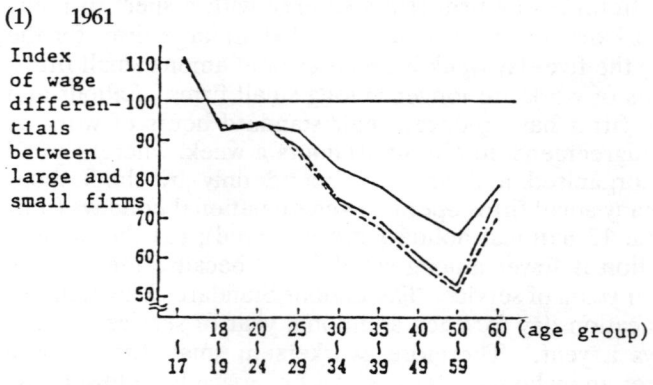

(2) 1972

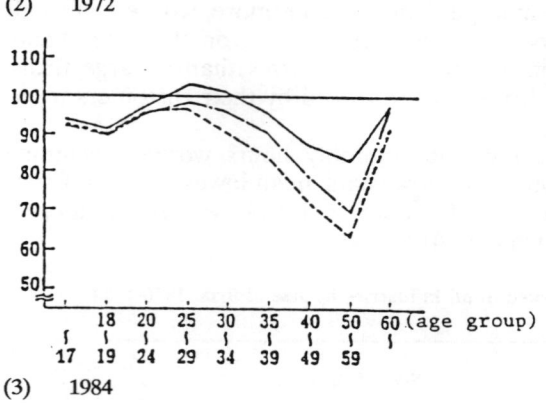

(3) 1984

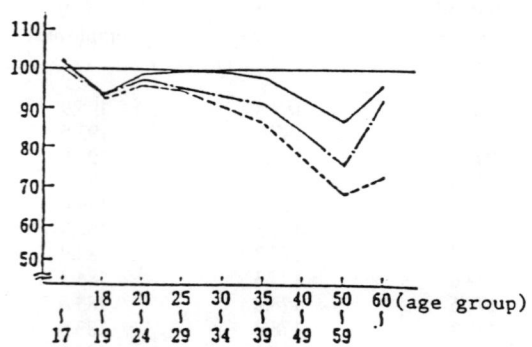

Notes: ---- shows the wage differentials by age group.
shows the wage differentials when the education levels and the occupations are controlled.
shows the wage differentials when the years of service are further controlled.

Source: The Agency of SMEs: *White paper on SMEs for 1986*, p. 22, based on Ministry of Labour: *Basic survey of wage structures*.

Japan

It follows from the preceding analysis that hourly earnings should be lower in small firms than in large firms. Table 22 shows that the differentials in terms of average total hourly earnings, including both overtime and bonus payments, have expanded since 1970 in firms of all size groups under 500 employees. The rate of decrease of relative earnings was largest in the smallest group of firms.

Table 22: Average hourly earnings in all industries by size of firm, 1970-1984

Year	500 and over	100-499 employees	30-99 employees	5-29 employees
		Average hourly earnings		
1970	467.8	403.4	367.1	288.1
1971	544.3	465.8	424.7	335.9
1972	634.7	543.0	495.7	389.5
1973	782.5	666.1	612.5	480.1
1974	1 025.8	876.2	800.6	623.7
1975	1 211.5	1 025.5	924.2	730.4
1976	1 330.8	1 135.0	1 045.9	789.0
1977	1 451.1	1 243.9	1 147.6	871.7
1978	1 550.2	1 329.4	1 230.3	934.4
1979	1 658.3	1 406.4	1 272.1	985.9
1980	1 775.4	1 506.3	1 346.6	1 046.9
1981	1 887.1	1 604.8	1 423.9	1 100.0
1982	1 977.7	1 657.0	1 481.8	1 145.9
1983	2 050.3	1 720.1	1 506.0	1 170.3
1984	2 109.9	1 791.3	1 552.3	1 227.0

	100-499 employees	30-99 employees	5-29 employees
	Differentials (size 500 and over = 100)		
1970	86.2	78.5	61.6
1971	85.6	78.0	61.7
1972	85.6	78.1	61.4
1973	85.1	78.3	61.4
1974	85.4	78.0	60.8
1975	84.6	76.3	60.3
1976	85.3	78.6	59.3
1977	85.7	79.1	60.1
1978	85.8	79.4	60.3
1979	84.8	76.7	59.4
1980	84.8	75.8	59.0
1981	85.0	75.5	58.3
1982	83.8	74.9	57.9
1983	83.9	73.5	57.1
1984	84.9	73.6	58.2

Source: Ministry of Labor: *Monthly labor statistics*.

3. Differentials in other benefits

There are considerable size-related differentials in other benefits. Lump-sum retirement allowances, pensions and medical care have already been mentioned. Moreover, there are differentials in company welfare facilities, housing loans, and so on, and workers in small firms are also more vulnerable to work accidents. Furthermore, it is undeniable that workers in small businesses tend to have less social prestige and less psychological satisfaction. In a traditional society like Japan, these intangible factors are sometimes more important than pecuniary differentials, particularly in terms of social status and marriage relationships.

It is important to take into account the challenging views developed by Nakamura, Kiyonari and Koike, which emphasise the positive new aspects that have emerged among small businesses since the 1970s. But the conclusion seems unavoidable that the differentials in working conditions between large and small firms have been expanding considerably since the oil crisis.[14]

4. Causes of the wage differentials

It has been a long-established view among economists that the wage differentials between large and small firms resulted from differentials in value added per employee, which in turn was a result of differences in the capital/labour (K/L) ratio. The availability of capital has been limited for small businesses until recent years. Figure 4 shows these differentials between 1957 and 1984. The differentials in value added per employee (V/L) and K/L narrowed considerably between the 1960s and the middle of the 1970s but they have widened somewhat since then. Since wages are a function of value added per worker, the evolution of value added per employee seems closely related to that of wage differentials.[15]

---

14. In this respect, it may be worthwhile mentioning here an argument raised by Nakamura [1985]. He cites evidence showing that there are many well-paid job opportunities even among small firms. But the data he quotes is for 1978. In order to support his arguments further, it is necessary to update the figures to cover the 1980s. Time limitations do not allow the present author to undertake this task in this study.

15. On a more technical note, labour productivity is a function of the capital stock. Since capital's share in total output is typically higher in large firms (due to more capital-intensive technologies), it follows from a Cobb-Douglas production function that labour productivity will increase more in large firms for a given increase in K/L.

Japan 215

Figure 4: Differentials of labour productivity and capital intensiveness between large and small firms in the manufacturing industry, 1957-1984

Differentials between large (employing 1,000 and over) and small (employing 10-299 employees) establishments

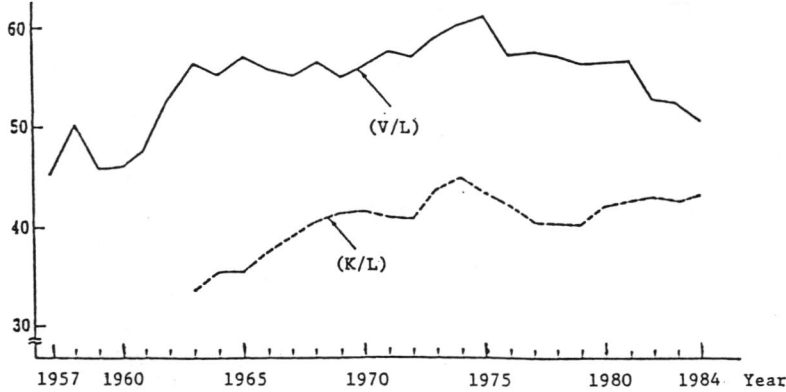

Note: (V/L) denotes the average added value per employee in a small firm as a percentage of that in a large firm, and likewise (K/L) denotes the average amount of asset value per employee in a small firm as a percentage of that in a large firm.

Source: Agency of SMEs: *White paper of SMEs in 1986*, p. 23, based on the MITI's *Census of Manufacture*.

VI. Attitudes and policies toward the small firm sector

1. Financial measures to help SMEs[16]

The Agency of SMEs within the Ministry of International Trade and Industry provides a wide range of financial measures to help small businesses. The Law to Promote Modernisation of SMEs was enacted in March 1963. It designates 185 industries and trades as the target of modernisation, 72 of which are the object of emergency measures. They include such traditional industries as soy-sauce brewing, sake brewing, small printing shops, etc. Two special governmental banks provide loans to firms in these designated industries and trades in order to modernise their production facilities and equipment. The SME Financing Bank provides ten-year loans of up to 350 million yen per firm at below-market interest rates. The National Financing Bank also provides low interest ten-year loans of up to 30 million yen per firm. When a group of SMEs in the designated

---

16. Descriptions in this section are taken from the Agency of SMEs [1985a].

industries or trades applies for financial aid to modernise their production facilities and equipment, a special loan to facilitate structural reform is available through the SME Financing Bank (maximum of 350 or 750 million yen) or the National Financing Bank (maximum of 35 million yen).

The government also established in 1980 the SME Undertaking, which has special judicial status and is intended to promote the structural reform and modernisation of SMEs. The Undertaking helps to develop land for groups of SMEs, integrate SMEs into co-operative unions, construct joint warehouses, and modernise shopping centres, etc. in co-operation with prefectural governments. The SME Undertaking and prefectural governments jointly provide SMEs with loans at low interest rates. The Undertaking also provides managerial expertise and consulting services.

The Agency of SMEs provides prefectural governments with financial aid to renovate local specialised industries. For those areas that suffered from structural changes, a special temporary law to help renovation and transformation of SMEs was enacted in 1983. The law provides special tax considerations, special loans through the SME Financing Bank and National Financing Bank, and a total of 220 million yen available through the prefectural governments in 55 areas.

In order to facilitate access to financial resources, special arrangements for SMEs are made through three kinds of institutions: 69 mutual banks (established by a special law in 1951) give loans to SMEs (those firms with fewer than 300 employees or capitalised with less than 800 million yen) up to a maximum of 15 billion yen; 561 credit banks (established by a special law in 1951) give similar loans to the members of credit co-operatives; 464 credit unions (established by SME Co-operative Law in 1949) give smaller loans, up to a maximum of 400 million yen, to their members.

Beside these special financial institutions, an association to guarantee credit for SMEs is set up in each prefecture. This is necessary because many SMEs lack sufficient security to get loans from ordinary banks. The association provides guarantees for loans without adequate security, which are further supported by the Public Insurance Institution for SMEs (*Chusho Kigyo Shinyo Hoken Koko*). A sum of 5.7 billion yen is now available for SMEs through this arrangement.

Furthermore, three governmental banks for SMEs provide loans directly to small businesses: (a) the SME Financing Bank, set up in 1953, fully capitalised by the government, and supplied with money from a special fiscal fund (postal savings and premiums of the Welfare Pension Plan) provides long-term (ten-year) loans at low interest rates up to a maximum of 250 million or 350 million yen. The loan balance amounted to 5.2 trillion yen by March 1985; (b) the National Financing Bank, set up in 1949, fully capitalised by the government, and supplied with money from the government and a special fiscal fund, provides a small amount of long-term loans to those small firms which cannot raise money from ordinary banks. The interest rate is also low and the maximum loan is limited to 25 million yen. The loan balance amounted to 4.9 trillion yen by March 1985; (c) the Central Bank for Commercial and Industrial Co-operatives was set up in

1936 by the government in co-operation with qualified co-operatives. It provides low interest loans to member co-operatives or their affiliates. The loan balance amounted to 7.7 trillion yen by March 1985. In addition, two government finance institutions (The Environmental Safety Finance Bank and the Finance Bank to Develop the Okinawa Islands) are providing special loans for specific purposes.

Finally, SME Investment Promotion Companies were established in 1963 in Tokyo, Nagoya, and Osaka. It is difficult for SMEs to raise capital through equity markets. In order to cope with this problem, these companies provide SMEs with capital as well as managerial and technological consulting services. The qualifications for receiving financial aid from SMEIPC are as follows: (a) capital less than 100 million yen; (b) operating in the designated 28 industries or trades; (c) having an intention to list stock on the exchange in the future; (d) paying dividends of more than five yen per share over the previous two years; (e) the stockholders do not have ability to raise money for increasing capital; and (f) having plans to modernise or rationalise equipment. Venture business firms which have unique technology or products and spend more than 3 per cent of revenue from sales for R & D have preferential access to SMEIPC money.

2. Tax exemptions and reductions[17]

Self-employed businessmen can choose between a "blue tax report" or a "quasi-corporation tax" system. The former allows tax exemptions on wages and salaries paid to family workers. The latter allows tax exemptions on remuneration to the owner of a business equivalent to that of a corporation.

Incorporated SMEs with capital of less than 100 million yen are treated more favourably than ordinary corporations in terms of corporate income tax. Ordinary corporations must pay a corporate income tax of 43.3 per cent, whereas small companies must pay 31.0 per cent on income less than 8 million yen and 43.3 per cent on income over 8 million yen. If companies pay dividends, large companies must pay 25.0 per cent on income of less than 8 million yen and 33.3 per cent on income of more than 8 million yen. There are various other tax reductions for SMEs, such as accelerated depreciation, tax exemptions for R & D, special treatment in cases of succession of businesses, etc.[18]

---

17. Descriptions in this section are taken from the Agency of SMFs [1985a].

18. For more details, see the Agency of SMFs [1985a], pp. 154-202.

VII. Conclusions

Labour market duality between large and small firms has been a subject of serious discussion among economists and sociologists in Japan since the 1930s. The low standard of living of the working class and the misery of exploited small businesses in the early days engendered considerable sympathy among intellectuals. Moreover, political oppression by the militarist government angered pre-war Marxists, with the result that Marxist economists and sociologists paid a great deal of attention to the problem of SMEs in Japan. This pre-war tradition has continued to the present day and, as a result of such a tradition, the overwhelming majority of studies in this field have been strongly tinged with a stereotypical Marxist flavour. However, on a more positive note, the strong criticisms by Marxist scholars have made government economists in charge of the SMEs, as well as other labour problems, highly sensitive to the seriousness of the state of workers in small businesses. As a result, they have undertaken a series of voluminous statistical surveys designed to clarify the situation of SMEs. This information has provided Japanese scholars with to material to aid their analysis of many aspects of the problems of SMEs. Unfortunately, most of their studies have been largely descriptive, and few empirical studies have been undertaken in this field except for publications by governmental agencies.

This study has attempted to bring out the various important features relating to the small business sector within the Japanese economy and to explain the complicated industrial matrix which links small and large firms. Explaining the role and relevance of small firms in any economy is a difficult task as the nature of this sector may change over time. This study has attempted to clarify the Japanese situation in a number of ways. First, it has been pointed out that the definition of the small firm is a conceptual problem in itself, and that any study of this sector must begin by using the statistical sources which are relevant to the analysis at hand.

Second, the importance of small businesses in the Japanese economy and their contribution to employment generation have been emphasised. About 99 per cent of the total establishments in the private sector belong to the small and medium-sized sector (where this sector is defined to be employing fewer than 300 employees in general, but fewer than 100 in the wholesale trade and fewer than 50 in the retail trade). In total, SMEs in 1981 employed more than 80 per cent of the 46 million people employed in the private sector,[19] and the employment share of SMEs in 1982 was 53 per cent. If the analysis is confined to incorporated firms, then 58 per cent of total value added in the fiscal year 1985 was produced by SMEs [Agency of SMEs, 1987, Appendix, p. 19]. Therefore, approximately 60 per cent or more of Japan's GNP can be accounted for by small businesses. The

---

19. Compiled in Agency of SMEs [1987], Appendix, pp. 2-3. Table 3 in the text includes the establishments of government enterprises in several industries besides "public service" so that the figure here does not coincide with those in Table 3. On the other hand, Table 16 of this paper does exclude all the public enterprises.

corresponding figure in the United States is estimated to be almost 40 per cent.[20] Almost all of the increased employment opportunities created in the secondary and tertiary industries between 1972 and 1981 (6.8 million out of total 6.93 million people) were attributable to SMEs. In particular, the retail trade and the service industries accounted for 72.2 per cent of this employment growth [Agency of SMEs, 1985a, pp. 96-97].

Third, the study has shown that the small business sector is not a homogeneous entity but varies according to many factors. The growth and performance of small businesses depend on whether they are traditional firms or "venture" businesses with higher R & D capabilities. However, dynamic changes have been identified which occur even within the so-called traditional businesses.

Fourth, it has been noted that the health of the small business sector depends partly on aggregate demand for goods and services, but also on the subtle inter-relations between large and small businesses. In many sectors the technological gap between the small subcontractor and large parent firm has narrowed as technology "cascades" from large to small businesses. Profit rates based on a return on capital measure shows that many small businesses have performed well vis-à-vis large firms. Flexibility and intelligent dependence have been the key to the health and survival of SMEs.

Fifth, the study has attempted to address the problem of "duality" in Japan's industrial structure. Workers in small businesses are relatively less well off in terms of medical care, pensions, union representation, hours of work and status than workers in larger firms, and this is a problem which still needs to be considered in more depth. Wage differentials also exist between small and large enterprises, although the gap narrows when workers of the same educational background and experience level are compared.

Sixth, the response of government to the problems of small businesses shows that some attempt has been made towards solving certain resource bottlenecks frequently faced by small enterprises.

Finally, there is the issue of "monopolist capital exploitation", a phrase still used to describe large firms' dominance over their smaller counterparts. This relationship has also been described as symptomatic of a "premodern" era. If this simple definition is accepted, then it would be difficult to avoid defining most modern industrialised countries as being to some extent "premodern". Japan is not unique in having a structure based on a foundation of small firms, although the volume of statistics collected in Japan on this subject appears to be more comprehensive, and thus more open to discussion, than in other countries [see Bannock, 1980]. The key to research on this subject is further international comparative study whic would permit a meaningful assessment of the small firm sector's contribution to economic performance and to meeting workers' aspirations.

---

20. John A. Cicco's correspondence with the author, dated 6 November 1987. His paper "Small business and the large corporation: The emerging critical linkage" will soon appear in the *Harvard Business Review*.

Bibliography

Bannock, G. 1980. *The promotion of small business: A seven-country study*, London, Shell.

Agency of SMEs (Chusho Kigyo Cho). 1984a. *Bencha Bijinesu Jittai Chosa Hokoku* (A survey of venture businesses), Tokyo, Agency of SMEs, February (mimeo).

---. 1984b. *Bencha Bijinesu he no Kitai to Kadai* (Expectations for and tasks of venture businesses), An interim report of a study committee on venture businesses, Tokyo, Toyo Hoki Shuppan.

---. 1985a. *Chucho Kigyo Seisaku no Aramashi* (Outline of the measures for SMEs) in FY 1985, Tokyo, Chusho Kigyo Chosakai.

---. 1985b. *Gijutsu Kakushin to Chusho Kigyo* (Technological innovation and SMEs), A report of the Deliberation Committee on Modernisation of SMEs), Tokyo, Tsusho Sangyo Chosakai.

---. 1986. *Chusho Kigyo Hajusho* (A White Paper for SMEs for 1986), Tokyo, Okurasho Insatsukyoku.

---. 1987. *Chusho Kigyo Hajusho* (A White Paper for SMEs for 1987), Tokyo, Okurasho Insatsukyoku.

Fei, J.; Ranis, G. 1964. *Development in the labour surplus economy: Theory and policy*, Homewood, Ill., Richard D. Irwin, Inc.

Fujita, Keizo (ed.). 1943. *Shitauke-sei Kogyo* (Subcontract systems in manufacturing), Tokyo, Yuhikaku.

---. 1957. "Nihon Sangyo ni okeru Kigyo Keiretsu" (Enterprise series in Japanese industry), in *Keiei Kenkyu*, No. 29, July.

Ichikawa, Hirokatsu. 1948. "Tekkogyo ni okeru Chusho Kigyo Mondai" (Problems of SMEs in the iron and steel industry), in *Shakai Kagaku*, No. 19, Tokyo, University of Tokyo.

---. 1957. "Kikan Sangyo ni Okeru Keiretsuka no Doko: Tekkogyo" (A trend of subordination in a basic industry: The iron and steel industry), in *Kosei Torihiki*, No. 78.

Ichikawa, H.; Hirozumi, Iwao (eds.). 1972. *70 Nendai no Nihon Chusho Kigyo* (Japanese SMEs in the 1970s), Tokyo, Shinhyoron.

Ikeda, Masataka. 1972. "70 Nendai no Shitauke Sei no Kozo Henka" (Structural changes in the subcontract system in the 1970s) in Ichikawa, H.; Iwao, H. (eds.) 1972.

---. 1982. "Sangyo no Kokusaika to Shitauke Saihensei" (Internationalisation of industries and the restructuring of subcontract firms), in Watanabe, M. (ed.), 1982.

Ito, Mitsuharu. 1963. "Niju Kozo Ron no Tenbo to Hansei" (Outlook for and reflections on discussions of the dual economy), in Kawaguchi; Nagasu (eds.) *Nihon Keizai no Kiso Kozo* (The basic structure of the Japanese economy), Tokyo, Shunju Sha.

Keizai Kikaku Cho (Economic Planning Agency). 1957. *Keizai Hakusho for 1957* (Economic White Paper for 1957), reprinted in 1976 by Nihon Hyoron Sha.

Kiyonari, Tadao. 1967. *Gendai Nihon no Chusho Reisai Kigyo* (SMEs and very small businesses in modern Japan), Tokyo, Bungado Ginko Kenkyu Sha.

---. 1972. *Gendai Chusho Kigyo no Shintenkai* (New developments in modern SMEs), Tokyo, Nihon Keizai Shinbun Sha.

---. 1980. *Chusho Kigyo Dokuhon* (Textbook on SMEs), Tokyo, Toyo Keizai Shinposha.

Kiyonari, T. et al. (eds.). 1972. *Bencha Bijinesu - Zuno wo Uru Chisana Kigyo* (Venture businesses - small firms selling intelligence), Tokyo, Nihon Keizai Shinbun Sha.

Kobayashi, Yoshio (ed.). 1958. *Kigyo Keiretsu no Jittai* (The present situation of the enterprise series), Tokyo, Toyo Keizai Shinpo Sha.

Koike, Kazuo. 1981. *Chusho Kigyo no Jukuren* (Skills in SMEs), Tokyo, Dobunkan.

Kokumin Kinyukoko Chosabu (Research Division, National Financing Bank). 1985. *Bencha Bijinesu* (Venture businesses), Tokyo, Chusho Kigyo Risaachi Senta.

Komiyama, Takuji. 1941. *Nihon Chusho Kogyo Kenku* (A study of the Japanese small and medium-sized industry), Tokyo, Chuo Koron Sha.

Kosai, Yutaka. 1981. *Kodo Seicho no Jidai* (The era of high economic growth), Tokyo, Nihon Hyoron Sha.

Koshiro, Kazutoshi. 1981. *Nihon no Roshi Kankei* (The era of high economic growth), Tokyo, Nihon Hyoron Sha.

---. 1983a. *Personnel planning, technological changes, and out-sourcing in the Japanese automobile industry*, Discussion paper 83-3, Center for International Trade Studies, Yokohama National University, May. Also reproduced in *International Journal of Technology Management*, Vol. 2, No. 2, 1987, pp. 279-297 and Vol. 2, Nos. 3/4, 1987, pp. 473-499.

---. 1983b. *Nihon no Roshi Kankei* (Japanese industrial relations), Tokyo, Yuhikaku.

---. 1984. "Gijutsu Kakushin ka ni okeru Chusho Kigyo no Koyo Mondai" (Employment problems of SMEs under technological innovation), in *Kokumin Kinyu Koko Chosa Geppo*, No. 282, October.

---. 1985a. *Chusho Haiteku Kigyo no Rodo Shijo ni kansuru Jisshoteki Kenkyu - Bencha Bijinesu no Rodo Shijo* (Empirical studies in the labour market of SMEs with high-technology - The labour market of venture businesses), Interim Report, Tokyo, Koyo Shokugyo Sogo Kenkyujo.

---. 1985b. "Dento Sangyo no Gijutsu Kakushin" (Technological innovation in the traditional industries), in *Kyoto no Rodokeizai*, No. 85 (Kyoto Prefecture), October.

---. 1986. *Bencha bijinesu no Rodo Shijo* (Labour markets of venture businesses), unpublished mimeo. Later published as "Chusho Kigyo Rodosha no Kinro Iyoku to Rodoshijo" (Work morale and the labour market in the small firm sector), in *Economia*, No. 92, Yokohama National University, March, pp. 1-53.

Koshiro, Kazutoshi; Nagano, Jin. 1985. "Jidosha Sangyo" (The automobile industry), in Mikio Sumiya (ed.): *Gijutsu Kakushin to Roshi Kankei* (Technological innovation and industrial relations), Tokyo, The Japan Institute of Labor.

Kuwahara, Yasuo. 1987. *The job creation and job destruction process in Japan*, Paper submitted to the OECD's Programme on Job Creation and Human Capital Investment in the Context of Technological and Other Structural Changes, January (mimeo). The essence of this paper is included in OECD: *Employment Outlook*, September 1987.

Minami, Ryoshin. 1970. *Nihon Keizai no Tenkan Ten* (The turning point of the Japanese economy), Tokyo, Sobunsha.

Mitsui, Itsutomo. 1985. "Bencha Bijinesu" (Venture businesses), in Takizawa, Kikutaro (ed.), 1985.

Miyazawa, Kenichi. 1961. "Keizai Kozo to Kinyu Kozo" (The economic structure and the financial structure), in Ichiro Nakayama (ed.): *Shihon Chikuseki to Kinyu Kozo* (Capital accumulation and the financial structure), Tokyo, Toyo Keizai Shinposha.

Nakamura, Hideichiro. 1962. *Nihon no Chusho Kigyo Mondai* (Problems of SMEs in Japan), Tokyo, Godo Shuppan Sha.

---. 1964. *Chuken Kigyo Ron* (On the medium standing firms), Tokyo, Toyo Keizai Shinpo Sha.

---. 1977. *Kakushin-teki Kigyoka Seishin no Ninaite* (Bearers of innovative entrepreneurship), Tokyo, Nihon Keizai Shinbun Sha.

---. 1985. *Chosen suru Chusho Kigyo* (Challenging SMEs), Tokyo, Iwanami Shoten.

Ohkawa, Kazushi; Rosovsky, Henry. 1965. "A century of Japanese economic growth", in Lockwood, W. (ed.): *The state and economic enterprise in Japan*, Princeton NJ, Princeton University Press.

*Osaka Keizai Daigaku Chusho Kigyo Keiei Kenkyu Jo (Institute of SME Management, Osaka University of Economics) (ed.). 1978. *Chusho Kigyo Kenkyu* (Research on SMEs), Tokyo, Nichigai Associates.

Shinohara, Miyohei. 1959. *Sangyo Kozo* (The industrial structure), Tokyo, Shunju Sha.

Taira, Koji. 1970. *Economic development and the labour market in Japan*, New York, Columbia University Press.

*Takizawa, Kikutaro (ed.). 1985. *Nihon no Chusho Kigyo Kenkyu* (Studies in SMEs in Japan), 3 vols., Tokyo, Yuhikaku.

Tasugi, Kisou. 1941. *Shitauke-sei Kogyo Ron* (On the subcontracting industry), Tokyo, Yuhikaku.

Umemura, Mataji. 1964. *Sengo Nihon no Rodo Ryoku* (The labour force in post-war Japan), Tokyo, Iwanami Shoten.

Watanabe, Mutsumi. 1972. "Chusho Kigyo no Kozo Henka" (Structural changes in SMEs), in Ichikawa, H; Iwao, H. (eds.), 1972.

Watanabe, Mutsumi (ed.). 1982. *80 Nendai no Chusho Kigyo Mondai* (Problems of SMEs in the 1980s), Tokyo, Shinhyoron.

Watanabe, Mutsumi; Kyoichi, Maekawa. 1984. *Gendai Chusho Kigyo Kenkyu* (Studies on the modern SMEs), 2 vols. Tokyo, Otsuki Shoten.

Watanabe, Yukio. 1982. "Daitoshi ni okeru Reisai Kogyo no Yakuwari" (The role of very small businesses in large cities), in Watanabe, Mutsumi (ed.), 1982.

---. 1985. "Shitauke Keiretsu Chusho Kigyo" (Subordinate subcontractor SMEs) in Takizawa, Kikutaro (ed.), 1985.

* The books marked with an asterisk are bibliographical studies.

6 United Kingdom

David Marsden

I. Introduction and summary

The role of small firms in the economy and their influence on labour markets has engendered a good deal of controversy recently. The idea that small firms, or at least some small firms, might hold the key to economic regeneration may have seemed eccentric 15 years ago, but now such ideas appear attractive to many at various points on the political spectrum. This paper has two main aims: the first is to examine the development of small firms in the United Kingdom and to look at some of the implications of recent changes; and the second is to review some of the existing material on small firms.

Piore and Sabel [1984] have argued that many developed countries have now reached a point at which there is a choice between pursuing economic prosperity by further development of mass production, reinforced by the economic institutions and policies required to make such systems viable, and encouraging the development of a small firm sector using different forms of economic and social co-operation. A renewed emphasis upon market as opposed to hierarchical co-ordination can be found in their argument, but it is a market supported by a strong body of social institutions. These institutions enable market co-ordination and competition to be combined with a greater degree of "high trust" relationships between firms than is normally associated with free market competition in which the contract is supposed to dominate trust. As will be seen in the course of this chapter, their argument leads one to highlight one of the weaknesses of the small firm sector in the United Kingdom compared, for example, to the Federal Republic of Germany, or their own examples from Italy; namely, the apparent absence of strong social organisations of small firms. Although many of the hallmarks of Piore and Sabel's theory seem absent or underdeveloped in the United Kingdom, there has nevertheless been a marked growth in the employment share, and some decline in the size of units of production used by large firms. Whether or not Piore and Sabel's thesis is borne out for the United Kingdom - and most of the existing data reviewed in this paper cannot give a clear answer - it is still important to assess the implications of this change in the structure of the British economy for labour market policies and for regulation of labour markets.

This paper seeks, as far as possible, to follow the standard format used for all the countries involved, thus facilitating comparisons. It falls into five sections. Section II deals briefly with typologies of small firms and their relations with other firms. It also compares the numerical importance of small firms in the United Kingdom with that in some other European countries, showing this to be smaller in the United Kingdom, although the gap has been reduced in recent years. The evidence that small firms are commonly "satellites" of larger ones receives only limited support, and this accounts for the inapplicability of some of the "dual labour market" theories developed in other countries. Nevertheless, the problems of low pay and poor working conditions have proved more difficult to tackle among small firms, although such firms have often been competitors with, rather than satellites of, larger, better paying, and more strongly unionised firms.

Section II also examines some of the institutional arrangements for the representation of small firms, which is much weaker than in many countries of continental Europe. In several cases, such representation has arisen from the feeling among small firm owners that organisations designed to represent all firms are inadequate for their special needs, and they subsequently break away. Part of the weakness of small firms organisations could stem from their diversity, but if this is so, it would be interesting to know how such problems have been overcome in, for example, the Federal Republic of Germany.

Union recognition is less common in small establishments,[1] and there is a greater tendency than elsewhere for reliance upon multi-employer bargaining arrangements. But even among small establishments, establishment level bargaining is often the norm, perhaps reflecting the weakness of collective representation of small firms noted earlier.

Section III deals with the long-term historical, and recent, evolution of small firms in the United Kingdom. In manufacturing, for which the data are best, small establishments declined in share of output and employment until the late 1960s. Evidence of a similar decline in small retail shops could also be found for the post-war period. In manufacturing, one of the most important developments was the rise of giant multi-establishment firms. Many of the reasons commonly put forward for the decline of small firms, such as those relating to marketing, finance, transportation, and technical economies of scale appear to explain the decline of small firms as the inverse of factors explaining the rise of giant firms, and so implicitly presume that the provision of many such services from within the firm is more efficient than from outside.

As concerns changes during the 1970s, Section III documents in particular the resurgence of small establishments, especially after the deep recession of 1979-82. Within manufacturing, this resurgence affected all branches, but in retail distribution - the services sector for which the information is clearest - it seems that although the decline stopped, such increases did not occur. The structural aspects of the changes of the 1970s

---

1.   The terms "establishment" and "plant" are used interchangeably in this chapter, as are those of "enterprise", "firm", and "business". For stylistic reasons, the less cumbersome terms "plant" and "firm" are used frequently.

are also considered, notably the characteristics of new firms, and the questions of concentration and dependency. Production, construction, the retail and catering trades account for most business starts, and in these sectors the median completed life of firms is about four years. Most small firms deal with local markets, and many depend on a few major customers.

Ownership concentration increased during the 1970s, continuing a much longer-standing movement, and the number of establishments owned by the 100 largest firms increased by about 14 per cent. However, the average size of these establishments decreased in line with the overall decrease in average establishment size. Small firms appear to have played a bigger role in job creation, as in the United States, but this occurred in a period of employment shake-out in large establishments, and so may not be typical.

Section IV examines factors in the economic and social background to the development of small firms, and the reasons for their development. Labour costs have been lower in smaller establishments, and unit labour costs may also have been lower in the early 1970s. However, any unit labour cost gap appears to have been eliminated by 1983. If this is sustained by a more rigorous analysis, it may suggest that the labour cost advantage of smaller establishments has been a factor in the move to smaller establishments, at least in the United Kingdom. At the same time, the elimination of the unit labour cost differential could have been the purpose of heavy labour shedding by many large establishments after 1979, of which the car, steel, and shipbuilding industries provide some good illustrations (and also show the role of industrial relations in such changes).

Section V covers aspects of small firm development, but it was not possible to include much evidence of small firm communities in the United Kingdom, despite the historical importance of industrial districts. This weakness may be related to the comparative weakness in the United Kingdom of small firm collective organisations.

Section VI looks at government attitudes and policies towards small firms. In terms of government influence, employment law does not appear to have harmed small firms, although the present government has removed small firms from coverage under some provisions. The government has also acted to help small firm finance, one of the most important steps being its fiscal support of the unlisted securities market since its foundation in 1980.

The chapter concludes by arguing that the resurgence of small establishments may be an important development, but that much depends upon the reasons for it. If it is primarily because unit labour costs escaped management control in large establishments during the 1960s and 1970s, then the apparent reduction of the cost disadvantage of large establishments may neutralise further development. But the reasons for this loss of control are complex, and a return of the unit labour cost disadvantage depends on the reversibility of the changes occurring in labour and product markets and in management methods and industrial relations since 1979.

Small firm development has been favoured by a number of other factors, including changes in the cost and the flexibility of some capital equipment, new forms of management organisation for small firms, and moves by governments and by some large employers to "deregulate" labour markets. These, too, have important consequences for labour protection and collective bargaining, and the difficult problem of potential trade-offs between these issues and employment promotion.

II. Characteristics and extent of small firms

1. Definition of small firms

There is no institutional definition of the small firm sector in the United Kingdom arising from any special legal status similar to that of the West German *Handwerk* or the French *Artisanat* sectors. The Bolton Committee, which reported in 1971, established a statistical convention for its own purposes by taking small firms in manufacturing as those with under 200 employees. But with the gradual change in the concerns of policy and research, this definition has slowly become less influential, and the OECD's convention of 100 employees, because of its wider reference, is likely to become more widely accepted. In any case, a crude statistical threshold is bound to be arbitrary, and unsuited to the investigation of certain problems.

2. Volume and employment share of the small firm sector

During much of the post-war period, the United Kingdom has had a relatively weak small business sector in numerical terms. In the early 1960s, its share of small establishment (fewer than 100 employees) manufacturing employment was the lowest of the 13 advanced industrial countries surveyed by the Bolton Committee, at 31 per cent, against 34 per cent for the Federal Republic of Germany, 39 per cent for the United States, and 66 per cent for Italy. Ganguly's [1982] estimates for a period 10-15 years later suggest that the gap has narrowed owing to a faster decline in small firms in the other countries, except the United States and Canada. The results of the 1981 Eurostat Labour Cost survey show the United Kingdom to be closer to the position of the largest EEC economies, especially in manufacturing, but still very different in retail distribution, banking and insurance. In the latter sectors, the dominance of large firms in the United Kingdom is very striking.

The picture in Table 1 is somewhat distorted by exclusion of establishments and firms with fewer than 10 employees. In the United Kingdom, in 1982, these accounted for 5 per cent of manufacturing employment, but 31 per cent of retail employment. In addition, recent comparisons of the small firm sectors in the United Kingdom and the

Federal Republic of Germany reveal many more very small firms in the latter [Bannock, 1976; Prais et al, 1981; Doran, 1984]. It may, therefore, understate the difference between the United Kingdom and other countries. This might explain the rather different emphasis in research on small firms to that found in, for example, Italy or the Federal Republic of Germany.

The boundary between small firms and other forms of employment activity is not a clear one in economic terms, and so it is worth comparing also the level of self-employment in the United Kingdom (Table 2) with some other countries. Self-employment is also less developed in the United Kingdom than elsewhere, even when agriculture is excluded, but there has been a marked increase since the severe recession of 1979-82.

Table 1: Employment share by enterprise size, 1981

Sector	Enterprise size		
	less than 100	10 - 199	more than 1000
Industry + construction	25.9	37.4	32.7
Manufacturing	27.1	36.9	29.2
Wholesale distribution	42.2	48.4	38.6
Retail distribution	35.3	39.1	50.1
Banking	0.8	1.5	95.5
Insurance	2.6	4.8	80.0

Notes: Industry = establishments, services, enterprises; Industry and construction = NACE 1-5; Wholesale = NACE 61, 64, 653-56; Retail = NACE 64 + 65 except 651 and 652; Banking = NACE 812/813; Insurance = NACE 82. Establishment = "local unit".
Source: Eurostat/LCI.

Table 2: Percentage self-employed in industry and services, by gender, 1979 and 1983

Year	Industry		Services		All workers
	Male	Female	Male	Female	('000s)
1979	2.1	0.1	3.3	1.1	23 804
1983	2.8	0.2	4.2	2.1	22 473

Source: Eurostat Labour Force Survey.

One contributory factor to the lesser development of small firms and self-employment in the United Kingdom is the relative concentration of taxation upon wages and salaries instead of upon firms. The proportion of total labour costs represented by statutory social charges in the United Kingdom remains light by EEC standards, so there is correspondingly less incentive to avoid tax by subcontracting to moonlighting firms and individuals. For industry and construction, statutory social charges in 1981 accounted for 17 per cent of total labour costs in the Federal Republic of Germany, 19 per cent in France, and 23 per cent in Italy, but only 9 per cent in the United Kingdom.

3. Types of small firms

As in all countries, there is great diversity among small firms in the United Kingdom. Some of this has been given institutional expression through the organisations created to represent small firms but, as will be seen later, there is no institutional equivalent to the organisations of the German *Handwerk* sector, nor to those of the French *artisanat*. There is a variety of legal forms of small firms running from those quoted on the stock exchange, through partnerships, to sole proprietorships, and self-employment (Table 3). But many of the collective organisations, for example in those sectors where partnerships are strong, are based primarily on the type of activity (legal, medical, etc.) and not the scale or type of organisation. If such lines of cleavage are weak in the United Kingdom, what other bases of typologies have been discussed?

There are two strands to thinking about small firms in relation to labour market segmentation. One relates to theories of dependence of small firms producing for larger ones, providing them with a greater degree of cost flexibility in recession. The second strand relates to the problem of low pay. For many years it seemed doubtful that there was any simple identification that could be made between small firms and "secondary labour market" conditions. In the early 1970s there was not much evidence that small firms were fulfilling such functions in the economy. Indeed, the Merrett Cyriax survey [1970] found that 78 per cent of small (fewer than 200 employees) firms in manufacturing were in competition with large firms, 16 per cent were specialists, and only 6 per cent were what they called "satellites" of large firms. Only 35 per cent of small firms were dependent for more than 25 per cent of their business on a single customer [Bolton, 1971, p. 32]. The proportion of "satellites" would diminish further if the sample included retail shops and partnerships in many services.

According to the second strand, small firms have been seen as part of the problem of low pay (see Tables 5 and 6), but this is a separate question from that of the links between large and small firms [for a recent discussion see Craig et al., 1984]. Indeed, often such small firms have been seen as a threat to larger firms offering union rates and conditions, a point raised in the defence of the Wages Councils and the Fair Wage Resolution (forms of minimum wage protection) by several members of the Confederation of British Industry in its consultations on minimum wage policy in 1984 [see Chronicle, *British Journal of Industrial Relations*, November, 1984].

Table 3: The legal status of small enterprises by economic sector, 1970

Enterprise size	Quoted companies	Non-quoted limited companies	Unlimited companies	Partnerships	Sole proprietorships	Total
Manufacturing						
Enterprise size						
1 - 24	0.0	77.4	2.6	7.4	12.6	100.0
25 - 99	1.0	94.6	1.1	2.3	1.0	100.0
100 - 199	5.4	91.7	1.6	0.7	0.7	100.0
Non-manufacturing	0.3	33.3	0.4	20.3	45.8	100.0
Retail	0.4	34.5	0.6	22.6	41.8	100.0

Notes: Definition of small firms: manufacturing, fewer than 200 employees; non-manufacturing: construction, fewer than 25 employees; motor trades, turnover less than £100,000; retail, less than £50,000; wholesale, less than £200,000; catering, all excluding multiples and brewery managed public houses; road transport, fewer than 6 vehicles.
Turnover values in real terms using 1963 prices.
Source: Bolton [1971, p. 6], based on questionnaire sample survey.

Reflecting the concerns of the time, the Bolton Committee's chief interest in small firms arose from their potentially beneficial role in the economy as a source of innovation and new ideas, and in maintaining competition; in particular, what Lydall [1979] later characterised as "entry and product market competition". Completed shortly afterwards, Boswell's [1973] study of small firms stressed the "two-edged" nature of the sector: on the one hand, a source of vitality and renewal; and on the other, an area of inefficiency and decay, something which had also been of concern to Bolton.

Interest in small firms has revived recently because of changes in some employers' policies, and the present government's policy to "deregulating" labour markets. For example, in October 1985, the Director General of the Engineering Employers' Federation (EEF) James McFarlane, boldly stating many of the points on the EEF's negotiating agenda with the engineering unions, urged further moves towards more flexible employment patterns. Notably, he urged contracting out such functions as security and catering; offering temporary contracts to semi-skilled workers when orders so justified; employing easily acquired staff, such as telephonists and truck drivers, on standard terms; and offering superior conditions of employment, including job security, to key permanent workers, electricians and toolmakers, who would be expected to offer complete job flexibility. Beyond statements of bargaining intention, Atkinson's [1986] case studies suggest that a number of firms have been seeking to adopt more flexible employment patterns.

Firms have sought flexibility of deployment between jobs for core employees, and a range of practices from temporary contracts to contracting work out for activities the demand for which is likely to fluctuate, or which are not central to the firm's main business. In these examples, the reason for contracting out is one of cost, but it is a cost arising from under-utilisation of labour due to fluctuating output demands and the difficulties of redeploying labour within the firm, rather than one arising from subcontracting to individuals or organisations which can avoid taxes and social charges.

The present government has also come to regard small firms as a source of vitality and job creation. It has pursued a variety of policies designed to alter the environment in which small firms work, including changes in industrial relations, dilution of social legislation for small firms (e.g. maternity benefits), removal of impediments to firms taking on new labour, plus measures to boost youth employment which small firms have utilised a great deal. This emphasis on small firms is particularly strong in the government's 1986 white paper on deregulation [*Building business ... not barriers*, United Kingdom Government White Paper] and this has been sustained in the Government's 1988 Industry White Paper.

Recently there has also been much discussion of particular types of small firms, for example those organised by "franchising", especially in distribution, and technological "spin-offs" in which small firms are established by former employees of large R & D-based firms. It is, however, very difficult to assess the extent of these developments (see for example *Financial Times* special supplement 1 April 1986).

4. The collective organisation of small firms

The *Handwerk* sector in the Federal Republic of Germany plays an important institutional role in regulating the life of small businesses by defining the training content and minimum standards for a particular trade, and by providing comprehensive sectoral representation for its businesses. No such comprehensive arrangements exist in the United Kingdom. They are much more piecemeal, and much less comprehensive in their coverage, their representation, and their regulation of standards. There is no compulsory registration of small firms other than that arising from legislation affecting all firms, such as the 1961 Factories Act which regulates health and safety in all establishments employing manual workers, the obligation to register for Value Added Tax (VAT) if annual turnover exceeds a certain limit, for taxation, and for filing annual reports under the Companies Acts.

Differences in the legal status among small firms provide an illustration of the diversity of the small business sector. In manufacturing, sole proprietorships are important only among the very smallest firms, and the predominant form is that of limited companies not quoted on the Stock Exchange (Table 3). Outside manufacturing, sole proprietorships are more important, except in construction and in wholesale distribution, which are closer to the pattern for manufacturing.

Small firms are represented by a number of organisations including trade associations, employers' associations, chambers of commerce, and some organisations specially for small businesses. Particularly important for small engineering firms is the Engineering Industries Association (EIA), and the Engineering Employers Federation (EEF). The latter negotiates minimum rates of pay, overtime provisions, standard hours and training provisions with the Confederation of Engineering and Shipbuilding Unions for the whole industry. Although not specifically intended for small firms, many large engineering firms have left the EEF on the grounds that it represents more the interests of smaller firms. Small firm participation in such bodies is not very great. Doran estimated that the small firm membership density in the EIA was only 5 per cent, although it is higher in some other activities (as high as 60 per cent for the British Printing Industries Federation). He estimated that over all sectors, only about 7.5 per cent of small firms were members of a trade association or an employers' organisation [Doran, 1984, pp. 38-39].

Broader forms of representation are provided by the Confederation of British Industry (CBI), which has a long-standing interest in small firms through its Small Firms Council, and the Association of Independent Businesses, which broke off from the CBI in 1968. Another important organisation is the National Federation of the Self-Employed and Small Businesses, set up in 1974. Its foundation was stimulated by the self-employed sector's protest against the Social Security Amendment Act (1974), which required them to pay a National Insurance contribution of 8 per cent of gross profits. It also stimulated the formation of two other bodies, the National Association of the Self-employed (NASE), and the Association of Self-employed People (ASP). VAT and employment legislation provided major campaign issues notably in connection with complaints about harassment by the tax authorities, unfair dismissal compensation and maternity rights [McHugh, 1979]. For these and other representative associations for small businesses, political and economic influence is greatly weakened by their relatively small and diverse membership. This may not appear surprising in the light of the desire of many small business owners for independence, but it seems unlikely that small businessmen in other countries have any lesser preference for independence.

A. Industrial training

A system of industry training boards was set up by the 1966 Industrial Training Act, and revised by the Employment and Training Act (1973). It provided for a training levy to be raised on all employers within the scope of a particular board, and the money to be used to reimburse employers providing apprenticeship training. Small firms were exempt from the levy, but the benefit to such firms has been reduced over time. The levy was reduced in 1973, and several training boards were abolished in 1981. On the other hand, small firms have been major beneficiaries of a number of government employment subsidies, especially for young workers, such as the Young Workers' Scheme, and the Youth Training Scheme.

5. Employment and work in small firms

Information on management and employee relations in new firms is not readily available, but as most new firms are small ones, an approximation may be obtained by looking at evidence on employee representation and pay and conditions in small firms. Unfortunately, much of the statistical material on management and industrial relations in small firms does not distinguish between new and established small firms.

A. Labour costs and wage levels

It has often been argued that small firms play an important part in secondary labour markets, offering lower labour costs and poorer working conditions than larger firms. On the labour supply side, small firms can recruit lower wage groups who are prevented, by family obligations, from travelling to work in higher paid firms. The small firms thus offer convenient location instead of good pay. On the demand side, many small firms are more closely tied to local markets, and if they do supply a local large firm, a degree of monopsony may enter their relations, restricting the small firm's capacity to offer better wages. In addition, small firms are less highly unionised, and so are less likely to pay the union mark-up. Recent estimates in the United Kingdom suggest a mark-up of about 8 per cent in aggregate [Stewart, 1983].

Labour costs are lower in smaller establishments, as is shown by Eurostat's labour cost survey (Table 4): £363 a month in establishments with 10-49 employees, against £420 in those with 50 or more employees. The structure of labour costs is broadly similar, the main difference arising from a smaller proportion of voluntary social payments and payment for days not worked in the small establishments. The voluntary social payments include redundancy payments, plus all other non-statutory social payments, and probably reflect the stronger degree of unionisation of larger establishments (see Table 8).

There is evidence that expenditure on vocational training is higher both absolutely and as a proportion of labour costs, in small firms (Table 4). This may be because smaller firms make greater use of apprenticeships than do larger firms, as they employ a higher proportion of skilled and craft labour (Table 5). The larger firms employ a higher proportion of semi-skilled workers whose main training takes place informally on the job, and as such is unlikely to figure in company accounting systems. This would reduce the real difference in training expenditures, but might not eliminate it, as apprenticeships are more expensive and provide a higher quality of skill.

Table 4: The structure of labour costs in small establishments in industry and construction (NACE 1-5), 1978

Labour cost component	Size of establishment (no. of employees)	
	10 - 49	50 or more
Direct earnings	75.4	71.8
Periodic bonuses	1.7	1.0
Payment for days not worked	7.1	8.5
Pay in kind	0.3	0.3
Total direct costs	84.5	81.6
Statutory social security	(10.1)	8.7
Voluntary social payments	(3.2)	6.8
Total social payments	12.6	15.5
Vocational training	2.5	1.8
Other	2.9	2.9
Total labour cost (£ Sterling)	363	420

Note: Estimate for 10-49 size range obtained by extracting range less than 50 from that less than 10. Vocational training expenditure includes apprentices' pay.
Source: Eurostat Labour Cost Survey.

Table 5: Weekly earnings and skill composition of manual workers in the engineering industry, by establishment size, 1970 and 1980

	(% of all engineering)							
Skill group	Average weekly earnings (1)				Employment share			
	1970		1980		1970		1980	
	Establishment size (no. of manual employees)							
	25-99	500 or more	25-99	500 or more	25-99	500 or more	25-99	500 or more
Maintenance	99.5	121.9	105.8	120.6	4.4	4.9	3.4	5.9
Toolroom	101.8	118.3	109.1	113.2	4.7	4.2	4.8	3.7
Other skilled	93.7	110.9	100.6	110.5	49.0	34.8	53.5	33.1
Semi-skilled	83.9	100.0	85.3	95.6	32.6	50.3	31.2	52.4
Unskilled	69.7	81.2	74.9	87.6	9.3	5.9	7.1	5.0
All manual	88.9	104.5	94.6	102.2	100.0	100.0	100.0	100.0
Total ('000s)					107.4	643.8	166.4	441.5

Note: (1) Average gross weekly earnings in all engineering: 1970 £28.67; 1980 £105.93.
Source: UK/GB/EESC.

However, earnings and labour cost data from the production census and the labour cost survey say nothing about the possible effect of differences in the type of workforce used. The engineering industry is particularly interesting because it provides a degree of homogeneity both in terms of the industrial activities undertaken and of the types of skill used, although it is confined to male manual workers. Thus, if larger firms were considering decentralising production, or subcontracting major activities to other firms, they might well do it within the same industry.

In engineering, it is clear that differences in pay levels and in working conditions prevail even for workers with the same skill level between small and large establishments. Surprisingly, if one remembers the growth in small firm employment during the 1970s, pay differences between large and small establishments were considerably reduced during that period (Table 5), and the reduction in the differential in weekly hours shows that this also occurred in hourly pay rates.

Two factors may be relevant. First, incomes policies of the 1970s, combined with the two periods in which bigger percentage increases were allowed for the lower paid (1972-73 and 1975-77), may have held back pay increases in larger establishments (especially because more visible) and also pushed up the lower paid small establishments. It may seem ironic that employment should also have increased in small establishments. However, the second factor may be that the crisis of 1979 and after hit large establishments hardest (see below).

For a view of non-manual workers' earnings it is necessary to turn to the workplace industrial relations survey. Differentials by plant size within occupations appear slightly larger than in engineering, but the present survey covers the whole economy and includes women. Table 6 shows that clerical pay increases about the same amount with plant size as it does for manual workers, but pay increases most for middle management. The advantage small firms have in labour costs must be considered together with their relative disadvantage in labour productivity. Labour costs and labour productivity together determine unit labour costs, which are discussed later (Table 13). Nevertheless, despite offering lower pay at each skill level than large plants, in the early 1980s, small firms did not pay so much less as to constitute a low paid sector.

B. Working conditions

Another important change is that the differential in hours of work between small and larger engineering firms has narrowed considerably. Payment by results (PBR) systems have often been associated with unpleasant working conditions, and a work environment in which co-operation between workers is undermined. In this respect, small firms might appear to offer better working conditions than larger ones (Table 7). Here again, differences have narrowed between large and small establishments, with the decline in PBR in large establishments and a small increase in small ones. One reason for the move away from PBR in large firms was the increasing difficulty that management had in controlling such schemes, a factor which could be related to the higher levels of strike activity in large plants (Table 10).

C. Differences in skill composition

One final point worth noting is the difference in structure of the workforce in small and large plants, especially with regard to skilled and semi-skilled labour. Unfortunately, 1980 was probably too soon to see the effects of microelectronic technology on skills, but the difference in fixed capital investment can surely be seen in the higher proportion of semi-skilled workers in the larger engineering establishments (Table 5).

The different skill composition may also be indicative of a different relation with labour markets. Smaller firms rely more on workers with readily identifiable skills who can be hired directly from their local labour markets, instead of relying on their internal markets. The latter option is more available to larger establishments. However, as has been argued elsewhere [Marsden et al, 1985], the existence of occupational labour markets for skilled labour in the United Kingdom, coupled with the patterns of occupational defence used by skilled workers, has meant that many British firms have much less scope for organising strong internal markets based on upgrading even in large establishments.

D. Patterns of worker representation

It has long been known that unionisation has been weakest in small firms. The reasons for this difference include the less bureaucratic and more personalised relations in small firms, and the fact that unions have only limited resources to service members scattered in small firms. The 1980 workplace industrial relations survey confirms this view, showing that union recognition (for bargaining purposes) declines sharply with establishment size, from nine out of ten establishments with more than 200 employees, to only one in four among those with under 25 employees. In small establishments which were not part of a larger firm, it fell to only one establishment in six (Table 8).

For establishments which do recognise unions, the Warwick survey [Brown (ed.) 1981] showed that, in manufacturing, multi-employer bargaining predominated among small establishments (fewer than 100 employees, Table 9). Nevertheless, the amount of single employer bargaining was high even among small establishments, and higher still for non-manual workers. Allowing for differences in size definition and coverage, the importance of single-employer bargaining may help explain the low participation by small firms in employers' organisations and trade associations mentioned earlier. Nevertheless, the Warwick finding that 44 per cent of establishments with 50-99 employees had multi-employer bargaining seems to be high compared with Doran's [1984] estimates of small employer participation in multi-firm organisations.

Table 6: Weekly earnings (1) of non-manual workers, by skill level and establishment size, 1980

Skill level	Establishment size (no. of employees)							
	25-49	50-99	100-199	200-499	500-999	1000-1999	2000+	All sizes
Semi-skilled	67	76	75	80	83	85	88	74
Skilled	90	97	95	103	104	107	110	96
Clerical	69	72	73	75	75	75	84	72
Middle management	117	121	121	125	132	135	143	121

Note: (1) £ per week.
Source: Workplace Industrial Relations Survey [1980], Daniel W.W. and Milward N. [1983] p. 266.

Table 7: Working hours and payment systems in engineering, by establishment size, 1970 and 1980

	Working hours				Payment systems			
	1970		1980		1970		1980	
	Establishment size (no. of manual employees)							
	25-99	500 or more	25-99	500 or more	25-99	500 or more	25-99	500 or more
Time rates	46.1	44.5	42.6	41.6	72.0	50.2	68.0	65.2
PBR (1)	44.6	42.6	40.7	40.7	28.0	49.8	32.0	34.8
All workers	45.7	43.5	42.0	41.3	100.0	100.0	100.0	100.0

Note: (1) Payment by results.
Source: UK/GB/EESC.

Table 8: Trade union recognition by type and size of establishment, 1980 (proportion of establishments that recognised manual trade unions)

Type of establishment	Size of establishment (Number of manual workers employed)					
	Total	1-24	25-49	50-99	100-199	200+
All establishments	50	25	43	63	78	91
Independent establishments	31	16	24	50	66 (1)	67(1)
Establishments part of a group	58	28	55	68	81	92

Note: Union recognition for manual workers; private sector.
Source: Daniel and Millward [1983], p. 25.

The union weakness in small firms has caused many unions to regard government policies which favour small firms as part of a wider policy to undermine collective bargaining and to weaken the unions' influence on the economy. The main response by the unions so far to the rise of employment in firms in which they are most weakly represented has been twofold. First they have campaigned against contracting-out, with some success in the public sector, notably the National Health Service and local government, but less success in the private sector. Indeed, a number of the recent flexibility agreements have specifically included a provision for use of contractors, but with a common proviso that the existing workforce should not be available to do the work. The second response, again as much motivated by public as by private sector considerations, has been the decision to press for a national minimum wage, adopted, after long preparation, at the Trade Union Council's annual congress on 3 September 1986.

E. Industrial relations in small firms

Strike patterns might be taken as a very crude indicator of the climate of industrial relations. It has been observed in a number of countries that strike frequency increases with plant size, and this has been taken as an indicator of the more difficult nature of industrial relations as the size of production units increases. Strike frequency increases with plant size, but only up to plants with about 500 employees, after which it levels off. This could indicate that in larger plants there is some tendency to organise action into larger disputes, and to group grievances together which in smaller plants could lead to a stoppage. Working days lost per thousand employees shows a more continuous rate of increase with plant size (Table 10).

Prais et al. [1981] take the analysis further providing comparisons with strike patterns by plant size in the United States and the Federal Republic of Germany. They show that, for 1965-75, strike activity increased most with plant size in the United Kingdom, followed by the United States, with the Federal Republic of Germany a long way behind. At least one of the authors has taken this to be an indicator of management's lesser ability to run large plants in the United Kingdom, given their pattern of industrial relations as compared with the other two countries [Jones, 1981]. This point has been further supported by an analysis of the United Kingdom's productivity gap with the United States [Davies and Caves, 1987]. These observations perhaps call for some qualification of Bolton's argument that the rise of large firms in the United Kingdom had been helped by the development of expertise in managing large production units.

Table 9: Bargaining patterns in manufacturing by worker status and establishment size, 1977-78

Worker status *Level of agreement*	50-99	100-199	200-499	500-599	1000+
			% of establishments		
Manual workers					
Multi-employer	44	33	32	23	15
Single-employer	39	59	60	70	84
of which:					
Corporate	7	11	15	16	32
Establishment	32	48	45	54	52
Other	-	2	1	2	1
No bargaining	17	5	6	4	-
Total	100	100	100	100	100
Non-manual workers					
Multi-employer	23	18	15	9	4
Single-employer	43	56	64	72	85
of which:					
Corporate	7	16	23	22	39
Establishment	36	40	41	50	46
Other	2	1	3	3	2
No bargaining	32	25	18	15	8
Total	100	100	100	100	100

Source: Brown [1981], pp. 9 + 14.

Table 10: Industrial stoppages in manufacturing by size of establishment, 1971-1973

Establishment size (no. of employees)	Working days lost per 1,000 employees	Number of stoppages per 100,000 employees
11-24	14.8	8.0
25-99	72.4	19.2
100-199	155.0	23.0
200-499	329.1	25.4
500-999	719.4	29.7
1000-1999	1127.8	26.7
2000-4999	2075.4	29.4
5000 +	3708.0	31.7

Note: Annual average 1971-73, Great Britain.
Source: Smith et al. [1978], p. 57.

III. Quantitative development of the small firm sector

1. Long-term trends

The Bolton Committee [1971] reported towards the end of a long period of decline of small firms in the British economy. It was a period in which many of those concerned with economic and industrial policy still looked to giant enterprises as the way to rationalise and restore the economy. The British car firms had been amalgamated to form the ill-fated British Leyland Motor Corporation (later to become BL) in 1968, and the steel industry was still to embark upon a huge investment in large-scale production facilities intended to capture the economies of scale enjoyed by large firms in Japan and South Korea. Consequently, much of its evidence documented the decline of small firms, especially in manufacturing, but later also in certain services, and sought to explain the decline and suggest policies that could sustain the small firm sector as a spur to competition.

After a small rise during the 1920s, the number of small manufacturing firms declined sharply after 1935. Whereas the employment share of *establishments* with fewer than 200 employees stood at about 44 per cent between 1924 and 1935, it declined to 37 per cent by 1948, and to 31 per cent by 1963. Their share of net output similarly fell from about 40 per cent to 27 per cent. The employment share of small *enterprises* fell from 38 per cent in 1935 to only 20 per cent in 1963 [Bolton, 1971, pp. 58-9]. A similar decline in employment share of small manufacturing establishments between the 1950s and the middle 1960s occurred in a number of other countries, including the Federal Republic of Germany, Sweden, France and Japan, but not in the United States and Canada. In the United States, part of the increase was the result of a move to more multi-plant enterprises [Bolton, 1971, p. 70].

Equally striking was the growth of giant firms. Between 1958 and 1970, the number of employees in firms employing more than 50,000 people more than doubled from 547,000 to 1,181,000 [HRCP, Table 15]. Over the same period, the concentration of industrial output increased as the share of net output by the 100 largest firms (defined in terms of net output) increased from 22 per cent of manufacturing net output in 1949 to about 40 per cent in 1970 [Prais, 1976]. It remained at more or less that level through the 1970s, and early 1980s (41 per cent in 1983, Census of Production). Merger activity remained through the early 1980s at a level well below that reached in 1972-73.

Also important within manufacturing have been changes in the relationship between establishments and enterprises. Prais [1976, p. 62], using the "local unit" definition of establishment, showed that the average number of establishments belonging to the 100 largest enterprises increased greatly between 1958 - the first year such data were available - and 1972, rising from 27 to 72. But, at the same time, the average plant size in these enterprises declined from 750 employees to 430. Employment per enterprise increased from 20,300 to 31,180, again showing the increased importance of large employers in the economy. However, as shown in Table 9, for establishments of all sizes the establishment level is more common for bargaining than the corporate level, indicating a good deal of independence for plant level management. Since 1970 the number of establishments owned by the largest 100 (in terms of employment) enterprises has further increased rising from 36 establishments in 1970 to 41 in 1983. And the average size of these establishments has continued to fall, dropping from 774 employees in 1970 to 429 in 1983, with nearly two-thirds of the fall coming after 1979 (Census of Production, see Table 15).

Table 11: Employment and share of net output in manufacturing, by enterprise size, 1930-1983

Year	\multicolumn{6}{c}{Enterprise size (no. of employees)}
	1-24	25-99	100-499	500-999	1000+	Total ('000s)
Employment						
1930	12.8	16.1	32.7	38.4		5 554
1948	9.9	16.9	32.2	13.5	27.5	7 080
1954	8.4	15.7	32.4	13.1	30.4	7 672
1963	8.0	12.2	30.7	14.2	34.9	7 952
1970	7.3	11.1	27.0	13.9	40.6	8 033
1974/5		19.7	25.3	13.3	41.8	7 467
1983		26.2	27.0	13.3	33.5	5 079
Share of net output						
1930	12.3	15.4	30.6	41.6		1 191
1948	9.4	16.9	32.6	13.6	27.4	3 954
1954	7.6	13.7	30.9	13.7	34.2	6 235
1963	7.1	10.5	28.6	14.8	39.0	10 820
1970		16.4	25.7	14.4	43.5	18 531
1974/5		16.7	24.2	14.3	44.9	36 948
1983		22.3	25.8	14.2	37.7	80 804

Note: In 1970 the establishment definition changed from that of "local unit" to "smallest unit for which information required in a production census can be made". Prais [1976] estimated that in 1970 there were roughly 1.5 times as many local units as establishments.

Source: HRCP: *Historical record of the census of production 1907-1970*, updated from later production censuses. Results for 1930-70 not shown for less than 200 range.

Retail distribution is another important employment sector. Here, too, the importance of small establishments and, by implication, small businesses has declined, although satisfactory data are available only for the post-war period. The decline of small businesses was no less striking in the retail trade in terms of both their shares of employment and of turnover. Applying the Bolton definition, Bannock [1976] showed that the employment share of small retail shops had declined to 65 per cent in 1971.[2] Up to the late 1960s, employment in small shops remained fairly steady at between 1.6 million and 1.7 million, so the loss of employment share could be attributed to the growth of new larger shops, notably supermarkets and discount stores. In contrast, their declining employment and turnover shares in the 1970s were associated with absolute decline, as employment declined in the sector as a whole. The decline slowed in the late 1970s, but does not appear to have been reversed, in contrast to manufacturing (see below). The Bolton Report also revealed some decline in small organisations between 1950 and 1965 in wholesale distribution [Bolton, 1971, p. 66].

The share of self-employed also declined, although as Bannock [1976] has shown, it roughly halved between 1911 and 1951 (12.8 per cent to 7.2 per cent of the labour force), but declined only half a percentage point between then and 1965. Only recently has it started to grow again (Table 2).

Table 12: **Small firms in retail distribution since 1950**

A. **Small establishments defined by turnover** (1)

	Employment all establishments ('000s)	% employment in small establishments	% of turnover small establishments
1950	2 348	72	63
1957	2 472	70	63
1961	2 485	66	59
1966	2 556	67	60

B. **Small establishments defined by no. of outlets and employment size**

	emp. all estabs ('000s)	shops with 1 outlet % share of employment	shops with 1 outlet % share of turnover	shops with fewer than 10 employees % share of employment
1971	2 541	49.5	40.8	56.2
1976	2 503	39.8	34.0	31.7
1979	2 429	36.6	31.7	30.1
1982	2 264	36.6	30.2	31.3

Note: Establishments with an annual turnover of less than £50,000 in 1963 prices.
Sources: Part A, Bolton Report Tables 5.VI and 5.VII based on Censuses of Distribution and Other Services. Part B, Census of Distribution 1971 and Business Monitor Retailing 1976+.

---

2. The Bolton definition of small retailing establishments could not be applied for 1976 and later because the size ranges of annual turnover in published data were too great.

The image of decline painted by the Committee did not pass uncontested. Boswell [1973], from his own research, argued that a declining employment share could also be caused by an increase in the dynamism of small firms expressed in increased "birth" and "death" rates, and in increased rates of expansion. The cross-sectional data used so far does not give any information on such developments, but the data now most widely used, based on VAT registrations, only started with the introduction of VAT in 1973 (see Table 16).

2. The recent period: Since 1970

The decline of small firms in manufacturing appears to have ceased by the middle 1970s. The recent sharp increase in the employment and output shares of small firms started in 1979 with the worst recession to hit British industry since the 1930s, as a 20 per cent rise in the value of Sterling against other major currencies coincided with the arrival of recession in the United Kingdom's main export markets.

Between 1979 and 1983 the number of small manufacturing establishments increased, as did their share of employment, whereas that of the largest establishments declined (Table 13). Moreover, the employment share of small establishments increased in every branch of manufacturing (Table 14), and in some branches, despite the overall decline in employment, numbers increased in small establishments. Throughout the period, small firms and small establishments have been roughly synonymous, the average number of establishments per enterprise being only 1.2 in each year from 1970 to 1983.

On the whole, changes in net output were smaller than those in employment, hence the increase in the labour productivity gap between small and large establishments. Taken with the observation (Table 15) that the size of the average establishment of the 100 largest firms decreased, this would suggest that one important factor has been the employment shake-out in large establishments since 1979. These may have been harder hit by the Sterling overvaluation due to their greater involvement in products which are traded internationally. Job losses in the car and steel industries after 1979 would be good illustrations of this explanation.

3. Concentration and dependency

Although employment in small establishments and small firms had increased, especially after 1979, the number of establishments per enterprise has hardly changed since 1970, remaining at 1.2 establishments throughout (Table 15). Thus, these figures might be interpreted as showing a growth in the importance of legally independent small establishments. However, the picture has to be qualified by changes among the top 100 firms, whose average number of establishments increased from 36 in 1970 to 41 in 1983, with much of the increase occurring after 1979. As these are only snapshots

United Kingdom

it is impossible to tell whether large firms are decentralising production into smaller establishments by breaking up their own operations, or whether they are buying up existing small and medium-sized firms. Either way, the average size of establishments belonging to them declined from 774 employees in 1970 to 429 in 1983, again with much of the fall occurring after 1979. As mentioned earlier, at least part of this change seems to be due to the employment shake-out in large firms after 1979. If the change were due solely to this factor, then it would follow that the employment share of the 100 largest firms would have fallen. However, it fell only modestly, from 37.3 per cent in 1979 to 36.0 per cent in 1983, while the average number of establishments per firm rose. This leaves room for other explanations, including the buying up of smaller firms and the subdivision of existing operations. Unfortunately, the production census gives no indication as to the nature of such changes.

Table 13: Distribution of employment, net output, and productivity in manufacturing, by establishment size, 1974-1983

Establishment size (no. of employees)	Establishments (in %) 1974/5	1979	1983	Employees (in %) 1974/5	1979	1983
1-10	51.9	55.7	51.8	3.5	4.0	4.5
11-19	16.1	15.9	23.1	3.2	3.5	6.5
20-49	14.0	12.3	11.8	6.0	6.0	7.5
50-99	7.2	6.2	5.4	7.0	6.8	7.7
100-199	4.7	4.4	3.5	9.3	9.5	10.1
200-499	3.7	3.4	2.7	16.0	16.1	16.9
500-999	1.4	1.2	1.0	13.3	13.2	13.3
1000-1499	0.4	0.4	0.3	7.2	8.0	6.7
1500 +	0.6	0.5	0.4	34.6	32.9	26.8
Total	100.0	100.0	100.0	100.0	100.0	100.0
Numbers ('000s)	104.1	107.4	102.4	7 467.0	6 925.6	5 078.8

	Net output (in %) 1974/5	1979	1983	Net output per head (% of all sizes) 1974/5	1979	1983
1-99	16.7	17.8	22.3	83.7	87.6	85.4
100-199	8.5	8.8	9.2	92.0	92.9	90.9
200-499	15.7	16.2	16.6	98.2	100.1	98.4
500-999	14.3	13.6	14.2	107.4	103.3	106.5
1000-1499	7.2	8.2	6.9	100.0	102.6	102.9
1500 +	37.7	35.4	30.8	108.9	107.7	114.7
Total	100.0	100.0	100.0	100.0	100.0	100.0

Note: 1974/5 and 1979 SIC 1968, 1983 SIC 1980.
Source: UK Census of Production.

The re-emergence of small enterprises

Table 14: Distribution of small establishments(1) by branch of manufacturing,(2) 1979, 1983

NACE	manufacturing branch	Numbers of small establishments ('000s) 1979	1983	Per cent small establishments within branch 1979	1983
21	Extraction metal ores	0.4	-	25.0	-
22	Metal manufacture	31.7	29.0	9.2	16.3
23	Extraction other minerals	9.9	9.0	42.1	68.2
24	Manufacture non-metal mineral products	62.4	57.3	22.4	27.5
25	Chemicals	42.3	41.8	11.7	14.5
26	Man-made fibres	0.5	0.5	1.6	2.5
31	Manufacture metal goods nes.	175.1	163.0	35.2	47.4
32	Mechanical engineering	242.2	220.0	25.0	32.5
33	Office and data processing equipt.	3.2	4.3	6.8	10.7
34	Electrical engineering	69.7	73.7	10.1	13.5
35	Motor vehicles and parts	34.1	33.8	6.9	11.2
36	Other transport equipment	22.2	21.7	5.8	6.7
37	Instrument engineering	28.2	30.3	27.0	37.3
41/42	Food, drink, tobacco manufacture	96.5	95.5	13.3	15.8
43	Textiles	69.3	60.1	18.8	25.6
44	Leather and leather goods	17.4	14.1	56.3	65.0
45	Footwear and clothing	138.2	109.3	33.1	36.7
46	Timber and wood furniture	130.3	120.9	53.1	59.8
47	Paper and printing	155.2	150.9	29.1	33.8
48	Rubber and plastics	57.0	59.8	21.3	29.8
49	Miscellaneous manufacturing	37.5	32.3	39.6	56.2
50	Construction	626.6	686.2	46.9	57.8
2-4	Manufacturing	1 423.6	1 327.4	20.6	26.1
2-5	Manfacturing and construction	2 050.2	2 013.6	24.9	32.1

Notes: (1) Establishments with more than 100 employees; (2) SIC 1980.
Source: UK Census of Production.

Table 15: Employment and number of establishments of the 100 largest enterprises and of all enterprises, 1970-1983

Year	100 largest enterprises Average no. establishments	Average establishment size (employees)	All enterprises Average no. establishments	Average establishment size (employees)
1970	36.2	774	1.2	85.8
1975	38.4	695	1.2	82.2
1979	37.5	644	1.2	68.6
1983	40.7	429	1.2	49.6

Note: 100 largest firms by employment size.
Source: Census of Production.

One attempt to estimate the extent to which larger firms have been contracting-out work has been based on an analysis of expenditure on non-industrial services by manufacturing firms. Ray [1986] showed that the purchase of non-industrial services increased from 4.5 per cent to 8.0 per cent of gross manufacturing output between 1973 and 1983. However, Ray pointed out that part of the growth in spending probably arose from the need for new services not hitherto provided by existing manufacturing firms. Hence at least part of the increase does not seem attributable to contracting-out of established in-house activities.

The Bolton report's evidence suggested that a relatively small percentage of small firms was engaged as satellites of larger firms, although many were heavily dependent upon a few large customers. Without citing specific figures, studies by Lloyd and Mason [1985] and by Gould and Keeble [1985] suggest that many small new manufacturing firms serve local markets, and have a few major customers.

4. Characteristics of new firms

An increase in employment and output shares of small firms does not, by itself, say much about the nature of new firms. The introduction of Value Added Tax (VAT) in 1973 and the obligation on all firms, except the very smallest, to register, has created a new source of information on new enterprises.

In which sectors are most new firms established, and what is their initial size? About 45 per cent of starts occurred in three branches: production industries, construction, and the retail trade, although when starts are compared to the existing stock of firms, these branches appear to be about average (Table 16). Thus, no branches stand out as being especially fertile in the rise of new firms, except for the rag-bag of "other services". If median sales turnover can be taken as an indicator of entry costs, it is perhaps suprising that there is no strong tendency for new firms to have started more frequently in branches in which median turnover was lowest, although too much should not be made of one year's figures. It is also clear that not all new firms are small ones. The upper quartile turnover of new firms in some branches were £129,600 in production, and £204,600 in wholesale distribution, which were in both cases well above the median turnover for the branch as a whole.

The median age of firms which deregistered for VAT in 1981 was nearly four years. This might understate the true age of some very small firms which may deregister for tax reasons by keeping their turnover below the VAT threshold. This can be done in small-scale construction, for example, by getting the client to pay directly for all building materials used so that turnover consists solely of labour-related costs.

On the other hand, median ages on deregistration in 1981 may overstate the survival potential of new firms because many firms which registered in 1973 had already been going for a considerable time.

According to VAT registrations, in 1982, about two-thirds of new businesses fail within the first two-and-a-half years [*British Business*, 12 Aug. and 7 Oct., 1983]. Nevertheless, the ages on deregistration in Table 16 show a surprising consistency between branches if agriculture, motor trades and "other services" are excluded.

Table 16: New firms by sector and turnover in 1982

Sector	Stock '000s	Starts % of stock	Starts % of starts	Median stock	Median starts	Q75 starts	Median age at "death"(1) (months)
			Turnover (£'000s)				
Agriculture	181.1	3.6	4.0	35.1	16.8	40.7	less than 84
Production	131.2	12.9	10.4	81.2	44.5	129.6	50.3
Construction	199.3	11.8	14.4	37.5	34.1	49.6	45.4
Transport	56.0	13.1	4.5	42.6	35.3	54.2	43.2
Wholesale	104.5	14.2	9.1	100.4	48.6	204.6	40.9
Retail	264.6	12.5	20.7	61.7	45.3	84.5	51.5
Finance	86.6	11.1	5.9	39.4	31.9	47.8	45.7
Catering	118.9	13.5	9.8	57.5	45.2	80.9	46.1
Motor trades	71.4	13.2	5.8	76.0	42.1	97.7	38.3
Other services	145.4	17.3	15.4	35.6	33.5	49.4	37.1
All sectors	1 359.0	12.0	100.0	46.5	39.2	77.8	47.2

Notes: Based on VAT registrations.
(1) Median age of businesses deregistering in 1981, in months.
Source: *British Business*, 18 May 1984, and 7 Oct. 1983.

These figures are compatible with those of the Merrett and Cyriax survey [1970] which found that once firms survive the early years, their life can be quite considerable. They found that the median ages of small firms interviewed in 1970 which had been active seven years earlier were quite high, ranging from 19 years in retail and in motor trades to 22 years in manufacturing and 69 years in construction.

5. Job creation by small firms

The opening of a new small firm creates new jobs in that firm, and the higher birth rate of small firms has aroused widespread interest in the contribution by small firms to job creation in aggregate. However, their higher mortality rate, as compared with larger firms, also has to be considered to measure *net* job creation properly.

The work in the United States by Birch [1979], which showed that small firms (with fewer than 20 employees) there had been responsible for 66 per cent of all net new jobs between 1969 and 1976, has stimulated similar work in the United Kingdom. Gallagher and Stewart [1984] also found that small firms were responsible for a greater than proportionate share of net new job creation in the United Kingdom. They compared information on firms from a commercial credit rating and market research agency for 1971 and 1981: firms present in 1971 but not in 1981 were counted as "deaths", those present in 1981 but not in 1971 as "births", and those whose employment size changed between the two dates as "contractions" or "expansions". Their study showed a lower annual rate of "births" of new firms in the United Kingdom compared with the United States (2.4 per cent against 5.9 per cent), but also a lower annual rate of "deaths" (3.8 per cent against 5.1 per cent). Likewise, British firms expanded and contracted more slowly than those in the United States. One factor they mentioned, borne out by other studies of firms' hiring practices, is that British firms are more likely to lose jobs by closure than by smaller scale lay-offs - at least this was the case in the 1970s [Bowers et al., 1982]. Gallagher and Stewart also showed that rates of job loss between 1971 and 1981 were greater in large firms (48 per cent for those with more than 500 employees against 14 per cent for those with between 1 and 19 employees), but recall that the employment shake-out of 1979-82 hit large establishments especially hard (see above).

Table 17: Net job creation by firm size, between 1971 and 1981

Enterprise Size (no. of employees)	% of job creation in sample	"Fertility" ratio (1)
1-19	31	2.4
20-49	11	1.4
50-99	10	1.2
100-199	21	0.9
500-999	10	0.8
> 1000	17	0.5

Note: (1) Ratio of % of job creation to % of employment in sample.
Source: Gallagher and Stewart, in *British Business*, 13 July 1984.

Gallagher and Stewart's estimates of net job creation by small firms show a strong relative advantage for small firms, but in view of the higher birth and death rate of such firms, it is likely that many such jobs are of shorter duration and less secure than those in larger firms. This aspect of job creation by small firms has also been stressed by Storey [1985]. His study of employment change in Northern England 1965-78 used a number of local authority sources, and found that although small establishments had contributed more than large ones to employment creation, in many cases they were not independent, but part of larger groups based outside the region, and often attracted by regional subsidies. Hence he was less sanguine about the impact of small firms on net job creation. Finally, the studies brought together by Storey [(ed.), 1985] show considerable regional variation in patterns of new firm formation.

IV. The economic and social background to recent changes

Surveying the changes up to 1970, the Bolton Committee identified a number of economic and social factors responsible for the decline of small firms. The factors it analysed are interesting both as an analysis of the causes of the decline of the small firm sector in the United Kingdom up to the early 1970s, and as a summary of the accumulated research and knowledge at that time.

The factors included:

- technical change and optimum plant size;
- economies of research and development;
- improved management for large firms;
- economies of transport and communication;
- economies of marketing;
- greater social appeal of large organisations;
- state intervention.

In their view, in a broadly competitive economy the decline of small firms for such reasons may not be harmful. These should be examined in greater detail.

Although technical change had favoured the growth of large plants in some industries, the studies carried out for the Bolton Committee suggested that in many cases technical economies of scale had not changed greatly since the 1930s, and stressed instead economies in marketing and finance. In retailing, the economies of "self-service" have been less readily available to small shops, as have been new techniques of warehousing and stock control. Nevertheless, many small shops have been able to pool resources whilst retaining some independence - for example, in purchasing and advertising - and many small stores have been able to organise their layout on self-service lines.

Research and development expenditures have risen sharply since the last war, and there are industries in which considerable economies of scale exist, such as the automobile industry and certain defence industries. However, in many sectors, such as the new science-based ones, small size has proved an advantage. Indeed, more recently in the biotechnology area, several large firms have preferred to buy up successful small innovating firms, rather than do all the research themselves and face the associated risks.

Managerial factors were also put forward, notably the increased skill in managing large organisations in such areas as financial control, plus the possibilities opened up by modern communication methods. These factors could favour co-ordination by "hierarchies" rather than by "markets", and hence facilitate the growth of very large organisations. Any advantages from these factors could, however, be partly offset by the disadvantages of greater specialisation within such organisations, and a possible loss of flexibility.

Changes in transport and communication were thought to favour larger firms because of the way in which they turned previously local markets into national markets and, in turn, opened up international markets. Because larger firms are better placed to deal with national and international markets, primarily because of economies of marketing and of production for export, such changes were thought to favour large firms relative to small firms.

The importance of marketing in the Committee's thinking is already clear, but social factors deserve some consideration, particularly in relation to countries with a strong small firm culture such as the Federal Republic of Germany and Italy. In the United Kingdom, small firms do not have the social organisations equivalent to those of the *Handwerk* sector in the Federal Republic of Germany, nor do they have the effective pressure-group organisations like the French General Confederation of Small- and Medium-Sized Firms (CGPME). The social image of small firms has also proved less attractive to highly trained manpower. This is because higher education graduates have mostly sought jobs in larger organisations. Furthermore, technical training in the United Kingdom is generally weak. There is, for example, no equivalent to the middle-level technical training for engineers found in the Federal Republic of Germany. The absence of such training restricts the availability of technical expertise to small firms.

The State has, until the 1980s at least, contributed to the rise of large organisations, in part by virtue of being a large employer itself either directly through government and social services (the National Health Service is the largest employer in Western Europe), and indirectly through the nationalised industries. But the State has partly also played a role through the way government policies for labour markets and for industrial development can affect firms. The Committee argued that the growth of the public sector restricted the areas of activity open to small firms: the state's purchasing policy had often unwittingly militated against small firms; government intervention in industrial reorganisation had concentrated on creating large units (for example in automobiles and shipbuilding, but also in coal and steel); state regulation of environmental problems could also hurt small firms, for example by planning controls and increased social regulations, such as redundancy payments; and finally, taxation policies, through their impact on incentives and on the transmission of wealth between generations, could discourage small firm development.

From these factors, it is clear that the decline of small firms, and the rise of giant enterprises are closely, but not necessarily inversely, related phenomena. The Committee's view that these factors did not call for urgent remedial action depended, in part, on their belief that there was no major discrepancy between public and private benefits involved. Yamey [1972] criticised the report for failing to distinguish adequately between the fate of the relatively few high-fliers, rewarded for their merit, and the decline of the overall population of small firms.

Implicit in the Committee's reasoning (and indeed also their terms of reference) was the idea that change is not irreversible. Of the reasons put forward, optimal plant size could decline, and there is a good deal of evidence of such a decline in certain sectors. In the automobile industry, for example, the technical pressure for large plants has declined. Process and product changes have made it possible to work with smaller volumes for each model, although the minimum efficient production of certain parts, such as gearboxes, could require the same basic gear box to be used in several different models [Altshuler et al, 1984].

Economies of transport and communication, marketing, and possibly even improved management are also not necessarily irreversible. Hannah [1980] stressed the importance of the sophistication of intermediate markets in nineteenth century Britain in explaining why it developed patterns of vertical integration later than the United States, and then on a smaller scale. Should the forms of intermediate business service activities, and of marketing organisation stressed by Piore and Sabel [1984], develop further in the United Kingdom, it is conceivable that firms would find it more efficient to contract-out a number of activities internalised by the growth of large firms.

The rise of small firms in manufacturing during the 1970s, but especially since 1979 in the United Kingdom, could owe something to a shift in relative costs between large and small establishments. It was noted earlier that wage levels had been lower in small establishments in the early 1970s, and that the gap had narrowed somewhat by 1980. Output per head, however, is higher in large establishments. A very crude way of adjusting for differences in the quality of labour in large and small establishments is to give output per head as output per unit wage cost: in other words, to take labour costs as a proportion of net output. In 1983, labour costs as a percentage of net output in manufacturing were 46 per cent in establishments with under 100 employees, and 45 per cent in those with over 1,000 employees, suggesting that lower pay was slightly more than offset by lower labour productivity. A full analysis would require taking account of the capital stock in large and small establishments. Nevertheless, it suggests that there is no great advantage currently on straight unit labour cost grounds.

However, in earlier years there appears to have been such an advantage: in 1975 the comparable figure for establishments under 100 employees was 51 per cent, while for 1,000 and over it was 53 per cent; and in 1979, 45 per cent and 49 per cent, respectively. Could this explain part of the decline in large establishments? Clearly, if large and small establishments were in equilibrium and operating at their desired production levels in both periods, then a higher labour share would indicate higher labour productivity. But if management and industrial relations difficulties in large establishments were such as to prevent the achievement of output levels for which the plants were designed, then the reduced labour cost differential could be interpreted as indicating an improved position for large establishments.

It was suggested earlier that strike rates were higher in large than in small establishments, and that this difference was greater than in other countries, such as the Federal Republic of Germany or the United States.

This argument has been used to suggest that the United Kingdom has a comparative disadvantage in the management of large plants [Jones, 1981; Davies and Caves, 1987]. The major management and industrial relations changes which have occurred in large plants when facing major job losses, and the decline in private sector strike activity in the United Kingdom, both point to improved management as a factor in the improved performance of large plants in that country. Without further evidence, however, such an interpretation must remain tentative.

1. Small firms and technical change

It is in the area of technical change where the balance of the argument has perhaps shifted more. Piore and Sabel's [1984] argument rested mostly on new flexible forms of automated equipment, but small firms may also contribute more directly to innovation. Reviewing work by SPRU, Rothwell [1986] shows that in the United Kingdom small and medium-sized firms (1-499 employees) have played a major part in technical innovation, as have very large ones (over 10,000 employees). Intermediate sized firms did less well. Moreover, he showed that the performance of small firms had improved between 1955-59 and 1975-80 (measured as innovations per employee). One of the reasons for the bimodal pattern, Rothwell argued, was that many large firms encourage innovation in small firms if they are component suppliers, and many also enter into joint technological ventures with innovative small firms which supply them with sophisticated goods, or which complement their product range.

V. Special studies on small firm development

Small firms have received a great deal of attention in studies of regional and inner city regeneration but, as already noted, a good deal of the literature has been somewhat sceptical, perhaps in response to the excessive expectations.

One irony raised by the studies of British business in the nineteenth century is that the sophistication, by contemporary standards, of intermediate markets, and the importance of the "industrial districts" that played an important part in Alfred Marshall's thinking [Bellandi, 1986], should not have given rise to a stronger small firm sector akin to the German *Handwerk* sector.

Small firms have, however, had an important part to play in the development of what might be thought of as contemporary forms of Marshallian industrial districts in some of the "hi-tech" areas in the United Kingdom; notably in Scotland's "Silicon Glen", around Cambridge, or in the Thames Valley. In such cases, the firms involved are not all small, but they could be said to group into industrial districts in so far as they provide services to each other, work in competition and, perhaps most important, develop a pool of qualified and experienced labour on which they can all draw. Beyond this, Marshall's conception of an industrial district implied a certain intensity of exchange between firms *within* the district so that they become an alternative to large firm organisation. Whether this is true of the science-based growth areas, or whether they simply provide a convenient location for particular activities of larger firms, is hard to assess.

VI. Attitudes and policies towards small firms

British governments have influenced small firm development mainly through employment law, and through financial support. The main support from business has come from the establishment of new forms of access to equity finance, notably through the Unlisted Securities Market and, more recently, the new Third Market. Unions under pressure from a declining membership base in large firms have recently been seeking ways to increase recruitment of workers in small firms and in non-standard forms of employment, both of which are traditionally difficult areas for recruiting and retaining new members. One area of interest has been the recent establishment of training schools by two unions with important craft memberships.

1. Role and impact of government

As was noted above, the two main ways in which government has had an impact on small firm development have been through employment laws and financial support.

A. Employment law

One way in which government activity has been thought to influence, and perhaps harm, small firms has been employment legislation, especially in areas of unfair dismissal, maternity leave, redundancy, health and safety, and the support for collective bargaining and trade union activities. Several of these measures had been reinforced during the 1970s, and this generated some concern that they would discourage new employment. In particular, it was feared that they would disadvantage smaller enterprises which are unable to afford specialist personnel managers, to arrange cover for absent workers (e.g. on maternity leave), and to carry inefficient workers.

A survey of firms with under 50 employees carried out by the Department of Employment in 1978 [Clifton and Tatton-Brown, 1979] revealed that 54 per cent of their sample had had no experience with the employment legislation provisions. Of those which had, the most important were health and safety (28 per cent), unfair dismissal (15 per cent), need to pay workers temporarily laid off (10 per cent), maternity provisions (8 per cent), and union-related provisions (5 per cent). On the whole, these experiences were not considered to be among the major difficulties of the firms, although provisions such as unfair dismissal had caused many small firms to increase care in recruitment (47 per cent), and to reduce numbers recruited (26 per cent - prompted answers). So the survey showed that employment legislation up to 1979 had had some effect on the policies and recruitment by small companies, but a modest one.

Nevertheless, since 1979 the emphasis in employment legislation has moved sharply in the direction of reducing trade union power and individual employment rights, especially in the more weakly unionised small firm sector. The 1980 and 1982 Employment Acts restricted picketing and outlawed the use of secondary picketing (picketing the premises of an employer not directly involved in the dispute), which, it could be argued, reduced the likelihood of small firms being drawn into disputes in larger firms they were supplying. The termination of legal encouragement of trade union recognition in 1980 perhaps reduced the likelihood of further extension of unionisation to small firms, although it had in fact been a small firm, Grunwick, which proved the inefficacy of the earlier legislation in this area. Removal of small firms from the coverage of maternity protection in 1980, and the extension of the minimum period for an employee to qualify for unfair dismissal protection, could also be seen as measures to help job creation in small firms. These moves are soon to be reinforced by the government's new white paper on deregulation [UK Government White Paper, 1986].

B. White Paper on deregulation, 1986

In May 1986, the Government published its White Paper on further deregulation measures to promote employment. It emphasised that the way to reduce unemployment is to promote more businesses, more self-employment, and greater wealth creation, and to direct the Department of Employment to encourage the development of an enterprise economy. Among the main proposals of the White Paper were recommendations: to review the impact of VAT on small businesses; to review planning regulations to allow a wider range of changes of use without planning permission; to reject the idea that small companies should be exempted from having their accounts audited, or from compliance with health and safety provisions; to deter "ill-founded" unfair dismissal claims by charging applicants £25 to appear before an industrial tribunal; to restrict the range of industrial relations duties for which lay union officials must be allowed time off with pay; to consult on the amount of information companies are required to file with the registration offices.

Key aspects of the Department's new role should include: promoting enterprise and job creation in growth areas such as small firms, self-employment and tourism; helping businesses to grow by cutting red tape, improving industrial relations by ensuring a fair balance under the law, and encouraging employee involvement; improving training arrangements; helping the young and the long-term unemployed to find work.

C. Government help

After publication of the Bolton Report in 1971, the then government set up the Small Firms Service within the Department of Industry, and this has evolved into a counselling and consultancy service for small firms with 50 area offices around the country. A similar service is provided in rural areas by the Council for Small Industries in Rural Areas (CoSIRA). Local government has since also become involved, sponsoring projects such as the pioneering London Enterprise Agency set up in 1978. Direct public sector finance has been fairly limited in the United Kingdom. Doran [1984] estimated that in 1981 the total public sector loans to small- and medium-sized businesses were about £66 million, and reached only one in 500 firms. The bulk of the finance came from CoSIRA, the Scottish and the Welsh Department Agencies. The government also planned to allocate £20 million in 1982/3 through the Department of Industry's Small Engineering Firms Investment Scheme, for firms employing under 200 people.

Private sector finance has been promoted through the Industrial and Commercial Finance Corporation, jointly owned by the English and Scottish clearing banks and the Bank of England. It provides loans and loan/equity arrangements between £5,000 and £2,000,000, and in 1982 had advanced about £400 million. Another important joint public and private sector initiative has been the government's Loan Guarantee Scheme, designed to encourage banks to lend to small firms.

D. Financial help

The Enterprise Allowance Scheme was set up in 1983 to help unemployed people set up on their own account, or to start small businesses. It is run by the Manpower Services Commission, and can provide a subsidy of £40 a week to people starting their own ventures.

Moving up the scale, the Small Business Loan Guarantee scheme, introduced in 1981 initially as a three-year experiment, is designed to encourage participating banks and financial institutions to make additional loan finance available to small businesses when they would otherwise not have lent the money. It provides a 70 per cent government guarantee for a 2.5 per cent premium over the normal small business lending rates. A report commissioned by the Department of Industry [*British Business*, 6 April 1984] suggested that the scheme had been fairly successful in encouraging greater support by financial institutions, but that it had encouraged the use of loan finance when often equity finance would have been more appropriate. By January 1986 it had helped over 17,000 businesses with loans totalling £554 million. However, the restrictive rules attached to the scheme caused many to predict its demise at the last Budget. In fact, it was renewed for a further three years.

2. Industry and unions

For the larger small firms, the City's launching of the Unlisted Securities Market (USM) in 1980 has provided a new source of equity finance especially adapted for smaller firms. By 1986, the USM had 113 fund management organisations, plus a large number of smaller organisations operating at its fringes [*Financial Times*, 3 July 1986]. Since 1980, institutional investors have put in about £700 million into venture capital funds. The USM has been boosted also by the Government's Business Expansion Scheme (BES), set up in 1983, which permits private investors to claim tax relief for supporting unlisted companies. The 1986 Budget made the first sale of BES shares exempt from capital gains tax.

Union interest in small firms has been mainly representational, although initiatives to recruit among small firms and in the new "hi-tech" assembly plants, have been of fairly recent origin. This has been a difficult area in which to establish membership, and has to some extent required new methods, such as the highly controversial "no strike" agreements [Bassett, 1986]. Other union initiatives which could prove important include those of the electricians' and the engineers' unions to establish training schools in new technology skills for their members. In view of the reluctance of private employers to undertake training, and the decline of apprenticeships, one avenue for the future would be the re-establishment of craft labour markets with greater union control over training. One of their prime interests would be to preserve the transferability of skills of use to their members, but also useful to small firms which are not in a position to have high overheads. However, so far, these schools are of limited capacity, and the unions' main concern has been to help their members keep their skills up to date.

VII. Conclusions

1. Permanency of the changes

One of the most important ideas recently put forward has been that technical change has enabled smaller scale organisations to thrive, because the flexibility of "electronically controlled" capital goods enables firms to spread their cost over more varied and smaller markets, obviating the need to capture homogeneous mass markets. This argument may place too much emphasis on the technical side of production, as distinct from the economies of scale in finance and marketing that have been stressed by Bolton [1971] and later by Prais [1976]. The financial and marketing factors put forward by Prais are not inconsistent with Piore and Sabel's [1984] concept of "flexible specialisation". But in this case the economies of scale in finance and marketing are provided by the continued existence of giant firms, and the advantages of more flexible capital equipment give a further push to the decline in establishment size (a trend which has continued even in the 100 largest enterprises). It may be that Piore and Sabel's argument runs into trouble in the United Kingdom over the structure of ownership rather than the structure of production. This recalls the apparent weakness of the institutional organisation of small firms in the United Kingdom, but this is only part of the problem. It is also necessary to explain why intermediaries, specialising in marketing or financial risk-spreading, have not developed at the expense of giant firms which provide these services internally.

Nevertheless, there are important forms of market organisation geared to smaller firms, such as the importance of occupational markets for skilled labour which enable small employers to hire ready-trained skilled workers without having to develop their own internal labour markets. In addition, multi-employer bargaining, although not predominant, remains an important feature of industrial relations in smaller firms in industries such as engineering. But in recent years this form of bargaining has declined somewhat in favour of enterprise based systems.

One potentially important factor behind the revival of small firms and establishments in manufacturing has been their unit labour cost advantage (measured as the proportion of labour costs in net output, to take account of lower wages and social contributions in small firms). The reversal of this cost differential by 1983 raises the possibility that further growth of small establishments may be limited. The reasons for this change need to be analysed in greater depth and, in particular, this has to be set in the context of a rise in small firms in several other countries during the same period. Again, these developments are not necessarily inconsistent with Piore and Sabel's hypothesis because more flexible capital goods can help multi-establishment firms as much as single establishment ones. But there is another potentially important factor: that the decline in employment share of large establishments arose because management regained control of industrial relations and manning levels, and so was able to introduce major manpower cuts.

The likely impact of increased production flexibility requires an assessment of economies of market size, in which marketing and financial costs are also a component, but it is beyond the scope of this paper. At least as far as the technical side is concerned, it seems probable that the adaptability of capital goods will increase further and their cost continue to fall, and this could further enhance the position of small production units, however organised.

Assessing the internal management and industrial relations problems of large and small plants in the United Kingdom is equally difficult. Controlling the growth of workplace "custom and practice" needs constant management attention, because the employment relation is at heart a bargaining relation. Large plant managers in the United Kingdom have been greatly assisted in their negotiation over changing working practices by high levels of unemployment, and the acute awareness of many workers that even many large firms faced closure. A major change in product or labour markets could well reverse some of the changes which have taken place.

A third force promoting small firms has been government policy aimed at reducing regulations applying to small firms, and also at making labour markets more flexible, especially as concerns weaker groups of workers. The Department of Employment survey [Clifton and Tatton-Brown, 1979] showed evidence of a modest side-effect of employment protection legislation on employment in small firms, and the removal or weakening of some of these provisions would seem likely to have helped employment in small firms. Similarly, removing young workers from the coverage of wages councils (which set industry-specific minimum wages), plus the special youth employment and training subsidies, could prove advantageous to small firms, although it is common for many such schemes to have a fairly high "deadweight effect" as employers can claim them for people they would have recruited anyway. On the whole, it seems likely that these measures will produce some increased employment in small firms, but not a prolonged growth of the sector at the expense of larger firms and plants.

One factor which could have a more prolonged effect is the encouragement of the unlisted securities market, offering a permanent, and possibly growing, source of finance for small and medium-sized firms. It seems possible that this could offset some of the financial factors favouring giant firms, and possibly even encourage the development of marketing organisations which would provide services to many small firms as an alternative to the multi-plant firm with internally provided services. However, Ray's [1986] analysis of non-manufacturing services purchased by manufacturing firms shows that the growth of such services has so far been limited.

Overall, therefore, it seems possible that employment in small manufacturing plants and in small firms will continue to grow, if not at the rate of the last five years. This has a number of implications for economic and labour market policy, some of which are discussed below.

2. Some implications

As concerns the *quality of jobs and employment*, there has been a long-standing concern that workers in small firms receive lower pay and less security than workers in larger firms, although there may be some compensation through more personal contact. Smaller firms offer fewer opportunities for internal advancement, particularly for managerial staff, and this point is visible in the greater differentiation of management pay between small and larger establishments (Table 6), especially if the small ones are independent. However, the pay differential, within engineering at least, declined greatly during the 1970s, as did the differential in hours of work and payment systems. The growth of small firm employment may have accentuated the problems of low pay to some extent, but the question of low pay should be kept separate from that of poverty, as there are strong economic arguments for attacking poverty through improved social security.[3]

As concerns *labour market structure*, perhaps the most important point relates to skills and training. If small firms are to contribute to, and to draw from, a pool of well-trained manpower, it is important to maintain a system of occupational labour markets rather than to rely upon company internal labour markets. In the latter case, skills are often non-transferable, and even if similar equipment is used, training often lacks the degree of standardisation required to facilitate mobility between firms. Indeed, employers often wish to restrict this in order to reduce labour turnover. In the United Kingdom, apprenticeship linked to craft labour markets developed originally as a form of training suitable to small organisations. It would be ironic if the system finally decayed just when small establishments and small firms appeared to be reviving.

Much policy on *worker representation* in the United Kingdom has been based on the idea that collective bargaining is the norm, but if small firms continue to increase, given the organisational problems that unions have in small firms, there may be other methods which can be used. The British TUC and the Labour Party have opted for a national minimum wage in order to protect workers in the growing areas outside the reach of collective bargaining. But although it may be possible to fix pay by remote control, it is not usually possible to deal with individual workers' grievances in this way. It may be preferable to offer workers in small firms in the United Kingdom rights, similar to those of workers in the Federal Republic of Germany, to have a works council if there are more than five employees, or to have a statutory elected representative as in France. Given the very large number of small employers outside any form of representative institution in the United Kingdom, it is unlikely that a general framework for representation in small firms could be set up by voluntary agreement.

Growth of small firms, if sustained, could also raise new demands on the *social welfare system*. Direct regulation of employment conditions by law could be more damaging in small firms than larger ones because the marginal recruit or employee represents a much larger proportion of the existing workforce. Provisions for maternity benefit or for training which can be easily dealt with by large organisations can impose severe burdens, particularly on very small firms. One solution is to exempt small firms from such provisions, but this may harm the employees concerned. An alternative would be to spread the burden across all employers or across society as a whole. As they increase their demands for functional flexibility of their core workforces, larger firms may be less willing than before to take on workers

---

3. There remain, however, three main arguments for removing low pay: that it is an affront to people's dignity (claiming social security remains a humiliating process for many); it can undermine the efforts of better paid workers to maintain their own conditions; and it reduces the opportunities of unscrupulous employers to take advantage of unequal bargaining power.

in more vulnerable groups or who need training, thus pushing these groups more into areas of employment where small firms predominate. Exempting small firms from employment protection provisions could thus have a disproportionate effect on these sections of the workforce. Providing for these workers could be by a form of levy on all employers which would fund certain social benefits and training, or by direct State intervention.

Bibliography

Altshuler, A. et al. 1984. *The future of the automobile: report of MIT's International Automobile Program*, London, George Allen and Unwin.

Atkinson, J.; Meager, N. 1986. *Changing working patterns: How companies achieve flexibility to meet new needs*, London, National Economic Development Office.

Bannock, G. 1976. *The smaller business in Britain and Germany*, London, Wilton House Publications.

Bassett, P. 1986. *Strike free: New industrial relations in Britain*, London, Macmillan.

Bellandi, Marco. 1986. *The Marshallian Industrial District*, Working paper, Department of Economics, University of Florence, No. 42, July.

Birch, A. 1979. *The job generation process*, Final Report to the Economic Development Administration, Cambridge, MIT Program on Neighborhood and Regional Change (mimeo).

Bolton, J.E. 1971. *Report of the Committee of Inquiry on Small Firms*, London, UK Committee of Inquiry on Small Firms.

Boswell, J. 1973. *The rise and decline of small firms*, London, George Allen and Unwin.

Bowers, J. et al. 1982. *Labour hoarding in British industry*, Oxford, Blackwell.

Brown, W.A. (ed.). 1981. *The changing contours of British industrial relations*, Oxford, Blackwell.

Clifton, R.; Tatton-Brown, C. 1979. *Impact of employment legislation on small firms*, London, Department of Employment Research Paper No. 6, Department of Employment, July.

Craig, C. et al. 1984. *Payment structures and smaller firms: Women's employment in segmented labour markets*, London, Department of Employment Research Paper No. 48, Department of Employment.

Curran, J. et al. (eds.) 1986. *The survival of the small firm*, Aldershot, Gower.

Daniel, W.W.; Millward, N. 1983. *Workplace industrial relations in Britain: The DE/PSI/SSRC Survey*, London, Heinemann.

Davies, S.; Caves, R. 1987. *Britain's productivity gap*, Cambridge, Cambridge University Press.

Doran, A. 1984. *Craft enterprises in Britain and Germany: A sectoral study*, London, Anglo-German Foundation.

Gallagher, C.; Stewart, H. 1984. "Major share of job generation is by small firms", in *British Business*, 13 July.

Ganguly, P. 1982. "Small firms survey: The international scene", in *British Business*, 19 November, pp. 486-491.

Gould, A.; Keeble, D. 1985. "New firms and rural industrialisation in East Anglia", in Storey, D. (ed.): *Small firms in regional economic development: Britain, Ireland, and the USA*, Cambridge, Cambridge University Press.

Hannah, L. 1980. "Visible and invisible hands in Great Britain", in Chandler, A.; Daems, H. (eds.): *Managerial hierarchies: Comparative perspectives on the rise of the modern industrial enterprise*, Cambridge, MA, Harvard University Press.

Jones, D.T. 1981. 1981. *Maturity and crisis in the European car industry*, Sussex European Papers, No. 8, Brighton, University of Sussex.

King, R.; Nugent, N. (eds.) 1979. *Respectable rebels: Middle class campaigns in Britain in the 1970s*, London, Hodder and Stoughton.

Lloyd, P.E.; Mason, M. 1985. "Spatial variations in new firm formation in the UK", in Storey, D. (ed.): *Small firms in regional economic development: Britain, Ireland, and the USA*, Cambridge, Cambridge University Press.

Lydall, H. 1979. *A theory of income distribution*, Oxford, Oxford University Press.

McHugh, J. 1979. "The self-employed and the small independent entrepreneur", in King, R.; Nugent, N. (eds.): *Respectable rebels: Middle class campaigns in Britain in the 1970s*, London, Hodder and Stoughton.

Marsden, D. et. al., 1985. *The car industry: Labour relations and industrial adjustment*, London, Tavistock.

Merrett Cyriax Associates. 1970. *Dynamics of small firms*, Research Report for the Bolton Committee, No. 12, London, HMSO.

Piore, M.J.; Sabel, C. 1984. *The second industrial divide: Possibilities for prosperity*, New York, Basic Books.

Prais, S. 1976. *The evolution of giant firms in Britain*, Cambridge, Cambridge University Press.

Prais, S. et al. 1981. *Productivity and industrial structure*, Cambridge, Cambridge University Press.

Ray, G. 1986. "Services for manufacturing", in *National Institute Economic Review*, No. 3, pp. 30-32.

Rothwell, R. 1986. "The role of small firms in technological innovation", in Curran, J. et al. (eds.): *The survival of the small firm*, Aldershot, Gower.

Smith, C.T.B., et al., 1978. *Strikes in Britain*, Department of Employment Manpower Paper No. 15, London, HMSO.

Stewart, M. 1983. "Relative earnings and individual union membership in the UK", in *Economica*, Vol. 50, pp. 111-125.

Storey, D. 1985. "Manufacturing employment change in Northern England 1965-78", in Storey, D. (ed.): *Small firms in regional economic development: Britain, Ireland, and the USA*, Cambridge, Cambridge University Press.

Storey, D. (ed.) 1985. *Small firms in regional economic development: Britain,Ireland, and the USA*, Cambridge, Cambridge University Press.

UK Government White Paper. 1986. *Building business ... Not barriers*, London, HMSO, Cmnd 9794.

Yamey, B. 1972. "The Bolton Committee Report on Small Firms", in *Three Banks Review*, September.

7 United States of America

Michael J. Piore

This paper reviews research on the role of small business in the United States economy and on its organisation and structure. It focuses upon three principal questions: (1) Is there in fact evidence of a shift toward smaller business units? (2) What is the nature of the organisational context in which small business units operate? (3) What are the contextual factors which make these units effective?

I. Small business as a concept in the United States

Small business is salient in American political rhetoric and iconography but it is not a distinct category in the actual organisation of the United States, politically, economically, or socially, and it has achieved only limited and precarious recognition as a category of social and economic legislation. Moreover, in and of itself, small business is not an organised political force. The two major business lobbies are the National Association of Manufacturers and the Chamber of Commerce. Smaller businesses are more important in the latter than in the former, but neither is exclusively, or even particularly, concerned with the needs of small companies.

1. The Small Business Administration

The only really enduring institutional manifestation of the country's concern with small business is the Small Business Administration (SBA). This agency was created in 1953 within the Department of Commerce. It offers technical assistance and low interest loans under a variety of categorical programmes and helps small businesses in the competition for federal government contracts. The SBA defines a small business as "one which is independently owned and is not dominant in its field".[1]

The specific criteria defining eligibility for SBA aid are summarised in Chart I. As can be seen there, the criteria vary from industry to industry: in manufacturing, for example, a small business eligible for SBA loans can have a maximum of 500 to 1,500 employees; in retail trade, the criteria is annual sales or receipts not exceeding $3.5 to $13.5 million. Most of the loan money thus goes to firms which in other countries would be classed as medium sized, or even large. The SBA certainly does not cater to the

---

1. *Your business and the SBA*, SBA Public Communications Departments, October 1981.

American equivalent of the artisanal sector in countries like Italy and Japan. And it is not the major channel through which any significant category of business gets either funds or technical assistance. In recent years, a very large part of its activities has been concerned with promoting minority business enterprises.

2. Legal framework

American law has a variety of special provisions designed either to favour small business directly or to exempt it from one or another form of government regulation. These legislative provisions are apparently similar to those existing in countries like France and Italy, but they do not appear to have an important influence upon business decisions and hence do not seem to influence the size distribution of enterprises or establishments in and of themselves. They do not create an artisanal sector as they do in Italy, for example; nor do businesses resist employment expansion above legal thresholds as seems to be the case in France.

Indicative of the role which these legislative exemptions play on business decisions is the fact that it is virtually impossible to find a summary of them. Even legal handbooks for small businessmen neglect to mention some of these provisions and refer to the rest only casually as an aside.

Why have these provisions played such a minor role in the structuring of the United States economy? The most plausible answer is their heterogeneity: they have been neither stable in time nor uniform across different pieces of legislation. The rhetorical commitment to small business surrounded these legislative provisions when they were initially introduced and thus facilitated their introduction, but the most important factor historically in generating such provisions is a peculiarly American institution, the "Commerce Clause" of the United States Constitution. This clause limits the capacity of the Federal Government to regulate the economy to that part of economic activity which is involved in interstate, as opposed to intrastate, trade. The courts, and Congress, have often used size as a surrogate for a real measure of involvement in interstate trade and the exemptions in the laws were thus thought necessary to guarantee their constitutionality. The legal inhibitions upon Federal economic regulation were much more important in early regulatory legislation. Over time, the courts have become more willing to sanction Federal activity; arguably, the national economy has become more integrated as well.

In the early legislation, particularly that which dates from the 1930s, the Commerce Clause interacted with the other factors: one was the political problem of garnering support for the legislation; a second was the administrative problem of setting up a new regulatory system. Both of these factors led the initial sponsors of the legislation to accept exemptions for smaller enterprises, but both also led them to conceive such exemptions as temporary, to be reduced over time. And, over time, they moved in fact in this direction. These moves were facilitated by the increasingly liberal construction of the Commerce Clause by the courts.

Chart 1: Definitions of small business in United States Labor Legislation and administrative practice

Small business administration loan programmes

Manufacturing:	500-1500 employees (depending on industry)
Wholesaling:	500 employees
Services:	$3.5-14.5 million annual sales or receipts (depending on industry)
Retailing:	$3.5-14.5 million annual sales or receipts (depending on industry)
Construction:	$17 million average annual receipts for three past fiscal years
Special trade construction:	$7 million for three past fiscal years (depending on industry)
Agriculture:	$0.1-3.5 million annual receipts

Source: SBA, Business loans from the SBA, GPO publication, 1984, 0-453-353, OPC-6, September 1984

The third factor differentiating the American structure from that of other countries was that many state and city governments supplemented Federal regulation with legislation of their own, legislation which was designed precisely to cover intrastate commerce. This legislation was most common, and most comprehensive, in the most industrial states. This fact, of course, makes it even more difficult to summarise the legal climate in which small business operates. And it has tended to undermine the political resistance to the expansion of Federal regulations, since by the time the expansion was proposed, most of the exempted groups were already covered by state law. Recent legislation (for example, the laws governing the hiring of women and minorities) have tended to programme the expansion of coverage in the initial legislation.

A last factor, which should be mentioned in differentiating the American case, is that union organisation of small businesses in a number of industries (notably construction, garment, printing, and trucking) long predates governmental protections for the right to organisation and the law has, if anything, acted to restrain union organisation in these areas by substituting the union election for economic weapons such as strikes and, most importantly, boycotts. Thus, there was little point in trying to stay small in order to avoid unions, as has been the case in France and Italy.

The legal discussions about small business in the United States thus do not focus upon government regulation of internal operations. They seem to be primarily concerned instead with so-called "fair trade" laws, which protect small retail establishments by limiting price competition. This form of regulation has tended to diminish greatly in recent years.

II. The statistics[2]

1. The distribution of employment

There are two major sources of statistics in the United States on the distribution of employment by size of the business unit: *The country business patterns* provides annual data on establishments. The Bureau of the Census conducts a census of business every five years, and the results, published in *Enterprise statistics*, provide data on the distribution of employment by size of enterprise. An enterprise is roughly equivalent to a business or a company: a given enterprise may have more than one establishment. Given available resources, it was impossible to make an exhaustive analysis of this data; the results of the analysis which was feasible, supplemented by other recent work on the characteristics of the size distribution (which, however, is rather limited) yield the following results.

1. There has been a redistribution of employment toward small units in the last decade. This constitutes a reversal of the pattern of the earlier postwar period in which employment shifted toward larger units. The pattern is most pronounced in the establishment data. Here the shift seems to be largely one in which the share of units of 250 or more declines and that of units of under 100 rises. The middle class of establishments, units with 100 to 250 employees, retains a fairly steady share. The pattern is less marked in the enterprise data: through 1977, the share of employment in large enterprises continued to expand and that of smaller enterprises to decline. This suggests that the early shift in the establishment distribution reflected decentralisation of employment within large business, or possibly a merger and conglomeration process in which larger companies bought up smaller, independent producers. By 1982, however, the pattern seems to have changed, and the enterprise distribution also shows a very marked shift toward smaller units. The percentage of total employment in firms with fewer than 100 employees, for example, jumps from 40.1 per cent in 1977 to 45.7 per cent, a figure which is higher even than the figure for 1958 (41.3 per cent). Thus, it does not appear that current trends can be attributed to decentralisation of large business alone.[3]

---

2. Sources of data on small business in the United States are summarised by Candee S. Harris with Nancy O'Connor and Kirk Kummil, in the *Handbook of small business data: A sourcebook and guide for researchers and policy-makers* (The Brookings Institute, January 1983).

3. Other studies bearing on this question are presented by Barry Bluestone and Bennett Harrison in their book *The deindustrialisation of America* [1982]. Their work suggests that the concentration of ownership is continuing. There is, however, some contradictory evidence, which Bluestone and Harrison do not cite. For example, an analysis of unemployment insurance data in California, suggests that enterprises with a single establishment *in that state* (although not necessarily in the nation as a whole) are growing more rapidly than enterprises with more than one establishment in the state [Teitz et al., 1981].

2. These shifting trends could reflect changes in the industrial composition of employment away from manufacturing, where the typical establishment is much larger than average. This, however, does not appear to be the whole story. For the establishment distribution we made a shift-share analysis, calculating what the distribution of employment by size class would have looked like in 1983, assuming that the distribution of employment *across* industries had remained as it was in 1977 and only the size distribution *within* industries had shifted. This analysis suggests that roughly half of the shift toward units of less than 100 employees could be explained by the changes in the industrial composition of employment. The remainder was due to a shift in the pattern *within* industries. Most of that "internal" shift occurred within manufacturing. A shift-share analysis within the manufacturing sector itself (at the two digit level) suggests that the deconcentration within manufacturing is fairly evenly spread across sectors: almost none of the manufacturing shift, in other words, can be explained by the relative growth of industries where employment has traditionally been concentrated in smaller units. In certain respects, the trends in the manufacturing distribution are quite dramatic. For example, between 1977 and 1983, while overall employment in manufacturing fell from 20.6 million to 18.2 million, and declined in the larger size class below 250 (i.e. 1-4 employees, 5-9, 10-19, 20-49, 50-99, and 100-249), the shifts in manufacturing were partially offset by services where the distribution is moving in the other direction. But within services, there are significant exceptions. In the rapidly growing business service sector, the pattern resembles that in manufacturing.

We did not undertake a comprehensive analysis of the compositional effects in the enterprise statistics, but it is clear that the shift in the distribution which occurred in 1982 cannot be readily explained by the industrial composition of employment. It is evident not only in the aggregate statistics but also in both the "manufacturing" and the "selected services" categories taken separately.

Table 1: Distribution of employment by size of establishment for the economy as a whole, 1974-1985

Year	1974	1975	1976	1977	1978	1979	1980	1981	1982	1983	1984	1985
Emp.	63 488	60 564	62 648	64 976	70 289	74 681	74 836	74 850	74 297	72 971	77 995	81 119
< 100	52.5	53.9	54.1	54.5	54.5	54.1	54.2	54.4	55.2	56.1	55.9	55.9
> 250	33.9	32.8	32.3	31.8	31.6	31.8	31.3	30.9	30.4	29.7	29.5	29.3
< 20	25.8	27.1	26.9	27.1	26.6	26.0	26.0	26.1	26.8	27.6	27.1	26.9
20-99	26.7	26.9	27.3	27.4	27.9	28.1	28.3	28.4	28.5	28.5	28.8	29.0
100-249	13.6	13.3	13.6	13.7	13.9	14.1	14.4	14.6	14.4	14.2	14.5	14.8
250-499	9.6	9.3	9.5	9.4	9.3	9.4	9.4	9.4	9.1	8.9	9.0	9.1
500-999	8.3	8.0	8.1	7.9	7.9	7.7	7.6	7.3	7.3	7.1	7.2	7.0
> 999	16.0	15.4	14.8	14.5	14.4	14.7	14.3	14.2	14.0	13.8	13.4	13.1

United States of America

Table 2: Employment shares by establishment size: Time series for manufacturing sector, 1974-1985

Year \ Emp.	1974	1975	1976	1977	1978	1979	1980	1981	1982	1983	1984	1985
Emp.	20 380 740	18 374 397	18 965 344	19 638 852	20 612 389	21 483 353	21 151 842	20 428 330	19 572 113	18 231 529	19 325 352	19 433 606
< 100	24.4	25.7	25.4	25.5	25.3	24.9	25.2	25.6	26.9	28.0	27.4	27.6
> 250	58.1	56.8	57.0	56.8	57.0	57.4	57.1	56.5	55.1	53.5	54.0	53.8
< 20	6.2	7.0	6.9	7.0	6.7	6.4	6.5	6.7	7.3	7.7	7.3	7.4
20-99	18.1	18.7	18.5	18.5	18.6	18.6	18.6	18.9	19.6	20.3	20.1	20.2
100-249	17.5	17.5	17.5	17.7	17.7	17.7	17.8	17.9	18.1	18.4	18.6	18.6
250-499	15.3	15.0	15.3	15.1	15.3	15.5	15.3	15.2	15.0	15.2	15.3	15.3
500-999	13.7	13.2	13.5	13.5	13.7	13.5	13.6	13.2	13.4	12.8	13.0	12.7
> 999	29.1	28.6	28.2	28.2	28.0	28.4	28.2	28.0	26.7	25.5	25.7	25.8

Table 3: Shift-share analysis of entire United States economy: Employment shares by establishment size

Employment size class	1984 actual	1984 using 1973 weights	1973 actual
< 100	55.9	52.9	50.1
< 250	29.5	33.4	35.7
< 20	27.1	26.5	24.3
20-99	28.8	26.4	25.9
100-249	14.5	13.7	14.1
> 250	29.5	33.4	35.7

Table 4: Shift-share analysis of manufacturing sector: Employment shares by establishment size

Employment size class	1984 actual	1984 using 1974 weights	1974 actual
< 100	27.4	24.5	24.4
< 250	54.0	58.2	58.1
< 20	7.3	6.4	6.2
20-99	20.1	18.1	18.1
100-249	18.6	17.3	17.5
250-499	15.3	15.0	15.3
500-999	13.0	13.6	13.7
> 999	25.7	29.6	29.1

United States of America

Table 5: Employment shares by establishment size - selected industries, 1978 and 1984

Number of employees	All establishments 1978	All establishments 1984	Manufacturing 1978	Manufacturing 1984	Retail trade 1978	Retail trade 1984	Fire 1978	Fire 1984	Services 1978	Services 1984	B-services 1978	B-services 1984	Contract construction 1978	Contract construction 1984
< 20	26.6	27.1	6.7	7.3	41.2	38.8	31.9	29.9	31.7	30.3	23.7	23.0	43.3	41.2
20-99	27.9	28.8	18.6	20.1	39.4	41.4	29.6	29.1	25.0	24.4	29.1	29.0	30.9	33.6
100-249	13.9	14.5	17.7	18.6	10.3	12.2	11.9	13.1	13.8	14.3	19.8	20.8	10.3	11.4
250-499	9.3	9.0	15.3	15.5	4.6	4.2	7.4	8.4	8.5	8.4	12.4	12.3	4.8	5.2
500-999	7.9	7.2	13.7	13.0	2.7	2.0	6.8	6.7	7.9	7.6	7.3	7.8	3.1	2.7
1000 >	14.4	13.4	28.0	25.7	1.9	1.3	12.5	12.9	13.5	15.1	7.7	7.0	7.4	5.9

Source: US Bureau of the Census: County Business Patterns, HC101.A185.

Table 6: Average payroll per employee indices by employment size class: Entire economy. Overall average payroll/employee = 100

Employees	1974	1975	1976	1977	1978	1979	1980	1981	1982	1983	1984
	16 817	16 597	16 727	16 885	16 566	16 215	16 203	16 341	16 143	741	16 722
< 100	90	89	88	88	87	87	87	87	87	87	87
> 250	117	119	121	121	123	123	123	125	125	126	126
< 20	89	86	85	85	85	85	86	85	85	85	85
20-99	91	92	91	91	90	89	89	88	89	88	88
100-249	97	98	98	98	97	98	97	98	98	97	97
250-499	101	102	103	103	104	104	105	106	107	109	107
500-999	108	110	111	111	112	114	115	117	118	119	119
> 999	132	135	137	139	141	140	139	140	140	142	143

Table 7: Average payroll per employee indices by employment size class: Manufacturing sector. Overall average payroll/employee in this sector = 100

	1974	1975	1976	1977	1978	1979	1980	1981	1982	1983	1984
Overall annual payroll per employee ($1,982)	19 504	19 573	19 980	20 300	20 336	19 939	19 603	20 209	19 695	20 995	21 072
Employment size class											
< 100	89	88	87	86	84	84	84	83	83	83	82
> 250	108	109	110	110	111	111	111	112	112	113	113
< 20	96	89	87	85	83	84	84	83	80	79	80
20-99	87	88	87	86	84	84	84	84	84	84	83
100-249	87	89	88	88	87	87	87	87	88	88	87
250-499	90	90	90	90	90	91	91	91	91	93	91
500-999	99	100	100	99	101	101	101	102	101	103	102
> 999	123	123	125	127	128	127	127	128	129	130	132

Table 8: Employment shares by size of enterprise, by sector, for selected years between 1958 and 1982

Year	All industries	Mineral	Construction	Manufacturing	Transportation	Warehousing	Wholesale trade	Retail trade	Selected services
				% of employment in companies with fewer than 100 employees - excluding owner					
1958	41.3	44.2	-	20.6	-	67.7	78.6	65.4	69.5
1963	39.9	51.0	-	19.1	73.6	-	79.4	62.9	67.3
1967	39.9	45.0	68.8	16.3	78.5	-	75.8	60.2	65.4
1972	41.3	34.1	69.6	16.2	-	-	76.9	56.9	63.5
1977	40.1	-	68.9	16.1	-	-	-	53.9	59.1
1982	45.7	40.5	67.5	17.6	-	-	70.6	52.0	60.1
				% of employment in companies with fewer than 100 employees - including owner*					
1958	46.8	46.9	-	21.7	-	69.8	80.5	71.5	77.2
1963	45.3	54.1	-	20.2	75.4	-	81.2	68.9	75.3
1967	45.6	47.7	74.6	17.2	77.7	-	77.7	66.0	73.9
1972	47.0	36.6	74.9	17.2	-	-	78.9	62.8	72.3
1977	43.3	-	72.2	17.2	-	-	-	57.3	63.1
				% of employment in companies with fewer than 500 employees - excluding owner					
1958	55.1	61.1	-	37.1	-	86.1	94.1	72.5	84.0
1963	52.9	68.1	-	34.5	90.7	-	93.7	69.4	81.7
1967	53.2	61.5	86.5	30.4	92.0	-	92.0	67.8	81.0
1972	53.5	48.6	85.7	28.9	-	-	91.7	64.4	79.3
1977	52.5	-	85.3	29.0	-	-	-	62.3	75.7
1982	58.7	55.8	81.4	30.3	-	-	87.6	61.7	77.2

Note: *Not available for 1982

Table 8 (continued)

Year	All industries	Mineral	Construction	Manufacturing	Transportation	Warehousing	Wholesale trade	Retail trade	Selected services
			% of employment in companies with fewer than 500 employees - including owner*						
1958	59.4	63.0	-	38.1	-	87.1	94.7	77.4	88.1
1963	57.1	70.1	-	35.5	91.4	-	94.3	74.4	86.2
1967	57.6	63.4	89.0	31.3	92.7	-	92.6	72.6	85.7
1972	58.1	50.6	88.2	29.8	-	-	92.4	69.3	84.3
1977	55.0	-	86.9	29.9	-	-	-	65.2	78.1
			Gini coefficient for employment - excluding owner						
1958	0.726	0.719	-	0.853	-	0.571	0.478	0.503	0.509
1963	.737	.680	-	.861	.525	-	.468	.532	.525
1967	.738	.724	.542	.883	.494	-	.494	.466	.542
1972	.731	.789	.541	.883	-	-	.484	.606	.566
			Gini coefficient for employment - including owner						
1958	0.756	0.713	-	0.843	-	0.534	0.468	0.581	0.590
1963	.763	.681	-	.858	.500	-	.444	.586	.606
1967	.780	.615	.656	.878	.465	-	.465	.642	.622
1972	.781	.794	.656	.881	-	-	.505	.686	.642

Note: * Not available for 1982.

Source: US Department of Commerce, Bureau of the Census: *Enterprise statistics*, various years. Original table from White, pp. 36-37, updated from 1977 by Piore.

3.   A second possible explanation for the shifting distribution is "cyclical effects" associated with rising levels of unemployment in the last decade relative to earlier postwar periods. It is very difficult to separate out this effect without a detailed specification of the manner in which the economy responds to changes in economic activity and labour market conditions. We made a crude effort to separate the cyclical and trend effects by regressing the shares of employment in the less than 100 and the greater than 250 size classes against unemployment and a time trend. The results are presented in Tables 9-12. Basically, they show:

(a) Both the time trend and the unemployment rate are significant: in other words, there is a trend toward smaller units which appears to be separate and distinct from the tendency for higher levels of unemployment to reduce the size of the business unit.

(b) The trend in the period 1973-1984 is a reversal of a trend in the other direction which was also significant in the 1964-1974 period.

(c) While unemployment shifts the distribution toward smaller units in both sub-periods, it appears to have a stronger impact prior to 1974 than after 1975. In the 1974-1984 period, the qualitative results of the regressions of size shares against unemployment and time are the same for the economy as a whole and for most individual two-digit manufacturing industries. An exception is the garment industry, which we have been studying for other reasons: in this industry, however, when a variable reflecting imports is added to the equation, both the time trend and the unemployment rate become statistically significant.

4.   Finally, we examined the distribution of average earnings across size-class. This distribution of earning is of interest for two reasons. First, earnings differentials might explain the movement of employment: economic activity might be shifting toward smaller units because labour is cheaper there. Second, earnings distributions might indicate the welfare effects of the change in the size distribution: one might be less favourably inclined toward these trends if they were having an adverse effect on earnings. It is, however, difficult to separate the effect of establishment size upon earnings from other factors which might be expected to vary systematically with size such as the skill requirements and educational levels of the labour force. The OECD collected a variety of disparate pieces of evidence on this question for the United States and concluded that there was a substantial differential between conditions in small and larger enterprises, even after correction for worker characteristics [OECD, 1985, p. 78-81].

The establishment data yielded figures on annual earnings per employee by size class. These figures are uncorrected for any determinants of earnings; they treat part-time and full-time work indiscriminately. The differentials, as can be seen in Tables 6 and 7, are large and tend to have increased over the period not only for the economy as a whole but also in individual manufacturing sectors. A secondary finding is that in a number of industries, establishments of fewer than 20 employees tend to have higher earnings than the subsequent two or three size classes, but the differential advantages tend to decline or even disappear over time. We tried to explain the pattern of the wage differentials through regression analysis using the unemployment rate and the minimum wage, without success.

Table 9: Coefficients on time in small establishment regressions, 1974-1984

	A	B		A	B
Total economy	0.22* (4.4)	0.29* (2.2)	SIC 29	0.31* (4.9)	0.31 (1.3)
Manufacturing sector	0.18* (3.3)	0.23 (1.7)	SIC 30	0.69* (17.9)	0.71* (5.0)
SIC 20	-0.45* (6.4)	-0.34* (2.1)	SIC 31	0.21* (2.3)	0.31 (1.0)
SIC 21	-0.19* (4.2)	-0.17 (0.7)	SIC 32	0.36* (3.8)	0.50 (1.6)
SIC 22	0.09 (1.9)	0.13 (0.7)	SIC 33	0.46* (4.2)	0.48 (1.4)
SIC 23	-0.17 (1.6)	-0.29 (1.1)	SIC 34	0.59* (6.2)	0.63 (2.7)
SIC 24	-0.17 (1.6)	-0.10 (0.2)	SIC 35	0.55* (4.6)	0.65 (2.1)
SIC 25	-0.09 (1.3)	-0.06 (0.2)	SIC 36	0.03 (0.6)	0.14 (0.8)
SIC 26	0.16* (3.2)	0.16 (0.8)	SIC 37	0.01 (0.6)	0.00 (0.0)
SIC 27	0.26* (4.9)	0.29 (1.9)	SIC 38	0.16* (2.8)	0.23 (2.0)
SIC 28	0.19* (3.1)	0.26 (1.6)	SIC 39	0.32* (3.3)	0.53 (1.7)

Note: A: not differenced, B: first differenced

Table 10: Coefficients on unemployment rate in small establishment regressions, 1974-1984 (t statistics in parentheses)

	A	B		A	B
Total economy	0.21* (1.8)	0.26 (2.9)	SIC 29	-0.08 (0.5)	-0.20 (1.2)
Manufacturing sector	0.43* (3.3)	0.39 (4.3)	SIC 30	0.10* (11.8)	1.03* (10.6)
SIC 20	-0.28* (1.7)	0.20 (1.8)	SIC 31	0.37 (1.7)	0.30 (1.5)
SIC 21	-0.10* (0.0)	-0.05 (0.4)	SIC 32	0.55* (2.4)	0.56* (2.6)
SIC 22	0.42 (3.4)	0.43* (3.6)	SIC 33	0.58* (2.2)	0.42 (1.8)
SIC 23	0.49* (2.7)	0.65* (3.6)	SIC 34	0.93* (4.1)	0.79 (4.9)
SIC 24	1.40* (7.6)	1.90* (5.7)	SIC 35	0.26 (0.9)	0.14 (0.7)
SIC 25	1.27* (7.7)	1.36* (3.8)	SIC 36	0.43* (3.1)	0.42* (3.5)
SIC 26	0.43* (3.6)	0.50* (3.8)	SIC 37	0.15* (2.6)	0.14 (1.9)
SIC 27	0.00 (0.0)	0.04 (0.4)	SIC 38	0.32* (2.3)	0.18* (2.4)
SIC 28	0.07 (0.5)	0.02 (0.2)	SIC 39	0.90* (3.8)	0.82* (3.9)

Note: A: not differenced, B: first differenced

Table 11: Coefficients on time in large establishment regressions, 1974-1984 (t statistics in parentheses)

	A	B		A	B
Total economy	0.36* (11.0)	0.41* (4.6)	SIC 29	-0.52* (3.4)	-0.30 (0.5)
Manufacturing sector	-0.27* (3.7)	0.34 (1.9)	SIC 30	1.11* (16.7)	-1.08* (4.8)
SIC 20	-0.57* (8.1)	0.42* (2.2)	SIC 31	0.48 (1.9)	-0.66 (0.7)
SIC 21	-0.23* (2.5)	0.39 (1.0)	SIC 32	0.48* (7.1)	-0.55* (2.4)
SIC 22	-0.18* (2.3)	-0.27 (0.9)	SIC 33	1.02* (5.3)	-1.07* (2.1)
SIC 23	0.17 (1.6)	0.31 (0.7)	SIC 34	0.69* (7.0)	-0.74* (3.5)
SIC 24	-0.03* (0.4)	-0.02 (0.1)	SIC 35	-0.73* (5.0)	-0.80 (1.9)
SIC 25	0.02 (0.3)	-0.08 (0.3)	SIC 36	-0.18* (2.1)	-0.34 (1.4)
SIC 26	-0.15* (2.3)	-0.20 (0.8)	SIC 37	-0.05 (1.5)	-0.07 (0.5)
SIC 27	-0.36* (7.3)	-0.41* (2.5)	SIC 38	-0.45* (4.6)	-0.57* (2.7)
SIC 28	-0.22* (2.3)	-0.33 (1.4)	SIC 39	-0.40* (3.4)	-0.62 (1.4)

Note: A: not differenced, B: first differenced

Table 12: Coefficients on unemployment rate in large establishment regressions, 1974-1984 (t statistics in parentheses)

	A	B		A	B
Total economy	0.1?* (1.4)	0.14* (2.3)	SIC 29	-0.91* (2.5)	-0.80 (1.8)
Manufacturing sector	-0.46* (3.6)	0.38* (3.1)	SIC 30	-1.10* (6.9)	-0.98* (6.4)
SIC 20	-0.31 (1.8)	0.28* (2.2)	SIC 31	-0.69 (1.1)	-0.79 (1.2)
SIC 21	0.14 (0.6)	0.26 (1.0)	SIC 32	-0.60* (3.7)	-0.67* (4.2)
SIC 22	-0.61* (3.3)	-0.67* (3.2)	SIC 33	-0.77 (1.7)	-0.41 (1.2)
SIC 23	-0.54* (2.1)	-0.75* (2.4)	SIC 34	-1.00* (4.2)	-0.80* (5.5)
SIC 24	-0.91* (4.7)	-0.72* (4.0)	SIC 35	-0.33 (1.0)	-0.15 (0.5)
SIC 25	-1.51* (10.7)	-1.59* (8.2)	SIC 36	-0.49* (2.4)	-0.50* (3.0)
SIC 26	-0.18* (1.1)	-0.17 (1.0)	SIC 37	-0.32* (4.1)	-0.33* (3.6)
SIC 27	-0.04 (0.3)	-0.01 (0.0)	SIC 38	-0.23 (1.0)	-0.01 (0.1)
SIC 28	-0.17 (0.7)	-0.09 (0.5)	SIC 39	-0.98* (3.5)	-0.90* (3.0)

Note: A: not differenced, B: first differenced

Table 13: Average wage by employment size class regressions

Wage_small ≡ wage index for workers in small establishments

Wage_large ≡ wage index for workers in large establishments

U-rate ≡ wage index for workers in small establishments

(1) Wage_small = β_0 + 0.34*U_rate - 0.70*trend
         (1.6)   (8.1)

Differenced:

(1') Wage_small = 0.17*U_rate - 0.69*trend
          (1.2)   (3.6)

(2) Wage_large = α_0 - 0.10*U_rate + 0.50*trend
         (1.2)   (14.2)

Differenced:

(2') Wage_large = -0.08*U_rate + 0.51*trend
          (1.0)   (4.4)

2. Small business and job creation

The most active area of public policy discussion and debate in the United States concerns the role of small business in job creation. This discussion was sparked by a 1979 study by David Birch, who began his work at the Harvard Business School and is now in the MIT Department of Urban Studies. Birch purported to show that small business was responsible for a major portion of net new job creation in the United States (establishments under 20 created 66 per cent of new jobs, establishments under 100, 88 per cent in the period 1969-1976) [Birch, 1979]. These figures were widely used to support the policy conclusion that the government should give special aid and encouragement to small business.

The figures have generated enormous controversy. There is no analytical literature which would create strong expectations about the role of size and the job generation process, but Birch's findings nonetheless apparently violate a widely-held set of prior beliefs. The controversy has also been fueled by people who oppose the notion of government intervention in the economy (although the policy conclusions do not follow directly from the figures: one might in fact argue that small business is doing a fine job generating jobs without government help).

The Birch data have been refined and reworked by a group of analysts at The Brookings Insitute, which was generally sceptical of his results. The findings show a relatively large contribution of smaller companies to total job creation, although the Brookings' numbers are somewhat smaller than Birch's.

The issues in this debate are extremely complex and technical but I would draw the following tentative conclusions.

1. The initial scepticism about the Birch results was based, in part, upon the belief that the size distribution of business units was stable. They are most plausible, however, in the light of recent data which appears to exhibit, as we have noted above, a trend toward smaller units. Nonetheless, the concentration of net job creation in smaller units revealed by even the Brookings studies, which reworked the original Birch data, is incompatible with the magnitude of the shift in the distribution of employment revealed by the County Business Survey. For example, between 1975 and 1983, employment covered by the County Business Survey grew 12.4 million with a stable distribution over size classes, employment in establishments of fewer than 100 employees would have been 29,404 million, a growth of 6.7 million and such establishments would have counted for 54 per cent of the growth. In fact, employment was 40,936 million, a growth of 8.2 million or 66 per cent of the total net increase in employment. This 66 per cent compares to figures of 78 per cent, 88 per cent and 82 per cent reported in Brookings and MIT studies. Those studies, it is true, cover somewhat different time periods, but they also cover time periods in which the change in the underlying distribution was less dramatic, or even the reverse of that required to produce these results. These figures also demonstrate, incidentally, that the bulk of employment is in small units, and small units are likely to account for the bulk of employment growth.

2. It would be possible to reconcile the County Business Pattern data with the Birch-Brookings results if a sizeable number of establishments under 100 employees moved through employment growth into larger size classes. There is some evidence that this is the case, but it is not conclusive [Harris, 1983, p. 9].

3. Jonathan Leonard has argued that the Birch results reflect a statistical phenomenon known as regression toward the mean [Leonard, 1986]. In essence, the argument is that at any given time, the tails of a distribution include a large number of observations which are "out of place" relative to their "real", "permanent", or "long-term" position in the economy. In the case of the size distribution of enterprises, the smallest size classes will include a disproportionate number of firms which are experiencing temporary employment loss and the largest size classes, a disproportionate number with temporary gains. Over a long period of time, these temporary or transitory factors will "go away". As a result of the process through which they "go away", one will observe larger rates of growth in the smaller classes and smaller rates of growth in the larger classes. Leonard investigates these phenomena with a special data set constructed from Equal Employment Opportunity Reports for the period 1974-1980, which seems to confirm his hypothesis. On the other hand, Bronwyn M. Hall, using another data set focusing on the manufacturing sector alone, rejects Leonard's hypothesis. Her findings imply that the rapid growth of small firms is a real

phenomenon, and she is able to explain them by such variables as investment and R & D expenditures [Hall, 1986].

4.   There is now a growing literature on the data base which Birch and the analysts at the Brookings Institute used to study job generation. It suggests that the data which Birch has been using are too unreliable to draw any firm conclusions about the job generation process at this time. There is a real question as to whether it will ever be a useful research instrument.

Birch's data consists of a file of establishments created by Dun and Bradstreet, a private company which sells information on individual firms to clients who use it primarily for credit rating. The biggest problem appears to be that the data under-report the branches of multi-establishment firms. All of the analysts have made some attempt to correct for this bias, and much of the literature debates these corrections. The corrections, however, are substantial, and none of the procedures would appear to render the data adequate for analysing the job generation process.

Other important problems with the Dun and Bradstreet data include: reporting lags, particularly in recording the death of firms which have merged or gone out of business (D & B clients do not usually request credit ratings for "dead" establishments), under-reporting of small retail and service establishments, and random coding errors.

There are several other sources of data which are just emerging and may enable more precise answers to the questions asked in this literature in the future. These include the Equal Employment Opportunity Commission (EEOC) data which Leonard has been working with and the data base of publicly-rated manufacturing firms used by Hall. Unemployment and social security tax records are also a ready potential source of data on job creation by firm size.[4]

5.   There is a growing literature in industrial organisation, an applied field in the discipline of economics, on the relationship between firm size and firm growth. Much of the recent work is essentially theoretical (see, for example, Lucas [1978] and Jovanovic and Rob [1987]), but the latest empirical contributions examine the growth of a panel of firms over time. These studies indicate that employment growth is most rapid for small and new firms and that firms then tend to stabilise [Dunne et al., 1988; Evans, 1987]. This finding is essentially consistent with Birch's contention although it does not focus on small firms per se and it is not yet able to shed light on the changes in patterns of firm growth over the post-war period.

---

4.   This data is presumably more reliable than the Dun and Bradstreet records or EEOC because it is generated by a payroll tax collection process to which are attached stiff legal penalties (both civil and criminal) for reporting errors. Unemployment insurance is a state programme (although operating with Federal guidelines). So far as I know, only one study has made use of this data. The study was for the State of California; a problem with the California data is that it cannot distinguish among establishments of the same company in the state or establishments which are parts of much larger companies which span more than one state [Teitz et al., 1981].

III. Potential explanations

These trends in the size distribution of business units are not the salient facts of American economic life, and the number of analysts who have attempted to explain them is limited. Nonetheless, there would appear to be two distinct theories of what is happening. One of these is the thesis about the need for flexibility and the move toward flexible specialisation developed in *The second industrial divide*. The second is the effort of large companies to increase their power and control over the labour process through the decentralisation of economic activity. The most forceful statement of this view is by Barry Bluestone and Bennett Harrison in *The deindustrialisation of America*. Bluestone and Harrison place particular emphasis upon efforts of large corporations to buy up and milk establishments in older industrial regions by diverting profits and depreciation reserves from reinvestment in these establishments themselves toward investment in other corporate activities in newer regions and even totally different industries. Their argument thus focuses upon trends in the size of enterprises - rather than size of establishments. The trend toward larger enterprises - if indeed there is such a trend - is obviously more striking if the average size of establishments is growing smaller. But the latter has not been a major focus of the Bluestone/Harrison work. Presumably, they see it, however, as part of the effort of employers to avoid concentrations of worker power. And at this point, their argument does join the flexible specialisation debate in the sense that it implies that the declining productivity in older (and presumably larger) establishments is due not to the inefficiency of such enterprises but rather to management's refusal to reinvest in plant and equipment and hence to maintain them up to date.

The potential debate has never, however, been joined. Bluestone and Harrison themselves have directed their attention toward an argument with conventional economists at the Brookings Institution about the inevitability of the decline in traditional manufacturing activities and the desirability of state industrial policy to forestall it [e.g. Lawrence, 1983]. To the extent that flexible specialisation is a way of sustaining manufacturing activity, it can be seen as strengthening Bluestone and Harrison's position in the Brookings debate. The Bluestone/Harrison argument about otherwise viable enterprises being milked by distant corporate owners has been an important factor in union bargaining and regional industrial policy in some specific situations. And in the one case with which I am personally familiar, New Bedford, the continued viability of local producers does indeed appear to be due to the fact that they have moved into specialised niches in their markets, using more flexible production techniques than their competitors in newer industrial regions. Whether the parent companies who had apparently written them off and were milking them for cash, understood this or not is hard to say. There is also some evidence on this point in the study of a central Massachusetts industrial region discussed below [Doeringer et al., 1987].

The argument about decentralisation and the reassertion of managerial authority, particularly in large companies is, it should be noted, very widely accepted [Kochan et al., 1986]. It may be difficult to document it precisely but there is considerable evidence to support it in the business press - and indirectly in studies of the changing strategy of American industrial relations. The question is thus not so much whether it exists but how it relates to flexible specialisation.

Three other views about trends toward smaller business units may be distinguished in United States commentary although it is not easy to identify explicit expositions of them. One of these is related to the product life cycle model: the argument essentially is that small size is related to early stages in the life of an industry when the products are new and the market small and that the optimal productive unit grows as the industry matures. In this view, the down-sizing of the enterprise distribution is associated with the rapid movement of the United States economy out of mature manufacturing industries into new high technology manufacturing and newer services [Dorfman, 1983]. This view would also be consistent with some of the latest work in industrial organisation cited earlier [i.e. Dunne et al., 1988]. The theoretical branch of that literature would probably yield other hypotheses were it to focus on the apparent discontinuity in the postwar growth patterns. A second view is that the deregulation of economic activity and the "supply-side" reforms associated with Reaganomics have encouraged entrepreneurial activity (Friedlander). A third view, prominent in business schools, is that there has been a break-through in managerial science, and the newly discovered techniques favour smaller business units [Horwitch, 1988].

IV. Institutional studies

There is a wide variety of institutional studies of small business which shed some light on the trends in organisational structure and the various explanations and debates associated with them. By and large, however, the studies do not speak directly to these issues. They were engendered by different and largely orthoganal concerns. They are presented here under six headings. The headings are somewhat arbitrary, but by and large they do group together studies whose authors see their work as closely related.

1. Studies of the relationship between large and small companies

I have been studying changes in the organisational structure of major United States corporations as part of the "Management of the 1990s Project" of the Sloan School of Management of MIT. My own view of the shifting relationship between small and large companies is based largely on that work. Thus, I tend to see this question in terms of the broader set of organisational reforms and experiments in which major American corporations are currently engaged. Broadly speaking, developments suggested by that study, as well as reports in the business press and in a growing managerial literature from business scholars and scholar-practitioners, may be summarised in the following points.

1.   Most major American corporations are engaged in a conscientious effort to alter their relationship with the external business units with whom they do business. This includes their subcontractors, vendors of capital equipment, wholly or partly-owned subsidiaries, consultants and the like. Most of these extra-organisational units are smaller than the corporation and have traditionally seen themselves as in one way or another subordinate, but they are not necessarily, or even typically, "small business" in any meaningful sense of that term. The relationships of the large companies to each other are also changing [e.g. Von Hippel, 1986].

These changes are a response to what are perceived as competitive pressures emanating from the external environment. The threat of Japanese competition is felt to be especially strong, and many of the reforms are modelled on Japanese practices. The reform movement began in the 1970s but it was catalysed by the recession of 1981-82.

2.   The reforms are generally characterised by those responsible for them as an effort to "increase flexibility", but this term is subject to a variety of different interpretations by those who employ it. Those interpretations are roughly captured by the contrast between the Bluestone/Harrison version of decentralisation and the Piore/Sabel one. Some executives are seeking to reduce costs by forcing their subordinates to bear them, through lower wages in the case of the workforce and reduced profit margins in the case of subcontractors, vendors, and other external business collaborators. Other executives seek to improve efficiency by reforms in the nature of the collaborative relationship with subordinates: generally, they are seeking more flexibility to adjust quickly to the shifting business environment, although not necessary to institute what Sabel and I describe as flexible specialisation. Typically, the flexibility they are seeking is built into the productive apparatus by pre-programming automated equipment and cross-training workers to operate on several distinct products. Thus, it is a kind of flexible mass production as distinct from flexible specialisation, where the production set is open-ended. Nonetheless, it is very different from classic mass production and from simple cost-cutting tactics within the traditional production strategy. The contrast and conflict among different views of flexibility can be found within almost every organisation and although one may dominate at any moment of time, many organisations vacillate among them.

3.   The specific organisational reforms include:

(a)   A reduction in the number of subcontractors and the development of a more permanent long-term relationship with those which remain.

(b)   A reduction of in-process inventories within the parent company and a movement toward the Kan-Ban system in which parts producers deliver closer to the time at which their supplies actually go into production.

(c) Closer collaboration in the product design with vendors and external parts manufacturers.

(d) The granting of considerably greater freedom to subsidiaries to make business decisions on their own and to pursue business policies which are independent of, even at variance with, those of the parent company. As part of this tendency, companies who used to purchase external business units outright and integrate them wholly often now simply purchase equity.

(e) Encouraging employees to establish their own companies by providing capital and commitments to purchase in whole or in part the new company's output.

(f) A trend, particularly marked in the last year, to recentre the company on its basic business activity; to sell off businesses not directly related to that activity; and to purchase highly specialised services, even those related to the company's main line of business, from outside companies or individual consultants. This is a sharp reversal of earlier trends to diversify risk and maintain historic growth rates through conglomeration.

4. Virtually all of these policies can be used either to increase competition and shift cost or to increase efficiency by promoting flexibility. In the competitive-cost shifting strategy, the reduction in the number of subcontractors is used as an occasion to orchestrate a more intensive competition among them and thus drive down the price of parts; the Kan-Ban system is used to shift inventory costs to the subcontractor; the new independence of subsidies is used to enable them to establish lower wages than the parent and to escape fringe benefits and personnel policies which inhibit (or increase the cost of) discharge, early retirement and the like; the aid to employees to form their own business is used to increase the subcontracting options, etc. In the flexibility strategy, the reduction in subcontractors facilitates the establishment of permanent, collaborative relationships; the Kan-Ban system reduces in-process inventories and thus facilitates a shift from one product to another and promotes lateral information flows and co-ordination: the independence of subsidies and promotion of employee entrepreneurship fosters product diversification.

It is much too early to say where these reforms are headed in the long run and which of the two strategies will ultimately predominate. It is, however, worth noting that the reforms as part of a new "high road" approach are the subject of a growing body of managerial literature and the focus of an increasing body of research. Unfortunately, for our purposes, most of this research is prescriptive rather than descriptive and no-one, to my knowledge, has tried to quantify these developments. Among the work which might be mentioned in this regard is: Abernathy et al., 1983;

Lawrence and Dyer, 1983; Kanter, 1983; Peters and Waterman, 1982; and Horwitch, 1988.

2. The classic small business industries: Garments and construction

The two industries in the United States which have been traditionally characterised by communities of small firms are garments and construction. The literature on the socio-economic structures of these two industries is limited, but both have drawn upon academic economists as arbitrators and mediators in labour relations and there is, therefore, a long oral tradition among industrial relations scholars about their structures. Sabel and I drew heavily upon this tradition in our attempt to understand and characterise industrial regions. The most salient features of the industries in the United States are twofold: (a) the role of particular immigrant groups in the industry and the consequent embeddedness of the industrial structure in the social structures of the immigrant community; and (b) the strength of trade union organisations and their key role, not only for the workforce - a role which trade unions play in most industries - but for industrial organisation more generally.

Both industries have historically been characterised by a multitude of very small firms. Capital requirements are minimal. Entry for new firms is easy, and existing firms can expand (and contract) their employment easily as well. As a result, the industry is extremely competitive. Firms are very interested in reducing the amount of competition - and the number of decision-making margins upon which competition takes place - but the ease with which new firms can enter the industry makes this very difficult to do. In construction, firms have an additional interest in predictability: they must bid on jobs and commit themselves to a price in advance for some relatively prolonged period in the future. The competitive nature of the industry makes the bidding precarious and creates a strong interest in a mechanism which will impose the same costs upon everybody in the industry and fix those costs in advance of the bidding process. For these reasons, employers welcome union organisations as the key to wage stabilisation in the industry provided that the union can enforce the same wage bargain upon all employers, potential as well as actual. And unions are often organised from the "top down", i.e. the firm commits its employees to membership. Contractors' associations may be organised in this way as well: with prime contractors (the general contractor is in construction; the manufacturer is in garments) obligated to impose labour conditions on the subcontractors or, as they are called in garments, "jobbers".

The immigrant community plays a central role in this process because it is able to bring community pressure to bear upon both workers and employers to adhere to the labour agreement. Without this kind of strong community sanction, apparently, competitive pressure makes it very difficult to maintain the requisite cohesion. In any case, both the union and the employer associations are closely tied to the political, religious and/or nationalist organisations of the immigrant communities, and the two organisations are often actually divided into sub-units (union locals and contractors' associations) along ethnic lines.

A key to community (and hence trade union) control in both garments and construction (although in somewhat different ways) is the skill involved in the work and the nature of the skill acquisition process. Labour skills depend almost entirely on on-the-job training in which senior workers teach novices in the process of production. Entrepreneurial skills appear to be acquired in this way as well: subcontractors "learn" how to manage from their contractors and expect over time to move "up-market" toward increasingly sophisticated and profitable lines of work just as employees move from low to high skilled tasks. The nature of skill enables the immigrant community to limit entry at least to its own members, although that control has been periodically breached in the United States by the entry of new immigrant groups with skills acquired abroad. In construction, this control is formalised in an apprenticeship system, but apprenticeship's main contribution seems to be in the training of managerial workers, and rank-and-file workers are largely trained more informally on the job. The garment industry has a training problem related to the generation of fashion designers similar to the problem of supervisory training in construction. In New York, this is resolved in part through formal educational institutions maintained under employer and union pressure by the municipality. The construction industry has additional problems of allocating labour with specialised skill which is required on demand for short periods of time and this has been resolved through the union-controlled hiring hall.

The hiring hall problem, or rather the technical problem which the hiring hall resolves, is a particular manifestation of a general problem which appears in industrial regions of this kind: the regional industry is composed of a variety of individuals and small enterprises, many of which have highly specialised skills or knowledge required for operations which, while often utilised regularly in the region as a whole, may be rarely needed by any particular employer. In construction, the union business agent at the hiring hall is the repository of knowledge about who has these skills and where they are required. In the garment industry, that knowledge is apparently more diffuse.

Because employers are small and often short-lived, the union - in combination with a limited group of stable contractors and operating through the municipality with the help of the ethnic community and ethnically controlled political institutions - has been responsible for the "industrial policy" and strategy. These include industrial standards (i.e. building codes in construction); the preservation of industrial space, through zoning requirements in garments; and, as we have seen, training. Both the garment and construction unions, alone or in co-operation with contractors, have also been active in industry research and development and the garment unions have been heavily involved in the development and maintenance of foreign trade protection (actually negotiating with foreign governments).

An important problem in the garment and construction industry has been the maintenance of wage and labour supply controls over time. It appears that in both industries, this has been done so as to foster product innovation but forestall innovation in the production technology. In the garment industry, wages have been controlled by an elaborate piece-rate system. In the construction industry, the system of work jurisdictions has inhibited certain kinds of technological change.

From these origins in the oral wisdom about garments and construction crafts, the literature on small-scale industry in the United States branches in three directions: (1) a still largely oral and increasingly thin thread of work updating our understanding of construction and garments; (2) a rich and growing literature on immigrant industries and immigrant entrepreneurship; and (3) a somewhat diverse and disjointed literature on particular industries and regional economies characterised by small-scale production.

3. Recent developments in garments and construction

In the last decade, practising lawyers have largely replaced academic economists as neutrals in labour relations, and the oral tradition out of which the preceding picture of the garment and construction industries is abstracted has languished. It would appear, however, that in the post-war period, both industries evolved away from the paradigmatic structures just described toward organisations and practices more typical of mass production. In the garment industry, this evolution began very early in the post-war era; in the men's clothing industry perhaps even before the war. Fairly standard items, which were not subject to fashion changes and hence for which relatively long production runs were possible (men's suits, for example, and sportswear, especially blue jeans) were broken into "section work", a division of labour reminiscent of the automobile assembly line. The shops moved out of the city centres, especially New York City, to rural areas, where they employed unskilled farm women in large units. A certain amount of specialised machinery was used in these shops, and they were increasingly non-union. New York City, however, continued to operate in essentially the old way, producing for the high fashion industry and "reorders", i.e. short runs of standard items which catered to peaks in demand which had not been anticipated in advance.

However, in the most recent years, for which our knowledge is least comprehensive, these trends may have been reversed or at least altered. The industry has come under intense foreign competition, but the impact has been greatest on the standard production segments which had already left the original New York City centre. In the City itself, output has fluctuated but around a more stable trend, and production organisation has changed little. A major change has, however, occurred in the ethnic composition of the industry. Second and third generation Jews and Italians have been reluctant to enter the industry labour force and they have been replaced by new immigrants from the Far East and Latin America. Most recently, the newer immigrant groups have replaced Jewish and Italian contractors as well. This ethnic transition has strained the structure of the trade unions and the contractors' association. The old organisation forms appear to be reemerging within the Chinese community; less so among Hispanics who, because of the diverse origins of Spanish-speaking immigrants, do not really constitute a community anyway. These pieces of the story have been more closely followed in the literature on immigrant entrepreneurship. In most recent years, the unions appear to have recognised the problems posed by the piece-rate system for technological dynamics, and have begun to experiment with other forms of wage controls. The unions themselves appear to be reasserting their traditional role in industrial strategy and leadership: they have become active in research and development of new technologies, a role which languished in the 1950s and 1960s; they are if anything more aggressive than ever in seeking protection from foreign competition; although their political power is no longer what it was, they continue to influence zoning and other forms of municipal regulation; finally, they have begun to formulate training policies for the industry, a function which previously took place within immigrant families and was largely ignored by the unions and contractors. A major development, however, which has accompanied the new immigration, is the creation of urban garment centres outside New York, especially in Los Angeles and Miami, where the union is much weaker. We know virtually nothing about the evolving industrial organisation in these newer areas.

The organisation in construction has also changed in the last decade and a half. Beginning in the early 1970s, several large national construction contractors began to operate either partly or wholly non-union. It appears that these non-union contractors have attempted to abrogate the old craft organisation of the industry. They employ a permanent core of broadly trained workers, who serve largely as supervisors and team leaders and hire, on the local labour market, a crew of unskilled or semi-skilled workers for each job. The work itself is divided into tasks and distributed without respect for old craft lines. These non-union, industrial-type companies must, however, have always had recourse to speciality subcontractors for certain highly-skilled specialists, and there is some indication that they are moving from direct employment and supervision toward progressively greater reliance on specialised subcontractors of this kind.

Meanwhile, some of the construction unions (most prominently the bricklayers), like their brothers and sisters in garments, have been revitalising their traditional roles in training and in research and development. The bricklayers, at least, are also reorganising the unions on a regional basis, which will presumably place the union in a better position to deal with large contractors which operate over broad geographic areas.

4. Immigrant industries and immigrant entrepreneurship

Most of the literature on migrant workers in Europe, and my own work on undocumented migration in the United States, has emphasised the flow of foreigners into unskilled, dead-end jobs. The contemporary literature on immigrant entrepreneurship developed in large measure in reaction to this characterisation.

The most coherent statement of an alternative position can be found in the work of Alejandro Portes comparing the experiences of Mexican and Cuban immigrants to the United States. He found that the Cubans experienced much higher incomes and much greater upward occupational mobility in both the first and second generations. He argues that this can be explained by the differences in the labour market structures into which they flowed. The Mexican labour market experience, Portes argues, is correctly captured by a dual labour market model with the migrants confined to a secondary sector, where the employing enterprises are owned and managed by United States nationals from other racial and ethnic groups. The Cubans who are concentrated in the city of Miami, however, managed to establish what Portes calls an ethnic enclave, where most enterprises were Cuban owned and managed. The enclave constitutes a kind of internal labour market in which unskilled workers are able to advance to progressively more highly-skilled and better paying positions which are elsewhere monopolised by United States nationals. This advancement provides a kind of social mobility for the first generation itself. But it also permits that generation to sustain the professional education of their children and thus enables the immigrant community to enter the mainstream of American life through the professions, at a high level of socio-economic status, in the second generation [Portes and Bach, 1985].

This model suggests that clusters of immigrant enterprises have a critical impact not only upon the entrepreneurs themselves but upon the whole ethnic group and points clearly toward community effects. But Portes' work has not described the structure of the Miami Cuban community in a way which would enable us to understand how it operates and how or why it developed in the first place, and I am not aware of other research which effectively does so.

In a sense, Roger Waldinger's work on the New York City garment industry can be viewed as an extension of Portes' efforts at theorisation. In these terms Waldinger produces several interesting findings. First, his work, as well as the earlier oral traditions about the old Italian and Jewish communities, suggests that the immigrants are not unskilled: on the contrary, they are able to enter the industry - indeed are initially recruited from abroad - precisely because they already possess the requisite skills. The reason that the old immigrants were replaced by new ones, rather than by United States nationals, was because the latter were not skilled and, in a piece-rate industry where earnings depended on skill and where novices learn only if experienced workers are willing to sacrifice their own earnings in order to teach them, never acquired enough skill to obtain income levels which were competitive with other opportunities. Second, Waldinger found substantial immigrant entrepreneurship among virtually all ethnic groups. Third, however, the kind of community structures that one might imagine underlie the Portes' enclaves were not universal. The Chinese entrepreneurs in New York employ exclusively Chinese workers and, as noted above, are regenerating the kinds of contractor and union structures that were characteristic of the industry when it was dominated by Jews and Italians. But the Hispanic entrepreneurs often pursue exactly the opposite policy, employing workers from diverse national and ethnic backgrounds in order to forestall organisation and communitarian effects. One would like to know then how one or the other of these alternatives was chosen and how the choice affects the future evolution of the industry [Waldinger, 1986].

A third type of industry study which further complicates this picture examines the relationship between the structures of the industry in the United States into which the immigrants move, and the structure of the industry at the point of origin abroad. I am aware of two studies of this kind, one looking at Mexicans in the shoe industry in Los Angeles [Runsten, 1985], and the other at the Colombians of the textile industry in New England [Glaessel-Brown, 1984]. In both cases, the immigration is highly structured and their arrival permits the perpetuation or, in the case of Los Angeles, the creation of an industry which is unable to attract the requisite skilled labour at home. The studies thus further undermine the simplistic dual labour market model of the immigration process. The Los Angeles shoe study, however, also calls into question Portes' enclave model, at least in so far as Portes draws upon the assumed unskilled nature of Mexican immigrants to explain their jobs in the United States. In neither industry does the immigration lead to the formation of particularly dynamic industrial regions in the United States. The firms do seem to survive by finding specialised niches within their own industry but they continue to lead a precarious and marginal existence. The immigration, if anything, facilitates this, because when employment turns down, the workers simply go home, thus reducing pressures upon their employers to find alternative market niches. One might hypothesise that it is this return flow which distinguishes the Mexicans and Colombians from the Cubans and explains why in the former case there is so little entrepreneurship or community.

The Mexican shoe industry, from which the Los Angeles workers came, is bifurcated into two parts: one producing relatively standard products in long runs using semi-skilled labour in large enterprises, the other producing high quality items with skilled labour in small shops. The latter sector, however, yields very low incomes and miserable working conditions. The skilled workers in Los Angeles are drawn from this small enterprise segment. The study does not provide a good explanation of why the Mexican industry has not been more dynamic although drawing on a comparison with Brazil it suggests that the stagnation in Mexico is related to the protected nature of the Mexican market and the lack of an effective industrial policy for the industry. One wonders whether the Mexican industry, had it been more dynamic, would have led to a more dynamic industry in Los Angeles as well, perhaps with more Mexican entrepreneurs. Alternatively, a dynamic Mexican industry might have paid high wages in Mexico, holding the workers there and using Los Angeles as an export market for its products, thus effectively precluding the kind of development of the Los Angeles industry which occurred.

These skilled textile workers in New England evidently come out of very large enterprises in Colombia with very extensive formal training programmes. In this case, it does not appear that one could have transferred entrepreneurial skills from one country to another although, of course, an industrial region might nonetheless have developed for other reasons had the immigrants themselves been less mobile.

I have not made a complete search of the literature. There are probably other immigrant industry studies - indeed, I am aware of several others myself [see, especially, Portes and Manning, 1986]. But the particular focus upon the relationship between the industry structure and the community structure, which is central to the dynamics of small-scale industry, is not common. The literature which we have does not suggest that the multiplication of case studies, by itself, is going to clarify the issues in this area. Generalisation seems to become more difficult, not less so, as the number of case studies expands. This implies that the problem may be conceptual and theoretical, not empirical, a point to which we return below.

5. Industry studies

The third strand, which follows from the garment and construction tradition, concerns studies of particular industries and/or regions in which small-scale production predominates. Roughly speaking, these divide into two groups. One focuses upon older, traditional industries, the second on high tech. The latter tend to have a regional focus and are discussed under that heading in the next section. The non high tech industrial studies are really a hodge-podge. Researchers become interested in them for a variety of different reasons. They are largely unaware of each other's activities. One could not say, therefore, that there is a literature here in the sense that it is accumulating knowledge or undergoing theoretical development over time. And for that same reason, there are undoubtedly a number of potentially relevant studies that I have missed. Nonetheless, in terms of the interests of this project, the following material seems relevant.

A group of researchers at the University of Illinois has recently developed a history of the organisational structure of the radio broadcasting industry in the United States. This industry is particularly interesting because organisationally it has shifted over time from a highly centralised to a highly decentralised structure. The transformation, moreover, was not linear and yielded various intermediate structures along the way. Initially, broadcasting was viewed as an adjunct to the sale of radios and the original centralisation of the industry was due to the concentration of the radio manufacturing industry which financed the broadcasting companies. When the market for radio equipment became saturated, the interest of the manufacturers subsided and a new source of financing was required. In the United States, this eventually became advertising. But the structure of the advertising market then evolved substantially over time. In the beginning, the advertisers bought radio time, and produced their own programmes. The intermediary in this transaction of radio time was the advertising agency. The agency gradually assumed responsibility for the production of the programmes which were being aired during the time it sold. And the programme then became the key commodity and the agency the central organisation unit. The next step in the evolution was towards a fee structure for programmes which was based upon the size of the audience so that, in effect, it was the size of the audience which became the basic commodity around which transactions took place and not the air time nor the programme itself. Once this change occurred, power within the industry increasingly shifted to the major networks. They began to produce and sell their own programmes and, at the same time, increased their power over their local affiliates so that the latter were obliged to air the network productions. The reversal of this trend appears to centre around the use of recorded programmes. The centralised industry developed in a period where there was a strong belief that audiences would only accept live programmes by major (and hence limited and expensive) talent. There was an ideological barrier to broadcasting prerecorded programmes and, especially, record music. But when local stations began to experiment successfully in the 1940s and 1950s with the disc-jockey/record format, it became economically feasible for them to produce their own programmes and sell local advertising time directly. As the local stations increased their autonomy in this way, they began to specialise on particular audience groups, further fragmenting and decentralising the industry. This final phase, however, was accompanied, somewhat ironically, by one critical countervailing trend: i.e. the creation of centralised rating services, which foreclosed fraud and permitted and assured measurement of the size of the audience, which was the metric for comparing and calculating charges for the specialised programming of the fragmented stations.

Three features of this particular study should be underscored. First, the relative instability of the product which is being produced and sold and the way in which the evolution of the definition of that product is bound up with the structure of the industry. Second, the fact that the shifting product definition and the related shifts in industrial structure have relatively little to do with technology. And three, the role of communal (centralising) institutional structures like the rating service in the consolidation of a decentralised organisational structure. (A piece of the history not well developed in the Illinois study but of great interest is Mutual Broadcasting, a network created during the centralised phase of the industry which, unlike NBC, ABC, and CBS (the major networks) was a syndicate of independent local stations designed to produce national programmes for their own use.)

The focus upon the changing nature of the "product" in the radio study reflects the theoretical concerns of the Illinois researchers. They are organisational theorists in a business school whose primary interest is in a reorientation of transaction-based organisational theory - a subject to which we will return below.

A different focus underlies a study of organisational decentralisation in the motion picture industry conducted by Michael Storper and Susan Christopherson at the University of California, Los Angeles [Storper and Christopherson, 1986a, 1986b]. The early history of this industry is also one of a highly centralised, vertically integrated organisational structure in which the key organisational unit was the major motion picture studio. The major studios owned chains of movie houses and held under contract virtually all important theatrical talent. The pictures produced in the studios utilised the talent under contract and were exhibited in the studios' own theatres. A sophisticated publicity operation, also controlled by the studios, promoted both the contracted performers and the pictures in which they appeared. The production process was also highly repetitive and routinised. Not only did the same stars reappear in film after film but the basic story lines, scenery, and costumes tended to repeat themselves, and the films were often produced in assembly-line fashion, breaking up a series of scripts into component scenes which could be grouped on the basis of their common production elements and shot in sequences totally unrelated to the particular films into which they were later incorporated. This pattern was overturned in the course of the 1950s and 1960s by two major "events": first, the court ordered break-up of the studio control over movie theatres and then, by the advent of television as a competitor to the movie theatre and a second consumer of motion picture products. The new structure, which Storper and Christopherson explicitly link to flexible specialisation, is one in which the major studio continued to maintain "a firm grip on the financing and distribution of high budget theatrical releases and also moved into production for television. But the production process itself became organised on the external market rather than within the firm." The films were produced by independent production companies which hired, rented, or subcontracted the necessary elements for each film from specialised experts or subcontractors and put them together film by film in a craft-like way.

Storper and Christopherson are geographers and what interests them is the fact that over the period of organisational decentralisation, the industry became, if anything, more geographically centralised in Los Angeles than it was in the days of the major studios. The paradox is easily explained, however, by the requirements of the resources, especially the workers, for continuity in employment as the institutional continuity of any particular employer becomes increasingly problematic and by the parallel need of the employer, whose labour requirements varied radically and unpredictably over time, to find specialised skilled manpower at short notice. A general rationale for an industrial district emerges directly from this explanation. Storper and Christopherson also identify several institutional structures which seem critical to the successful functioning of the district. In addition to the vestigial but critical role of the major studios in financing and distribution, they give a great deal of attention to the unions. The role and structure of the unions in motion pictures is remarkably similar to that in construction and garments. It appears, however, that the union functioned in a similar way under the older, vertically integrated studio structure, a fact which the authors do not emphasise and never analyse. They also note that union strength has been declining in recent years. This is discussed at some length by the authors but the discussion is not really satisfactory in the light of the critical functions which the unions seem to perform, not only in this industry but in garments and construction as well.

Because the Storper/Christopherson study derives from a set of theoretical concerns so different from those in the Illinois radio study, the parallels between them never emerge. But there are several. First, it seems that it is changes in the product, or the conception of the product, rather than in the technology of production (and, arguably, even the technology of the product) which generates the shift from mass production to flexible specialisation (to apply a term which the radio study does not use). Second, to the extent that there are exogenous changes in the environment in either case, it is in the legal structure facilitating (or inhibiting) the vertical integration of the industry. Finally, it should be noted that in both cases the decentralisation precedes the period upon which Sabel and I concentrate in *The second industrial divide*. And neither movies nor broadcasting are manufacturing industries in any standard sense of the term.

A third case study which can be read as a companion to movies and broadcasting is a study of the scholarly book industry by Walter Powell, an organisational sociologist at Yale. Powell identifies [1985] the critical organisational units in this industry as the "network" of scholars surrounding textbook editors. These networks move with the editor as the latter shifts among firms, and Powell traces this movement and shows how it is affected by various efforts at concentration within the publishing industry. Perhaps his most interesting finding is the ability of the large corporate organisation to adapt to this structure and incorporate it within itself. This study has led Powell to a more general concern with "networks" as a form of organisation intermediate between markets and hierarchies, and he is attempting a more general theoretical formulation of the properties of the "network" form [Powell, 1984].

6. Industrial regions

In addition to the industry and ethnic community studies, there is a certain amount of new work on local and regional economies. In some respects, this literature may be viewed as a continuation of a venerable tradition in economic geography and urban economics stressing economics of agglomeration, particular locational advantages, input-output relationships and the like. This line of reasoning was eclipsed in the 1950s and 1960s by the dispersion of American industry from the cities to the suburbs and by the geographic decentralisation of production, most notably industries which had once been associated with particular urban centres such as Detroit in car manufacturing, Akron, Ohio, in rubber, Chicago in meat packing, and the like.

A. Traditional industries

The most germane to the problematic of the "new industrial organisation" - not coincidently since it was directed by one of our colleagues in Boston - is a study of Montachusetts, an old industrial region in central Massachusetts. The study reveals that the region is adapting to a new economic climate by a strategy of "nicheism". The original industrial base of the region was spread over a rather wide variety of industries ranging from paper and paper products to furniture, garments, and plastics. In all of these industries, mass production is moving, or has already moved, out of the region. The remaining firms are small, often (although not always) locally owned, and are concentrating on special order production of either new or customised products or items where quality, workmanship, or speed of delivery are the key competitive factors. The study attempts to separate out the contribution of the "invisible" factors associated with business strategies of this kind from conventional and quantifiable competitive factors such as wages and labour productivity, and to trace the success to the regional heritage of skilled labour, an entrepreneurial tradition, and certain interorganisational relationships.

Several factors seem to distinguish this regional economy from those identified in other studies. First, there does not seem to be a single dominant industry or industrial agglomeration. The closest candidate is a plastics complex, including plastic mould making, raw material production, and finished plastic goods (there is a possible comparison with the Oyonnax region in France) which appears to account for somewhat less than one-third of total manufacturing employment in the region (it is difficult to tell from the study because the employment in mould making is not specifically identified; about 25 per cent of total employment seems to be in resin manufacture and fabrication [Ibid., p. 120]; mould making and machine tools account for 21 per cent of total employment but the division between them is not given [Ibid., pp. 102 ff]). The importance of this concentration, as an explanatory factor, is somewhat reduced by the fact that all industries seem to be pursuing similar strategies. Second, ethnic ties do not seem to be important in the development of any of the industries. The region has the largest concentration of Finns in the United States, but this group is not mentioned at all in the study. Three, a number of small companies in the study have developed alliances with foreign producers to whom they provide marketing services, technical assistance, and apparently some supplementary production in the States. These foreign alliances are presented in the text in the context of the adjustment to the overvalued dollar, but they may also serve as a substitute for relationships with other firms in the region. Fourth, the small increasingly specialised enterprises in the Montachusetts region have not drawn heavily on modern technologies, such as robotics or numerically controlled machine tools. They feel that the skilled labour force in the region gives them a special advantage and enables them to obtain better quality and higher productivity out of conventional equipment than other producers obtained from the high tech alternatives. At the same time, the skilled craftsmen upon which the industry of the region is increasingly dependent are afraid of the new equipment and this deters its introduction. The policy conclusions of the Montachusetts study focus upon the problems caused by skill and technology and suggest that, for industry to survive in the future, the region will have to develop more formal education and training programmes to replicate the present generation of craftsmen and a system of re-education and technological assistance which will help the region overcome the technological gap which is emerging between it and its competitors abroad.

B. State development strategy

The changes occurring in business organisation are being accompanied by a shift in the economic development strategy of individual states. The dominant strategy in the postwar period has been an effort to attract national and, increasingly, multinational companies to locate branch manufacturing plants in the states. The strategy originated in the low wage, largely agricultural sites of the Old South. The first programme was developed in the lowest wage state, Mississippi, in 1936, under the name BAWI (Balance Agriculture With Industry) and was designed, as the name indicates, to diversify the State's cotton-based economy. The State, and its local subdivisions, provided tax incentives, subsidised land, direct subsidies (financed by tax-exempt municipal bonds), training assistance and, where necessary, specialised physical infrastructure and exemptions from local regulatory requirements. The policy was carried even further in Puerto Rico, which was the lowest wage area with free access to the United States market and, because of its special status, was able to exempt companies from minimum wage laws and corporate income taxes. By the 1970s, the competition of the low wage states was being strongly felt in the older industrial states which felt compelled to moderate their tax, regulatory and welfare provisions and, in some cases, to introduce special tax exemptions and financial subsidies of their own.

In the last ten years, there has been a major change in the philosophy of state economic development. This change has both a "negative" and a "positive" component. The "negative" component, signalled by a planning document very widely circulated by the National Governors' Association, emphasises what might be called internal economic development and the role of traditional government services. It is specifically critical of the older effort to attract branch plants of national companies, arguing that such a policy approach tends to create unstable, unskilled, low wage jobs that are eventually lost to foreign competition while, at the same time, eroding the financial base of state government and, hence, its ability to provide governmental services and maintain the state infrastructure. The report highlights instead the role of small business in job creation noted in the first section of this report, drawing the conclusion that most jobs are created by local business entrepreneurship. It argues that this kind of job creation needs the support of a strong educational system and sound physical infrastructure and that the erosion of the tax base through exemptions threatens the state's ability to provide this. The report also places great emphasis on the elimination of state regulations which may inhibit or deter entrepreneurship. It is particularly concerned with limitations on competition imposed by consumer protection legislation, banking regulations, barriers to entry of out-of-state producers, and the like. There is heavy emphasis on the creative force of destructive competition, which the report illustrates by reference to a small area study which found that "65 per cent of the influences leading to the start-up of new companies were negative: 'getting fired', 'boss sold the company', 'organisational changes', 'being transferred but did not want to leave the area', 'no future'; 'didn't like the job'" [Vaughan et al., 1985, p. 57].

The "positive" approach to the new state industrial policy is represented by a recent policy statement of the Committee for Economic Development [CED, 1986]. It starts from the presumption that spontaneous entrepreneurship is not sufficient in itself to generate growth: active government promotion is required as well. Such an active approach has been developed in several industrial states including Pennsylvania, New York, Michigan, and Massachusetts. The instruments of the positive policy include the state provision of venture capital, state "incubators" for small business which provide technical and managerial assistance for new start-ups and fledgling entrepreneurs, and export promotion through state-sponsored advertising and business representation abroad. In most programmes, these newer instruments are combined with traditional approaches such as industrial parks, training and vocational education, and university-based research and engineering activities.

These approaches are too recent to have been evaluated and it is premature to form a judgment about them. One obvious view is that they are simply turning internally the range of policy instruments which were previously directed at attracting institutions from out of state, and that the resources are largely dissipated by subsidising operations which would have happened anyway and/or moving activity around from one state to another without net addition to the national economy. Undoubtedly, there was much of this in the beginning although one can believe that over time, state officials are learning on the job and thereby giving some substantive meaning to such terms as "venture capital" and "entrepreneurial incubators" which will distinguish them from a simple subsidy, in cash or in kind. The expressed philosophy implies a much greater emphasis upon real education and education-related research and development than in the old state development policy which tended to short-run training, and one could attempt to measure the extent to which such a change has indeed taken place. Because the United States economy has become internationalised and the states are selling in the international market place, the new programmes are much less likely to be simply drawing activity from others parts of the country: the efforts by states at export promotion is a genuinely new dimension of their development activity.

C. High tech

Finally, there has been a lot of interest in the United States in high tech industrial regions. The amount of genuine research and scholarship on these regions which I was able to uncover, however, is limited. There are by common consensus two paradigmatic regions, Route 128, the circumferential highway around Boston, Mass., and Silicon Valley, in Northern California near San Francisco. A fairly large number of other United States cities and states have tried to reproduce similar phenomena (as well as a number of foreign cities and regions). Prominent on the United States list of such areas would be Austin, Texas; Chapel Hill, North Carolina; Pittsburgh, Pennsylvania; some areas of Southern California around Los Angeles. The literatures divides into two parts: studies which focus on the structure of Route 128 and Silicon Valley, and studies about the attempt to produce analogous development elsewhere.

Thus far, the literature seems basically to have identified a list of factors which are critical to success. The standard lists include (1) a major research university; (2) an academic tradition, or ethos, which encourages researchers to engage in practical activities and which is not hostile to linkage between the academic and business community; (3) venture capital or, more precisely, a local financial community with both the resources and the willingness to provide funds for start-up enterprises; and (4) a local entrepreneurial tradition and a reservoir of expertise in the management of start-up business. The attempts to create new regions have essentially tried to create the institutions on this list. They have, for that reason, virtually all occurred in areas which already had a research university. They have first moved to expand and/or redirect their activities toward high tech engineering. This has usually been combined with some efforts to provide venture capital and promote entrepreneurship. The experience has, as noted above, been rather disappointing. That development which has occurred appears largely due to the attraction of facilities, both research and production, of national corporations and a limited spin-off of people, projects and capital from these activities. There is, of course, nothing wrong with such development - indeed, quite the contrary. But it is not a reproduction of the pattern which the projects initially sought to imitate and suggests that our understanding of what those patterns are and how they develop is limited.

One possible explanation for the difficulties of the newer regions is that there is a very limited space within the economy for the kinds of activities in which these regions engage and that space is already occupied by the existing regions. But this is not a line of reasoning which, as far as I can tell, anyone has seriously pursued. People seem to operate with the notion that a good innovation can always find a niche in the market if it is properly managed and financed. Instead, researchers have sought to expand the list of institutional structures which are required to systematically generate and launch the innovations or increase the precision with which institutions already on this list are described. The literature along these lines is still very diffuse and not easily summarised. Part of it consists of elaborate regional histories emphasising the unique combination of people and events which produce Route 128 and Silicon Valley. There is a study now under way of the Route 128 region for the Austrian Government by an Austrian national with considerable experience in the United States which attempts to clarify the nature of the university-business link and compare it to the stylised picture which Europeans have created, working against the model of their own academic tradition. One of the things which she manages to show is that the strict boundary between research and production is maintained in Boston and, hence, the relationship between business and the academic world, while perhaps very different from that on the continent, does not provide anything like the merger between the two which is often pictured abroad.

Two graduate students at the Sloan School at MIT are working from the hypothesis that one of the critical factors in the Boston area is the existence of networks of individuals and institutions which link together the critical ingredients required for high-tech start-ups through complex social structures [Norhia, 1986; Kanai, 1986]. These students are seeking to identify what those structures are, how they develop and the kinds of information which flow through them by examining various high tech clubs which have grown up around MIT. The clubs are of special interest, however, because they are a new institution, or institution-like entity not previously on the "list" which may catalyse the other elements already present in the community. To understand how this catalytic action works, these students are particularly influenced by a notion of Granovetter's about the "strength of weak ties" [Granovetter, 1973; 1982]. The basic idea is that the most efficient informational network consists of people who are not so strongly tied to each other that they all process the same information. There must nonetheless be enough trust and commonality of language to permit communication to take place.

V. Conclusion

Taken together, the United States material confirms a shift toward smaller productive units. This is unquestionably true at the establishment level. The shift is indicated by both qualitative case study and interview findings and by quantitative evidence, including the distribution of employment across establishments classified by employment levels. The evidence at the enterprise level is less conclusive but it is consistent with a shift toward smaller enterprises as well. Looking at establishments, where there is complete data annually, it is clear that the shift toward smaller establishments is not merely a compositional effect: it is occurring *within* virtually all manufacturing industries and *within* certain service industries as well. Moreover, statistical tests indicate that it represents a secular trend, which began in the early 1970s, and represents a reversal of a trend toward larger establishments in prior postwar decades: the tests indicate that the movement toward small establishments is *not* simply a response to the relatively higher levels of unemployment in recent years.

The causes of this shift in productive activity are *not* clear. There are too broad classes of hypotheses in this regard. One class explains the shift as an effort to take advantage of lower employment costs in smaller productive units. The second class of hypotheses attributes the shifts to changes in productive and organisational technologies. The evidence examined for this study is inconclusive in this regard. In the United States, earnings are, on average, lower in smaller establishments; and the differential has increased in the last 15 years, but the data examined for this study did not permit us to distinguish part-time from full-time work, let alone to correct for skill levels, geographic location or other factors which might be correlated with size. Other evidence indicates that wage rates, corrected for these factors, are positively correlated with size, but we do not know whether the size differential has increased over time in a way which might have induced the shift toward smaller enterprises. Qualitative evidence indicates that business is shifting toward smaller productive units *both* in search of lower labour costs *and* to implement new productive techniques and organisational reforms and that these two developments are distinct. The organisational and technological trends would probably cause wages in smaller units to *increase*, but the relative magnitudes of the two effects are unclear.

A good deal of case study material was collected about dynamic small businesses that embody the organisational and technological forms likely to produce high wage employment. These studies suggest that more conceptual work is required in order to understand this phenomenon. The existing literature about business organisation is structured by the hypotheses that the modern business enterprise is a response to very large economies of scale, involving highly specialised capital equipment that is profitably employed only in mass markets for standaridsed products, and that efficient production and marketing under these circumstances thus requires extremely large, vertically integrated, hierarchical organisational structures. Small establishments exist only in the penumbra of this dominant organisational form, working either as specialised subcontractors without independent design or marketing capabilities; in narrow luxury markets; or at early stages in the product life cycle. Given that the dominant hypothesis creates a space for smaller enterprises in the economy, albeit a very restricted one, it is difficult to question that hypothesis through case study evidence alone. The studies do clearly undermine the unidirectional development which the hypothesis suggests: the two entertainment studies (broadcasting and movies) as well as the organisational reforms in large companies are about movements over time in a very different direction.

The collection of case study material also suggests that the dominant hypothesis is a very misleading way to organise our understanding of small business. When viewed in the light of that hypothesis, the case studies are of a piece, because they all suggest that hypotheses' limitations. But when removed from the debate structured by the large corporate form and read in the light of a more agnostic view, the case studies reveal a great diversity in the forms which dynamic, independent small business organisations can take. None of the studies indicated that the small organisations are successful in isolation: all seem to involve larger agglomerations. But the forms which those agglomerations take are various and to understand them we need a richer typology than the debate about the larger corporation has yielded. This is probably the most important finding of this review, and we conclude with some abbreviated suggestions about the construction of such a typology.

1. Toward a typology of small firms

There are two distinct approaches to developing typologies: one is theoretical: it abstracts a series of possible forms from some set of hypothesis or axioms which lay out the dimensions over which organisations can vary. The advantage of this approach is that it is in some sense exhaustive: all possible forms can be derived. On the other hand, the relevance of the typology depends completely on the theory: if the axioms are invalid or focus on dimensions of business organisation which are irrelevant or incomplete in terms of the issues of efficiency or welfare with which we are concerned, the typology itself will be irrelevant as well. In any case, at the present juncture there is simply no theoretical structure which provides this kind of closed typology of organisation forms.

The case material at hand lends itself to the second approach, which is empirical and inductive: it abstracts a set of types from the existing material. This approach is also limited: the typology is open in the sense that there is no way of knowing whether some other set of cases might generate additional types. And it is ad hoc, in the sense that one has no prior idea of what the relevant dimensions of the material might be and, as a result, cannot be sure whether the types reflect the underlying material or the investigators' preconceptions about what is interesting or relevant to look at. Ideally, however, inductive typologies of this kind lead to theory, in the sense that they stimulate the development of a theoretical structure which will link together and explain the variation across types. Such a theory, if it can be derived, will also suggest what additional types are possible and might be identified in a comprehensive search. For typology construction, the most important observations to emerge from the case study literature are as follows.

First, the decentralisation of business activity is not a movement from a tightly integrated hierarchical organisation to a market of isolated business units who communicate with each other indirectly through price signals (co-ordinated by impersonal price signals). The smaller, decentralised business units of the case studies are members of social networks, federations, or confederations of units who are in direct communication with each other, continually defining and/or redefining their inter-relationships and sharing a variety of communal services and functions. This does not necessarily mean that the isolated firms of competitive economic theory do not exist: this review, however, did not make a determined effort to find studies about them, and none turned up by accident along the way. The relationship among business units was, in other words, social rather than strictly economic.

Second, the economic functions of the social structure appeared to be extremely complex. Some of those economic functions seems to be related to trust, something which has recently received a good deal of emphasis within the economics literature. But, in other respects, the social structure appeared to function in a way which facilitated communication like a language community. The members of the community were likely to bond with each other rather than with outsiders because they understood each other better and hence could consummate the relationship more readily and rapidly. Trust and communications might thus constitute two dimensions in a typology but it is not clear that they are actually separable socially (although clearly they are separable in terms of their economic functions). They may actually be a dimension of a more fundamental aspect of human societies, like culture.

Third, to the extent we are talking about cultures, the cultures observed in the literature are of at least two kinds. One is organisational culture growing out of large business corporations. The second are geographically based cultures which are often ethnic in nature. A third cultural category might be that associated with Route 128 or Silicon Valley: in a sense, it is a professional culture but since it extends beyond members of the engineering profession in a narrow sense, "professional" is too limited a term to capture the essence of this third type. At any rate, the three types of culture clearly have different origins and different capacities to span geographic distance.

Fourth, the degree of direct co-ordination among the business units also seemed to differ substantially. In corporate organisations, there remained a managerial hierarchy. Its long run role in directing the organisation is debatable but is clearly an important factor now and seems likely to continue into the foreseeable future. In construction and movies, there was also clearly a general contractor who put the various components together, co-ordinated their activities, and mediated their relationship with each other. In the garment industry or in Route 128 ventures, or in the decentralised broadcasting industry, this kind of co-ordination was weaker (possibly even non-existent) and certainly less apparent.

Fifth, in some cases there was a central organisation which mediated the relationship between the community and the produce market whereas in others that was not apparent. The corporation was one such organisation. The general contractor did this in construction, the studios in the decentralised movie industry. It is harder to identify a single mediating organisation in the broadcasting industry although, at various times, advertising agencies and rating services played important roles. There is no mediating organisation in garments, or Route 128 and even the general contractor in construction is not a mediator in the sense that the studio is in the movies or the corporation is in manufacturing. The role of the mediating organisation is related to the idea of "economies of scope", a term much used in the literature but never tightly defined.

Finally, these small firms were linked together by other formal organisations which provided the community with social overhead capital, such as skill training, research and development, and physical infrastructure in the form of roads, sewers, industrial parks and the like. The organisations providing formal services were different from the mediating organisations. They tended to be trade unions, trade associations, or municipal governments.

Bibliography

Abernathy, William J. et al. 1983. *Industrial renaissance: Producing a competitive future for America*, New York, Basic Books.

Armington, Catherine; Odle, Marjori. 1982. "Small businesses - How many jobs?", in *Brookings Review*, Winter.

---. 1983. *Further examination of sources of recent employment growth: Analysis of USEEM data for 1976 and 1980*, Washington, D.C., Brookings Institution, March (mimeo).

Bearse, Peter J. et al. 1979. "A comparative analysis of state programs to promote new technology based enterprise", in *The New England Journal of Business and Economics*, Vol. 5, No. 2, Spring.

Benson, J. Kenneth. 1975. "The interorganizational network as a political economy", in *Administrative Science Quarterly*, No. 20, pp. 229-249.

Birch, David L. 1979. *The job generation process*, Cambridge, MA., MIT Program on Neighborhood and Regional Change, Final report to Economic Development Administration (mimeo).

---. 1981. *Corporate evolution, a micro based analysis*, United States Small Business Administration, January.

Birch, David L.; McCracken, Susan. 1982. *The small business share of job creation - Lessons learned from the use of a longitudinal file*, United States Small Business Administration.

Bluestone, Barry; Harrison, Bennett. 1982. *The deindustrialization of America*, New York, Basic Books.

Bonacich, Edna. 1978. *U.S. capitalism and Korean immigrant small business*, Riverside, CA, University of California-Riverside, Department of Sociology (mimeo).

Bonacich, Edna; Modell, John. 1980. *The economic basis of ethnic solidarity: Small business in the Japanese-American community*, Berkeley, University of California Press.

Bonacich, Edna et al. 1977. "Koreans in small business", in *Society*, No. 14, pp. 54-59.

Burt, Ronald S. 1980. "Models of network structure", in Inkeles, Alex et al. (eds.): *Annual Review of Sociology*, No. 6, pp. 79-141.

Carland, James W. et al. 1984. "Differentiating entrepreneurs from small business owners: A conceptualization", in *Academy of Management Review*, No. 9, pp. 354-359.

Castells, Manuel (ed.). 1985. "Technology, space and society", *Urban Affairs Annual Review*, No. 28.

Churchill, Neil C.; Lewis, Virginia L. 1983. "The five stages of small business growth", in *Harvard Business Review*, No. 61, pp. 30-50.

Committee for Economic Development (CED). 1986. *Partnership for state economic progress*, Confidential draft of proposed CED policy statement for discussion by the Subcommittee on Organizing for State Economic Progress at its meeting on 18 April 1986, Washington, D.C. (mimeo).

Conard, Alfred F. et al. 1977. *Enterprise organisation*, Miroda, N.Y., The Foundation Press.

Cooper, Arnold C. 1970. "The Palo Alto experience", in *Industrial Research*, No. 12, pp. 58-61.

Cummings, Scott (ed.). 1980. *Self-help in urban America: Patterns of minority business enterprise*, Port Washington, NY, Konnikat.

Cunningham, J.V.; Kotler, M. 1983. *Building neighborhood organizations*, Notre Dame, IN, University of Notre Dame Press.

Doeringer, Peter B. et al. 1987. *Invisible factors in local economic development*, New York, Oxford University Press.

Domhoff, G. William. 1975. "Social clubs, policy planning groups, and corporations: A network study of ruling-class cohesiveness", in *Insurgent Sociologist*, No. 5, pp. 173-184.

Dorfman, Nancy S. 1983. "Route 128: The development of a regional high technology economy", in *Research Policy*, No. 12, pp. 299-316.

Dunne, T. et al. 1988. "Patterns of firm entry and exit in U.S. manufacturing industries", in *The Rand Journal of Economics*, Vol. 19, No. 4, Winter, pp. 495-516.

Eaton, Thomas; Conant, Ralph W. 1985. *Cutting loose: Making the transition from employee to entrepreneur*, Chicago, Probus Publishing Co.

Evans, David S. 1987. "Tests of alternative theories of firm growth", in *Journal of Political Economy*, pp. 657-674.

Gartner, William B. 1985. "A conceptual framework for describing the phenomenon of new venture creation", in *Academy of Management Review*, No. 10, pp. 696-706.

Glaessel-Brown, Eleanor. 1984. *Immigration policy and Colombian textile workers in New England: A case study in political demography*, Unpublished Ph.D. dissertation, Political Science Department, MIT, Cambridge, MA.

Granovetter, Mark S. 1973. "The strength of weak ties", in *American Journal of Sociology*, Vol. 78, No. 6, pp. 1360-1380.

---. 1982. "Strength of weak ties: A network theory revisited", in Marsden, Peter V.; Lin, Nan (eds.): *Social structure and network analysis*, Beverley Hills, CA, Sage Publications, pp. 105-130.

---. 1984a. "Small is bountiful: Labor markets and establishment size", in *American Sociological Review*, No. 49, pp. 323-334.

---. 1984b. *Economic and social structure: A theory of embeddedness*, Working paper, Stony Brook, NY, State University of New York, Department of Sociology.

Greene, Richard. 1982. "Tracking job growth in private industry , in *Monthly Labor Review*, September.

Hall, Bronwyn H. 1986. *The relationship between firm size and firm growth in the U.S. manufacturing sector*, NBER Working Paper No. 1965, Cambridge, MA., National Bureau of Economic Research, Inc., June.

Harris, Candee S. 1982. *U.S. establishment and enterprise microdata: A data base description*, Washington, D.C., The Brookings Institution, June.

---. 1983. *Small business and job generation: A changing economy or differing methodologies?"*, Washington, DC, The Brookings Institution, 25 February (mimeo).

Harris, Candee, S. et al. 1983. *Handbook of small business data: A sourcebook and guide for researchers and policy-makers*, Washington, D.C., The Brookings Institution, January (mimeo).

Holmes, J. 1986. "The organisation and locational structure of production subcontracting", in Scott, A.J.; Storper, M. (eds.): *Production, work, territory: The geographical anatomy of industrial capitalism*, Boston, Allen and Unwin, pp. 80-105.

Horwitch, Mel. 1988. *Post-modern management: Its emergence and meaning for strategy*, Detroit, The Free Press.

Jorge, Antonio; Moncarz, Raul. 1981. "International factor movement and complementarity: Growth and entrepreneurship under conditions of cultural variation", in *REMP Bulletin*, Supplement 14, September.

---. 1982. *The future of the Hispanic market: The Cuban entrepreneur and the economic development of the Miami SMSA*, Discussion Paper 6, International Banking Center, Florida International University.

Jovanovic, Boyan. 1982. "Selection and evolution of industry", in *Econometrica*, No. 50, May, pp. 556-569.

Jovanovic, Boyan; Rob, Rafael. 1987. "Demand-driven innovation and spatial competition over time", in *Review of Economic Studies*, No. 54, January, pp. 63-72.

Kanter, Rosabeth Moss. 1983. *The change makers: Innovation for productivity in the American corporation*, New York, Simon and Schuster.

Kim, Illsoo. 1981. *New urban immigrants, the Korean community in New York*, Princeton, NJ, Princeton University Press.

Kimberly, John R. 1979. "Issues in the creation of organizations: Initiation, innovation and institutionalization, in *Academy of Management Journal*, No. 22, pp. 437-457.

Kochan, Thomas et al. 1986. *The transformation of American industrial relations*, New York, Basic Books.

Lane, Marc J. 1977. *Legal handbook for small business*, New York, Amacom (a division of American Management Association).

Lawrence, Paul R.; Dyer, Davis. 1983. *Renewing American industry*, New York, The Free Press.

Lawrence, Robert. 1983. "Is trade deindustrializing America?", in Perry, G.; Burtless, F. (eds.): *Brookings Papers on economic activity*, Washington, DC, The Brookings Institution, Vol. 1.

Leonard, Jonathan S. 1986. *On the size distribution of employment and establishments*, Working paper No. 1951, National Bureau of Economic Research, June.

Light, Ivan. 1972. *Ethnic enterprise in America*, Berkeley, University of California Press.

---. 1980. "Asian enterprise in America: Chinese, Japanese, and Koreans in small business", in Cummings, Scott (ed.): *Self-help in urban America*, New York, Kennikat Press.

Lucas, Robert E. 1978. "On the size distribution of business firms", in *Bell Journal of Economics*, No. 9, Autumn, pp. 508-523.

MacDonald, James M. 1986. "Entry and exit on the competitive fringes", in *Southern Economic Journal*, Vol. 52, January, pp. 640-652.

Maguire, Lambert. 1983. *Understanding social networks*, Beverley Hills, CA, Sage Publications.

Miller, Roger; Cote, Marcel. 1985. "Growing the next Silicon Valley", in *Harvard Business Review*, July-August, pp. 114-123.

Moore, Gwen. 1979. "The structure of a national elite network", in *American Sociological Review*, No. 44, pp. 673-692.

Norhia, Nitin. 1986. *Institutional innovations in high technology based entrepreneurial communities: The 128 venture group as a case study*, Cambridge, MA, Sloan School of Management, April (mimeo).

Norton, R.D.; Rees, J. 1979. "The product cycle and the spatial decentralization of American manufacturing", in *Regional Studies*, No. 13, pp. 141-151.

OECD (Organisation for Economic Co-operation and Development). 1985. "Employment in small and large firms: Where have the jobs come from", in *Employment Outlook*, Paris.

Perrow, Charles B. 1986. *Complex organizations: A critical essay*, New York, NY, Random House, 3rd edition.

Perrucci, Robert; Lewis, Bonnie L. 1985. *Continuity and change of interorganizational networks and community elite structure*, Paper presented at the 80th Annual Meeting of the American Sociological Association, 29 August, Washington, DC (mimeo).

Peters, Thomas J.; Waterman, Robert H., Jr. 1982. *In search of excellence: Lessons from America's best-run companies*, New York, Harper & Row.

Peterson, Richard A.; Berger, David G. 1971. "Entrepreneurship in organizations: Evidence from the popular music industry", in *Administrative Science Quarterly*, No. 16, pp. 97-107.

Pinchot, Gifford, III. 1985. *Intrapreneuring*, New York, Harper & Row.

Portes, Alejandro; Bach, Robert L. 1985. *Latin journey, Cuban and Mexican immigrants in the United States*, Berkeley, University of California Press.

Portes, Alejandro; Manning, Robert D. 1986. "The immigrant enclave: Theory and empirical examples", in *Competitive Ethnic Relations*, New York, Academic Press.

Portes, Alejandro; Mozo, Rafael. 1985. "The political adaptation process of Cubans and other ethnic minorities in the United States", in *International Migration Review*, No. 19, pp. 35-63.

Powell, Walter W. 1984. "Neither master nor hierarchy: Network forms of organization", in *Research in organizational behavior*, Vol. 12, pp. 295-336, New York, JIA Press.

---. 1985. *Getting into print: The decision-making process in scholarly publishing*, Chicago, The University of Chicago Press.

---. 1988. "Institutional effects of organizational structure and performance", in Zucker, Lynn (ed.): *Institutional pattern and organizations: Cultures and environment*, New York, Ballinger Press.

Ridgeway, Valentine F. 1978. "Administration of manufacturer-dealer systems", in *Administrative Science Quarterly*, No. 1, pp. 464-483.

Rogers, Everett M.; Larsen, Judith K. 1984. *Silicon Valley fever: Growth of high technology culture*, New York, Basic Books.

Runsten, David. 1985. *Mexican immigrants and the California-Mexico role in the US shoe industry*, San Diego, University of California (mimeo).

Saxenian, AnnaLee. 1985. "Silicon Valley and Rte 128: Regional prototypes or historical exceptions?", in Castells, Manuel (ed.): *Technology, space and society, urban affairs annual review*, No. 28.

Scott, A.J.; Storper, M. 1986. *Production, work, territory*, Boston, Allen and Unwin.

---. 1987. "High technology industry and regional development: A theoretical critique and reconstruction", in *International Social Science Journal*, Vol. 39, No. 2, pp. 215-232.

Storper, Michael; Christopherson, Susan. 1986a. *Flexible specialization and regional industrial agglomerations: The case of the U.S. motion picture industry*, Los Angeles, UCLA, Department of Geography and Graduate School of Architecture and Urban Planning, January.

---. 1986b. *Flexible specialization and new forms of labor market segmentation: The United States motion picture industry*, Los Angeles, UCLA Graduate School of Architecture and Urban Planning, February.

Taylor, Benjamin J.; Witney, Fred. 1983. *Labour relations law*, Englewood Cliffs, NJ, Prentice-Hall.

Teitz, Michael B. et al. 1981. *Small business and employment growth in California*, Working Paper No. 348, Berkeley, University of California, Institute of Urban and Regional Development, March.

Tilly, Charles (ed.). 1974. *An urban work*, Boston, Little Brown.

Turk, Herman. 1973. "Comparative urban structure from an interorganizational perspective", in *Administrative Science Quarterly*, No. 18, pp. 37-55.

Turk, Herman; Lefcowitz, Myron J. 1962. "Toward theory of representation between groups", in *Social Forces*, No. 40, pp. 337-341.

US Department of Commerce, Bureau of the Census. Printed annually. *County business patterns*, Washington, DC, US Government Printing Office.

US Small Business Administration. 1985. *Your business and the SBA*, Issued by Public Communications Division, OPC-2, February.

---. 1984. *Business loans from the SBA*, Issued by Public Communications Division, OPC-6, September.

Vaughan, Roger J. et al. 1985. *The wealth of States: Policies for a dynamic economy*, Washington, DC, Council of State Planning Associations.

Vernon, R. 1979. "The product life cycle hypothesis in a new international environment", in *Oxford Bulletin of Economics and Statistics*, No. 41, pp. 255-267.

Von Hippel, Eric. 1986. *Cooperation between competing firms: Informal know-how trading*, Working Paper WP 1759-86, Cambridge, MA, MIT Sloan School of Management.

Waldinger, Roger. 1986. *Through the eye of the needle*, New York, Columbia University Press.

Warren, Roland L. 1967. "The interorganizational field as a focus for investigation", in *Administrative Science Quarterly*, No. 12, pp. 397-419.

White, Lawrence J. n.d. *Measuring the importance of small business in the American economy*, Monograph Series in Finance and Economics, No. 1981-4, New York, New York University, Solomon Brothers Center for the Study of Financial Institutions, Graduate School of Business Administration.

Wilson, John W. 1985. *The new ventures: Inside high-stakes world of venture capital*, Reading, MA, Addison-Wesley.

Wilson, Kenneth; Martin, W. Allen. 1982. "Ethnic enclaves: A comparison of the Cuban and Black economies in Miami", in *American Journal of Sociology*, No. 88, pp. 135-160.

Wilson, Kenneth; Portes, Alejandro. 1980. "Immigrant enclaves: An analysis of the labor market experiences of Cubans in Miami", in *American Journal of Sociology*, No. 86, pp. 295-319.

Achevé d'imprimer
en septembre 1990